Letters From Your Loving Son

Wilson C. Lineaweaver

His Journey Through the CCC and U.S. Navy
Until His Death on the USS *Bunker Hill* in 1945

Thomas R. Lehman

*To Roger —
May we never take for
granted the freedom
we enjoy.*

Thomas R Lehman

On the front cover:
Wilson, about 1941, in a photo possibly taken in Norfolk, VA,
at "The Strip" where there were numerous
photo studios that catered to sailors.

On the back cover:
SB2C-1's turning into the pattern to land aboard the *Bunker Hill*, 1943.
navsource.org

ISBN-13:978-1541362536

ISBN-10:1541362535

Library of Congress Control Number: 2017901570
CreateSpace Independent Publishing Platform, North Charleston, SC

LettersFromYourLovingSon@hotmail.com

This book is dedicated to "HKL"
Harold Kenneth Lineaweaver

The youngest of "the kids" and one of his older brother Wilson's biggest fans.

All pictures on this page are of Harold Lineaweaver.

October 17, 1933-
May 23, 2015

U.S. Navy
1951-1953

TABLE OF CONTENTS

ABBREVIATIONS

ARM1c - Aviation Radioman First Class

ARM2c - Aviation Radioman Second Class

ARM3c - Aviation Radioman Third Class

ACRM- Aviation Chief Radioman

AS - Apprentice Seaman

BB - Battleship, after 1920

CASU - Carrier Aircraft Servicing Unit

CCC - Civilian Conservation Corps

CV - Aircraft Carrier

CVE - Aircraft Carrier, Escort

DD - Destroyer (ship), after 1921

FPO - Fleet Post Office

LT - Lieutenant

LT (jg) - Lieutenant, Junior Grade

LT CDR - Lieutenant Commander

NARA - National Archives and Records Administration

NAS - Naval Air Station

NOB - Naval Operating Base

PHTH - Pearl Harbor, Territory of Hawaii

QM3c - Quartermaster Third Class

SB2C - "Helldiver"; single-engine Navy scout-bomber (VSB), manufactured by Curtiss

SBD - "Dauntless"; single-engine Navy scout-bomber (VSB), manufactured by Douglas

SEA2c - Seaman Second Class

TBF - "Avenger"; single-engine Navy torpedo-bomber (VTB), manufactured by Grumman

USN - United States Navy

USNAS - United States Naval Air Station

USNRS - United States Naval Recruiting Station

USNTS - United States Naval Training Station

USS - United States Ship *(a commissioned ship of the United States Navy)*

V - Fixed-wing heavier-than-air aircraft squadron

> *(vs. H for a rotary wing, i.e. helicopter; heavier-than-air vs. lighter-than-air, i.e. dirigible)*

VB - Navy Bombing Squadron

VC - Navy Composite Squadron

VF - Fixed-Wing Fighter Plane

VGS - Navy Escort Scouting Aircraft Squadron

VSB - Navy Scouting Bomber Aircraft Squadron

VTB - Navy Torpedo Bomber Aircraft Squadron

INTRODUCTION

In October 1937, a mother in Lebanon, Pennsylvania, began saving letters her son wrote and sent home. The letters began when he joined the Civilian Conservation Corps. After his service in the CCC, he embarked on a worldwide journey in the U.S. Navy during World War II. Letters continued to be saved. Another son entered the U.S. Army in 1943. He wrote letters home which were also carefully saved. Her youngest son joined the U.S. Navy in 1951. His letters, too, were kept with the letters from the previous 14 years. Not only were letters saved, but among other things were cards, photos, newspaper clippings, and an assortment of papers.

Nettie Earlene Lineaweaver, "Mother" or Earlene to family and friends, kept hundreds of letters, cards, papers, and clippings, from her three sons in the service. Over 200 letters from Wilson beginning in 1937. Some 34 letters from Jim while in the Army. And at least 44 letters from Harold in the early 1950's. Fast forward a quarter century, when Earlene passed away, this treasure of keepsakes, memories and reminders, was passed to her youngest son Harold. The years following, Harold occasionally opened his large red military chest and carefully perused this collection of letters and memorabilia. He spoke with a sense of awe and pride of his older brother Wilson who gave his life for our country, and of the stories he had heard of Wilson's adventures in the Navy. Years passed and Harold has now left this chest and its contents for the next generation.

After my father-in-law Harold Lineaweaver passed away on May 23, 2015, while looking for pictures and memorabilia for his memorial service, I searched through that large red military chest. It was my first time viewing its contents, not because it was kept hidden, but because of my failure to inquire of all the memories it held. Overwhelmed by the amount of letters, cards, papers, awards, newspaper clippings, and other things, I thought something should be done to preserve this rich abundance of family history. Not knowing what would lie ahead, I plunged in to try to put together some sort of record of these memories. From almost two years of poring over the chest's contents, searching historical records, typing, scanning, proofing, and then doing some more of the same, the result has been this book. Two regrets, of course, were not previously realizing the scope of Wilson's service, and not asking Harold more questions about his brother, whom he rightly considered a hero.

When Wilson joined Bombing Squadron 84 in May 1944 at the age of 25, he was one of its oldest members, and one of the only three aircrewmen who had previous bombing experience. By that time he had served three years in the Civilian Conservation Corps (the third year as a Project Assistant and not a regular enrollee), and over three years in the United States Navy. He had twice been to the war zone in the Pacific, participating, among others, in the Battle of Santa Cruz and the Battle of Tarawa. These were a foreboding of what he would experience during his months on the *Bunker Hill*. One constant through all this time was his love for his family and his letters he faithfully sent home to his mother, including one he wrote on the very day he was killed.

I've 'picked the brain' of his only surviving sister, Lucille, numerous times. She has shared what she remembers, but said she "always had her nose in a book and wasn't paying much attention to what was going on." At the age of 90 she still has a sharp mind and a quick wit. She has always referred to her brother as Wils - pronounced with an 's' at the end and not a 'z' - and she mentioned that all her brothers and sisters called their dad 'Pop'.

Throughout this book when I mention their mother, I've spelled her name as Earlene. There does not seem to be much consistency in the spelling over the years. Some official records such as a birth record, and the bank account that she opened for Wilson with both their names on the account, used the spelling Earlene.

All the pictures and papers in this book are from the large red military chest, unless otherwise noted. There is more in the chest from her sons that 'Mother' (and Harold) saved, but to include it all would require another book of considerable length. Also in the chest is a stack of sympathy cards the family received after Wilson's death in World War II, and a pair of his WWII Navy shower shoes. The location of any medals Wilson received, except the Distinguished Flying Cross which was in the chest, is unknown.

The original spelling and punctuation in the letters in this book have been retained in the transcriptions. The letters in this book have for the most part been reduced from their original size, most to around 55-60%. Other papers, cards, photos, etc., have been reduced in size to utilize the space available. Many of the envelopes are missing their stamps. As a young boy from a poor family, Harold found an interest in stamp collecting. He could save stamps from his brother's letters, and other letters, for free. He said he later sold this stamp collection which, as time passed, he regretted.

In searching for information with which to expand the scope of the letters, I was able to contact Wilson's fiancé Bette (Knepper) Helling. She was suffering from some effects of a mild stroke, and I was never able to talk to her personally, but spoke to her daughter. At the age of 94, Bette was still living in her own home in Dubuque, Iowa. I also was able to contact Pam Blasingame of Medon, Tennessee, the widow of Sam McLean, one of Wilson's close friends in the Navy. Debra Goodale of Cleveland, Texas, provided some wonderful pictures of her father William Raymond Lamb who was Wilson's pilot on the *Bunker Hill*. A picture of Wilson and Lamb was especially exciting to receive from Debra. Trying to locate current family of Joe Wiley King, Carlos B. Stafford, and the Lane family in California, all of whom had contact with Wilson during World War II, was unsuccessful. Joe and Carlos both died relatively young at the ages of 46 and 66 respectively.

This book is not a complete record of all of Wilson's service activities. There were many training exercises on various ships, as well as other Navy related activities of which only he would have known.

A thank you to my daughter Anna for her interest, encouragement, excitement and help. To aunt Anne and cousins Ellen, Sharon, Suzanne, Faye, Becky, and others, who were a tremendous help. To Bethany for the outstanding cover design. Historians Mike Moy, Jim Krombach, and Gary Williamson, were invaluable in sharing with me their expert knowledge. And a special thank you to my very patient wife Beth who put up with me through all the months of working on this project.

TRL

God is our refuge and strength, A very present help in trouble.
Therefore we will not fear, though the earth should change
And though the mountains slip into the heart of the sea....
Psalm 46:1-2

Back Row, Left to Right: David, James, Mahlon ("Fat"), Wilson, Lucille
Front Row, Left to Right: Dorothy, Robert, Harold, Earlene, Nathan

This family picture was taken in December 1942 when Wilson was home on a 30 day leave. It was after Wilson had experienced his first full year in World War II, and had witnessed horrors such as friends and shipmates being killed, fellow airmen's planes shot down while in mid-air battles, and his ship the USS *Hornet* CV-8 being sunk.

Robert J. Lineaweaver, 1886-1952, married on January 4, 1912 to Nettie <u>Earlene</u> Haag, 1894-1977
Their Children:

David J., born October 24, 1913	Lucille M., born November 26, 1926
Mahlon R. ("Fat"), born August 13, 1916	Dorothy E., born October 29, 1929
Wilson C., born April 6, 1919	Nathan A., born November 3, 1931
James L., born October 20, 1923	Harold K., born October 17, 1933

Left: Wilson as a baby with his mother at Elizabeth, NJ, where he was born.

Right: Brothers, L-R, Jim, Wilson, Mahlon, David

(According to son Jim Lineaweaver, the family moved to Elizabeth, NJ in 1914, and then back to Pennsylvania in 1924 when the dray line closed.)

Right:
Back - Jim, Wilson, Earlene; Front - Lucille, Dorothy, Nathan

Left and below: Pictures of Wilson while in the Navy, including one with an unidentified girlfriend (see July 8, 1942 letter).

Above, L-R: "Mother", on the porches of 1240 East Cumberland Street; 1942 in Avon; 1942 portrait.

Right: "Mother" in Avon Heights; finally moved out of the "dump" on East Cumberland Street after son Harold got out of the Navy.

Uncle and Aunt Horace and Eva (Haag) Clemens; mentioned in several letters.

"Pop", at 1240 East Cumberland Street: Left - in the living room; Right - in the back yard.

Wilson's youngest brothers, two of "the kids"; Nathan (left) and Harold (right). Left photo shows them in their first suits bought by their mother and older sister Lucille. Nathan was sometimes called "Jake" in Wilson's letters.

Left: Wilson Haag (Haig), served in the U.S. Army in France and Germany during WWI. Wilson Lineaweaver was named after his uncle Wilson Haag (Haig), who was in Europe in 1919 when his nephew was born.

A letter written on Feb. 5, 1919 from Eitelborn, Germany, by Wilson Haag states: "Nov. 1917 I had my first experience on the front. The first division was the first American unit ordered into the trenches. It was during this short stay on the front that I witnessed the first American Artillerymen killed in the war. The shell that killed them came within a hairs breadth of picking me off."

THE LINEAWEAVER FAMILY TIMELINE

1912, January 4, Thursday, Robert Joseph Lineaweaver and Nettie Earlene Haag marry in Annville, PA, by Phares B. Gibble

1913, October 24, Friday, David Joseph Lineaweaver born at Lebanon, PA

c1914, Robert and Earlene move to Elizabeth, NJ, where Robert and his brothers John and Tom start a laundry business

1916, August 13, Sunday, Mahlon Robert Lineaweaver born at Elizabeth, NJ

1919, April 6, Sunday, Wilson Charles Lineaweaver born at Elizabeth, NJ

1923, October 20, Saturday, James Luther Lineaweaver born at Elizabeth, NJ

c1924, Robert and Earlene move back to Lebanon, PA

1926, November 26, Friday, Lucille Mae Lineaweaver born at Lebanon, PA

1929, October 29, Tuesday, Dorothy Erline Lineaweaver born at Lebanon, PA

1931, November 3, Tuesday, Nathan Alfred Lineaweaver born at Lebanon, PA

1933, October 17, Tuesday, Harold Kenneth Lineaweaver born at Lebanon, PA

1937 Wilson Lineaweaver joins the CCC to help support his parents and siblings

1941, January 6, Monday, Wilson Lineaweaver joins the U.S. Navy at Baltimore, MD

1944, November 24 letter, Wilson writes that he gave Bette Knepper an engagement ring

1945, January 21, Sunday, Wilson departs California on the USS *Bunker Hill*

1945, May 11, Friday, USS *Bunker Hill* hit by two kamikaze planes, Wilson killed

The Dump

1240 East Cumberland Street. This address was home to the Lineaweaver family from 1941 to 1955. It is often referred to as a "dump" in Wilson's letters. For a number of years the family rented a house at 1908 Chestnut Street, Lebanon, PA, and according to daughter Lucille, they had a big garden and ate "real good." Wilson's father Robert was a huckster and peddled fruits in the local area, owned his own truck, and made a good living. In the 1930's the Acme and A&P grocery stores came to Lebanon. Lucille said that her pop could not compete with their prices, so business declined and he lost his livelihood. In the fall of 1940, the owner of the row of houses along Chestnut Street wanted to sell 1908 Chestnut Street to the Lineaweaver's, but at a price they could not afford. With tough times at hand, the family had to move and next lived at 927 ½ Cumberland Street, a small apartment. Daughter Lucille had to live with a brother because the apartment wasn't big enough for all the children. Son Harold remembered it being a terrible place overrun with bed bugs. They lived there a couple months and then rented a house at 1240 East Cumberland Street, in Avon, which adjoins the city of Lebanon. Through their difficulties, Lucille said her mother lost her zeal for life and lost interest in canning, cooking, and baking which she had done while living on Chestnut Street. The house at 1240 was the end of a three house row. Converted from a hat factory, the middle of the factory was removed to create six houses, three each side facing back to back. There was one single spigot with cold water in the kitchen. The heat was from a coal oil heater, and an outhouse was in the tiny back yard. Harold said he remembered there being a hole in the wall on the staircase open to the neighbor's house, and at times an unpleasant smell would waft through. Baths at 1240 were sponge baths or in a tub. Harold only experienced his first shower when he joined the Navy in 1951. Though it wasn't much to look at, granddaughter Sharon said she always remembers her grandmother keeping the house clean and tidy. While living here, Robert ("Pop") died in 1952. In 1955 when Harold was discharged from the Navy, he built a house in nearby Avon Heights. It was then that their mother finally moved from the house Wilson called "the dump".

Bailing Out

In a letter dated February 8, 1942, from Norfolk, VA, Wilson told about his first parachute jump when he and his pilot, out on patrol, got lost at night, and then the plane ran out of gas. Just as the plane engine stopped running, they bailed out. Wilson hit a house's porch upon landing. Because of the bombs on the plane, they were unable to make a forced landing, and though Wilson didn't say, it's likely the plane crashed in the ocean. Non-combat aircraft accidents during World War II were not uncommon. In Wilson's letter dated April 13, 1941, also from Norfolk, VA, he mentions a Navy bomber that crashed nearby killing ten men. According to the Naval History & Heritage Command website at www.history.navy.mil, from 1941 to 1946 there were over 12,000 U.S. Navy deaths due to aviation accidents that were not due to enemy action.

The Doolittle Raid

The famous Doolittle Raid occurred on April 18, 1942. Led by Lt. Col. James Doolittle, sixteen B-25 Mitchell bombers launched from the deck of the USS *Hornet*, on which Wilson was serving. Though Wilson was not part of the actual raid, he surely was part of the excitement aboard ship. Headed for the Japanese cities of Tokyo, Nagoya, Osaka, and Kobe, the goal was a bombing raid on the Japanese homeland in retaliation for the bombing of Pearl Harbor, to show that Japan was vulnerable to an American attack, and perhaps more importantly, to provide a huge boost to American morale. Each B-25 bomber carried four bombs totaling two tons. Knowing that they would not be able to return to the *Hornet*, the sixteen bombers planned on landing in China. Fifteen crashed in China and one landed in the

Soviet Union. All but three of the eighty crew members initially survived. Eight airmen were captured by the Japanese Army in China and three were later executed. The crewmen that landed in the Soviet Union were interned for more than a year. The crewmen that landed in China and not captured by the Japanese were aided by the Chinese, and some American missionaries, and were able to return to the U.S. or to American forces. The fact that the Doolittle Raid originated from the USS *Hornet* was kept a secret for a year afterwards. In retaliation for aiding the Americans, the aftermath in China was that the Japanese Army committed horrendous atrocities on the Chinese people in the areas where the American crewmen were aided. In many instances women were rounded up and repeatedly raped, torture was not uncommon, and in some villages anything that was living was shot including cows and hogs. "In Nancheng, men had fed the Americans. The Japanese forced these Chinese to eat feces, then herded a group chest-to-back 10 deep for a "bullet contest," to see how many bodies a slug pierced before stopping. In Ihwang, Ma Eng-lin had welcomed injured pilot Harold Watson into his home. Soldiers wrapped Ma Eng-lin in a blanket, tied him to a chair and soaked him in kerosene, then forced his wife to set her husband afire."[1] In the end, the Japanese massacred 250,000 men, women, and children.

The Japs
In Wilson's letter dated July 7, 1943, he says he is "expecting to go Jap hunting once again, any day now." In a July 27, 1943, letter he refers to a sailor from Lebanon that he knew, James Gettle, who was killed on the USS *Juneau*, and says "This time when I go out I'll have to get a few for him." Before WWII, Wilson likely didn't know much about the Japanese or have an opinion about them one way or another, which was probably typical of most Americans. During WWII this sentiment quickly changed. An article profiling Charles Reddig, a WWII B-25 Bomber pilot, that appeared in the Lancaster (PA) *LNP* newspaper, reads:

> Reddig also has memories of the battles he fought in those [Pacific] islands."I remember my tail gunner," Reddig said, "who sometimes had tears running down his cheeks while he was firing on Japanese Zeros (fighter planes). "In the beginning, I didn't like killing anybody," Reddig said. But one day, he noticed an American soldier parachute from a plane, and watched Japanese soldiers riddle him with bullets. He saw other examples of the brutality of the Japanese military, as well. "And then I became what you might call a professional killer," Reddig said, lowering his voice. "I couldn't stand it. Maybe I shouldn't say that, but that's what made me feel that way." He and his crew bombed a lot of Japanese military targets.[2]

The Accident
On December 20, 1943, the USS *Sangamon* (CVE-26) arrived at San Diego, CA. According to Wilson's letters, he entered the U.S. Naval Hospital in San Diego on December 21, 1943. His December 25, 1943 letter states that he was "hit by a trailer". Years later, his youngest brother Harold said that he was hit by a general or colonel's wife. Perhaps the vehicle she was driving (a jeep?) was pulling a trailer. Was that something to be covered up? Probably. In any case, Wilson had a broken pelvic bone and spent the next four plus months in the hospital. It was during this time that he met a girl who would later become his fiancé, Bette Knepper.

The Flight Home
Fourteen Day Leave. September 1944. Plane Ticket. $300.00. Wilson had said that for his 30 day leave in December 1942, it took him nine days just for travelling from and to California by train (June 23, 1943

---

[1] Scott, James M. (27 July 2015). Aftermath: Doolittle Raid Reexamined. Retrieved from http://www.historynet.com/aftermath-doolittle-raid-reexamined.htm
[2] Wright, Mary Ellen. "A Hero's Story". *LNP* 11 Feb. 2016: A1, A8, A10. Print.

letter). In a letter dated June 11, 1945, Wilson's fiancé Bette told Wilson's mother, in referring to his leaving on the *Bunker Hill*, that he "knew his chance of a safe return was slim" from his third trip into the war zone. This is likely why Wilson splurged to purchase a $300.00 plane ticket to come home during his fourteen day leave in September/October 1944. He would have had a feeling that it may be the last chance for him to ever see his family again. Wilson had his mother withdraw money from his bank account with Lebanon National Bank and send it to him by Western Union. For comparison, $300.00 in 1944 is equal to more than $4,000.00 in 2016. Not a small sum, to be sure.

The Regret

Wilson's last visit home to Lebanon was on a fourteen day leave in September/October 1944. He paid $300.00 for a plane ticket and said that it would take about 20 hours to fly from San Francisco to Harrisburg. When he was leaving 1240 East Cumberland Street to return to duty in California, his youngest brother Harold did not want him to leave. Because Harold didn't want Wilson to leave, he hid behind their sofa, thinking he'd come back looking for him. Wilson was on a tight schedule and had to leave promptly. That was the last time Wilson was home and the last time his family ever saw him. Harold never said goodbye and never had a chance to at a later time. This was something that he regretted and felt remorseful about the rest of his life, mentioning it numerous times over the years.

The Big Actions

In Wilson's April 14, 1945 letter, he mentions some of "the big actions" in which he participated in 1945 while with the USS *Bunker Hill*. They included: the Tokyo Raids of February 16-17 and 25, 1945; the Iwo Jima campaign; Okinawa; and "what really scared me mostly was flying as far as 60 miles inland over Japan". The attack on Tokyo was aimed to assist operations against Iwo Jima by destroying Japanese air forces, facilities, and manufacturing. After the February 17th strikes on Tokyo, the Navy carrier forces gave more direct support to the Marine landing operations on Iwo Jima which began on February 19th. Tokyo was again attacked on February 25th, though the weather was very unfavorable. Numerous ground installations, aircraft plants, radar installations, etc. were heavily damaged or destroyed in these raids. Throughout March, U.S. aircraft continued to attack Japanese defenses in support of the invasion of Okinawa beginning on April 1st. Japanese aircraft that were destroyed in the air and on the ground far outnumbered American losses in the fighting. The fighting continued thru April into May. On May 11th another major air battle was fought, and this is when two Japanese suicide dives on the USS *Bunker Hill* claimed the life of Wilson. Though not sunk, the ship was badly damaged, and 396 men were killed, with 43 of those listed as missing in action.

During this time, a man named Louie Zamperini was an American POW in the Japanese camp of Omori at Tokyo. In her book *Unbroken*, Laura Hillenbrand relates Louie's description of the February 1945 Tokyo raids from the perspective of a prison camp. On February 16th at 7:15 a.m. the men had just finished breakfast at Omori POW camp when the air raid sirens sounded. Because of the time of day, the POWs knew it was probably carrier aircraft from the US Navy as land-based B-29s could not fly all night to reach Japan so early. "The entire sky was swarming with hundreds of fighters, American and Japanese, rising and falling, streaming bullets at one another. Over Tokyo, lines of dive-bombers bellied down like waves slapping a beach, slamming bombs into the aircraft works and airport. As they rose, quills of fire came up under them. Louie was standing directly underneath the largest air battle yet fought over Japan. ... The view was electrifying. ... Planes were sweeping over every corner of the sky, and all around, fighters were dropping into the water. Several hundred POWs watched from the camp fence, their eyes pressed to knotholes or their head poking over the top, hearts leaping, ears roaring. ... All told, fifteen hundred American planes and several hundred Japanese planes flew over the POWs that day. The following day, back the planes came. By the end of February 17, more than five hundred Japanese planes, both on the ground and in the air, had been lost, and Japan's aircraft works had been badly hit. The Americans had lost eighty planes. Seven days later *[February 25ᵗʰ]*, the hammer fell. At seven in the morning, during a heavy snowstorm, sixteen hundred carrier-based planes flew past Omori and bombed Tokyo."[3] Of the planes flying over Omori that Louie witnessed on the 25th, one of them had a young man from a small town in Pennsylvania named Wilson Lineaweaver as its radioman and gunner.[4]

Sharks

Sharks were a very real and present danger in the Pacific. One of the stories relayed by Harold Lineaweaver, about his older brother Wilson, happened during the war. Wilson's plane was shot down and he and two other crewmen were on a raft in the ocean, waiting for rescue. As they were steadily surrounded by sharks, the pilot panicked, losing control of himself. Fearing for their safety, they had to knock him out. Eventually, they were rescued.

The peril of sharks to the men in the Navy on the Pacific Ocean is graphically depicted in *Neptune's Inferno: The U.S. Navy at Guadalcanal*: "The dying [aircraft carrier U.S.S. *Wasp*] drew in her escorts in a feverish rescue effort. It was the way of the South Seas that episodes like this were well attended by sharks. As the escorting vessels moved in with cargo nets thrown over the gunwales [to rescue men in the ocean], the sailors were horrified. 'Sharks were everywhere,' wrote Ford Richardson, a sailor from the destroyer *Farenholt*. 'Dozens. Hundreds. A shark would catch a man by an arm or a foot and pull him under, cutting off his screams. The poor devil would pop up again, and again, like a cork on a fishing line. Each time his scream would be weaker than before. Finally, he would come up no more. Sometimes the shark would grab the poor man in the middle and shake him like a dog shaking a rat. Then the shark would back off, dragging the dying man's entrails behind him. The water would turn milky with blood.' "[5]

The Insurance

In Wilson's letter dated November 24, 1944, he states that he took out a $10,000.00 life insurance policy on himself. If he had married his fiancé Bette before he was killed, she would have been his beneficiary until she remarried. Since Wilson was not yet married, he named his mother Earlene as his beneficiary. She received a one-time death gratuity payment of $1,417.50 in June 1945. In addition, she received a monthly life insurance payment for the rest of her life of $53.90, and a monthly "mother's pension" which by 1974 was $75.00 per month. Though a sad and regular reminder of a son who gave his life for his country, these checks were a great help to a family living on a shoestring. [The death gratuity was an amount payable to the next of kin for a member of the armed forces who died while on active duty. This was based on six months of Wilson's monthly pay. The "mother's pension" was 'Parents' Dependency and Indemnity Compensation" which was a tax-free income-based monthly benefit for the parent(s) of military service members who died in the line of duty or veterans whose death resulted from a service-related injury or disease.]

---

[3] Hillenbrand, Laura. *Unbroken: A World War II Story of Survival, Resilience, and Redemption*. New York: Random House, 2010. 273,274.

[4] "World War II War Diaries, 1941-1945", housed at the National Archives, includes historical reports of Wilson's squadron VB-84. In the reports for the air strikes of February 16-17, 1945, Wilson is not listed as an aircrewman for the VB-84 flights taking off from the *Bunker Hill*. A week later on February 25th, pilot William R. Lamb and his radioman/gunner Wilson C. Lineaweaver were part of the 2nd Section of the 2nd Division to take off from the *Bunker Hill* at 8:30 a.m. They bombed the Nakajima Aircraft assembly plant at Koizumi, Japan.

[5] Hornfischer, James D. *Neptune's Inferno: The U.S. Navy at Guadalcanal*. New York: Bantam Books, 2011. 133.

12ᵗʰ GRADE REPORT CARD

FORM 9	LAST NAME	FIRST NAME AND INITIAL		LEBANON HIGH SCHOOL PUPIL'S REPORT CARD	
	LINEAWEAVER	WILSON		GRADE 12	ROOM ~~114~~ 111

SCHOOL YEAR 1936 1937	No. Tardy Marks Recorded	Days Absent	English	History	P. of D.	Plane Geom.	German II					Phy. Tr.	A - EXCELLENT / B - GOOD / C - AVERAGE / D - PASSING / I - INCOMPLETE / F - FAILURE	
1ST PERIOD	1	6	D		C	C	D					C	Mrs. R Lineaweaver	
2ND PERIOD	5		D		C	C	D					A	Mrs. R Lineaweaver	
3RD PERIOD	8		D		C	D	D					B	Mrs. R Lineaweaver	
4TH PERIOD	6		D	-	D	C	C					B	Mrs. R Lineaweaver	
5TH PERIOD	6		D		C	D	D					C	Mrs. R Lineaweaver	
6TH PERIOD	5		D		D	D	C					C		

U. Samuel Angle — HOME ROOM TEACHER

See Other Side   L. H. S. Press

Note: During Wilson's elementary and junior high school years he did well in his studies, receiving grades of mostly A's and B's. It wasn't until his senior high school years that D's and C's outnumbered the higher grades.

LODESTONE 1937, HIGH SCHOOL YEARBOOK

WILSON LINEAWEAVER   "Willy"

Why worry, tomorrow is another day.

SCIENTIFIC; Chess and Checker Club—1; Football—2, 3

"The Air Adventures of Jimmie Allen"
Radio adventure serial broadcast from 1933-1937
[Did this program pique Wilson's interest in flying?]

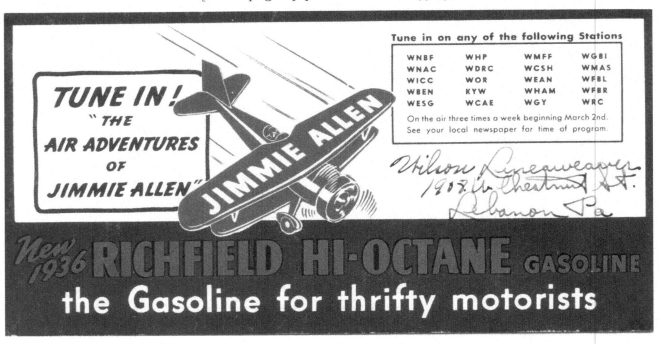

⚓ WILSON'S STUDENT PILOT CERTIFICATE, ISSUED JULY 25, 1940 ⚓

CIVILIAN CONSERVATION CORPS (CCC)

Wilson joined the Civilian Conservation Corps (CCC) in 1937 at the age of 18. Formed in 1933, and lasting until 1942, the CCC was one of President Franklin D. Roosevelt's New Deal programs during the Great Depression. As a public work relief program for unmarried young men, it was designed to promote environmental conservation and to build good citizens through hard, physical outdoor labor. Projects included planting millions of trees, building flood barriers, fighting forest fires, and building public roadways in remote areas. Corpsmen also dug canals and ditches, built wildlife shelters, stocked rivers and lakes, restored historic battlefields, and built and upgraded parks throughout the nation. It operated under the army's control. Camp commanders had disciplinary powers and corpsmen addressed superiors as "sir." The program provided the young men with shelter, clothing, and food. Most of their monthly wage of about $30.00 had to be sent home to their families, but they were allowed to keep about $5.00 for their personal use. In a March 1940 letter, Wilson mentions that his parents are receiving $22.00 a month from his CCC pay.

The first camp Wilson went to in October 1937 was Company 1324 in Scotland, PA. The second camp he went to in April 1939 was Company 2335 in Waynesboro, PA. After his service at Waynesboro, he joined the U.S. Navy in January 1941.

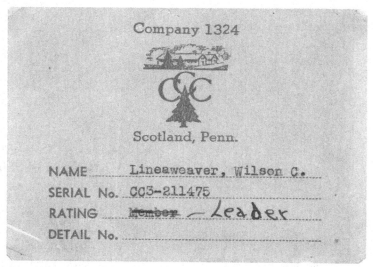

Wilson's CCC identification card at the Scotland, PA, camp.

Wilson Lineaweaver
Co. 1324, S.P. 18
Scotland, Pa.

Dear Parents:

I arrived in camp from Harrisburg about 4:00 P.M. Friday evening. The camp is located in Adams County about 6 miles from Shippensburg and 13 miles from Chambersburg, totally, about 76 miles from Lebanon.

Mr & Mrs. Fies were here and they said they were coming again in about 3 weeks and that they would fetch you along. Thanks for the fruit and there are a few things I need so when the Fiese's come, bring them along. I will write for what I need later.

All those that went with from the hill are in the same camp and also is Elijah Fox from over on the pike, I sleep right along side of him. I had two injections and the vaccination already and didn't mind them.

I saw the Shippensburg State Teachers and Kutsztown play foot ball and was in both towns already. I made the first string basket ball team already, we play on the Shippensburg College floor. The teams we are going to play are other camps and High Schools.

I am beginning to like camp because there are many here that I know. Hope everything is O.K. at home and please write with the above address. Me and Fox may come home over the week end shortly, expect me.

Your son
Wilson Lineaweaver

[Postmark is Gettysburg, P.A., Oct. 28, 1937, 8 AM]
Mr. & Mrs. Robt Lineaweaver
1908 W Chestnut St.
Lebanon Pa.

[Return Address:]
W.C. Lineaweaver
Company 1324, S.P. 18
Scotland, Pa.

HIGHLIGHTS FROM SOME OF WILSON'S LETTERS IN THE CCC

March 16, 1938 - In Scotland, Pa., and he decided to sign up for another six months.

May 19, 1938 - He was on a time keeper job, but it was too easy, and he decided to go on the road with a pick and shovel.

April 16, 1939 - He is now in CCC Camp No. 2335 SCS-4 (2335th Company, Project SCS-4-Pa.), Waynesboro, PA. It is 100 miles from home and 30 miles from Chambersburg. It's called Camp Glen Furney and is a "dump."

May 2, 1939 - His work is cracking rock with a 12 pound sledge all day in a quarry. He says of the camp: "This camp certainly is a dump, the buildings and landscape remind me of the city dump including the meals and I'm very sorry I came in but since I am in I'll try and stick it out."

September 11, 1939 - He signed for another 6 months in the CCC until March 31, 1940. He says he is sick of the CCC, and wrote to his mother that "I am only staying in to help you."

October 24, 1939 - The last two months he had been working in the area office in Waynesboro, and says "my work consists of mapping, surveying, and stripping farms."

February 23, 1940 - "I seen 'Gone With The Wind' the other night, it set me back $1.10 but it was very good." *[Note: A movie back home in Lebanon cost 25 cents.]*

Right: Wilson, standing on the right, in 1938 in the CCC with three buddies.

Sun. Jan. 28, 1940
Waynesboro, Penna.

Dear Mother & Family;

I just found out that I will have to leave camp at the end of march because regulations say you can't be in more than two years after 1937 so with a year at Scotland and a year (at the end of march) here at Waynesboro, my two years are up and I will have to get out. So in two month I'll be home and I have decided because I can't stand it loafing around home to join the army, soon after I do get home, that is if I don't get a fairly good job like in one of the steel mills or where Dave works. In the mean time if there is a chance to get a job Dad, Dave or you come across one let me know and I'll come home.

We started basketball last week and played two games getting beat in both 45-39 & 47-22. I was elected captain for the games but didn't make out so hot I scored 13 pts in the first game and only 6 pts in the second. We play two more the coming week and I hope we make out better.

I won't be home until the end of march

and that will be f
and the rest loo

The camp had
one of the rookies
(bed. night at the
two hours after
men are on sick g
one whole barracks
some how I'm luc
feel fine.

I think I'll
in radio this pay
and so until I he

Don't forget to write

[Postmark is Waynesboro, P.A., Jan. 29, 1940, 1:30 PM]
Mr. & Mrs. Robt Lineaweaver
1908 W Chestnut St.
Lebanon Penna.

[No Return Address]

Sun. Jan. 28, 1940
Waynesboro, Penna.

Dear Mother & Family:

I just found out that I will have to leave camp at the end of march because regulations say you can't be in more than two years after 1937 so with a year at Scotland and a year (at the end of march) here at Waynesboro, my two years are up and I will have to get out. So in two month I'll be home and I have decided because I can't stand it loafing around home to join the army, soon after I do get home, that is if I don't get a fairly good job like in one of the steel mills or where Dave works. In the meantime if there's a chance to get a job if Dad, Dave or you come across one let me know and I'll come home.

We started basketball last week and played two games getting beat in both 45-39 & 47-22. I was elected captain for the games but didn't make out so hot I scored 13 pts in the first game and only 6 pts in the second. We play two more the coming week and I hope we make out better.

I won't be home until the end of march and that will be for good so I do hope you and the rest look around for a job for me.

The camp had a lot of tough luck lately one of the rookies died from pneumonia last Wed. night at the Hagerstown Hospital about two hours after he arrived there and about 61 men are on sick quarters on account of colds, one whole barracks was made into a hospital. Somehow I'm lucky, I have a slight cold but I feel fine.

I think Ill start a correspondence course in radio this pay day, it cost 3 dollars a month. And so until I hear from you I remain

Your son
Wilson

Don't forget to write

have died if they would have got that much

I don't know when I'll come home next, sometime this summer, I was sorry to see Cli leave but I guess he was tired of the [...] a rumor going aro[...] I hope every[...] of anything else

Wilson C. Sniceweaver
CCC Co 2335 SCS-4
Waynesboro Penna

Dear Mother:
The last three or four letters that I wrote you, I told you that I was coming home, my two years up. The Superintendent Mr. Seamen offered me a P.A. (project assistant) and I accepted. I am not an enrollee anymore, but about the same. Ask Cli to explain it. You will still get the allotment of $22.00 every month.

I passed my driving test last Wednesday and got government license, the state cop that gave me the test was from Palmyra surname Whitey Onsbach, maybe pop knows him

I wish you would send me some hankerchiefs, I don't have one to my name, some tooth powder and if you wish to send tobacco get me union leader instead of the bag tobacco, and by the way I got the package you sent, the cake was very good and wasn't smashed and you know them few candy Easter eggs you sent was the only candy I had over Easter. I'll bet the kids would

[No envelope remains with this letter.]

Wilson C. Lineaweaver
CCC Co 2335 SCS-4
Waynesboro Penna

Dear Mother:

The last three or four letters that I wrote you, I told you that I was coming home, my two years up. The Superintendent Mr. Seamen offered me a P.A. (project assistant) and I accepted. I am not an enrollee anymore, but about the same. Ask Eli to explain it. You will still get the allotment of $22.00 every month.

I passed my driving test last Wednesday and got government license, the state cop that gave me the test was from Palmyra his name Whitey Ansbach, maybe pop know him.

I wish you would sent me some hankerchiefs. I don't have one to my name, some tooth powder and if you wish to send tobacco get me union leader instead of the bag tobacco, and by the way I got the package you sent, the cake was very good and wasn't smashed and you know them few candy Easter eggs you sent was the only candy I had over Easter. I'll bet the kids would have died if they would have got that much

I don't know when I'll come home next, sometime this summer. I was sorry to see Eli leave but I guess he was tired of the place. Right now theres a rumor going around of the camp breaking up. I hope everybodys well, can't think of anything else to say but good bye

Your son
Wilson

This is a brass CCC/Social Security identification card for Wilson. *(Part of the social security number was removed on this picture.)*

April 10, 1940
Waynesboro, Pa.

Dear Mother & Family,

The package came this evening and everything was alright. The cake it was smashed but it still tasted pretty good.

No doubt Ele & Ed told you the reason I stayed here, I couldn't see loafing around here when you are all busy. If dad would still be working I could stay but as it is really important the money is to the family that I sent, I am in position as a project assistant to use the money as I see fit, but you will continue getting $20.00 monthly...

CCC Company 2335
Camp Glen Furney, SCS-4
Waynesboro, Pa.

[Postmark is Waynesboro, P.A., April 11, 1940, 10 AM]
Mrs. Robt. Lineaweaver
1908 W. Chestnut St.
Lebanon Penna.

[Return Address:]
CCC Company 2335
Camp Glen Furney, SCS-4
Waynesboro, Pa.
W.C. Lineaweaver

April 10, 1940
Waynesboro, Pa.

Dear Mother & Family,

The package came this evening and everything was all right but the cake, it was smashed but it still tasted pretty good.

No doubt Eli told you the reason I stayed here, I couldn't see loafing around home while you are on relief. If dad would still be working I would be home and I realize how important the money is to the family that I sent. I am in position as a project assistant to use the money as I see fit, but you will continue getting $22.00 monthly and I hope you use it wisely and for the best purpose

I realize I have to get out of here sometime, I can't stay all the time and that money might come in handy, I really am working hard right now for it and after two years in the CCC I deserve it, but will not take it until conditions improve at home.

And Mother Ive often wondered if Harold and Jake miss me, do they often talk about me? Tell them I might be home to see them in the near future and I'll take them to the movie that I promised them.

I got government license now and have a crew of my own, most of my work are forms of surveying which include strip croping, marking drainage ditches, terraces and surveying for orchard planting. It is pretty important work and I am proud having a crew of men under me and supervising work of my own ingenuity. I am learning plenty and without bragging I have been commented often by the technical men which are a bunch of nice guys. Starting the latter part of this week we begin spring tree planting which include some 150,000 trees

If you come up over the summer I want to show you the blueprint I made of the camp, it rated excellent at district headquarters. I got a lot of credit for it and I pride it a lot, ask Eli about it, he didn't think I could make anything like that, in fact I didn't think so myself.

I imagine this is about the longest letter I ever wrote, it is sorty dull around here right now and I feel like writing, I hope your in the same mood about reading when you get this. I interrupt to tell that some forty rookies have just arrived from Reading and theres quite a rumpous going on, you should see the big brute that came in right next to me, I think Ill move.

It certainly is hell the way their acting over in Europe, right now flashes are coming in on the radio, I think the Germans are getting a little of their own medicine. And I pity poor Norway. It seems that nothing can stop Germany. I think Sweden is next or Holland. I hope we can stay out. so until I see or hear from you I'll close this novel

Your loving son
Wilson

P.S. Keep me informed how things are going and thank fat and Martha for me, for the birth day greetings and I also want to thank you for remembering. I wish I was home to argue with Dave and pop about the war situation.

June 17, 1940

Dear dad,

I am glad to here that you are working again and I hope it will last for a long time. The steel business should be pretty good right now with the war in Europe and the large defense program of this country.

Doesn't it look bad for the French and English right now and at the rate this country is going we will be in it shortly.

You know dad, I didn't buy a stitch of clothing for over 3 years. I am lucky I have a pr. of socks and an old pr. of shoes. If I went off some place I had to borrow clothing. I also want to get my teeth fixed beside getting some clothing so if you are able between now and the end of the month will you please send me $10.00 If you havent or can't spare the money it will have to be allright with me. If you decide to send the money send it by money order and I would appreciate it a lot for I believe I justly deserve it.

Your son
Wilson

Please answer

[Postmark is Waynesboro, P.A., 1940, 8 PM]
Mr. Robt. Lineaweaver
1908 W. Chestnut St.
Lebanon Penna.

[Return Address:]
CCC Company 2335
Camp Glen Furney, SCS-4
Waynesboro, Pa.
W.C. Lineaweaver

CCC Unit Certificates for First Aid, Elementary Surveying, and Current Events

Original size is 5 ½" x 3 ¼"

CIVILIAN CONSERVATION CORPS

C.C.C.

U.C. 999415

Unit Certificate

THIS CERTIFIES THAT ___WILLIAM LINEAWEAVER___ of
Company ___2335___ has satisfactorily completed ___12___
hours of instruction in ___FIRST AID___ and
is therefore granted this Certificate.

_____ Project Superintendent.   _____ Company Commander.
_____ Camp Educational Adviser.

Date ___JULY 8, 1940___   Place ___Waynesboro, Pa.___
gpo 6—9671

CIVILIAN CONSERVATION CORPS

C.C.C.

U.C. 67837

Unit Certificate

THIS CERTIFIES THAT ___WILLIAM LINEAWEAVER___ of
Company ___2335___ has satisfactorily completed ___12___
hours of instruction in ___ELEMENTARY SURVEYING___ and
is therefore granted this Certificate.

_____ Project Superintendent.   _____ Company Commander.
_____ Camp Educational Adviser.

Date ___JULY 8, 1940___   Place ___Waynesboro, Pa.___
gpo 6—9671

CIVILIAN CONSERVATION CORPS

C.C.C.

U.C. 67905

Unit Certificate

THIS CERTIFIES THAT ___WILLIAM LINEAWEAVER___ of
Company ___2335___ has satisfactorily completed ___12___
hours of instruction in ___CURRENT EVENTS___ and
is therefore granted this Certificate.

_____ Project Superintendent.   _____ Company Commander.
_____ Camp Educational Adviser.

Date ___JULY 8, 1940___   Place ___Waynesboro, Pa.___
gpo 6—9671

Aug. 17, 1940
Waynesboro, Pa.

Dear Mother & Family:

The package came last week and everything was O.K. The cake was flattened out a little but tasted good. I just finished reading your letter and was glad to hear from you, I am sorry about Harold's toothache, tell him not to eat so much candy.

Hows pops work, hope it last's, because I might be coming home next month, Ive been in here too long and I'm sick of it. What do you think of me coming home? Do you think I could get a job? Could you manage without that $22.00 a month, but I guess Ill be here for a while yet.

If you move, don't forget to send that letter* so I can come home and help to move and don't forget to send the new address. In your next letter let me know how you & dad feel about me coming home for good, or loafing around for a few months until I can get a job or Join the army, it just that I'm sick of the C.C.C. so until I hear from you I'll remain

Your son
Wilson   P.S. Hope pops still trying to get me that job.

[Postmark is Waynesboro, P.A., Aug. 18, 1940, 9:30 PM]
Mr & Mrs. Robt. Lineaweaver
1908 W. Chestnut St
Lebanon Penna.

[Return Address:]
CCC Company 2335
Camp Glen Furney, SCS-4
Waynesboro, Pa.
W.C. Lineaweaver

Sept. 28, 1940
Waynesboro Pa.

Dear Mother:

Hopping was pretty slow last Sunday, but I got back O.K. around supper time. Fat picked me up just outside of Harrisburg and took me about 18 miles. I am sorry I didn't write you sooner.

I guess you know that I won't have to come home and register as I thought I would, we will register right here in camp. I don't know whether I ought to join the army or wait till I am drafted. If drafted the time is only one year compared to four

If everything works out right next week I'll be at the world's fair. If you can manage early next week send me a package I need tooth powder, a tooth brush, soap, wash rag and whatever else you wish to send. Tell Jim to practice up in pool and when I come home again I'll play him

Your son
Wilson

[Postmark is Waynesboro, P.A., Sept. 29, 1940, 9:30 PM]
Mr & Mrs. Robt. Lineaweaver
927 ½ W. Cumberland St
Lebanon Penna

[No Return Address]

Oct 9, 1940
Waynesboro Pa.

Dear Mother & Family:

Just a few lines to let you know that I got back from the fair safetly. Where you surprised when you got my postcard? I should have told you I was going. We hopped to Phila. then took a Greyhound to N.Y. We slept in the Sloan Y.M.C.A. in N.Y. 75 cents a night on the 18th floor. When we went through the Holland tunnel my ears started to hurt, I guess that was due to the pressure. We went from N.Y. to the Worlds Fair by train.

Its impossible to describe the fair to you. I saw the Aquacade and was in the perisphere. General Motors was the best exhibit at the fair, I liked Duponts exhibit of chemical wonders and a hundred others. I might come home this weekend if a fellow from Harrisburg decides to go, he has a car so thats a ride to Harrisburg and back.

We ate our meals in Horn & Hardens Automats where you put your money in a slot and get what you want. Did you get the letter I sent last week?

Your son
Wilson

[Postmark is Fairfield, P.A., Oct. 10, 1940, 2 PM]
Mrs. Robt. Lineaweaver
927 ½ Cumberland St.
Lebanon Penna.

[Return Address (on back of envelope):]
Wilson C. lineaweaver
CCC Co. 2335 SCS-4
Waynesboro, Pa.

Nov 4, 1940
Baltimore Md.

Dear Mother:

I recieved the postcard and letter Saturday Morning and I was glad to hear from you and I want to thank you for the money. I borrowed the writing paper from a coast guard fellow that sleeps next to me. If you didn't send the cigarettes yet why don't bother because I think I can manage till I get home which may be this week sometime, I hope.

So Jim got a job (I can imagine him working) maybe he can get me one. Where did you say he was working? Is pop still working good and did you get a house yet? I wonder what my registration number is, were they listed in paper, if not see if you can find out

Its pretty lonely here at the hospital nothing to do all day. We have earphones at each bed so we can listen to the radio but the thing is we have to listen to what they have on down in the office. Dot should be here, stories all day and very little music. Sometimes there's a program on that Ill like and bang they switch stations. Boy! does that make me mad.

Your son
Wilson

(Wilson was in the hospital with pneumonia.)

[Postmark is Baltimore, MD., Nov. 4, 1940,12:30 PM]
Mrs Robt Lineaweaver
927 ½ Cumberland St
Lebanon Pa.

[No Return Address]

Honorable Discharge
from the
Civilian Conservation Corps

TO ALL WHOM IT MAY CONCERN:

This is to Certify That* ___Wilson C. Lineaweaver___ CC3-211475

a member of the CIVILIAN CONSERVATION CORPS, who was enrolled

___October 15, 1937___ at ___Harrisburg, Pennsylvania___, is hereby
(Date)

HONORABLY DISCHARGED therefrom, by reason of** Expiration term of service

Par. 1, SO#62, HS Co. 1324, SP-18, Scotland, Penna.

Said ___Wilson C. Lineaweaver___ was born in ___Elizabeth___

in the State of ___New Jersey___ When enrolled he was ___18___ years

of age and by occupation a ___Laborer___ He had ___Grey___ eyes,

___Brown___ hair, ___Fair___ complexion, and was ___5___ feet

___8___ inches in height. His color was ___White___

Given under my hand at ___SP-18 Scotland, Pa.___, this ___Thirtieth___ day

of ___September___, one thousand nine hundred and ___Thirty-eight.___

SAVERIO DIMEO, 1st Lt. Engr-Res., Commanding
(Name)   (Title)

* Insert name, as "John J. Doe."
** Give reason for discharge.

C. C. C. Form No. 2
April 5, 1937

RECORD OF SERVICE IN CIVILIAN CONSERVATION CORPS

**Served:

   a. From ___10-15-37___ to ___9-30-38___, under ___D.I.___ Dept. at ___SP-18 Scotland, Pa.___

      Type of work ___Park service___   *Manner of performance ___Satisfactory___

   b. From _____ to _____, under _____ Dept. at _____

      Type of work _____   *Manner of performance _____

   c. From _____ to _____, under _____ Dept. at _____

      Type of work _____   *Manner of performance _____

   d. From _____ to _____, under _____ Dept. at _____

      Type of work _____   *Manner of performance _____

   e. From _____ to _____, under _____ Dept. at _____

      Type of work _____   *Manner of performance _____

Remarks: Allotment of $22.00 per month to Mr. Robert Lineaweaver, 1908 W. Chestnut Street, Lebanon, Penna. Address of enrollee same. Selecting Agency notified of discharge. Enrollee notified of ineligibility to reenroll for period of 6 months. Provisions of Federal Compensation Act read to enrollee. FBI Fingerprint record taken.

RECORD OF INOCULATION

TYPHOID: 1st dose: 10-16-37   2nd dose: 10-22-37   3rd dose: 10-29-37

SMALLPOX: 10-16-37   RESULT: IMMUNE.

Paid in cash $8.00   by me.

Allotment to be paid by Finance Officer, U. S. Army, Philadelphia, Penna.

Discharged: Honorably, September 30, 1938 at Co. 1324, CCC, SP-18-Pa., Camp Still-House Hollow Scotland, Pennsylvania.

Transportation furnished from ___Not furnished, transportation waived.___, Penna.

Saverio Di Meo (signature)
SAVERIO DIMEO, 1st Lt. Engr-Res., Commanding

* Use words "Excellent" or "Satisfactory."
** To be taken from C. C. C. Form No. 1.

U. S. GOVERNMENT PRINTING OFFICE   3--10171

Honorable Discharge
from the
Civilian Conservation Corps

TO ALL WHOM IT MAY CONCERN:

This is to Certify That*   Wilson C. Lineaweaver,   CC3-211475

a member of the **CIVILIAN CONSERVATION CORPS, who was enrolled**

April 14th, 1939   at   Lebanon, Penna.   , is hereby
(Date)

HONORABLY DISCHARGED therefrom, by reason of**   Accept Employment,

per par. 44 a C.C.C. War Department REGS dated 1937.

Said   Wilson C. Lineaweaver   was born in   Elizabeth,

in the State of   Penna.   When enrolled he was   19   years

of age and by occupation a   Laborer,   He had   grey   eyes,

brown   hair,   fair   complexion, and was   five   feet

eight   inches in height. His color was   White.

Co. 2335th, SCS-4-Pa.,CCC

Given under my hand at   Waynesboro, Penna., this   27th,   day

of   November   , one thousand nine hundred and   Forty.,

                   (Name)   (Title)

* Insert name, as "John J. Doe."   JOSEPH LeMASURIER J.,
** Give reason for discharge.   CCC Company Commander

C. C. C. Form No. 2
April 5, 1937

RECORD OF SERVICE IN CIVILIAN CONSERVATION CORPS

**Served:

a. From 4-4-39 to 11-27-40 , under War C . 2335th, SCS-4-Pa., Dept. at Waynesboro Penna.

Type of work Soil Conservation *Manner of performance Satisfactory

b. From to , under Dept. at

Type of work *Manner of performance

c. From to , under Dept. at

Type of work *Manner of performance

d. From to , under Dept. at

Type of work *Manner of performance

e. From to , under Dept. at

Type of work *Manner of performance

Remarks: Rating at time of Discharge, (Assistant Leader)
The Project Superintendent, Mr. James A. Seaman, makes the following estimate of this enrollee as a workman., " He is a satisfactory leader and workman."

Educational Qualfications: 4th. Yr. High School.
Occupational Qualifications: Laborer.

Enrollee notified of ineligibility for reselection for a period of six months from date of Discharge.
Provisions of the Federal Employees Compensation Act have been read to this man.

Typhoid 1st. 4-6-39 2nd. 4-13-39 3rd. 4-21-40
Smallpox , April 6 1939 Result: Immune.

Discharged: November 27th, 1940 Co. 2335th, SCS-4-Pa., CCC, at Waynesboro, Penna.

Transportation furnished from none furnished. to

JAN 9 1941

PHILA., PA. 842

22.10

PAID IN FULL $

* Use words "Excellent" or "Satisfactory."
** To be taken from C. C. C. Form No. 1.

E. J. KELLY
LIEUT. COL., F. D.
FINANCE OFFICER, U. S. A.

(Name) (Title)
JOSEPH LeMASURIER J,
CCC Company Commander

U. S. GOVERNMENT PRINTING OFFICE 3—10171

UNITED STATES NAVY

WILSON'S NAVY SERVICE TIMELINE

Information for this timeline was taken primarily from Wilson's service records obtained from NARA, St. Louis, MO. Information gleaned from his letters is noted accordingly. The actions in which he was involved and listed here are not a comprehensive list, only what he mentioned in his letters. He would have been involved in many additional actions.

1941 January 6 - Enlisted in the U.S. Navy, USNRS Baltimore, MD, for a period of six (6) full years

1941 January 8 - Reported to U.S. Naval Training Station (USNTS) NOB, Norfolk, VA; Rate A.S.; Identification Number 258 32 24

1941 February 28 - Completed recruit training. Qualified in swimming. Indoor rifle range score: Max score 400, Qual. score 320, Actual score 290. Received gas mask instruction, gas mask size 2.

1941 February-March - Went home on nine day leave (February 17, 1941 letter)

1941 April 30 - Transferred to a Course of Instruction, Radio School, at NAS Jacksonville, FL

1941 May 1 - Reported to the U.S. Naval Air Station (USNAS) in Jacksonville, FL, from the USNTS in Norfolk, VA

1941 May 5 - Entered Radio School Class for a period of 16 weeks

1941 May 6 - Advanced to Sea2, from Rate A.S. [Apprentice Seaman]

1941 August 23 - Graduated from Class "A" Group IV Aviation Radio School (Qual-Air) in Jacksonville, FL. Graduated number 19 out of 68; Marks in various subjects ranged from 85 to 97 with a final mark of 94.2

1941 August - Went home on leave (September 2, 1941 letter)

1941 August 26 - Transferred to USNAS, Norfolk, VA, "for duty on USS *Hornet*"

1941 August 28 - Reported to USNAS NOB in Norfolk, VA, from USNAS in Jacksonville, FL

1941 September 30 - Listed as on 'temporary duty'

1941 October 22 - Transferred/reported to the USS *Hornet*, USNAS NOB Norfolk, VA

1941 October 24 - Transferred to Bombing Squadron 8 (VB-8) for duty, temporarily based on shore (with USS *Hornet*)

1941 November, approximately 9-19 - Went home on leave (November 20, 1941 letter)

1941 December 23 - Embarked on board USS *Hornet* with Bombing Squadron 8 (VB-8)

1942 February 1 - Temporarily based on shore with Bombing Squadron 8

1942 February 28 - Embarked on board USS *Hornet* with Bombing Squadron 8

1942 April 1 - Advanced to ARM3c from Sea2c, in Bombing Squadron 8

1942 April 29 - Transferred to the U.S. Naval Air Station, Pearl Harbor, for a course of instruction in Aerial Gunnery (temporary duty) in Carrier Aircraft Service Unit #1, from Bombing Squadron 8; transferred April 29 and received April 30

1942 June 8 - Commended by Commander-in-Chief, U.S. Pacific Fleet, as a member of the crew of Carrier Aircraft Service Unit #1 during the period of May 18, 1942 to May 29, 1942, when outstanding assembly and repair, ordnance, and radio work was accomplished on airplanes for duty on board combatant units of the fleet

1942 June 13 - Completed course of Instruction in Aviation Radio and Gunnery School

1942 June 17 - Reported to Bombing Squadron 8 from Carrier Aircraft Service Unit (CASU) #1 Ford Island, P.H.T.H.; "Temporary duty completed this date"

1942 October 1 - Listed "at sea" on beneficiary slip

1942 October 26 - Served with the USS *Hornet* during the Battle of Santa Cruz Island

1942 November 1 - Advanced to ARM2c from ARM3c

1942 November 14 - Transferred to Fleet Air West Coast, U.S. via the USS *Rochambeau*

1942 December - Thirty day leave (January 4, 1943 letter)

1943 January 6 - Reported to Carrier Aircraft Service Unit #6 from VB-8 ComFiar WC

1943 January 29 - Reported aboard Escort Scouting Squadron 37 (VGS-37) for duty *[The Escort Scouting Squadron 37 (VGS-37) had a designation change to Composite Squadron 37 (VC-37) on March 1, 1943.]*

1943 March 14 - Assigned to temporary duty to Red Bluff, California, Redding, California, and other places as necessary in connection with a search for missing aircraft; Wilson, ARM2/c, Composite Squadron 37

1943 May 1 - Designated Air Bomber to fill vacancy by authority of BuPers Manual Article D 5321 (5)

1943 May - Received a "few days special liberty" (May 10, 1943 letter)

1943 June/July - Ten day leave (June 23, 1943 letter)

1943 August 1 - Advanced to ARM1c from ARM2c, in Composite Squadron 37 (VC-37) (August 9, 1943 letter)

1943 October 10 - Embarked on USS *Sangamon* with Composite Squadron 37

1943 October 27 - Crossed equator, qualified shellback

1943 December 22 - Reported aboard (transferred to) U.S. Naval Hospital, San Diego, CA, from Composite Squadron 37. (Actually entered the hospital on December 21 according to his December 31, 1943 letter)

1944 May 5 - Discharged from the U.S. Naval Hospital (May 8, 1944 letter)

1944 May 5 - Reported aboard Bombing Squadron 84 from U.S. Naval Hospital, San Diego, CA

1944 September/October - Fourteen day leave (October 17, 1944 letter)

1945 January 24 - VB-84 reported aboard the USS *Bunker Hill* and departed Alameda, CA, at 1608

1945 March 1 - Advanced to ARCM from ARM1c, in Bombing Squadron 84. [*When Wilson made the rank of Aviation Chief Radioman, officers then addressed him as "Chief".*]

1945, May 11, Friday - USS *Bunker Hill* hit by two kamikaze planes; Wilson killed in the attack

In his book about the Battle of Midway, Craig Symonds gives a description of dive bombing: "The idea behind dive-bombing was for the pilot to approach his intended target at high altitude, say 20,000 feet, and preferably from out of the sun to avoid detection. ...After lining up on the target as best he could, the squadron leader deployed perforated 'dive brakes' on the trailing edge of his wings and went into a steep dive, around 70 degrees, with the pilots of his squadron following his lead *[about 5 seconds apart]*. During the dive, the pilots felt weightless, 'like you were floating,' as one put it. The Dauntless did not have shoulder straps, only a seat belt, so it was 'like you were hanging out on a string.' Between 2,000 and 1,500 feet, the pilot released his bomb. ...Then he pulled out of the dive, usually doing a 'snap pullout' that sometimes resulted in his briefly blacking out. Dive bombing an enemy ship that was twisting and turning at 25 or 30 knots was, as one pilot recalled, 'similar to dropping a marble from eye height on a scampering cockroach.' It was especially difficult because often during these steep dives, the windscreen would fog up at about 8,000 feet, all but obscuring the target. One pilot said it was 'like putting a white sheet in front of you and you have to bomb from memory.' 'Believe me,' he recalled, 'that's a helpless feeling when you try to dive bomb and [can] hardly see your target.' All in all, it was both a physical and mental challenge to dive almost three miles straight down at nearly three hundred miles an hour with a fogged windscreen and with the target ship throwing up a wall of antiaircraft fire. It was equally challenging for the enlisted man in the back seat, whose job during the dive was to call out the readings from the altimeter *[every 500 or 1,000 feet]*, especially important when the windscreen was fogged and the pilot could not see. The backseat crewman was also the radio operator and gunner. When the pilot released the bomb and pulled out of the dive, the rear-seat gunner was pushed down into his seat with, as one recalled, 'a force of one ton at eight G's,' or eight times the force of gravity. Nonetheless, he had plenty to do. 'Then the pilot tells you to go on the air, or switch to the homing frequency, or give hand signals to nearby crews in Morse code. All of this requires securing the guns, reaching forward, changing radio coils, and moving dials accurately and quickly.' Morse-code messages were sent by hand signal in order to maintain radio silence. The radiomen/gunners smacked their palm with their fist for a dot and slapped open handed for a dash. Those in nearby planes had to watch this and translate to their pilots. It required both intense concentration and a strong stomach to perform all these tasks flawlessly."[6]

A mid-war publicity photo posed for Navy recruiters to draw qualified young men into the combat aircrewman program. Photo from *SBD Dauntless Units of World War 2* by Barrett Tillman, Oxford: Osprey Pub., 1998, page 87.

In Wilson's letters he mentions three types of planes in which he was a radioman/gunner (also called radio-gunners, rear-gunners, back-seat men, or rear-seaters): the SBD-3 Dauntless dive bomber, the TBF Avenger torpedo bomber, and the SB2C Helldiver dive bomber. On

---

[6] Symonds, Craig L. *The Battle of Midway (Pivotal Moments in American History)*. Oxford University Press, 2011. 52-53.

these planes the radioman was responsible for communications, being trained in airborne radio, radar, sonar, semaphore, and Morse code. All radiomen/gunners at that time were enlisted men. When not on flight rosters, they worked on the hangar decks in the aircraft repair shacks, standing deck watches, or were belting ammunition, hauling ordnance, or pushing planes. In flight, they took the same risks as pilots and gave their lives in the same numbers.

The SBD-3 Dauntless dive bomber, and the SB2C Helldiver, each had a two-man crew of a pilot and radioman/gunner. On these Wilson would have manned the rear cockpit handling twin .30-caliber machine guns as well as the radio equipment.

The radioman/gunner of an SBD-3 Dauntless prepares to load his right-hand M-2 Browning. The .30-06 cartridges are belted with one in four tracer, distinguished by black -tipped bullets. Photo from *SBD Dauntless Units of World War 2,* by Barrett Tillman, Oxford: Osprey Pub., 1998, page 10.

The TBF Avenger torpedo bomber had a three-man crew of a pilot, turret or rear-seat gunner, and a radioman-bombardier-ventral/belly gunner. On the Avenger, Wilson could have been in the turret manning a .50 caliber machine gun, or in the belly of the plane manning the radio equipment and a .30 caliber machine gun. In the belly there was very little armor protection putting this crewman in constant danger of shrapnel wounds from enemy fire. The two crewmen could not wear their parachutes during operations, but the man in the belly had to first strap on his parachute and crawl out the small door before the man in the turret could drop down into the belly and follow suit. Also, neither of the crewmen could view or access the pilot's cockpit. Nerve-wracking for the two crewmen, particularly on a push-over, dive, and pull-out, was that they never knew if the pilot had been killed and if the plane was out of control or not.

In his book about the USS *Hornet* (CV-8), "*The Ship That Held The Line*", Lisle A. Rose writes: "The *Hornet* and her sister ships berthed the crew exclusively in the hull, not on the gallery deck. The men lived, sixty or more, in large compartments, sleeping on canvas-covered racks that were stacked four high and so close to each other that a man had to turn over carefully during the night to avoid bumping the sagging canvas above that held a shipmate. Each sailor had a locker just large enough for uniforms, dungarees, flat hats, white hats, shoes, and toiletries. One bulkhead contained a large locker for peacoats, and adjacent to each berthing compartment were the heads with showers, toilets, and shaving sinks. Three times daily at specified hours the men stood in long lines that snaked up ladders and along passageways and out onto the hangar deck, waiting for cafeteria-style meals in the large mess hall amidships on B Deck, two decks below the hangar. The crew's mess hall, which was adjacent to the ship's post office and laundry, was equipped with long benches and equally long tables.

San Diego Air and Space Museum

Men in line on the *Bunker Hill*.

"As the carrier and her escorts maneuvered ceaselessly, tension aboard the *Hornet* built steadily. After ten months at sea, several thousand men had become accustomed to a radical new life-style. But the stresses of daily life aboard a large carrier and of dangerous, unceasing work were compounded by the strains of war. Every American sailor in the Pacific in 1942 had learned to live with the odds against him, but the *Hornet* had become Japan's primary target. It was anyone's guess when an enemy bomber, torpedo plane, or submarine might turn the big carrier into a blazing torch like the *Wasp*, when a pilot might suddenly be killed or go down with engine failure hundreds of miles from base, when a flight deck crewman might be sawed in half by a propeller, run over, or thrown into the sea by a taxiing airplane. Such thoughts were stifled even as they formed, but they rattled even the strongest nerves."[7]

From the history of the USS *Sangamon*, Donald Schroeder writes: "She [*Sangamon*] was the first of four tankers converted into carriers, which became known as the Sangamon Class. She had a crew of 1100 including the aircrew. She had one catapult and two elevators to the hanger deck. The majority of the crew had quarters below the water line. On calm days or when in port, it was possible to open portholes for ventilation. At night no portholes or hatches could be open to maintain total black out while at sea. If you had to move around in these areas you would use a flashlight with red cellophane over the glass. The sick bay was in the after part of the ship. The ship was like a small city. It had a well-stocked sick bay with a surgeon. Injured sailors from the smaller ships were sent over by a stretcher on ropes. This was called a breeches buoy. They had a dentist, a barber, laundry, dry cleaning, post office and a machine shop. It also had a (GEDUNK) store where toilet articles were sold. On some days they sold ice cream. They were able to make 77 gallons a day when everything went OK. ... The profits were used to support the laundry, barber, cobbler, and tailor shop. When getting a hair cut, it was a good thing to tip the barber to get a better cut.

[7] Rose, Lisle A. *The Ship That Held the Line: The U.S.S. Hornet and the First Year of the Pacific War.* Annapolis, MD: Naval Institute Press, 1995. 24,207.

"While at sea the ships were always on a zigzag course in order to make it harder for an enemy submarine to attack. If another ship was alongside for fueling or transfer of mail or personnel this was not possible. In an emergency they would break off very quickly and resume zigzagging.

"It was not uncommon to have some type of accident when landing aircraft. There were men standing by in fire suits for every landing. There was a special vehicle for picking up planes that went onto the catwalk. It was called a 'cherry picker'. They also had jeeps for moving the planes about the flight and hanger decks. On launching operations, there were times when planes would not have enough speed and they would go into the sea. Destroyers would pick up the crew if they survived. In one case a pilot died shortly after landing his badly damaged plane. The Captain had them strip the plane of all-important parts and then pushed the plane over the side with the pilot in it for burial. Any time a fuselage of a plane was badly damaged they would dump them after removing all valuable parts. Sometimes planes would drop their bombs or rockets when landing. They were to get rid of all unused ones, but some of the time this was not possible because of damage to their plane by enemy fire. If they forgot or were not able to lock their 50 caliber guns, they would fire on landing. This would always send anyone topside scurrying."[8]

"The fact that the pilots were mostly officers and the rear-seat gunners were all enlisted men sometimes made for an awkward partnership. While in the air, the junior officer pilots depended heavily on their enlisted gunners, literally trusting them with their lives, yet aboard ship they were all but strangers. The gunners never came into the wardroom and seldom ventured into the squadron ready rooms. They never played cards with the pilots or sat around with them. ... In the air, the relationship was fraternal and interdependent; on the ship, each man went his separate way. The gunners called the pilots 'sir' or 'mister,' and the pilots referred to the gunners by their last names only. As one pilot put it, 'Pilots were treated as one class, gunners were treated as another class.' Another recalled, 'We hardly ever got to talk to our gunners until we were ready to climb into the cockpits.' "[9] While in aircraft, this formality of recognition was dispensed with to provide for team work and bonding of crews.

In addition to the segregation of officers and enlisted men, there was segregation among African-Americans, Filipinos, and whites. While the officers and enlisted men had their own separate bunking areas, whites also bunked separately from Filipinos who bunked separately from blacks. Blacks generally were assigned to mess hall duty, cleaning and sweeping duties, material and ammunition handling, etc. Filipinos were almost always assigned to various duties in the officer's quarters such as stewards and cooks.

With each deployment of the *Bunker Hill*, her third starting in January 1945, upgraded and new equipment was added to an already full ship. New equipment also required additional men. Originally designed to have about 2600 men, when Wilson was aboard for this third deployment, she had

San Diego Air and Space Museum

Bunks and men on the *Bunker Hill*.

[8] "USS *Sangamon* (CVE-26) by Donald T. Schroeder." Retrieved from http://www.navsource.org/archives/03/cve-26/history.pdf. 5,10,12.

[9] Symonds, Craig L. *The Battle of Midway (Pivotal Moments in American History)*. Oxford University Press, 2011. 54.

over 3400. Overcrowding meant some unfortunate sailors had to find space to bunk anywhere they could. Hammocks in the mess hall, cots stacked three high in an armory, and spaces in the boiler and engine rooms, were some of the options.

Maxwell Kennedy in his book "*Danger's Hour*" describes the *Bunker Hill*'s latrines for enlisted men: "The crewmen's latrine was dirty and extraordinarily public. Most of the men shared a lavatory in the center of the ship. ...[In the lavatory] two sets of benches ran along each side. A trough ran below each of the benches. A constant flow of seawater streamed down the troughs. The saltwater was carried in by pipes at the

San Diego Air and Space Museum

Haircuts on the *Bunker Hill*.

bow end, then drained by pipes at the stern end of the communal latrine. Dozens of men sat on boards atop these troughs, facing each other, twenty-four hours a day. The men sat crowded in their collective indignity, often reading the ship's newspaper *The Monument*."[10] Officers were treated differently and usually shared a bathroom with just a small group.

An aircrewman's life depended on the skill of his pilot. Sometimes in taking off for a mission a pilot would fail to get airborne and drop off the front of the ship. Or when returning from a mission, a

San Diego Air and Space Museum

Men playing cards on the *Bunker Hill*.

pilot would misjudge the wind speed, the speed of the ship, and his altitude, and would likewise land in the water in front of the ship. Few survived when this happened. These errors meant that they would likely be plowed over by the ship, which was not able to stop, then sucked into the path of the spinning and churning propellers.

It's been said that in combat waiting is the worst part. For pilots and their aircrewmen, this was often the case. Sometimes they waited in ready rooms for hours for their next mission only to find it delayed further because of weather, or other reasons perhaps not even known to them. Hours could drag on seemingly forever while under the overwhelming pressure of not knowing who may die that day. It could be you, a buddy from the ship, or someone you never met. While in the war zone, living

under these conditions of having periods of boredom with moments of fear could be very stressful.

While off the coast of Okinawa, the *Bunker Hill* was not alone. She was part of Task Group 58.3. This February 1945 diagram (right) shows the aircraft carriers *Bunker Hill*, *Essex*, and *Cowpens*, surrounded by a fleet of two battleships, two cruisers, and numerous destroyers. Task Group 58.3 was part of the larger Task Force 58. When the *Bunker Hill* was hit by kamikazes in May 1945, surrounding ships were able to come to her assistance. This fleet of ships worked together as a team in the war with Japan.

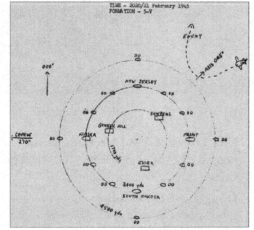

National Archives via fold3.com

_____

[10] Kennedy, Maxwell Taylor. *Danger's Hour: The story of the USS Bunker Hill and the kamikaze pilot who crippled her.* New York: Simon & Schuster, 2008. 170.

Wilson had three tours of duty into the active war zone: 1942 on the Hornet; *fall of 1943 on the* Sangamon; *and January-May 1945 on the* Bunker Hill. *He was on other ships, also. For instance, Bombing Squadron 84 (VB-84) had training exercises in November 1944 on the USS* Takanis Bay *(CVE-89) and the USS* Ranger *(CV-4). Except for the Helldiver photo which Wilson sent home, the photos of the planes are only examples of the type of planes in which he flew.*

Wilson was assigned to Bombing Squadron VB-8
USS *Hornet* (CV-8) and the Douglas SBD-3 Dauntless Dive Bomber, 1941-1942

Naval History and Heritage Command

San Diego Air and Space Museum

SBD-3 Dauntless

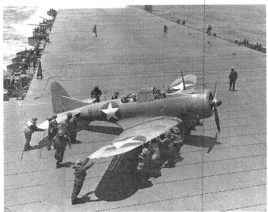

San Diego Air and Space Museum

USS *Hornet* CV-8 [Aircraft Carrier]:
Length - 824 ft. 9 in.; Beam - 114 ft.; Tonnage - 25,600 full; Crew - 2,919; Aircraft - 76+

Douglas SBD Dauntless:
[As changes were made to the SBD, these specifications varied.]
Length - 33 ft. 1 in.; Wingspan - 41 ft. 6 in.; Height - 13 ft. 7 in.; Max. speed - 256 mph; Max. range - 1370 miles; Carried 1,200+ lbs. of bombs; Crew of 2 - Pilot and Radioman/Gunner

A Dauntless of Bombing Squadron VB-8 on deck of the aircraft carrier USS *Hornet* (CV-8) during the battle of Midway, June 4, 1942. Wilson was on temporary duty in California during the battle of Midway.

Wilson was assigned to Composite Squadron VC-37, 1943
VC-37 embarked on the USS *Sangamon* (CVE-26) on October 10, 1943
The Grumman TBF Torpedo Bombers called "Avengers"*

Naval History and Heritage Command

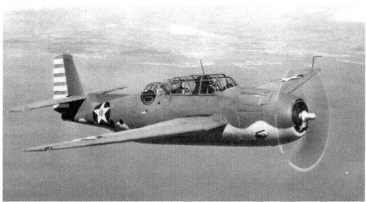

bluejacket.com

National Archives 80-G-418418

Above and left: TBF's

San Diego Air and Space Museum

NOTE: In his August 9, 1943 letter to his brother, Wilson stated that he had finished six months training in torpedo bombers [TBFs] and was now back in dive bombers. The Sangamon *carried both torpedo bombers [TBF's] and dive bombers [SBD's]. While he may have flown in an SBD when in combat, a record could not be found specifying in which type of plane Wilson actually flew while with the* Sangamon. *He would have been trained and qualified in both types, which made his skills versatile and valuable.*

USS *Sangamon* CVE-26 [Escort Carrier; Converted from an oil tanker]:
Length - 553 ft.; Beam - 114 ft. 3 in.; Tonnage - 24,275 full; Crew - 1080; Aircraft - 25+

Grumman TBF Avenger: *[As changes were made to the TBF, these specifications varied.]*
Length - 40 ft. 11 in.; Wingspan - 54 ft. 2 in.; Height - 15 ft. 5 in.; Max. speed - 275 mph; Range - 1000 miles; Carried 2,000 lbs. of bombs; Crew of 3 - Pilot, Radioman-Bombardier-Gunner, and Turret Gunner

Wilson was assigned to Bombing Squadron VB-84, 1944-1945
VB-84 embarked on the USS *Bunker Hill* on January 24, 1945
USS *Bunker Hill* (CV-17) and the Curtiss SB2C Helldiver

navsource.org

navsource.org

Island of the *Bunker Hill*

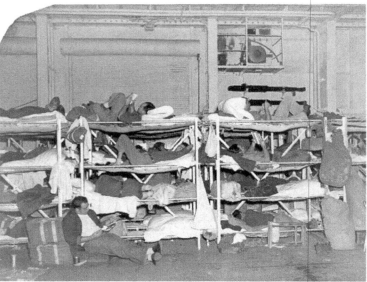

San Diego Air and Space Museum

Above: Bunks on the *Bunker Hill*. Enlisted air crew had racks that were attached so they didn't move in bad weather. By 1945 the sizes of air groups and their squadrons were larger, and perhaps this is how they handled the increased numbers.

U.S. Navy via wikimedia.com

Curtiss SB2C-4E Helldiver

USS *Bunker Hill* CV-17 [Aircraft Carrier]:
Length - 872 ft.; Beam - 147 ft. 6 in.; Tonnage - 36,380 full; Crew - 2,600+; Aircraft - 90+

Curtiss SB2C Helldiver: *[As changes were made to the Helldiver, these specifications varied.]* Length - 36 ft. 8 in.; Wingspan - 49 ft. 9 in.; Height - 14 ft. 9 in.; Max. speed - 295 mph; Range - 1165 miles; Carried 3,000 lbs. of bombs; Crew of 2 - Pilot and Radioman/Gunner

This is a photo that Wilson sent home of his plane in 1944. It is a Curtiss SB2C-3s Helldiver. He flew in Helldivers while with VB-84 and when on the USS *Bunker Hill* CV-17, 1944-1945. He says that "in the rear is the old dive bomber I used to fly." That plane is a Douglas SBD Dauntless Dive Bomber. Wilson flew in a Dauntless while with VB-8 and on the USS *Hornet* CV-8, 1942. Both sides of the photo are reproduced here actual size. This photo may have been taken at a naval station in San Diego or Hawaii.

My new plane in front H-24

This is a picture of my new plane - the Helldiver - in the rear is the old dive bomber that I used to fly. 970 & Thought you'd like to know.

Your loving son
Wilson

NRB Form No. 24 (Revised)

258822?

OCT 8 1941

This application blank will be forwarded for file with papers in the Bureau in cases of men accepted for enlistment.

APPLICATION FOR ENLISTMENT

__19th__ Congressional District, County of __Lebanon__ _____ State of __Pennsylvania__ _____
(This information to be supplied by Recruiter)

Last school grade completed: __12__ _____   MARTINSBURG VA. _____
Reason for enlistment: __CAREER__ _____   (Place)
Language qualifications: __ENGLISH__ _____   __OcT 22__ _____ , 1940
What is your trade? __NONE__ _____   (Date)   *Finished-File-Jacket*

I desire to submit my application for an enlistment of __6__ years in the United States Navy, and declare that I am of good habits and character in all respects; that I have never deserted from the U. S. Navy, Marine Corps, Army, Coast Guard or Civilian Conservation Corps. Having been informed that any false statements made by me would bar me from enlisting, I certify that the following statements are correct:

Name in full: __WILSON__ _____ __CHARLES__ _____ __LINEAWEAVER__ _____
    (First)   (Middle)   (Last)
Date of birth: __APRIL__ __6__ __1919__ __ Place of birth: __ELIZABETH N.J.__ _____
    (Month) (Day) (Year)   (City and State)
What is your race? __GERMAN WHITE__ __ If you were born in foreign territory, how did you acquire citizenship?
_____ Are you now a U. S. citizen? __YES__

Have you anyone solely or partially dependent upon you for support? __NO__ _____

Are you married? __NO__ _____ Have you ever been married? __NO__ _____
    (Yes or No)   (Yes or no)
Home Address: __927½__ __CUMBERLAND St__ __LEBANON__ __PA.__ __/MONTH__
    (Street No.) (Name of Street) (City or Town)   (State)
Former address: __1908 W. CHESTNUT St__ _____ Length of time lived at residence __16 YRS__
Former address: __CCC CAMP WAYNESBORO, PENN.__ Length of time lived at residence __3 YRS__
Where was your father born? __PA.__ _____ Where was your mother born? __PA.__ _____
Is your father living? __YES__ _____ Is your mother living? __YES__ _____
    (Yes or no)   (Yes or no)
Are your parents divorced? __NO__ Separated? __NO__ Have you a stepfather? __NO__ stepmother? __NO__
    (Yes or No)   (Yes or No)   (Yes or no)   (Yes or no)
Name and relationship of next of kin or legal guardian: __ROBERT JOSEPH LINEAWEAVER__
    (Full name)
__FATHER__ _____ Home address of next of kin or legal guardian: ____
    (Relationship)
__927½ CUMBERLAND St LEBANON__ __LEBANON__ __PA.__
(Street No.) (Name of Street) (City or Town)   (County)   (State)
Do you drink intoxicating liquors? __NO__ If so, to what extent? _____
    (Yes or No)
Have you ever been arrested or in the custody of police? __NO__ If so, for what? _____
_____

Have you ever been in a reform school, jail, or penitentiary, or have you ever been convicted of any crime?
__No__

Have you ever served in the U. S. Navy, Marine Corps, Army or Coast Guard? __NO__
If so, how long? _____ What is the date of your last discharge? _____
Character of discharge _____ Are you now or have you been a member of the National Guard, Naval Militia, Naval Reserve, or Marine Corps Reserve, or Civilian Conservation Corps? __YES__
__C.C.C.__ If so, what company or unit __CO.2335 SCS-4__ Produce discharge _____
__WAYNESBORO PA.__

(Applicant sign full name here) *Wilson Charles Lineaweaver*

Accepted: _____ Cause of rejection: _____
_____

Date: _____   *S/ Howe*
    G. T. HOWE, Lt. Cdr. USN. (Ret.)
    Officer-in-Charge

APPLICANT'S PHYSICAL QUESTIONNAIRE

Wilson Charles Lineaweaver
(Name of applicant)

927½ Cumberland Ave, Lebanon, PA   Oct 22, 1940
(Address)   (City)   (State)   (Date)

THESE QUESTIONS MUST BE ANSWERED HONESTLY BY THE APPLICANT, AND SIGNED
BY HIM AND HIS NEXT OF KIN OR THE APPLICANT'S LEGAL GUARDIAN

HAVE YOU EVER HAD THE FOLLOWING:		OTHER INFORMATION:
Asthma	NO	Have you lost or gained weight during
Heart trouble	NO	the past 6 months? SAME
Head injuries	NO	If so, how much?
Ear trouble	NO	
Trouble breathing	NO	
Hay fever	NO	
Fits	NO	
Dizzy or Fainting spells or walking in sleep	NO	
Lung trouble (any form)	NO	Family Doctor's Name:
Chronic tonsillitis (sore throat) SORE THROAT, NOT CHRONIC	YES	None
Are tonsils out	NO	
Rheumatism	NO	Address:
Venereal diseases	NO	
Rupture or hernia — Did you ever wear a truss	NO	
Piles	NO	
Spitting of blood	NO	
Urinated in bed in last five years	NO	
Broken bones SPRAINED LIGAMENT RT ARM	NO	I certify that, to the best of my
Stutter	NO	knowledge, the information given
Chronic rash or pimples	NO	hereon is correct.
Do your legs or feet tire easily	NO	
Operations (kind)	NO	Wilson Charles Lineaweaver
Depressed arches or any indication of same or previous foot injuries	No	(Signature of Applicant)
Have you ever worn arch supporters	NO	Robert Joseph Lineaweaver
Any insanity in family	NO	(Signature of next of kin or Legal Guardian)
Do you wear or have you ever worn glasses	NO	
Have you ever had a serious illness or been in a hospital? If so, give particulars US MARINE Hospital Oct. 25, 1940. DISCHARGED FROM Hospital Nov. 6, 1940 No Further hospitalization considered necessary, condition improved	NO	REF. LETTER FROM HOSPITAL
Are you well	YES	

U. S. NAVY RECRUITING STATION

Martinsburg, W. Va.

In spaces below, please write names and addresses of references together with the length of time they have employed or known you. The names of the following persons are desired:

(a) Principal of the last school attended.
(b) Last teacher in school.
(c) Chief of Police, if he knows you.
(d) Parish Priest, Minister, or Bishop.
(e) Scout Master (if you are or have been a scout).
(f) Last employer.
(g) Other employers.
(h) Family Doctor.
(i) Postmaster (if he knows you).
(j) Public Officials or Business men who know you.

(The names of relatives cannot be accepted as references).

EMPLOYERS REFERENCE (Leave blank if you have never been employed)

Name __Company Commander__

Address __Co. 2335- SCS-4, CCC,__ __Waynesboro, Penn.__

Occupation __Company Commander__ Length of time known __3 yrs.__

You were employed as __Laborer__

SCHOOL REFERENCE

Name of last school attended __Lebanon High School__

Address __Lebanon, Penn__

Length of time attended __2 years__ From __1935__ To __1937__

CHARACTER REFERENCES

Name __Victor Parks__

Address __RFD., Lebanon, Penn.__

Occupation __Shoe Worker__ Length of time known __Life__

Name __George Boltz__

Address __Center St., Lebanon, Penn.__

Occupation __Steel Worker__ Length of time known __Life__

Name _____

Address _____

Occupation _____ Length of time known _____

Name _____

Address _____

Occupation _____ Length of time known _____

__Wilson Charles Lineaweaver__
(Name of Applicant)

NRB Form 62

OCT 24 1940

NRB—25768—4-27-39—60M

U. S. NAVY RECRUITING STATION

Post Office Building
Martinsburg, W. Va.

Date __Oct. 23, 1940__

The Bureau of Vital Statistics,

State of __New Jersey__

__Trenton, New Jersey__

Dear Sir:-

It is necessary that the Navy Recruiting Service verify the age of all applicants for enlistment in the United States Navy. Since the below named man cannot produce documentary evidence substantiating his statement as to age, we are requesting that you check against your records and kindly give us such information as you may have.

NAME __Wilson__ __Charles__ __Lineaweaver__ RACE __White__

(First)   (Middle)   (Last)

HE STATES HE WAS BORN IN THE CITY OF __Elizabeth__

COUNTY OF __Union__ STATE OF __New Jersey__

ON __6__ __April__ __1919__

(Day)   (Month)   (Year)

THAT HIS FATHER'S NAME IS __Robert Joseph Lineaweaver__

MOTHER'S MAIDEN NAME WAS __Nettie Erlene Haag__

ADDRESS OF PARENTS __Elizabeth, New Jersey.__

It is respectfully requested that you refer to your records and give us the information as outlined below. Thanking you in advance, I am,

Yours very truly,

__J. S. Holloway, TM 1/c__, U. S. Navy
Navy Recruiting Service.

NAME IN FULL AS REGISTERED __Wilson Charles Lineaweaver__

MOTHER'S MAIDEN NAME __Earlene Haag__

DATE OF BIRTH __6__ __April__ __1919__

(Day)   (Month)   (Year)

PLACE OF BIRTH __Elizabeth__ __New Jersey__

(City)   (State)

WERE BIRTHS RECORDED AT THIS TIME? __Yes__

Please sign in ink and
affix seal of office.

__Walter R. Scott__ State Registrar.

(Signature and title of person furnishing information).

CBC

SELECTIVE SERVICE REGISTRATION CARD

REGISTRATION CERTIFICATE

This is to certify that in accordance with the
Selective Service Proclamation of the President of the United States

Wilson Charles Lineaweaver
(First name)   (Middle name)   (Last name)

927½ Cumberland Lebanon Pa.
(No. and street or R. F. D. No.; city or town, county and State)

has been duly registered this 16 day of October, 1940

John R. Earnest
(Signature of registrar)

Registrar for N. Cornwall Leb. Pa.
(Precinct)   (Ward)   (City or county)   (State)

BE ALERT { Keep in touch with your Local Board.
           Notify Local Board immediately of change of address.
CARRY THIS CARD WITH YOU AT ALL TIMES

D. S. S. Form 2   16—17105

[Reproduced here at actual size.]

DESCRIPTION OF REGISTRANT

RACE		HEIGHT (Approx.) 5 ft. 8 in.	WEIGHT (Approx.) 147	COMPLEXION	
				Sallow	
White	X	EYES	HAIR	Light	X
		Blue	Blonde	Ruddy	
Negro		Gray X	Red	Dark	
		Hazel	Brown X	Freckled	
Oriental		Brown	Black	Light brown	
		Black	Gray	Dark brown	
Indian			Bald	Black	
Filipino					

Other obvious physical characteristics that will aid in identification _____

_____

_____

Envelope for U.S. Navy Recruiting Station Letter on next page.

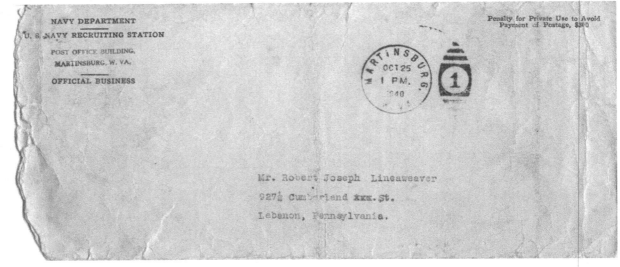

NAVY DEPARTMENT

U. S. NAVY RECRUITING STATION

POST OFFICE BUILDING,
MARTINSBURG, W. VA.

OFFICIAL BUSINESS

Penalty for Private Use to Avoid
Payment of Postage, $300

MARTINSBURG
OCT 25
1 P.M.
1940
1

Mr. Robert Joseph Lineaweaver

927½ Cumberland xxx St.

Lebanon, Pennsylvania.

U.S. Navy Recruiting Station Enlistment Letter to Parents

NRB Form 60.   NRB—22362—11-14-38—60M

U. S. NAVY RECRUITING STATION
Post Office Building
Martinsburg, W,Va.

October 25, 1940

Mr. Robert Joseph Lineaweaver
927 ½ Cumberland Ave.,
Lebanon, Pa.

Dear sir

I am pleased to inform you that your son, Wilson Charles Lineaweaver   ,
has successfully passed the preliminary examinations for enlistment in the United States Navy.
Before he can be enlisted, however, there are other conditions which must be met:

    He must be unmarried,
    He must be over 17 years of age,
    He must have no dependents, and
    He must have your unqualified consent.

            Non Dependency
Enclosed you will find a complete set of consent papers filled out and ready for your signature.

Please sign your name in ink, just as it appears in type as " Robert Joseph Lineaweaver" "

on the line marked "Signature of parent or guardian". This must be done in the presence of a NO-
TARY PUBLIC who will act as a witness to your signature and sign his name and title in the space
provided. Also, please read the information on the reverse side of the consent papers and sign each
copy.

As soon as these papers are complete, please forward them to this office, using the enclosed envelope which requires no postage.

Your signing the enclosed papers in no way obligates your son to enlist in the Navy.

Very truly yours,

H. I. Holloway, TM 1/c, USN
Recruiter.

P.S.
    Sign at all points indicated by red arrow on all papers. Please
have the Notary Public Official affix his seal to the Baltimore Form (NRB)
Form C. The seal must be on all three papers and all signatures must be
in ink.

Thanks for your kind cooperation,

NRB FORM NO. 28
NR9—19319—8-27-26—50M (A24G)

U. S. NAVY RECRUITING STATION
Post Office Building

Martinsburg, W. Va.

Date: Oct 26 1940

TO WHOM IT MAY CONCERN:—

I certify that I will not at any time during the enlistment of my son, named below, request his discharge from the United States Navy.

Wilson Charles Lineaweaver
(Name of applicant)

Robert Joseph Lineaweaver
(Signature of parent or guardian)

(Signature of witness)

Court House Lebanon, Pa.
(Address of witness)

Left: Form signed by Wilson's father Robert certifies that he will not request his son's discharge from the Navy during his enlistment. Signed and witnessed on October 26, 1940, at the Court House in Lebanon, PA. This copy was from Wilson's military service records file at the National Archives.

BALTIMORE
(NRB) FORM C

From: Robert Joseph Lineaweaver

To: Navy Recruiting Station, Martinsburg, W. Va.

Subject: Statement relative to dependency or possible future dependency upon my son, Wilson Charles

Lineaweaver .

1.   The following information pertaining to my son's enlistment in the U.S. Navy is furnished herewith:

(a) I am not now dependent, and barring unforseen circumstances I will not during the next six years become dependent upon my son for support of myself or my family.

(b) To the best of my knowledge and belief the applicant is not married, has never been married, and is not subject to the support or partial support of a wife, child, or any other person.

Robert Joseph Lineaweaver
(Signature of parent, guardian, or next of kin):

WITNESSED SIGNATURE Oct 26 1940

(SEAL)
(Notary Public or Justice of Peace)
My Commission expires: Feb 7 1941

Right: Form signed by Wilson's father Robert stating that he, nor his family, is dependent upon Wilson for support, and does not foresee dependency during the next six years, and that Wilson "is not married, has never been married, and is not subject to the support or partial support of a wife, child, or any other person." It was witnessed and notarized on October 26, 1940. This copy was from Wilson's military service records file at the National Archives

N. Nav. 511
(Mar. 1920)

RECRUIT IDENTIFICATION CARD
U. S. NAVY RECRUITING STATION
310 POST OFFICE BUILDING
BALTIMORE, MD.

TO IDENTIFY

Name LINEAWEAVER, Wilson Charles. 258 3224

Rate App. Sea.   *U. S. N.*   *Color of hair* Lt. Brown.

Color of eyes Hazel   *Height* 67 *in.*   *Weight* 141 *lbs.*

Prominent marks ANT: PS rt temple; S½" rt knee;
RS rt knee; Bmk rt foreleg; PS lt temple; S½"
lt knee; 3PS lt knee; POST: VS lt arm; S3/4"
lt scapula; PS½"D lt elbow; S½" lt wrist;
Countersigned

G. T. HOWE, Lt. Cdr. USN. (Ret.)
B. Howe   *Recruiting Officer.*
(OVER)
HW   4—5097

Wilson Charles Lineaweaver

INSTRUCTIONS—Keep this card carefully and deliver it to the officer to whom you report at the Training Station. If you fail to do so, you and others will be **seriously** inconvenienced.

G P O   4—5097

[Reproduced here at actual size.]

Notice that the card states that if enlistee loses this card "you and others will be **seriously** inconvenienced"!

JAN 25 1941

N. Nav. 351
(Apr. 1934)

United States | Navy
~~Naval Reserve Corps~~

Finished File Layers
Fold with this face o

ENLISTMENT of ___LINEAWEAVER, Wilson Charles 258-32-24___ ; ___$21.00___
(Full name, surname to the left) (Service number) (Pay per month)
Accepted for enlistment at ___Martinsburg, W.Va.___ ___Apprentice Seaman___
(Rating in which enlisted)
Enlisted at ___USNRS, Baltimore, Md.___ Date ___January 6, 1941___
Transferred to _____
Occupation ___None___ • Citizenship ___U.S.___ Place of birth ___Elizabeth, N.J.___
Date of birth ___April 6, 1919___ Home address ___1240 E. Cumberland St.,___ ___Lebanon___
(Street and number) (Town)
___Lebanon___ , ___Pennsylvania___
(County) (State)
Credited to ___19th___ Congressional District, State of ___Pennsylvania___
Married or single ___Single___ ; Name and address of next of kin ___Father___
(Relation)
___Robert Joseph Lineaweaver, 1240 E Cumberland St., Lebanon, Pa.___
(Name) (Address)
**Continuous Service Certificate ___None___ Previous service {Navy} {Reserve} (___None___). First enliste
(Number) (Years) (Months) (Days)
_____ at _____ and was last discharged _____
(Date) (Place) (Date)
from the U.S.S. _____ with _____ discharge as _____
(Character) (Rate)
Previous Coast Guard Service (___None___). Previous Marine Corps Service (___None___). Previou
(Years) (Months) (Days) (Years) (Months) (Days)
Army Service (___None___). Age ___21___ years ___9___ months. Height ___5___ feet ___7___ inches. Weight ___14___
(Years) (Months) (Days)
pounds. Eyes ___Hazel___ Sex ___Male___ . Hair ___Lt. Brown___ Complexion ___Ruddy___ Color ___White-U___
Personal characteristics, _____ marks, etc ___ANT: PS rt temple; 3½" rt knee; RS rt k___
___Bmk rt foreleg; PS lt temple; 5½" lt knee; 2PS lt knee; POST: VS lt arm; S 3/4"___
___Lt scapula; PS ½"D lt elbow; 5½" lt wrist; PS 3/4"D rt calf.___

I CERTIFY that I have carefully examined, agreeably to the Regulations of the Navy, the above-named recruit, and find that, in my opinion, he is free from all bodily defect and mental infirmity which would, in any way, disqualify him from performing the duties of his rating and that he has stated to me that he has no disease concealed o likely to be inherited.

___H. L. WHEELER, LT. CDR. MC USNR___ , Examining Surgeon.

For and in consideration of the pay or wages due to the ratings which may from time to time be assigned me during the continuance o my service, I agree to and with ___G.T. HOWE___ of the United States Navy, as follows:
(Name of commanding officer)
First: To enter the service of the Navy of the United States and to report to such station or vessel of the Navy as I may be ordered t join, and to the utmost of my power and ability discharge my several services or duties and be in everything conformable and obedient to th several requirements and lawful commands of the officers who may be placed over me.

Second: I oblige and subject myself to serve { ___6___ years from ___January 6, 1941___ , 1
{ during minority until _____ , 1

unless sooner discharged by proper authority, and on the conditions provided by the act of Congress of March 3, 1875, as follows:

Sec. 1422. That it shall be the duty of the commanding officer of any fleet, squadron, or vessel acting singly, when on service, to send to an Atlantic or to a Pacific port o the United States as their enlistment may have occurred on either the Atlantic or Pacific Coast of the United States, in some public or other vessel, all petty officers and pe sons of inferior ratings desiring to go there at the expiration of their terms of enlistment, or as soon thereafter as may be, unless, in his opinion, the detention of such pe sons for a longer period should be essential to the public interests, in which case he may detain them, or any of them until the vessel to which they belong shall return t such Atlantic or Pacific port. All persons enlisted without the limits of the United States may be discharged, on the expiration of their enlistment, either in a foreign po or in a port of the United States, or they may be detained as above provided beyond the term of their enlistment; and that all persons sent home, or detained by a comman ing officer, according to the provisions of this act, shall in all respects to the laws and regulations for the government of the Navy until their return to an Atlant or Pacific port and their regular discharge; and all persons so detained by such officer, or reentering to serve until the return to an Atlantic or Pacific port of the vessel t which they belong shall in no case be held in the service more than thirty days after their arrival in said port; and that all persons who shall be so detained beyond their ter of enlistment, or who shall after the termination of their enlistment, voluntarily reenter to serve until the return to an Atlantic or Pacific port of the vessel to whic they belong and their regular discharge therefrom, shall receive for the time during which they are so detained or shall so serve beyond their original terms of enlistmen an addition of one-fourth of their former pay: Provided, That the shipping articles shall hereafter contain the substance of this section.

I also oblige myself, during such service, to comply with and be subject to such laws, regulations, and articles for the government of th Navy as are or shall be established by the Congress of the United States or other competent authority, and to submit to treatment for th prevention of smallpox, typhoid (typhoid prophylaxis), and to such other preventive measures as may be considered necessary by nava authorities.

Third: I am of the legal age to enlist; I have never deserted from the United States Navy, Army, Marine Corps, or Coast Guard; I hav never been discharged from the United States Service or other service on account of disability or through sentence of either civilian or mi itary court; and I have never been discharged from any service, civil or military, except with good character and for the reasons given b me to the recruiting officer prior to enlistment. I am not a member of the National Guard, Naval Reserve, or Marine Corps Reserve.

Fourth: I have had this contract fully explained to me, I understand it, and certify that no promise of any kind has been made to m concerning assignment to duty, or promotion during my enlistment. I understand that if I become a candidate for the Naval Academy an fail to pass the entrance examinations, I will be returned to general service.

Oath of Allegiance: I, ___Wilson Charles Lineaweaver,___
do solemnly swear (or affirm) that I will bear true faith and allegiance to the United States of America, and that I will serve them honestl and faithfully against all their enemies whomsoever, and that I will obey the orders of the President of the United States and the orders o the officers appointed over me, according to the rules and articles for the government of the Navy.

And I do further swear (or affirm) that all statements made by me as now given in this record are correct.

___Wilson Charles Lineaweaver___
(Signature in own handwriting, surname to right)

Subscribed and sworn to before me this ___6th___ day of ___January___ , A. D. 1941
and contract perfected.

United States citizenship substantiated.

___S/ Howe___

___G.T. HOWE, Lieut.Comdr., U.S. Navy (Ret.___

Commanding, U.S.S. N.R.S. Baltimore, Md.

* CITIZENSHIP.—Native born, use initials U. S.; Naturalized, N. U. S.; Alien, intention declared, A. D. I.; Alien, A; Guam, Guam; Philippine Islands, P. I.; Samo Samoa; and Virgin Islands, V. I.
** For reenlistments with continuous service note Art. D-1002, Bureau of Navigation Manual.

U. S. GOVERNMENT PRINTING OFFICE 4—4730

OATH OF ALLEGIENCE

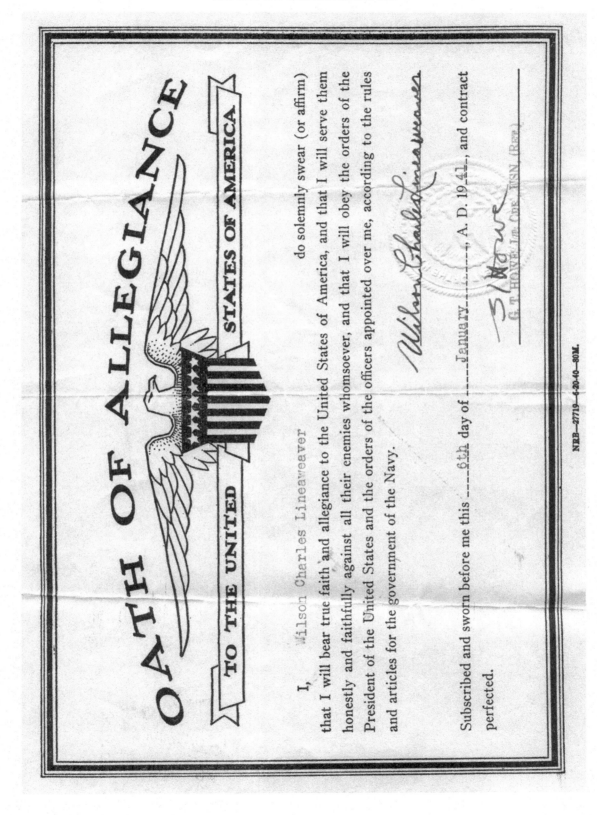

ENLISTMENT STATEMENT

NRB Form No. 30   NRB—25775—4-27-39—60M

STATEMENT

Date _____ JAN 7 1941 _____

Having made application for enlistment in the U. S. Navy, I hereby certify that the following points of information have been thoroughly explained to me:

1. That my records and fingerprints will be thoroughly checked and that if I have ever been discharged, under other than honorable conditions, and under continuous service, from the Army, Navy, Marine Corps or Coast Guard; or if I am concealing a police or juvenile record, I will be subject to discharge as undesirable from the Naval Service.

2. Any operations that I may have performed to correct any minor physical defects to qualify me for enlistment will be at my own expense and risk and that no promises have been made that if a physical defect has been corrected I will be enlisted.

3. Upon completion of my physical examination it will be necessary for me to return home until all necessary papers and investigation are satisfactorily completed, at which time I will be placed on the waiting list for enlistment, and that no assurance can be given as to the probable date of my enlistment.

4. I understand that the filling out of first papers makes me an APPLICANT and that ENLISTMENT is not executed until I have completed my final physical and other examinations, and have taken the OATH OF ALLEGIANCE, at which time I will be transferred to a NAVAL TRAINING STATION immediately.

I am aware that circumstances may arise beyond the control of the Recruiting Service that will prevent my ENLISTMENT even after my application papers are completed, and I have been advised to continue my present employment, and not to dispose of my personal effects, until after my ENLISTMENT.

I understand that I have the privilege to change my mind about enlisting in the Navy at any time before I take the OATH OF ALLEGIANCE.

I thoroughly understand the difference between applying for enlistment and enlisting in the Navy.

5. I hereby acknowledge the receipt of a copy of this statement, and I have had all points thoroughly explained to me by the recruiter.

Wilson Charles Lineaweaver
(Signature of Applicant)

H. Holloway
(Signature of Recruiter)

MAIL ADDRESS
Naval Training Station
Naval Operating Base, Norfolk, Va.
IN REPLY REFER TO

U. S. NAVAL TRAINING STATION
Naval Operating Base,
Norfolk, Virginia

Dear Sir:

    I am glad to inform you that your son has reported on this station and is undergoing training and instruction in the duties of the Naval Service.

    A letter of information regarding the training period for Apprentice Seaman is enclosed.

                 Very truly yours,

                 H. A. McCLURE,
              Captain, U. S. Navy,
                Commanding.

                 J. E. REZNER,
        Lieutenant Commander, U. S. Navy,
                 By direction.

U. S. NAVAL TRAINING STATION
Naval Operating Base,
Norfolk, Virginia

INFORMATION REGARDING TRAINING PERIOD FOR APPRENTICE SEAMEN

Apprentice Seamen are assigned to Naval Training Stations for a period of training and instruction in the fundamentals of the Naval Service. This period of training lasts _____ weeks. At the end of this time, the apprentice seaman is entitled to _____ days leave prior to assignment to his regular duties in the Navy, provided that he has sufficient funds to defray expenses of travel, and that his conduct has been satisfactory.

The Navy endeavors, in the training of apprentice seamen, to instill discipline, to arouse ambition, and to develop sturdy, well balanced men who will be useful in civil life as well as in the service. Particular attention is paid to their physical, mental and morale welfare. Regular habits of living are established immediately upon their arrival; wholesome exercise constitutes a part of the daily routine, and their health is constantly guarded through personal observation and necessary medical and dental treatment. They receive excellent food; daily amusement and recreation, religious counsel, and are required to attend Divine Services on the Sabbath during the training course.

All apprentice seamen are instructed to write home frequently, but failure of a recruit to write is generally due to thoughtlessness on his part and should not be considered cause for worry, since in case of serious illness or injury, the next of kin is immediately notified. Frequent, cheerful letters from home are a benefit to the apprentice seaman, and are the best means of encouraging him to write frequently. Letters addressed to him at "U. S. Naval Training Station, Norfolk, Va.," with "Platoon No. 5 " in the lower left corner will be delivered promptly while he is in training. Recruits are advised to inform their parents or nearest relatives each time they are transferred to new duties after they leave this station but such communications are sometimes slow in reaching their destination due to travel involved. Parents may, however, forward emergency communications to their sons via the Bureau of Navigation, Navy Department, Washington, D. C., at any time their address is unknown and communication is urgent.

A comfortable Hostess House on the station provides social center where enlisted men may receive their relatives and friends. A limited number of sleeping accomodations are available to parents who desire to visit their sons for which there is a charge of one dollar ($1.00) per person per night. To obtain these accomodations it is advised that reservations be written for in advance addressed Hostess House, Naval Training Station, Norfolk, Va. There are no facilities for serving meals in the Hostess House, but arrangements can be made for parents to have the Sunday noon meal with their sons. This letter should be shown when calling.

Civilian clothing of a recruit is not mailed home until after his first pay day. Shipment is normally made about three weeks after a recruit reports.

National Service Life Insurance may be applied for by each apprentice seaman within one hundred and twenty days after enlistment. This Insurance is the cheapest insurance available, and all recruits are encouraged to obtain some within the specified period. Many recruits, however, fail to take advantage of this opportunity because of their youth, inexperience and limited pay. Parents are therefore advised to study the information as given on the reverse side of this letter, and to express their attitude concerning the advisability of applying for National Service Life Insurance by writing direct to their son.

Inquiries regarding apprentice seamen should be addressed to the "Commanding Officer, U. S. Naval Training Station, Norfolk, Virginia."

NTSNV—11-2-40—30M.

INFCRMATION REGARDING
THE NATIONAL SERVICE LIFE INSURANCE

All National Service Life Insurance is issued upon the Five Year Premium Term Plan with the right that it can be converted or exchanged by the person taking out the insurance any time after the policy has been in effect for one year and provided it is converted or exchanged for another type of insurance before five years. The Five Year Level Term Policy can be exchanged or converted to one of the following types: Ordinary Life, Twenty-Payment Life or Thirty-Payment Life, but if not converted at the end of five years will lapse.

Insurance under this policy is paid to a beneficiary or beneficiaries named by the person taking out the insurance such as: wife, child, including those adopted or step children, parents and brother or sister. Upon death of the insured, the insurance may be paid to the beneficiary or beneficiaries in 240 monthly installments at the rate of $5.00 for each $1,000 insurance carried if the beneficiary is under 30 years of age. If the person named as beneficiary is 30 years of age or older benefits are payable in equal monthly installments over a period of 120 months with such payments continuing during the time that the beneficiary lives.

The monthly premium rate for $1,000 insurance upon the Five Year Level Premium Plan, same monthly premiums for five years without any increase, are as follows:

AGE	MONTHLY PREMIUM	AGE	MONTHLY PREMIUM
18	$ .64	27	$ .69
19	.65	28	.69
20	.65	29	.70
21	.65	30	.71
22	.66	31	.72
23	.66	32	.73
24	.67	33	.74
25	.67	34	.75
26	.68	35	.76

To determine the proper monthly premium to be paid each month the age of the person applying for insurance is the age of the birthday nearest the date the policy goes into effect.

This insurance will be granted upon application in writing to persons who are accepted and enrolled into the active service, but men must make application while in the active service and within 120 days after entrance in the Navy.

National Service Life Insurance will be granted to any one person in the service at policy value of $1,000 to $10,000 in units of $500.00.

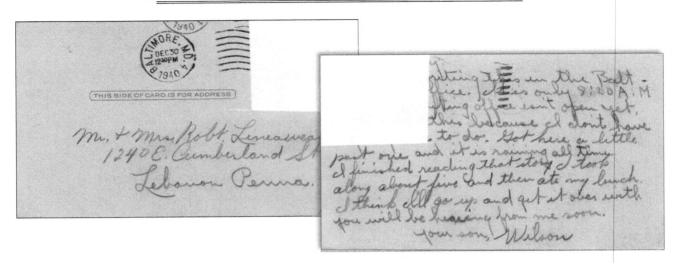

Mr. & Mrs. Robt. Lineaweaver
1240 E. Cumberland St.
Lebanon Penna.

...uting this in the Balt-
...fice. It is only 8:20 A.M
...ting office isn't open yet.
...this because I don't have
... to do. Got here a little
past one and it is raining all time
I finished reading that story I took
along about five and then ate my lunch.
I think I'll go up and get it over with
you will be hearing from me soon.
Your son, Wilson

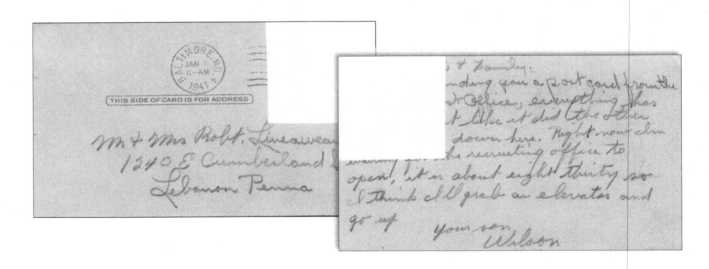

Mr. & Mrs. Robt. Lineaweaver
1240 E. Cumberland St.
Lebanon Penna.

...s & Family:
...nding you a post card from the
... Office, everything has
... like it did the other
... down here. Right now I'm
waiting for the recruiting office to
open, it is about eight thirty so
I think I'll grab an elevator and
go up
Your son
Wilson

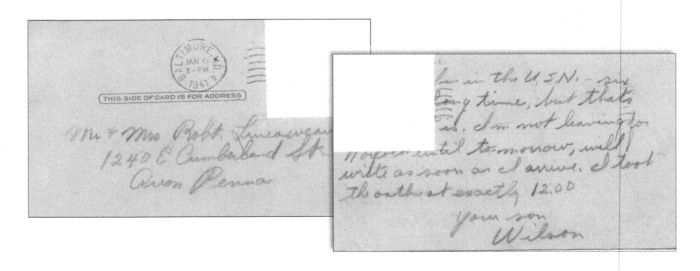

Mr. & Mrs. Robt. Lineaweaver
1240 E. Cumberland St.
Avon Penna.

... in the U.S.N. - six
... any time, but that's
... is. I'm not leaving for
...ow until tomorrow, will
write as soon as I arrive. I took
the oath at exactly 12:00
Your son
Wilson

[Postcard - Postmark is Baltimore, MD, Dec. 30, 1940, 12:30 PM]
Mr. and Mrs. Robt. Lineaweaver
1240 E. Cumberland St
Lebanon Penna.

... [w]riting this in the Balt[imore] ... [o]ffice. It is only 8:00 A.M. ... [recru]iting office isn't open yet. ... this because I don't have ... to do. Got here a little past one and it is raining all time. I finished reading that story I took along about five and then ate my lunch. I think I'll go up and get it over with
you will be hearing from me soon.
Your son, Wilson

****

[Postcard - Postmark is Baltimore, MD, Jan. 6, 1941, 11 AM]
Mr and Mrs Robt. Lineaweaver
1240 E Cumberland St.
Lebanon Penna

[Dear Parent]s & Family:
... [se]nding you a post card from the ...st Office, everything has ... like it did the other ... down here. Right now I'm waiting for the recruiting office to open, it is about 8:30 so I think I'll grab an elevator and go up
Your son
Wilson

****

[Postcard - Postmark is Baltimore, MD, Jan. 6, 1941, 3 PM]
Mr and Mrs Robt. Lineaweaver
1240 E. Cumberland St.
Avon Penna

... I'm in the U.S.N. – six ... long time, but that's ... is. I'm not leaving for Norfolk until to-morrow, will write as soon as I arrive. I took the oaths at exactly 12:00
Your son
Wilson

W. C. Lineaweaver
U. S. Training Station
Platoon No. 5
Norfolk, Va.
Jan. 9, 1941

Dear Parents:
Well I'm finally settled here and am writing. If you got the money yet from the CCC please send some of it to th above address.

I can't very well tell you about things here because I'm still in a fog, but will tell you later on when I know better. This I will tell you, its not what I expected - its tough, I guess I wish I was home and another thing, they make a man out of you, so they say if you can stick it out.

Please write. Later on I'll write a more detail letter.

Your son
Wilson

Don't forget th Platoon No 5 in my address.

W. C. Lineaweaver
Platoon No. 5 E.
U S Naval Training Station
Norfolk, Va.

Dear

Mr. + Mrs. Robt Lineaweaver
1240 E Cumberland St
~~Lebanon~~ Penna.
Picture

LEBANON JAN 10 2 PM 1941 PA.

NORFOLK JAN 9 2 8 PM 1941 VA.

W.C. Lineaweaver
U.S. Training Station
Platoon No. 5
Norfolk, Va.

Jan 9, 1941

Dear Parents,

Well Im finally settled here and am writing. If you got the money yet from the CCC please send some of it to the above address.

I can't very well tell you about things here because I'm still in a fog, but will tell you later on when I know better. This I will tell you, it's not what I expected. Its tough. I guess I wish I was home and another thing, they make a man out of you, so they say if you can stick it out.

Please write. Later on I'll write a more detail letter.

Your son,
Wilson

Don't forget the Platoon No 5 in my address.

[Postmark is Norfolk VA., Jan. 9, 1941, 8 PM]
Mr. and Mrs. Robt Lineaweaver
1240 E Cumberland St
Avon Penna

[Return Address:]
W. C Lineaweaver
Platoon #5
U.S. Naval Training Station
Norfolk, Va.

The Naval Base at Norfolk, Virginia

The Naval Operating Base and Naval Air Station at Norfolk, VA, were collectively referred to as Naval Base Norfolk until 1953. At that time it was renamed Naval Station Norfolk. The station at Norfolk was first developed in 1917 as part of a large program of naval base facility construction in that area. It first consisted of temporary or semi-permanent buildings. However, in line with the development of the area as the major naval base on the Atlantic Coast, the years following WWI saw the temporary facilities gradually replaced by permanent structures. In early May of 1940, the German army outflanked France's Maginot Line and quickly thereafter had overrun Western Europe. On May 16, 1940, President Roosevelt delivered a special message to Congress on the emergency needs of national defense, and he called for a huge increased program of defense activity. When Wilson joined the Navy in 1941 and was stationed at Norfolk, it was the largest of the Navy's four training stations. In 1939, the U.S. Navy's station at Norfolk had facilities for up to 10,000 men. By June of 1941, the personnel count at Norfolk was approximately 10,000 new recruits, over 15,000 officers and enlisted personnel, and over 14,000 sailors assigned to ships homeported there. For the U.S. Navy as a whole, in September 1939 its enlisted strength was about 110,000 men. Six years later, in September 1945, Navy personnel numbered over 3,000,000.

Jan. 12, 1941

Dear Parents & Family,

Now that I have a few minutes to spare I think I'll write and tell you a few things about the navy & what I did since I left home.

I was not shipped down here on Monday but slept in a Y.M.C.A. the expenses on the Government and was shipped by boat on Tuesday night. We arrived at Norfolk 6:30 in the morning. It took all day to get examined and boy did they go over us, even X-rayed us for T.B. plus a vaccination and a shot in the arm.

This is the toughest experience I ever went through, we are on the go 12 hrs. a day and can't even sit down. All our clothing must be rolled, tied and put in a small seamens bag, you'd think it was impossible to get it all in, but it

must be done. We are in Detention for 3 weeks behind a 12 ft. fence guarded every minute you'd think we are a bunch [...] These 3 weeks are to keep us from everybody else in case [of] some disease and they [...] try to see if we can take [...] have 7 weeks training and af[ter] I may be able to come [home?] being shipped to sea, just [...] to how I make out.

Please write and let [me know] how things are. and pop, [...] let me know how you [...] with the money proposit[ion] Did you get all of the [...] Will be writing again soon.

Your son
Wilson

Wilson E. Lineaweaver
U.S. Naval Train[ing] Station
Platoon No. 5
Norfolk, Va.

NORFOLK
JAN 11
2   8 PM
1941
VA.

Mr & Mrs. Robt. Lineaweaver
1240 E. Cumberland St.
Avon, Penna.

Jan. 12, 1941

Dear Parents and Family:

Now that I have a few minutes to spare I think I'll write and tell you a few things about the navy & what I did since I left home.

I was not shipped down here on Monday but slept in a Y.M.C.A. the expenses on the Government and was shipped by boat on Tuesday night. We arrived at Norfolk 6:30 in the morning. It took all day to get examined and boy did they go over us, even X rayed us for T.B. plus a vaccination and a shot in the arm.

This is the toughest experience I ever went through. we are on the go 12 hrs. a day and can't even sit down. All our clothing must be rolled, tied and put in a small seamens bag, you'd think it was impossible to get it all in, but it must be done. We are in Detention for 3 weeks behind a 12 ft barb wire fence guarded ever minute by marines. (you'd think we are a bunch of convicts). These 3 weeks are to keep us isolated from everybody else in case we have some disease and they drive us all day to see if we can take it. We have 7 week training and after that I may be able to come home before being shipped to sea, just according to how I make out.

Please write and let me know how things are. and pop, write and let me know how you are making out with the money proposition.

Did you get all the postcards? Will be writing again soon

Your son
Wilson

[Postmark is Norfolk VA., Jan. 11, 1941, 8 PM]
Mr. & Mrs. Robt. Lineaweaver
1240 E. Cumberland St.
Avon, Penna.

[Return Address:]
Wilson C. Lineaweaver
U.S. Naval Training Station
Platoon No. 5
Norfolk, Va.

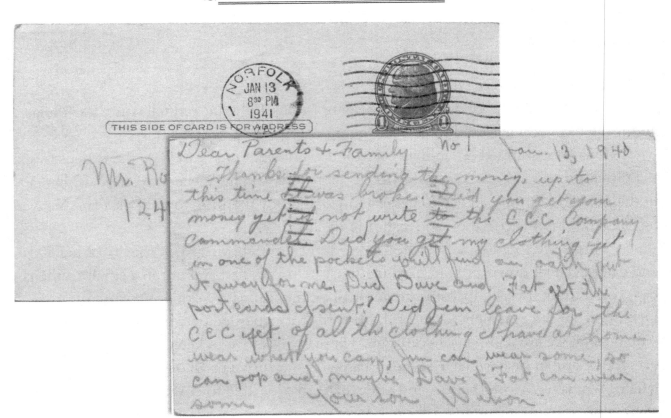

Dear Parents & Family   No 1   Jan. 13, 1941

Thanks for sending the money, up to this time I was broke. Did you get your money yet? If not write to the C.C.C. Company Commander. Did you get my clothing yet in one of the pockets you'll find an oath put it away for me. Did Dave and Fat get the postcards I sent? Did Jim leave for the C.C.C. yet. Of all the clothing I have at home wear what you can, Jim can wear some, so can pop and maybe Dave & Fat can wear some.

Your son Wilson

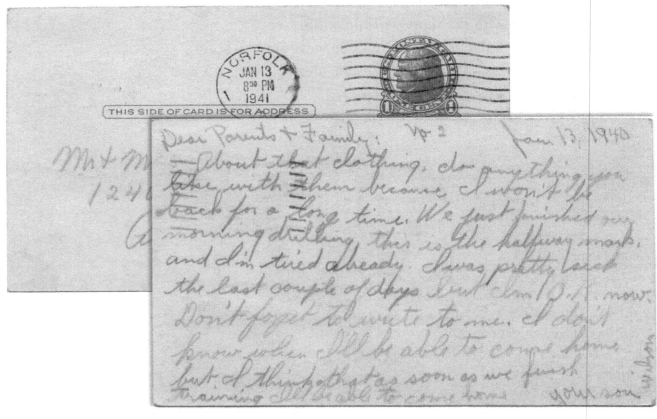

Dear Parents & Family: No 2   Jan. 13, 1941

— About that clothing, do anything you like with them because I won't be back for a long time. We just finished our morning drilling, this is the halfway mark, and I'm tired already. I was pretty sick the last couple of days but I'm O.K. now. Don't forget to write to me. I don't know when I'll be able to come home but I think that as soon as we finish training I'll be able to come home.

Your son Wilson

[Postcard - Postmark is Norfolk VA., Jan. 13, 1941, 8:30 PM]
Mr. Robt Lineaweaver
1240 E Cumberland St
Avon, Penna.

No. 1   Jan. 13, 1940 *[Postmarked 1941, so "1940" is an error]*

Dear Parents & Family
        Thank you for sending the money, up to this time I was broke. Did you get your money yet if not write to the CCC Company Commander. Did you get my clothing yet, in one of the pockets you'll find an oath, put it away for me. Did Dave and Fat get the postcards I sent? Did Jim leave for the CCC yet. of all the clothing I have at home wear what you can. Jim can wear some, so pop and maybe Dave & Fat can wear some

Your son
Wilson

****

[Postcard - Postmark is Norfolk VA., Jan. 13, 1941, 8:30 PM]
Mr. & Mrs. Robert Lineaweaver
1240 E Cumberland St.
Avon Penna.

No. 2   Jan. 13, 1940 *[Postmarked 1941, so "1940" is an error]*

Dear Parents & Family:
        About that clothing, do anything you like with them because I won't be back for a long time. We just finished our morning drilling, this is the halfway mark, and I'm tired already. I was pretty sick the last couple of days but Im O.K. now. Don't forget to write to me. I don't know when I'll be able to come home but I think that as soon as we finish training Ill be able to come home

Your son
Wilson

The weather down here is very cold, a
different cold from up home, I guess it's
because we are practically surrounded by
All the fellows here don't like me
because I'm from Penna. and then for
the south (they still think the war is
going on). The fellows from my platoon
from Florida, Alabama & Georgia. It's
hard to understand their talk. I guess
by the time I get out of here I'll be
talking like them. Of the many that's
here I believe that I'm the only one
from Penna, because I've yet to come
across one.

Will you please send me a can
Pebeco tooth powder, I can't buy it
here until I get out and mine is
about all. I got a card from Jim
Don't forget to write

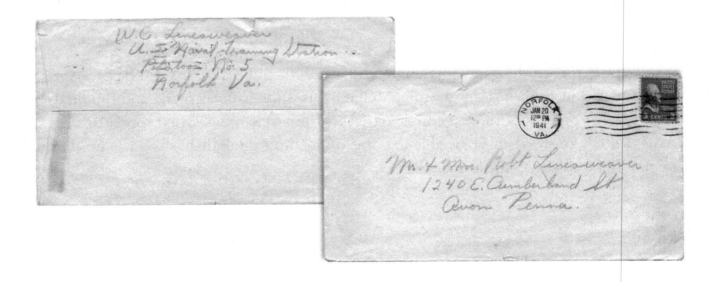

Dear Parents & Family:
This makes two weeks since I
left home and it seems like two years.
We just got our second shot yesterday
morning and my arm is swollen and
sore, on top of that I got a bad cold.
We still have another shot to get which
will probably be next Saturday.

I still have two weeks detention
behind this wire fence, then we get another
medical examination, if physical fit we
get out and will I be glad, this is like
being in a jail.

We spend all day marching and
drilling with rifles (you would think I'm
in the army instead of the navy)
Sometimes its a little dangerous with bayonets
on and you don't know how to use it.
We also go through hard exercises everyday

W.C. Lineaweaver
U.S. Naval Training Station
Platoon No. 5
Norfolk Va.

Mr. & Mrs. Robt Lineaweaver
1240 E. Cumberland St.
Avon, Penna.

Jan. 20, 1941

Dear Parents and Family:

This makes two weeks since I left home and it seems like two years. We just got our second shot yesterday morning and my arm is swollen and sore, on top of that I got a bad cold. We still have another shot to get which will probably be next Saturaday.

I still have two weeks detention behind this wire fence, then we get another medical examination, if physical fit we get out and will I be glad, this is like being in jail.

We spend all day marching and drilling with rifles (you would think I'm in the army instead of the navy). Sometimes it's a little dangerous with bayonets on and you don't know how to use it. We also go through hard exercises every day.

The weather down here is very cold, a different cold from up home. I guess it's because we are practically surrounded by water.

All the fellows here don't like me because I'm from Penna. and their from the south (They still think the civil war is going on). The fellows from my platoon are from Florida, Alabama & Georgia. It's hard to understand their talk. I guess by the time I get out of here I'll be talking like them. Of the many thousand here I believe that I'm the only one from Penna. because Ive yet to come across one.

Will you please send me a can of Pebecco tooth powder. I can't buy any here until I get out and mine is just about all. I got a card from Jim. Don't forget to write

-----

[Postmark is Norfolk VA., Jan. 20, 1941, 12:30 PM]
Mr. & Mrs. Robt Lineaweaver
1240 E. Cumberland St.
Avon Penna.

[Return Address:]
W. C. Lineaweaver
U.S. Naval Training Station
Platoon No.5
Norfolk Va.

1943 Pebeco Tooth Powder Ad

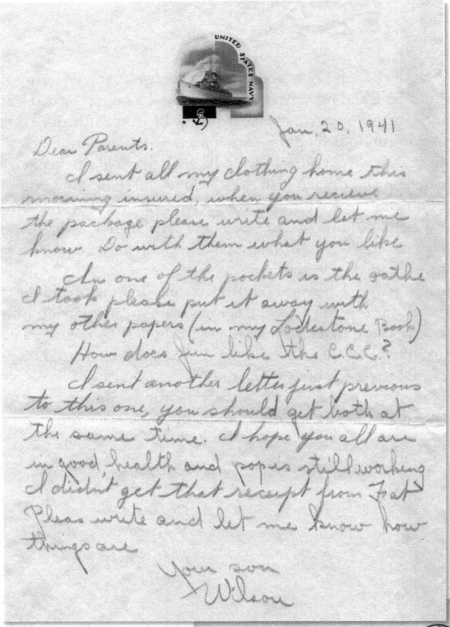

Jan, 20, 1941

Dear Parents:

I sent all my clothing home this morning insured, when you receive the package please write and let me know. Do with them what you like

In one of the pockets is the oath I took please put it away with my other papers (in my Lockstone Book)

How does Jim like the C.C.C.?

I sent another letter just previous to this one, you should get both at the same time. I hope you all are in good health and pop is still working I didn't get that receipt from Fat Pleas write and let me know how things are

Your son
Wilson

Mr. & Mrs. Robt. Lineaweaver
1240 E Cumberland St
Avon Penna.

Jan. 20, 1941

Dear Parents and Family:

I sent all my clothing home this morning insured, when you receive the package please write and let me know. Do with them what you like.

In one of the pockets is the oathe I took please put it away with my other papers (in my Lodestone Book)

How does Jim like the C.C.C.?

I sent another letter just previous to this one, you should get both at the same time. I hope you all are in good health and pop is still working. I didn't get that receipt from Fat. Please write and let me know how things are

Your son
Wilson

[Postmark is Norfolk VA., Jan. 20, 1941, 4:30 PM]
Mr. & Mrs. Robt. Lineaweaver
1240 E Cumberland St
Avon Penna.

[No return address]

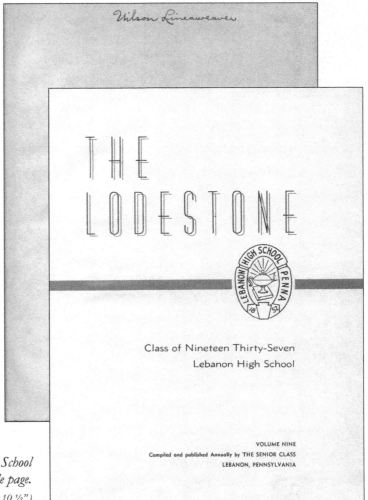

Wilson's 1937 Lebanon High School
Lodestone yearbook flyleaf and title page.
(Reduced from original size of 8" x 10 ½".)

drilling and go to different classes in seamanship, rowing, weaving and handleing gas masks. Then we go out the fering range practiseing rifle, machineigun and cannon firing + bayonet drills. We also must qualify in swimming. This includes several weeks of training. Then we take a written test to see if we go to trade school, if not we are shiped with the fleet. After our training period is over we are given ten days leave (be home) if you wish them, so don't be surprised if I come home in M... I'll soon think that I'm suppose to be a soldier instead of a sailor the way they drill us here. Well I guess I'll sign off

I got a tooth filled today and boy did it hurt but I'm glad its filled

Your son
Wilson

Please excuse the writting, I wrote this in bed (we have beds not hammocks)

Did pop get his money yet. Did he pay Fat for...

                                        Jan. 24, 1941

Dear Parents + Family

Received the package you sent this afternoon and am very gratefull for it. Thanks a lot.

Tell Fat I got that reciept. I got a post card from Jim and he said he was sick. Did he write you?

Well tomorrow we get our last shot and I'm glad that will be over with. We drill that much that I got two big blisters on my right foot. You ought to see the exercises we have to go through each day. Did you get my clothing yet.

I am sorry about Harold and the rest of the sick ones. I hope they get well fast. Pop ought to see a Doctor about that knee.

In a week or two we will stop

W. C. Lineaweaver
Platoon No. 5
U.S. Naval Training Station
Norfolk, Va.

Mr. & Mrs. Robt. Lineaweaver
1240 C. Cumberland St
Avon Penna.

Jan. 24, 1941

Dear Parents and Family:

Received the package you sent this afternoon and am very grateful for it. Thanks a lot.

Tell Fat I got that receipt. I got a post card from Jim and he said he was sick. Did he write to you?

Well tomorrow we get our last shot and I'm glad that will be over with. We drill that much that I got two big blisters on my right foot. You ought to see the exercises we have to go through each day. Did you get my clothing yet?

I am sorry about Harold and the rest of the sick ones. I hope they get well fast. Pop ought to see a Doctor about that knee.

In a week or two we will stop drilling and go to different classes in seamanship, rowing, wearing and handling gas masks. Then we go out on the firing range practiceing rifle, machine gun and cannon firing & bayonet drills. We also must qualify in swimming. This includes seven weeks of training. Then we take a written test to see if we go to trade school, if not we are shiped with the fleet. After our training period is over we are given ten days leave (I'll be home) if you wish them, so don't be surprised if I come home in March. I'll soon think that I'm supposed to be a soldier instead of a sailor the way they drill us here. Well I guess I'll sign off. I got a tooth filled today and boy did it hurt, but I'm glad it's filled.

Your son
Wilson

Please excuse the writing. I wrote this in bed (we have beds not hammocks) Did pop get his money yet. Did he pay Fat & Dave

-----

[Postmark is Norfolk VA., Jan. 25, 1941, 1:30 PM]
Mr. & Mrs. Robt. Lineaweaver
1240 E. Cumberland St
Avon Penna.

[Return adress:]
W C Lineaweaver
Platoon No 5
U.S. Naval Training Station
Norfolk, Va.

The past week end I got out of
detention and went down to the d___
I seen the aircraft carrier "Wasp"
about seven destroyers and a ta___
sea plane tender which I was on, the
also was a bunch of other kinds of ___
It was a pretty sight.

I hope the kids are having a goo___
time sleigh riding we didn't have ___
enough snow down here to make ___
snow ball.

How is the High School basket ba___
team making out? Do they have a goo___
team? I'll bet it seems strange aro___
the house with just a few kids, ___
of us gone. Was Jim home yet ___
expect to be home next month for a ___
while but theres nothing sure. D___
forget to write.

Your son
Wilson

P.S. This is the next morning and
I am getting ready to leave the
hospital. I feel fine. Hope you all feel the ___

Feb. 3, 1941

Dear Parents:
I received your letter the other
day and was glad to hear from you.
Right now I'm in the Hospital with a
cold fever but its nothing serious, I hope
to be out by the time you get this
letter.

You know that fire you read about
was only a half block below my
dormitory, we had to stand out in the
cold for four hours waiting to be
called for fire or police duty. Stuff
from the fire was falling on us
faster than a heavy snow. I
didn't hear anything about sabotage
but their was 275,000 damage, the
biggest fire I ever seen.

W. C. Inceawater
Battery 10-5
U.S. Naval Training Sta.
Norfolk, V.

Philadelphia, Pa.
Air mail office as soon
as Theo

Mr & Mrs Robt. Inceawater
1240 E Cumberland St
Avon Penna

Feb. 3, 1941

Dear Parents:

I received your letter the other day and was glad to hear from you. Right now I'm in the Hospital with a cold fever but its nothing serious. I hope to be out by the time you get this letter.

You know that fire you read about was only a half block below my dormitory, we had to stand out in the cold for four hours waiting to be called for fire or police duty. Stuff from the fire was falling on us faster than a heavy snow. I didn't hear anything about sabatoge but their was $275,000 damage, the biggest fire I ever seen.

The past week end I got out of detention and went down to the docks. I seen the aircraft carrier "Wasp", about seven destroyers and a large sea plane tender which I was on, there also was a bunch of other kinds of ships. It was a pretty sight.

I hope the kids are having a good time sleigh riding we didn't have enough snow down here to make a snowball.

How is the High School basketball team making out? Do they have a good team? I'll bet it seems strange around the house with just a few kids, four of us gone. Was Jim home yet? I expect to be home next month for a while but theres nothing sure. Don't forget to write.

Your son
Wilson

P.S. This is the next morning and I am getting ready to leave the hospital. I feel fine. Hope you all feel the same.

[Postmark is Norfolk VA., Feb. 5, 1941, 4:30 PM]
Mr. & Mrs. Robt. Lineaweaver
1240 E Cumberland St
Avon Penna.

[Return Address:]
W.C. Lineaweaver
Platoon No. 5
U.S. Naval Training Station
Norfolk, Va.

"You know that fire..."
Newspapers at the time reported that the fire Wilson mentions in this letter occurred on Sunday, January 26, 1941, in the 'huge' administration and communications office building at the Norfolk Naval operating base. The blaze started in the radio room at 9 a.m. destroying the central section of the building, and caused the base to be without telephone and radio communications for five hours.

I am captain of our platoon basketball team, we beat platoons 4 + 6 I scored 23 pts in both games. For other athletics we box, have swimming races, tug of [war] between platoons (this is fun) and st[arting] next week we will have boat races, [rowing] + sailing.

On the 27 of this month we [will] or complete training and I migh[t] be home for a few days.

Your son
Wilson

P.S. I got a bloody nose in my fir[st] boxing match and I had to qu[it] the doctor won't allow me to bo[x] anymore because of my nose (I wa[s] beating the other guy)
We didn't have any snow yet and [I] don't think we'll get any!
Don't forget to write

Feb. 12, 1941

Dear Mother + family,
I just received your letter and was glad to hear from you. I am glad everyone is feeling O.K. and I am glad [Jim] is making out O.K., tell him to stick it out. The camp I was in is a mile below the camp he is in. Was he home yet?

How much money did pop get? I'd like to know. Since I last wrote you we did a lot of rowing + sailing and went to a lot of classes where we learned about flags, signaling, tying knots, parts of ships and a lot of other things in general. But on the rifle range my score of 290 was ninth in my platoon of 74 men which I think was pretty good I shot left handed but must learn to shoot right handed in the future

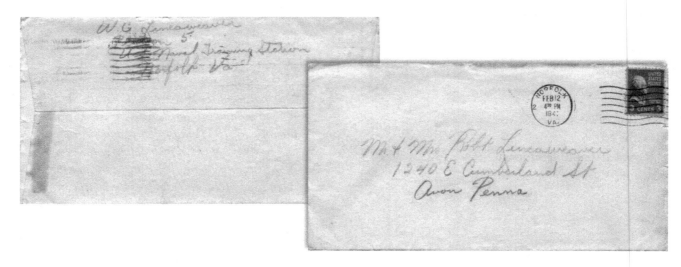

W. G. Linceaweaver
5th [ ] Naval Training Station
Norfolk Va.

Mr + Mrs Robt Linceaweaver
1240 E Cumberland St
Avon Penna

NORFOLK
FEB 12
4 PM
194[1]
VA.

Feb. 12, 1941

Dear Mother & family:

I just received your letter and was glad to hear from you. I am glad everyone is feeling O.K. and I am glad Jim is making out O.K., tell him to stick it out. The camp I was in is a mile below the camp he is in. Was he home yet?,

How much money did pop get? I'd like to know. Since I last wrote you we did a lot of rowing & sailing and went to a lot of classes where we learned about flags, signaling, tying knots, parts of ships and a lot of other things in general. Out on the rifle range my score of 290 I was nineth in my platoon of 74 men which I think was pretty good. I shot left handed but must learn to shoot right handed in the future.

I am captain of our platoon basketball team, we beat platoons 4 & 6 I scored 23 pts in both games. For other athletics we box, have swimming races, tug of war between platoons (this is fun) and starting next week we will have boat races, rowing & sailing.

On the 28th this month we break or complete training and I might be home for a few days.

Your son
Wilson

P.S. I got a bloody nose in my first boxing match and I had to quit. The doctor won't allow me to box anymore because of my nose (I was beating the other guy)
We didn't have any snow yet and I don't think we'll get any.
Don't forget to write

[Postmark is Norfolk VA., Feb. 12, 1941, 4:30 PM]
Mr. & Mrs. Robt. Lineaweaver
1240 E Cumberland St
Avon Penna.

[Return Address:]
W. C. Lineaweaver
Platoon 5
U.S. Naval Training Station
Norfolk Va.

There are a lot of things that I
could write about but I think I'll
wait until I get home and tell
to you. So I'll close hoping eve
is feeling allright

Your son
Wilson

Don't forget the buck, I'll rep
you when I get home
We were sailing today, I w
a lot of fun. I will mail this
letter on the way to the show,
are falling in to march there righ
now

Feb. 17th 1941

Dear Parents:
We have just received word that
after we break on the 28th, that means
finishing training we are allowed 9 days
leave, so that means I'll be home this
coming Saturday a week for 9 days. I'll
travel by bus by way of Washington
D.C., Baltimore & Harrisburg. Don't
keep me locked out because I'll
get there between 2 & 3 o'clock
Saturday morning.
I wish you would send me a
dollar till I get home. so I can
get some things and if you would add
a couple packs of cigarettes I wouldn't
mind a bit We don't get paid until
next Thursday so I wish you would
send these things right away.

W. C. Lineaweaver
U.S. Naval Training Station
Norfolk Va.
Platoon No

Mr & Mrs Robt. Lineaweaver
1240 E. Cumberland St.
Avon Penna.

Feb. 17, 1941

Dear Parents:

We have just received word that after break on the 28th, that means finishing training we are allowed 9 days leave, so that means I'll be home this coming Saturday a week for 9 days. I'll travel by bus by way of Washington D.C., Baltimore & Harrisburg. Don't keep me locked out because I'll get there between 2 & 3 o clock Saturday morning.

I wish you would send me a dollar till I get home, so I can get some things and if you would add a couple packs of cigarettes I wouldn't mind a bit. We don't get paid until next Thursday so I wish you would send these things right away.

There are a lot of things that I could write about but I think I'll wait until I get home and tell them to you. So I'll close hoping everyone is feeling allright.

Your son
Wilson

Don't forget the buck, I'll repay you when I get home
We were sailing today, It was a lot of fun. I will mail this letter on the way to the show, we are falling in to march there right now

-----

[Postmark is Norfolk VA., Feb. 18, 1941, 12:30 PM]
Mr. & Mrs. Robt. Lineaweaver
1240 E. Cumberland St.
Avon Penna.

[Return Address:]
W. C. Lineaweaver
U.S. Naval Training Station
Norfolk Va.
Platoon No. 5

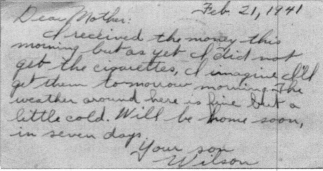

[Postcard - Postmark is Norfolk VA., Feb. 21, 1941, 8:30 PM]

Mrs. Lineaweaver
1240 E Cumberland St.
Avon Penna.

Feb. 21, 1941

Dear Mother:

I received the money this morning but as yet I did not get the cigarettes. I imagine I'll get them tomorrow morning. The weather around here is fine but a little cold. Will be home soon, in seven days.

Your son
Wilson

****

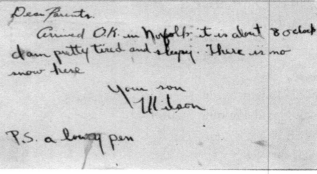

[Postcard –
Postmark is Norfolk VA., March. 10, 1941, 11:30 AM]
Mr. & Mrs. Robt. Lineaweaver
1240 E. Cumberland St.
Avon Penna.

Dear Parents,

Arrived O.K. in Norfolk it is about 8 oclock darn pretty tired and sleepy. There is no snow here

Your son
Wilson

P.S. a lousy pen

March 18th, 1940
[Postmarked 1941, so "1940" is an error]

Dear Parents:

I am sorry I didn't write sooner and I didn't hear from you yet. Did you get the postcard I sent soon after I arrived in Norfolk?

Enclosed you will find a money order for $6.50. Three of them you are to give to fat for my lodge fees. Two and a half goes to pop for the cigarettes and the money I borrowed. The other dollar is yours for fixing and pressing my clothing.

Your son
Wilson

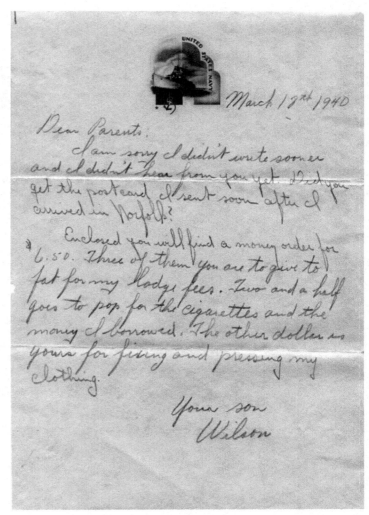

[Return Address:]
W C. Lineaweaver
U.S. Naval Training Station
Norfolk Va.
  Unit J

*[Postmark is
Norfolk VA., March 19, 1941, 12:30 PM]*
Mr. & Mrs. Robt. Lineaweaver
1240 E Cumberland St.
Avon Pennsylvania

not until the 1st of April. All
we do is a little walk around
the base and correct papers.

The rest of the fellows in
my platoon were sent to Phila.
to ship on the U.S.S. Washington
I would be with them if I
wouldn't be going to school. It
is a new Battleship just
finished.

School lasts four months so
that means I'll be home in Au—
sometime if everything goes all—

Is sour puss still sour or did
she get over it. I hope you see
a good show with the dollar I
gave you and not the kids.

Your son
Wilson

NAVY
YMCA
130 BROOKS AVE.
NORFOLK
VIRGINIA

THE SERVICE MEN'S CLUB
WHEN ASHORE

March 23, 1941

Dear Family,
I hope you received the letter
and money order I sent last
week. I got your letter yesterday
morning and was glad to hear
from you. I hope Pop is better.

Enclosed you will find some
of the pictures I had taken.
The fellow with me on two of
the pictures is a fellow ship
mate of mine by the name
of Eddy from West Va. You
can keep some and give the
others away to Dave or Fat or
anybody you wish.

I haven't started school yet,

W. G. Lineaweaver
U.S. Naval Training Station
Norfolk Va.
Unit J

Mr & Mrs Robt Lineaweaver
1240 C Cumberland St
Avon Penna.

March 23, 1941

Dear Family:

I hope you received the letter and money order I sent last week. I got your letter yesterday morning and was glad to hear from you. I hope pop is better.

Enclosed you will find some of the pictures I had taken. The fellow with me on two of the pictures is a fellow ship mate of mine by the name of Eddy from West Va. You can keep some and give the others away to Dave or Fat or anybody you wish.

I haven't started school yet, not until the 1st of April. All we do is a little work around the base and correct papers.

The rest of the fellows in my Platoon were sent to Phila to ship on the U.S.S. Washington. I would be with them If I wouldn't be going to school. The [Washington] is a new Battleship just finished.

School lasts four months so that means I'll be home in August sometime if everything goes all right.

Is sourpuss still sour or did she get over it. I hope you seen a good show with the dollar I gave you and not the kids.

Your son
Wilson

[Postmark is Norfolk VA., March 23, 1941, 6:30 PM]
Mr. & Mrs. Robt Lineaweaver
1240 E Cumberland St
Avon Penna.

[Return Address:]
W. C. Lineaweaver
U.S. Naval Training Station
Norfolk Va.
Unit J

[In this envelope was a paper titled "NAVY LETTER / TIME SAVER FOR BUSY SAILORS". A copy of this paper appears on the following page.]

A note from Wilson at the top reads: "What do you think of this kind of letter. I worked it out and the fellows down in the print shop printed it." *This paper was included with the letter on the previous page.*

[handwritten at top:] What do you think of this kind of a letter I worked it out and the fellows down in the print shop printed it

NAVY LETTER
TIME SAVER FOR BUSY SAILORS
(Use a check mark to avoid writer's cramp and
allow more time to eat and sleep)

Dear
- —Sweetie,
- X Ma,
- X Dad,
- X Sis,
- —Friend,
- X Brother,
- —Shipmate,

and I am very
- —sorry.
- X glad.
- —defatigated.
- —tight.
- —sober?

It is very
- —stormy.
- X Pleasant. *here (sometime)*
- —hot.
- —cold.
- —unusual.

The meals are
- —fierce.
- —irregular.
- —nourishing.
- —poor.
- X effective.
- —worse.

I need
- —loving.
- X money. *as usual*
- —YOU.
- —clothes.
- X sleep. *all the time*

Thanks for the
- —Gin.
- —tooth-paste.
- X letter.
- —food.
- —money.
- —Listerine.
- —advice? ?

I spend my spare time
- —at Church;
- —in bed;
- X studying;
- X WORKING; *but not hard*
- X at picture shows; *there is three here*
- X thinking of you;
- X eating;

Am having a wonderful time!
Wish YOU were here!
Regards to every one!
Going on Leave ...*August Maybe*...

and I am
- —well.
- —hungry.
- X broke. *all the time*
- —lonesome.
- —sleepy.

Yours
- —cordially.
- X with Love?
- —and YOURS only!
- —always.
- —respectfully.

!write soon!

My work is
- X enjoyable;
- —tiresome;
- —rotten;
- —long;
- —boring;
- —insidious;

[signature] W. C. L.............

[Return Address:]
Wilson C. Lineaweaver, U.S. Naval Training Station
Norfolk Va., Unit J

[Postmark is Norfolk VA.,
April 1, 1941, 8:30 PM]
Mrs. Robt. Lineaweaver
1240 E. Cumberland St
Avon Penna

April 2, 1941

Dear Mother:

Money is a hard thing for me to hold on to so I've decided each pay to send you a few dollars to keep for me so in case of an emergency I can send for it or when I come home on leave I have some to spend.

Enclosed is $3.00, put them away in some safe place for me. In case you would have to need some bad, why go ahead and use some. So each pay day expect a few dollars. By August when I come home on leave (if I get it) I should have a nice little sum. Don't be afraid to use some of it.

I hope you get the other letter I am sending with this one. Don't forget to write.

Your son
Wilson

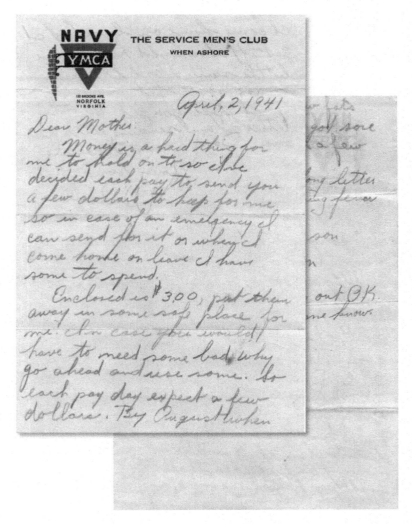

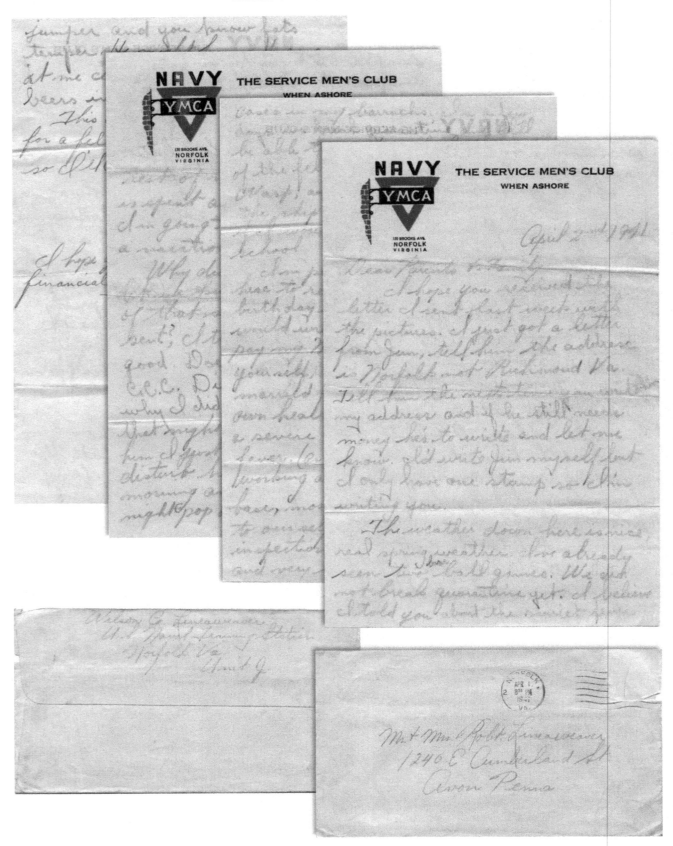

April 2nd 1941

Dear Parents & Family,

      I hope you received the letter I sent last week with the pictures. I just got a letter from Jim, tell him the address is Norfolk not Richmond Va. Tell him the next time you write him my address and if he still needs money he's to write and let me know. I'd write Jim myself but I only have one stamp so I'm writing you.

      The weather down here is nice, real spring weather. Ive already seen two base ball games. We did not break quarantine yet. I believe I told you about the scarlet fever cases in my barracks. In a few days we break quarantine and I'll be able to go to school. The rest of the fellows go on the U.S.S. Wasp, and aircraft carrier. This is the ship I would have gone on if I wouldn't have made service school.

      I'm putting a few lines in here to remind you I have a birthday shortly and I wish you would write me more. Did Fat pay my Moose dues? I hope pop, yourself, the kids and the married folks are O.K. As to my own health, I'm sick. I have a severe case of acute spring fever. (as usual) They have us working at odd jobs around the base, most of the time we have to our self. We only have one inspection a week, no drilling and very little discipline. If the rest of my time in the navy is spent as easy as this month I'm going to like it. This is a vacation compared to Training.

      Why didn't you write and let me know what you thought of that screwball letter I sent? I thought it was pretty good. Does Jim still like the C.C.C. Did Fat ever ask you why I did not sleep at his place that night we bowled, tell him I just didn't want to disturb him at 3 in the morning and besides that's the night pop helped me out of my jumper and you know fats temper. He might have got sore at me coming in with a few beers in me.

      This certainly is a long letter for a fellow having spring fever so I'll close.

Your loving son
Wilson

      I hope you are making out O.K. financially if not let me know.

[Postmark is Norfolk VA., April 1, 1941, 8:30 PM]
Mr. & Mrs. Robt. Lineaweaver
1240 E Cumberland St.
Avon Penna.

[Return Address:]
Wilson C. Lineaweaver
U.S. Naval Training Station
Norfolk Va., Unit J

don't hesitate to let me know.
Did Fat pay my lodg[...]
He didn't send the reciept [...]
in your next letter send [...]
address. I think its 329 S.
but I'm not sure.

Since papa is out of work [...]
would be a good idea if Jun[...]
stay in the CCC. The othe[...]
one of the navy bombers c[...]
killing ten men. All that [...]
left of them filled two se[...]
so you can imagine how the[y were]
mutilated.

I guess I'll have to sign o[ff]
Your son
Wilson

NAVY YMCA
130 BROOKE AVE.
NORFOLK
VIRGINIA

THE SERVICE MEN'S CLUB
WHEN ASHORE

April 13, 1940

Dear Parents & Family;
Well this is Easter, just
another day for us. They had us
working awhile this morning
(but not hard) I wish I
could have been home for just
this day.

I hope you had a very
enjoyable Easter with plenty of
candy for the kids. The weather
down here was very nice so I
imagine you had nice weather.

I am sorry to hear that
dad is laid off. I can't imagine
how you are going to manage but
if I can be of any assistance why

NAVY YMCA
130 BROOKE AVE.
NORFOLK
VIRGINIA

AFTER FIVE DAYS RETURN TO
W. [...] eaweaver
[...]

NORFOLK
APR 14
12:00 PM
1941
VA.

Mr. & Mrs. Robt Lineaweaver
1240 E Cumberland St
Avon ~~[...]~~ Penna.

April 13, 1940 *[Postmarked 1941, so "1940" is an error]*

Dear Parents & Family,

Well this is Easter, just another day for us. They had us working awhile this morning (but not hard) I wish I could have been home just for this day.

I hope you had a very enjoyable Easter with plenty of candy for the kids. The weather down here was very nice so I imagine you had nice weather.

I am sorry to hear that dad is laid off. I can't imagine how you are going to manage but if I can be of any assistance why don't hesitate to let me know.

Did Fat pay my lodge dues? He didn't send the receipt yet. in your next letter send Fat's address. I think its 329 S. tenth St but Im not sure.

Since pop is out of work it would be a good idea if Jim would stay in the CCC. The other day one of the navy bombers crashed killing ten men. All that was left of them filled two sea bags so you can imagine how they were mutilated.

I guess I'll have to sign off

Your son
Wilson

[Postmark is Norfolk VA., April 14, 1941, 12:30 PM]
Mr. & Mrs. Robt. Lineaweaver
1240 E. Cumberland St.
Avon Penna

[Return Address:]
W. C. Lineaweaver
U.S. Naval Training Station
Norfolk Va.
Unit J

> **"...one of the navy bombers crashed..."**
> *While thousands of men were killed in non-combat accidents during the World War II era, the crash mentioned by Wilson in his above letter occurred on April 7, 1941. A PBY-1 bomber with ten men was heading from Norfolk, VA, to Quonsett Point, RI, when it crashed into the ocean two miles off the coast of Virginia. All ten men aboard were killed. The pilot and co-pilot were Ensigns George Nelson Blackburn and Gerald W. Marson (age 22). Eight enlisted men were Theodore F. Mueller, Louis C. Luton (age 38), Boyd A. Taylor (age 24), Wallace Broadhurst, Fred W. Crows, Lecil L. Gurganus, Frank McElrath, and Anthony P. Fasano. Only two bodies were recovered and identified (Blackburn and Mueller). Additional parts of two or three other bodies were also recovered, but eight men were listed as lost at sea.*

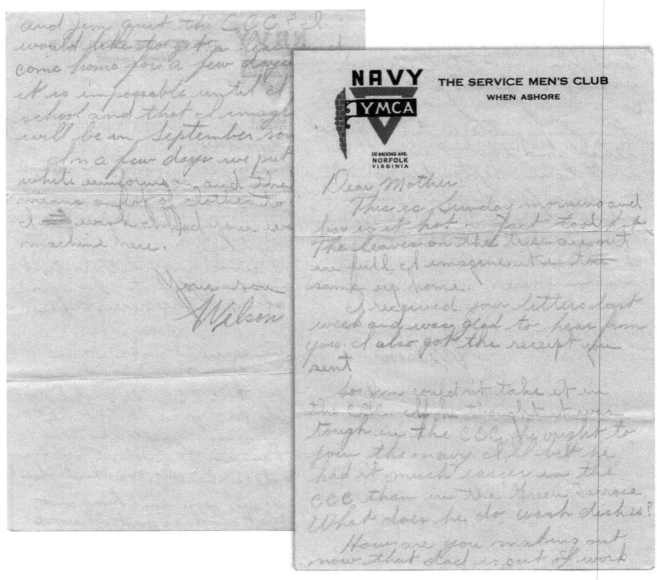

and Jim quit the C.C.C.? I
would like to get a ____
come home for a few days.
It is impossible until I
school and that I imagine
will be in September so—

In a few days we put
white uniforms on and that
means a lot of clothes to
I wish I had a w____
machine here.

Your son
Wilson

NAVY YMCA
THE SERVICE MEN'S CLUB
WHEN ASHORE
130 BROOKE AVE.
NORFOLK
VIRGINIA

Dear Mother:
This is Sunday morning and
how is it hot — fact too hot.
The leaves on the trees are out
in full. I imagine it is the
same up home.

I received your letters last
week and was glad to hear from
you. I also got the receipt you
sent.

So Jim couldn't take it in
the C.C.C. _____ I thought it was
tough in the C.C.C. He ought to
join the navy. I'll bet he
had it much easier in the
C.C.C. than in the Navy I know.
What does he do, wash dishes?

How are you making out
now that dad is out of work

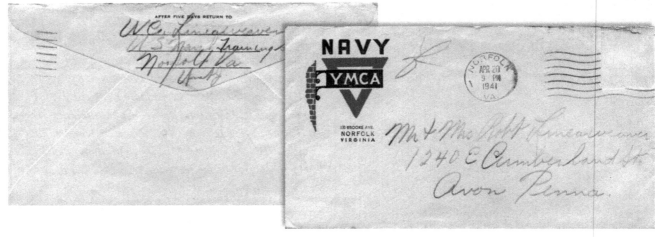

AFTER FIVE DAYS RETURN TO
W. C. Linaweaver
U.S. Navy Training
Norfolk Va
Unit ___

NAVY YMCA
130 BROOKE AVE.
NORFOLK
VIRGINIA

NORFOLK
APR 20
9 PM
1941
VA.

Mr & Mrs _____ Linaweaver
1240 E Cumberland St.
Avon Penna.

[No date on letter, but April 20th, 1941 was a Sunday]

Dear Mother:

This is Sunday morning and boy is it hot in fact too hot. The leaves on the trees are out in full, I imagine it is the same up home.

I received your letter last week and was glad to hear from you. I also got the receipt you sent.

So Jim couldn't take it in the CCC. If he thought it was tough in the CCC, he ought to join the navy. I'll bet he had it much easier in the CCC than in the "Green Terrace". What does he do, wash dishes?

How are you making out now that dad is out of work and Jim quit the CCC? I would like to get a leave and come home for a few days but it is impossible until I finish school and that I imagine will be in September sometime.

In a few days we put our white uniforms on and that means a lot of clothes to wash. I wish I had your washing machine here.

Your son
Wilson

[Postmark is Norfolk VA., April 20, 1941, 9 PM]
Mr. & Mrs. Robt Lineaweaver
1240 E Cumberland St.
Avon Penna.

[Return Address:]
W. C. Lineaweaver
U.S. Naval Training Station
Norfolk Va.
Unit J

maytagclub.com

Washing machine typical of what Wilson's mother may have used.

I am sorry to find out that things are going pretty tough, _____ I could help you. I hope p_____ finds work soon

And so until I get sit___ at my new place I'll cl___

Your son
Wilson

P.S. I hope I like radio s____ What do you think of the ___ studying radio?

Wilson C Lineaweaver
U.S Naval Training Station
Norfolk, Va.

April 28, 1941

Dear Mother & Family:

I recieved your letter this afternoon and was very glad to hear from you. Your letter arrived just in time because I am being transferred Wednesday to Jacksonville, Florida.

By the time you get this letter I'll be in Jacksonville so don't write any letters to the training station. I'll send my new address as soon as possible.

I am being transfered to the radio school at the Naval air station in Jacksonville. I will go to school for sixteen weeks than possibly advanced training I don't know.

Wilson C Lineaweaver
U.S. Naval Training Station
Norfolk Va
Unit J Bldg. 18

Mr. & Mrs. Robt. Lineaweaver
1240 E Cumberland St.
Cirron Penna.

Wilson C Lineaweaver
U.S. Naval Training Station
Norfolk, Va.

April 28, 1941

Dear Mother & Family:

I received your letter this afternoon and was very glad to hear from you. Your letter arrived just in time because I am being transferred Wednesday to Jacksonville, Florida.

By the time you get this letter I'll be in Jacksonville so don't write any letters to the training station. I'll send my new address as soon as possible.

I am being transferred to the radio school at the Naval air station in Jacksonville. I will go to school for sixteen weeks than possibly advanced training I don't know.

I am sorry to find out that things are going pretty tough, I wish I could help you. I hope pop finds work soon

And so until I get situated at my new place I'll close

Your son
Wilson

P.S. I hope I like radio school
What do you think of the Idea studying radio?

[Postmark is Norfolk VA., April 28, 1941, 8:00 PM]
Mr. & Mrs. Robt. Lineaweaver
1240 E Cumberland St.
Avon Penna

[Return Address:]
Wilson C Lineaweaver
US. Naval Training Station
Norfolk Va
Unit J   Bldg. 18

home working but I gue[ss]
used to this life. It [looks]
if our country is just ab[out]
war and I'll be right o[ut in]
front. I don't hear ver[y much]
because they have us g[oing to]
school day and night.

If I can complete [this]
course I'll graduate so[metime]
in September, these co[urses]
will be the toughest [I've]
spent.

I know you have [had it]
tough at home, not h[earing from]
you lately. I hope cond[itions have]
improved. Please write [and let]
me know how every one [of]
you are making out. Do[n't forget]
to use my correct addr[ess.]

Your son
Wil[son]

This is my →
correct address

Wilson C. Lineaweaver
Trade School
Barracks #2
Jacksonville Fla.

May 5, 1941

Dear Mother & Family,
        I am sorry I didn't write
you sooner, they have us on the
go all the time but I finally
found time. Boy is it hot
down here! I can just about
stand it.
        If I haven't told you before,
the school I am going too is
aviation radio at the naval
air station here in Jacksonville.
The course is plenty tough, I
don't think I'll be able to
finish it. Some of the subjects
that we are studying now are
Type writing, spelling, code &
semaphore signaling. We go to
school nine hours a day, two of
the hours are after chow from 7:30 to
9:30.
        A lot of times I wish I was

W.C. Lineaweaver
Barracks #2
Trade School
Jacksonville, Fla.

HOTEL WILLIAM BYRD
Richmond, Va.

Mrs Erlene Lineaweaver
1240 E Cumberland St
Avon Penna

This is my correct address

 Wilson C Lineaweaver
 Trade School
 Barracks #2
 Jacksonville, Fla.

May 5, 1941

Dear Mother & Family:

 I am sorry I didn't write you sooner. they have us on the go all the time. Boy is it hot down here! I can just about stand it

 If I haven't told you before, the school I am going too is aviation radio at the naval air station here in Jacksonville. The course is plenty tough. I don't think I'll be able to finish it. Some of the subjects that we are studying now are typewriting, spelling, code & semaphore signaling. We go to school nine hours a day, two of the hours are after chow from 7:30 to 9:30.

 A lot of times I wish I was home working but I guess I'll get used to this life. It looks as if our country is just about in war and I'll be right out in the front. I don't hear very much because they have us going to school day and night.

 If I can complete the course I'll graduate some time in September, these coming months will be the toughest I ever spent.

 I know you have it pretty tough at home, not hearing from you lately I hope conditions have improved. Please write and let me know how everyone is and how you are making out. Don't forget to use my correct address

Your son
Wilson

[Postmark is Jacksonville, Fla., May 6, 1941, 8:30 AM, Naval Air Sta.]
Mrs. Erlene Lineaweaver
1240 E Cumberland St
Avon Penna

[Return Address:]
W.C. Lineaweaver
Barracks #2
Trade School
US Naval air Station
Jacksonville Fla.

REPORTING TO TRADE SCHOOL LETTER TO PARENTS

IN REPLY REFER
TO FILE No.

UNITED STATES NAVAL AIR STATION
JACKSONVILLE, FLORIDA
May 6, 1941

Mr. Robert Lineaweaver
1240 E. Cumberland St.
Avon, Pennsylvania

Dear Mr. Lineaweaver:

I am glad to inform you that your son has reported for instruction at the Trade Schools, U.S. Naval Air Station, Jacksonville, Florida.

He and you are to be congratulated on the fact that he has been selected for additional instruction in a specialty at the Trade Schools. Such training is not available to every person who enlists, and his selection is an indication that he has already shown aptitude for the Service. His training here will be invaluable in his future Naval Career, and should enable him to advance more rapidly and also to render a greater service to his country as a trained man in U.S. Naval Aviation. Of course, his progress here at the Trade Schools will depend in large measure on his own application to his studies.

While a student, your son will continue to receive excellent food, daily recreation and religious counsel. His regular habits of living will be daily routine. Particular attention will be given to his physical, mental and moral welfare. Every effort is made to provide a well-rounded course of instruction, so as to develop men who will be useful in civil life as well as in the service.

The regulations of the Trade Schools require each student to write home at least each week. Should any occasion require it, the next of kin is immediately notified in case of serious illness or injury. Frequent, cheerful letters from home are not only a source of pleasure to the student and encourage him to write frequently, but also aid in maintaining morale; and therefore you are urged to correspond freely with your son. Letters to him should be addressed:

> Wilson C. Linewweaver
> Trade Schools,
> Barracks No. 2
> U.S. Naval Air Station,
> Jacksonville, Florida.

Inquiries regarding students should be addressed to Personnel Officer, Trade Schools, U.S. Naval Air Station, Jacksonville, Florida.

Sincerely,

J. L. COTTEN,
Commander, U.S. Navy,
Officer-in-Charge.
TRADE SCHOOLS.

[Souvenir cards' actual size is 3 ½" x 2 ½"; Duvall News Company, Jacksonville, Fla.]

It really is a pleasure,
When Mother's Day draws near,
To send you my best wishes,
And Greetings most sincere.
****

U. S. NAVAL AIR STATION
Jacksonville, Florida

MOTHER'S DAY

Dear Mother:

     We have been reminded that Sunday, May 11, will be Mother's Day.
Special services will be held at the Naval Air Station. The Secretary of
the Navy always sends out a letter to all ships and stations and Marine Corps
activities calling attention to the significance of Mother's Day and the duty
of everyone to render tribute to his mother. In view of this, the Chaplain
has prepared this letter with the idea that it will provide opportunity for
us to send greetings to our homes on this occasion. He hopes that we will
add personal messages of our own.

     The Naval Air Station is nearing completion and it is really a
pleasure to work in such beautiful surroundings. It is practically a city
in itself with the Ship's Service Store, Movies, Church, and many other activities. The latest is a block of two hundred homes for married personnel.
These families will soon be moving in and their advent will add much to the
home-like character of the station.

     I am enjoying my work here and getting a great deal from the ex-
cellent training and discipline provided.

                        Affectionately,

                        Wilson

Mr & Mrs Robt Linneaweaver
1240 E Cumberland St
Avon Penna

W. C. Linneaweaver
Barracks # 4
Trade School
Jacksonville Fla

It really is a pleasure,
When Mother's Day draws near,
To send you my best wishes,
And Greetings most sincere.

****

U.S. NAVAL AIR STATION
Jacksonville, Florida

MOTHER'S DAY

Dear Mother:

We have been reminded that Sunday, May 11, will be Mother's Day. Special services will be held at the Naval Air Station. The Secretary of the Navy always sends out a letter to all ships and stations and Marine Corps activities calling attention to the significance of Mother's Day and the duty of everyone to render tribute to his mother. In view of this, the Chaplain has prepared this letter with the idea that it will provide opportunity for us to send greeting to our homes on this occasion. He hopes that we will add personal messages of our own.

The Naval Air Station is nearing completion and it is really a pleasure to work in such beautiful surroundings. It is practically a city in itself with the Ship's Service Store, Movies, Church, and many other activities. The latest is a block of two hundred homes for married personnel. These families will soon be moving in and their advent will add much to the home-like character of the station.

I am enjoying my work here and getting a great deal from the excellent training and discipline provided.

Affectionately,
Wilson

[Postmark is Jacksonville, Fla., May 8, 1941, 8:30 AM, Naval Air Sta.]
Mr & Mrs Robt Lineaweaver
1240 E Cumberland St
Avon Penna

[Return Address:]
W.C. Lineaweaver
Barracks #4
Trade School
Jacksonville Fla.

School is getting tougher all the time, we must learn in half a year what should take a year and a half. Code is especially hard and typing takes a long time to learn but I'm working hard and hope to get it.

I have just made my first [rate] Wednesday from Apprentice seaman to seaman second class. The increase is from $21. to $36. The next rate is class seaman which pays $54. which I'll get during the latter part of the year.

Coming home is out of the question for a long time but I hope I can get home at least once sometime this [year].

How are all the kids, they've probably forgot about me already. Are they still wearing that white hat I gave them and are they feeling allright? I'll bet he is a [ ] brat. Tell Dave I received his letter yesterday morning, he had it sent from Norfolk, tell him my new address is [ ].

In the future I'll be sending money to you which I want you to keep for me, I guess you still have that [ ]. When I come home I'll have something to spend if you save it for me.

Please write. Your [ ]

Wilson C. Lineaweaver
Barracks #2
Trade School
Jacksonville, Fla.

May 11, 1941

Dear Mother

Today is Mothers day and I am sorry my financial standing is not adequate enough to send some fitting present but will in the near future. Did you get my letter that I sent a few days ago?

So Jim couldn't take it. Why did he desert, getting a job as he did he should have got an honorable discharge or did he do something wrong in camp or just couldn't take it (what would he do if he had six years)

We did not get paid since the beginning of April but will soon because the pay accounts were being transferred so after I get some money I am going to see what Florida is like especially the beach.

It seems to be getting hotter every day, I can just about stand it. This being only May I'm wondering what it will be like only in August I'm almost as black as a nigger already.

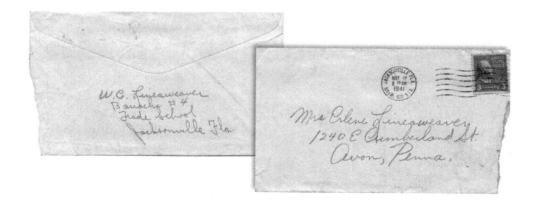

W.C. Lineaweaver
Barracks #4
Trade School
Jacksonville Fla.

Mrs Arlene Lineaweaver
1240 E Cumberland St.
Avon, Penna.

Wilson C. Lineaweaver, Barracks #2, Trade School, Jacksonville, Fla.

May 11, 1941

Dear Mother:

Today is Mother's day and I am sorry my financial standing is not adequate enough to send some fitting present but will in the near future. Did you get my letter that I sent a few days ago?

So Jim couldn't take it. Why did he desert? getting a job as he did he should have got an honorable discharge or did he do something wrong in camp or just couldn't take it. (What would he do if he had six years.)

We did not get paid since the beginning of April but will soon because the pay accounts were being transferred so after I get some money I am going to see what Florida is like especially the beach.

It seems to be getting hotter every day. I can just about stand it. This being only May Im wondering what it will be like July and August. Im almost as black as a niger already.

School is getting tougher all the time, we must learn in a half a year what should take a year and a half. Code is especially hard and typing takes a long time to learn but I'm working hard and hope to get through

I have just made my first jump upward Wednesday from Apprentice seaman to seaman second class. The increase in pay is from $21. to $36.. The next rate is first class seaman which pays $54. which I hope to get during the latter part of the year.

Coming home is out of the question for a long time but I hope I can get leave at least once sometime this year.

How are all the kids, I'll bet they forgot about me already. Are they wearing that white hat I gave them? Is pop feeling allright? I'll be he has another boil. Tell Dave I received his letter yesterday morning, he had it addressed to Norfolk, tell him my new address.

In the future I'll be sending money to you which I want you to save for me. I guess you still have that three dollars. When I come home I'll have some money to spend if you save it for me.

Your son
Wilson

Please write

[Postmark is Jacksonville, Fla., May 11, 1941, 8:30 AM, Naval Air Sta.]
Mrs Erlene Lineaweaver
1240 E Cumberland St.
Avon, Penna.

[Return Address:]
W.C. Lineaweaver
Barracks #4, Trade School
Jacksonville Fla.

and you know mom he might be
able to wear that [...]
mine. Tell Jim I th[...]
puff, can't take it in [...]
would he do if he was [...]
its plenty tough beca[...]
we just have to grin [...]

We have just fi[...]
class, semaphore, [...]
by flags are rather to [...]
of flags, perhaps you [...]
show when they sh[...]
pictures. My final g[...]
was 3.8 which is ex[...]
equal to one hundred [...]
way our marks are [...]

You should see [...]
but you wouldn't kno[...]
black. The sun is [...]

In a few min[...]
chow (supper to you) [...]
was glad to hear fr[...]
you continue to write [...]

W. C. Lineaweaver
correct address   Trade School Barracks #2
U.S. Naval Air Station
Jacksonville Fla.
May 19, 1941

Dear Mother & Family:
I spent all of yesterday swimming
at the beach and in the amusement
section. Boy! is swimming in the
ocean fun especially diving through
the big waves that come in and
lying around in the sand. I wish
all of you could have been with me

I promised myself to send
some money to you every payday but
after going to the beach (It costs
plenty if you want to enjoy yourself, and
I did) and buying a lot of things I
needed, I went broke. Enclo[...]
bucks you can save for me and [...]
future you'll get larger amounts [...]

So Jim got an honorabl[...]
after all, eligh[...]
don't mind t[...]

fellow going [...]
going to school [...]
In the fu[...]
I get a little m[...]
I'll send you [...]
present
Take care [...]
and don't rul [...]
too many boys [...]

May 19 1941

Dear Sis:
Just a few lines to let
you know I was glad to
hear from you.
About that blonde, your
thinking of the wrong girl
Who is K.T.? Do I know her?
Right now it's a brunette
not a blonde and boy she's a
beauty.
So you finish school
in a few weeks. I finish
when you start again. I
never expected to go to school
again and this is tougher
than High school (you
cant play hooky)
Don't go around showing
every body those lousy
pictures of me. Eddy! The

Mr. & Mrs Robert Lineaweaver
1240 E Cumberland St
Avon Penna.

[No return address on envelope; two letters inside envelope]

[Postmark is Jacksonville, Fla.,
May 20, 1941, 8:30 AM, Naval Air Sta.]
Mr. and Mrs Robert Lineaweaver
1240 E Cumberland St
Avon Penna.

correct address
   W. C. Lineaweaver, Trade School Barracks #2, U.S. Naval Air Station, Jacksonville Fla.

May 19, 1941

Dear Mother & Family:
   I spent all of yesterday swimming at the beach and in the amusement section. Boy! is swimming in the ocean fun especially diving through the big waves that come in and lying around in the sand. I wish all of you could have been with me.
   I promised myself to send some money to you every payday but after going to the beach (It costs plenty if you want to enjoy yourself, and I did) and buying a lot of things I needed, I went broke. Enclose is a buck you can save for me and in the future you'll get larger amounts.
   So Jim got an honorable discharge after all, I'm glad to hear that. I don't mind him wearing my clothes and you know mom he might be able to wear that brown suit of mine. Tell Jim I think he's a cream puff. Can't take it in the CCC, what would he do if he was in the navy, here its plenty tough because I know but we just have to grin and bear it.
   We have just finished our first class, semaphore, which is signaling by flags are rather talking by means of flags, perhaps you seen it in the show when they showed naval pictures. My final grade in semaphore was 3.8 which is excellent. 4.0 is equal to one hundred. This is the way our marks are graded.
   You should see me mom, Ill bet you wouldn't know me, because Im black. This sun is terrific down here.
   In a few minutes we go to chow (supper to you) so Ill close. I was glad to hear from you and hope you continue to write often.

Your son
Wilson

****

May 19, 1941

Dear Sis: *[Likely sister Lucille, age 14]*
   Just a few lines to let you know I was glad to hear from you.
   About that blonde, your thinking of the wrong girl. Who is K.T.? Do I know her? Right now is a brunette not a blonde and boy she's a beauty.
   So you finish school in a few weeks. I finish when you start again. I never expected to go to school again and this is tougher than High school (you can't play hooky)
   Don't go around showing every body those lousy pictures of me. Eddy, the fellow posing with me is going to school in Norfolk.
   In the future when I get a little money together I'll send you some little present
   Take care of yourself and don't run around with too many boys.

Your Brother
Wilson

the fourth month we get actual flying. This course generally used to last a year but their jamming it all into four month. When we left Norfolk we took a special physical examination for flying so some of us may become pilots, perhaps me, you never can tell.

I don't mind going to school all day but this going to school at night is killing me, we also go to school on Saturday till four in the afternoon so you can see we don't have time to do anything such as going to town, writing letters ore washing clothes. Their certainly jamming it down our throats all on account of a funny man with a little mustache (I mean Hitl). And another thing believe it or not I must go to church in fact all of us must go Sunday.

I cant burn any more paper so I guess I must close. Mom Don't forget to write

Your son
Wilson
& Lucille
Let me know whats going on around Lebanon

Wilson C. Lineaweaver
U. S. NAVAL AIR STATION
JACKSONVILLE, FLORIDA

May 23, 1941

Dear Mother & Family:

I hope you recieved the letter I sent you & Lucille the other day. I am writing this letter in school, it is 2040, we will soon be going back to our dormitories to bed. I am suppose to be copying code.

We just received our marks for last week, I had 3.89 the fifth highest in my class of 75 men, I think thats pretty good, but its easy compared to what its going to be later on I hope I can keep it up

If I make high marks I may after graduation be sent to Lakehurst NJ. thats fairly close to home.

Maybe I haven't told you but I'm in aviation radio, besides learning all types of communication we will get machine gun training during our third month and during

(right margin, vertical): 4.0 is equal to 100 as they take back home

---

Mrs. Erlene Lineaweaver
1240 E Cumberland St.
Avon Penna.

[Postmark is Jacksonville, Fla., May 26, 1941, 8:30 AM, Naval Air Sta.]
Mrs. Erlene Lineaweaver
1240 E Cumberland St.
Avon Penna.

[No return address on envelope.]

Wilson C. Lineaweaver

May 23, 1941

Dear Mother & Family:

I hope you recieved the letter I sent you & Lucille the other day. I am writing this letter in school, it is 2040, we will soon be going back to our dormitories to bed. I am suppose to be copying code.

We just received our marks for last week, I had 3.87 [*note written on the side with an arrow pointing here:* 4.0 is equal to 100 as they grade back home] the fifth highest in my class of 75 men, I think that's pretty good, but its easy compared to what its going to be latter on. I hope I can keep it up.

If I make high marks I may after graduation be sent to Lakehurst N.J., that's fairly close to home.

Maybe I haven't told you but I'm in aviation radio, besides learning all types of communication we will get machine gun training during our third month and during the fourth month we get actual flying. This course generally used to last a year but their jamming it all into four month. When we left Norfolk we took a special physical examination for flying so some of us may become pilots, perhaps me you never can tell.

I don't mind going to school all day but this going to school at night is killing me, we also go to school on Saturday till four in the afternoon so you can see we don't have time to do anything such as going to town, writing letter are washing clothes. Their certainly jamming it down our throats all on account of a funny man with a little moustache (I mean Hitler). And another thing believe it or not I must go to church in fact all of us must go Sunday.

I can't bum any more paper so I guess I must close Mom Don't forget to write & Lucille

Your son
Wilson

Let me know whats going on around Lebanon
Are there many soldiers in Lebanon

best of your ability

Did you read about the young flying cadet that was killed here Saturday?

Some places around here you would think were in the Sahara desert, the terrain around here is all sandy and with no rain for months this sand is always blowing in your face. It's disgust Up home I always bragged about Florida but give me good old Penn

There goes the bell so like a good school boy I'm off to school The bad part of it is I can't play hooky.

Your loving son
Wilson

Wilson C. Lineaweaver
U. S. NAVAL AIR STATION
JACKSONVILLE, FLORIDA

May 27, 1941

Dear Mother & Family:

I received your letter this evening and was glad to hear from you.

Boy! is school getting tough, seven fellows were kicked out today, they were not able to come up to the standards of the school. Here's hoping that I get through. I never knew I was dumb until I started school here. The things is we have so many things to learn in a short time with no time to study. I'm putting my heart and soul into it and hope with a little luck I'll get through

Here, your soley on your own, They tell you what to do and you must learn it. That is the way of the navy, you must learn to do things by yourself They tell you what they want done and you do it to the

MRS. ERLENE LINEAWEAVER
1240 E. CUMBERLAND ST
AVON PENNA.

Wilson C. Lineaweaver

May 27, 1941

Dear Mother & Family:

I received your letter this evening and was glad to hear from you.

Boy! is school getting tough, seven fellows were kicked out today, they were not able to come up to the standards of the school. Heres hoping that I get through. I never new I was dumb until I started school here. The things is we have so many things to learn in a short time with no time to study. I'm putting my heart and soul into it and hope with a little luck I'll get through

Here, your solely on your own, they tell you what to do and you must learn it. That is the way of the navy, you must learn to do things by yourself. They tell you what they want done and you do it to the best of your ability

Did you read about the young flying cadet that was killed here Saturday?

Some places around here you would think were in the Sahara desert, the terrain around here is all sandy and with no rain for months this sand is always blowing in your face. It's disgusting. Up home I always bragged about Florida but give me good old Penna.

There goes the bell so like a good school boy Im off to school. The bad part of it is I can't play hooky.

Your loving son
Wilson

[Postmark is Jacksonville, Fla., May 28, 1941, 8:30 AM, Naval Air Sta.]
MRS. ERLENE LINEAWEAVER
1240 E. CUMBERLAND ST
AVON PENNA.

[No return address on envelope.]

appreciate it a lot

How is the little one
making out, does she make
money that you need with
With all the kids getting
you could make out a
letter if you got a job

was out Saturday
& Sunday just laying around
and taking things easy in
the bathing beauties I
relaxation did me good and
I was broke couldn't even
pepsicola I had to hitch

What does pop do with
all day and with no place to
should be home to a que

The pencil I got has my
name printed on it.
Maybe the next letter I'll
send it

Your son
W

6/2/41

Dear Mother & family

We just completed a three day
holiday from Friday through to
Monday and were back at the old
grind again, I mean school. But
they have a magazine store picture
in town I guess

I am glad to hear that all
the kids got through school ok I
thought Jake was going to flunk, he
must have improved a lot since I
left home. I hope I made out as
good as they did.

The other day I received a
Shaffer ever sharp pencil with
nothing inside to let me know
who the sender was, so I can't
thank him. Will you please try to
find out who sent it. I would

Mrs. Arlene Lincasseaner
124 E Cumberland St.
Lebanon
Pennsylvania

6/2/41

Dear Mother & family

We just completed a three day holiday from Friday through to Monday and were back at the old grind again, I mean school. Did they have a large parade in Lebanon on Memorial day?

I am glad to hear that all the kids got through school O.K. I thought Jake was going to flunk, he must have improved a lot since I left home. I hope I make out as good as they did.

The other day I received a Sheaffer eversharp pencil with nothing inside to let me know who the sender was, so I can't thank him. Will you please try to find out who send it, I would appreciate it a lot.

How is the little working girl making out, does she make any money that you could talk about? With all the kids getting big I think you could make out a hundred percent better if you got a job

I was out at the beach Saturday & Sunday just laying around on the sand taking things easy and watching the bathing beauties. I believe the relaxation did me good, another thing I was broke, couldn't even buy a pepsi cola. I had to hitch hike it out & back.

What does pop do with himself all day and with no place to go. I should be home to argue with him.

Your son
Wilson

The pencil I got has my name printed on it. Maybe the Neversink Fire Co send it.

[Postmark is Jacksonville, Fla., June 5, 1941, 8:30 AM, Naval Air Sta.]
Mrs. Erlene Lineaweaver
1240 E Cumberland St.
Avon Pennasylvania

[No return address on envelope.]

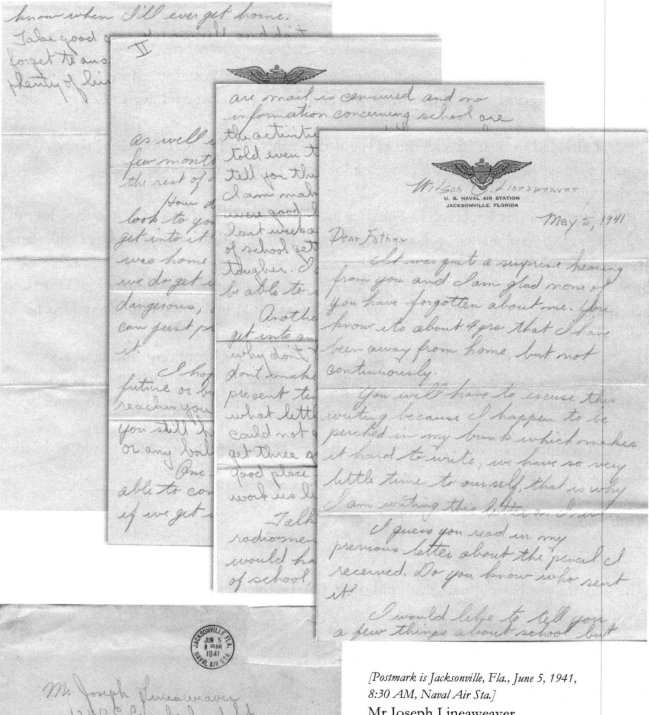

know when I'll ever get home.
Take good ...
forget to ans...
plenty of li...

II

as well ...
few month...
the rest of...

How d...
look to yo...
get into it...
was home...
we do get ...
dangerous, ...
can just p...
it.

I hop...
future or b...
reaches you...
you still ...
or any bal...

One...
able to co...
if we get ...

are mail is censured and no
information concerning school or
the activitie...
told even t...
tell you th...
I am mak...
were good...
last week a...
of school get...
tougher. I...
be able to...

Anoth...
get into an...
why don't...
don't make...
present te...
what little...
could not...
get three a...
food place...
work us li...

Talk...
radiomen...
would ha...
of school,

W. Son Lineaweaver
U. S. NAVAL AIR STATION
JACKSONVILLE, FLORIDA
May 5, 1941

Dear Father:
It was quit a surprise hearing
from you and I am glad none of
you have forgotten about me. You
know its about 4 yrs that I have
been away from home, but not
continuously.

You will have to excuse this
writing because I happen to be
perched in my bunk which makes
it hard to write, we have so very
little time to ourself, that is why
I am writing this ...

I guess you read in my
previous letter about the pencil I
received. Do you know who sent
it?

I would like to tell you
a few things about school but

[Postmark is Jacksonville, Fla., June 5, 1941,
8:30 AM, Naval Air Sta.]
Mr Joseph Lineaweaver
1240 E Cumberland St.
Avon Penna

[No return address on envelope]

Mr Joseph Lineaweaver
1240 E Cumberland St
Avon Penna

Wilson C. Lineaweaver

May 5, 1941   *[Envelope is postmarked June 5, 1941]*

Dear Father:

It was quite a surprise hearing from you and I am glad none of you have forgotten about me. You know its about 4 yrs that I have been away from home, but not continuously.

You will have to excuse this writing because I happen to be perched in my bunk which makes it hard to write, we have so very little time to ourself, that is why I am writing this letter as I rest.

I guess you read in my previous letter about the pencil I received. Do you know who sent it?

I would like to tell you a few things about school but are mail is censured and no information concerning school are the activities around here can be told even to our parents. But I will tell you this, at this stage of school I am making out fair. My marks were good but dropped some this last week and another thing instead of school getting easier its getting tougher. I don't know whether I'll be able to stick it out.

Another thing dad if you ever get into any bad financial trouble why don't forget to let me know. I don't make very much money at the present time but I would give what little I do make if you could not get along. At least here I get three good meals a day and a good place to sleep even though they work us like hell.

Talking to some of the radiomen, they told me I would have it easy after I get out of school, so I figure I might as well work like hell for these few months and have it easy for the rest of my naval career (I hope)

How does the war situation look to you? Do you think we'll get into it? I wish sometimes I was home to argue with you. If we do get into it my job will be dangerous, aviation radioman. We can just pray that we stay out of it.

I hope in the very near future or by the time this letter reaches you, you will have a job. Do you still have trouble with your leg or any boils lately.

One thing sure, I won't be able to come home this year and if we get into the war I don't know when I'll ever get home.

Take good care of yourself and don't forget to answer this letter. You have plenty of leisure time.

Your son
Wilson

about ready to leave for
Jacksonville so I will close
this letter and I will write you
tomorrow perhaps when I have
more time

Your loving son
Wilson

P.S. Please write immediately
so I know you got the money

Wilson Lineaweaver
U. S. NAVAL AIR STATION
JACKSONVILLE, FLORIDA
June
May 7th 1941

Dear Mother

Well we finally got another
pay and enclosed you will find $11.00
Please save it for me, put it with
the other money I sent you

If it wouldn't be too much
trouble you could start a bank
account for me in my name.
Ask dad to do it for me he has
plenty of time and knows how to
go about it. I hope he got the
letter I sent him. Please let
me know what you decide to do

I got your letter the other
day and the one from Lucille, I
was glad to here from you.

Being payday I am

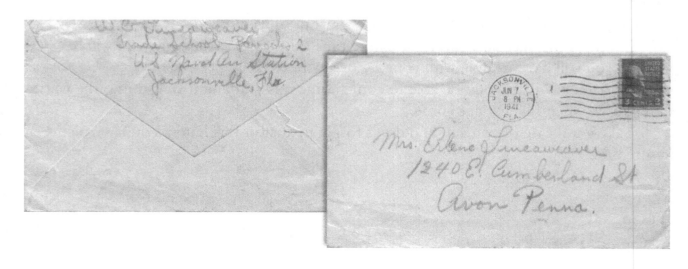

W. C. Lineaweaver
Trade School Barracks 2
U. S. Naval Air Station
Jacksonville, Fla.

JACKSONVILLE
JUN 7
8 PM
1941
FLA

Mrs. Arlene Lineaweaver
1240 E. Cumberland St
Avon Penna.

116

Wilson C Lineaweaver

May 7th 1941 *[Actually June not May]*

Dear Mother

Well! we finally got another pay and enclosed you will find $11.00 Please save it for me, put it with the other money I sent you.

If it wouldn't be too much trouble you could start a bank account for me in my name. Ask dad to do it for me he has plenty of time and knows how to go about it. I hope he got the letter I sent him. Please let me know what you decide to do

I got your letter the other day and the one from Lucille, I was glad to here from you.

Being payday I am about ready to leave for Jacksonville so I will close this letter and I will write you tomorrow perhaps when I have more time.

Your loving son
Wilson

P.S Please write immediately so I know you got the money

[Postmark is Jacksonville, Fla., June 7, 1941, 8 PM]
Mrs. Erlene Lineaweaver
1240 E. Cumberland St.
Avon Penna.

[Return Address:]
W.C. Lineaweaver
Trade School
Barracks 2
U.S. Naval Air Station
Jacksonville,Fla.

IN ACCT. WITH WILSON CHARLES LINEAWEAVER or EARLENE LINEAWEAVER, his mother No. 3060

	DATE	WITHDRAWAL	DEPOSIT	INTEREST	BALANCE	TRANS.
1	JUN10-41		**11.00		***11.00	
2	JUL-8-41	**10.00			****1.00	
3	OCT-7-41		***3.00		****4.00	
4	NOV18-41	***4.00			****0.00	
5	MAR-4-42		**20.00		**20.00	
6	MAY-2-42		**20.00		***40.00	
7	JUN-6-42			**0.03	***40.03	
8	JUN-6-42		**20.00		***60.03	
9	JUL-3-42		**20.00		***80.03	
10	JUL-6-42		**50.00		**130.03	
11	JUL13-42		**50.00		**180.03	
12	JUL10-42	**60.00	**20.00		**200.03	
13	AUG-6-42		**50.00		**250.03	
14	AUG17-42		**45.00		**295.03	
15	SEP-2-42		**20.00		**315.03	
16	SEP-4-42	***5.00			**310.03	
17	SEP10-42	**65.00			**245.03	
	NOV-5-42		**20.00		**265.03	
	DEC-1-42			**0.84	**265.87	
	DEC-1-42		**20.00		**285.87	
	DEC-9-42	*100.00			**185.87	
	DEC17-42	*100.00			***85.87	
	DEC21-42	**80.00			****5.87	
	DEC31-42	***5.87			****0.00	

LEBANON NATIONAL BANK
LEBANON, PENNA.
IT IS AGREED THAT THIS ACCOUNT IS OPENED SUBJECT TO THE RULES AND REGULATIONS CONTAINED HEREIN

Savings register for bank account opened for Wilson.

NO. 3060
SAVINGS DEPARTMENT
Lebanon National Bank
NINTH AND CUMBERLAND STREETS
Lebanon, Penna.

IMPORTANT
THIS BOOK MUST BE PRESENTED WHEN DEPOSITS ARE MADE OR MONEY WITHDRAWN. AND IF LOST OR STOLEN THE BANK MUST BE NOTIFIED AT ONCE.

get through school here.

So I think I'll let
this letter ...
I have a ...
does it ...
the salt ...

II   Florid...

like, se...
give the ...
Lebanon ...
my home ...
sorry abo...

We hav...
my class ...
second la...
that mea...
to go ...
who have ...
go to an ...
Washington ...
I'll be ...

There also is a big amusement
center here with a large wooden pier
running out ...
a lot of pe...
large glance ...
the Club ...
I think in ...
been them ...
of the club ...

Right in ...
passenger ...
10 miles ou...
pretty with ...
the large ...
horizon. th...
to 'Miam...

Tell ...
latter on ...
time. You ...
she thinks ...
I draged ...
to be hom...
see what ...

Florida, "The Land of Sunshine"
JACKSONVILLE, FLA.

June 8, 1941

Dear Mother & Family;

I am writing this letter
while sun bathing at the
Jacksonville Beach. I hope you got
my previous letter with the money
and I hope you comply with my
wish that you bank the money. Each
payday I'll send a few dollars

Its very nice here at the
beach and its fun diving through
the large waves that come rolling
in. I wish this bed could be
... I would say
playing in the sand and have
the water wash up on them

Mrs. Arlene Lineaweaver
1240 E. Cumberland St.
Avon Penna.

Jacksonville
Fla. U.S.A.

[No return address on envelope]

June 8, 1941

Dear Mother & Family,

I am writing this letter while sun bathing at the Jacksonville beach. I hope you got my previous letter with the money and I hope you comply with my wish that you bank the money. Each payday I'll send a few dollars.

Its very nice here at the beach and its fun diving through the large waves that come rolling in. I wish the kids could be here, I know they would enjoy playing in the sand and have the water wash up on them. There also is a big amusement center here with a large wooden pier running out into the ocean where a lot of people fish off of and a large dance floor is on it. Tonigh the Ink Spots are going to there, so I think me & the girlfriend will hear them. You must have heard of the Ink Spots.

Right now we can see a large passenger ship passing by about 10 miles out and it really look pretty with the blue ocean and the large ship sitting on the horizon. I imagine it's going to Miami

Tell Lucille I'll write her latter on when I can find some time. You know Mom she said she thinks Im homesick, well! I disagree but I would like to be home for a few days to see what the old town look like, see a few people and give the kids a few pennies but Lebanon doesn't seem like my home anymore. So don't worry about me getting homesick.

We have just found out that my class would graduate on the second last week in August. That means I have 11 weeks to go. Some of the fellows who have high marks will go to an advanced in Washington D.C. but I think I'll be satisfied just to get through school here.

So I think I'll close this letter and go in for a dip. I have a cut on my leg and boy! does it burn when I go the in the salt water

Your son
Wilson

[Postmark is Jacksonville, Fla., June...]
Mrs. Erlene Lineaweaver
1240 E. Cumberland St.
Avon Penna.

Wilson C. Lineaweaver

June 13th, 1941

Dear Mother:

I received your letter the other day, I am glad you got the money I sent, If I can manage there will be more coming each pay day.

We will have a few day's vacation over the fourth of July, but not enough so that I can come home. I think Ill spend the holiday roasting myself at the beach and save my money.

Right now I am on the injured list with an infected foot but I don't think its anything serious. I hurt my foot out at the beach

I hope by now pop is working. When do they expect to have the new bridge completed? Is Lucille still working?

My marks in school are still fair and I think I'll be able to get through. Typewriting is the hardest thing for me to get, but I guess it just takes plenty of practise, you can't get it overnight.

I heard the "Ink Spots" Sunday night and boy! they were swell. After the show I did quite a lot of dancing. It was swell out on the pier at night, quite romantic and I enjoyed myself immensely

Your loving Son
Wilson

P.S. The food lately is lousy, a boy friend by the name of Mclean suggest you send a package with eats. If you can manage we would appreciate it a lot.

[Postmark is Jacksonville, Fla., June 14, 1941, 11 AM, Naval Air Sta.]
Mrs. Erlene Lineaweaver, 1240 E. Cumberland St., Avon Penna.

[No return address on envelope]

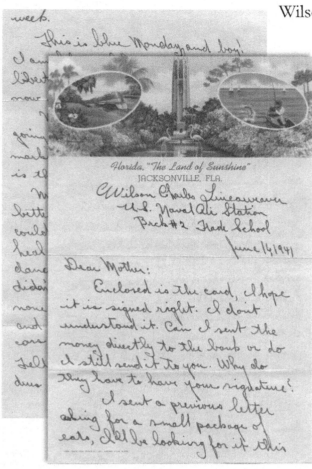

Wilson Charles Lineaweaver
U.S. Naval Air Station
Brck #2   Trade School

June 16, 1941

Dear Mother:

Enclosed is the card, I hope it is signed right. I don't understand it. Can I send the money directly to the bank or do I still send it to you. Why do they have to have your signature?

I sent a previous letter asking for a small package of eats, I'll be looking for it this week.

This is blue Monday and boy! I am blue, I had week end liberty and spent it in Jacksonville, now I am paying for it.

My marks in school are going down a little each week, my mark for this week is 3.62 which is the same as a C or about 85.

My foot is getting a little better but it is still sore. If I could keep off of it, it would soon heal and another thing, I was dancing all Sat. night and that didn't do it any good. I hope none of you are on the sick list and tell the kids to watch for cars while crossing the highway Tell fat I'll send him my lodge dues soon, I think it is due

Your son
Wilson

[Postmark is Jacksonville, Fla.,
June 17, 1941, 11 AM, Naval Air Sta.]
Mrs. Erlene Lineaweaver
1240 E. Cumberland St
Avon Penna.

[No return address on envelope]

⚓ JUNE 25, 1941 ⚓

[Left page — partial handwritten letter]

...pops working at the po[st]
house he always said he wo[uld]
get there some day (hope that [...])

I'll get to go ahead pay th[e]
lodge dues and I'll send it to h[im]
letter. (If it isn't too much trouble)

What's wrong with Harold?
getting into trouble, he ought t[o]
take it a little easy. Hope he's [...]

My foot is slowly healing
the infection is gone but [...]
tell [...]. I think I'll b[e able]
to go swimming on the fourth. [...]
going anyplace over the fourt[h]
did pop + Sara like the boat gam[e]
I wish I could have been with them [...]

[...] part took up [...] w[...]
it went up considerably [...]
it continues tomorrow, Thursday [...]
examination day and I am a litt[le]
shaky. Radio theory is subject [...]
[...] right now Don't [...]
write, tell pop to write and [...]
also
                    Your son
                    W. Pro[...]

[Right page — handwritten letter on stationery]

Wilson C. Loveweaver
U. S. NAVAL AIR STATION
JACKSONVILLE, FLORIDA
                         June 25 1941

Dear Moth[er]
        I received your letter a few
minutes ago and I was glad to
hear from you. I am sorry I didn't
write sooner.

        The package was allright, the
cake was good and not even smashed
Thanks a lot. I don't want to bother
you any more about packages but if
you are inclined to send them why I'd
hardly mind eating it, so don't go to
any extra trouble on account of me.

        I [...] buy a lot of extra clothing
this pay and I'll need some to
celebrate the fourth of July so I
won't send you any money this pay.

        I'll continue sending the
money to you and you can bank it and
if the occasion arises that I need
some I'll let you know.

[Envelope]

W. C. Loveweaver
U.S. Naval Air Station
Jacksonville Florida
[...]

JACKSONVILLE FLA.
JUN 25
8:30 AM
1941
NAVAL AIR STA.

Mrs. Aline Loveweaver
1240 C Cumberland St
Avon, Penna.

Wilson C. Lineaweaver

June 25, 1941

Dear Mother:

     I received your letter a few minutes ago and I was glad to hear from you. I am sorry I didn't write sooner.

     The package was allright, the cake was good and not even mashed. Thanks a lot. I don't want to bother you any more about packages but if you are inclined to send them Why! I don't mind eating it, so don't go to any extra trouble on account of me.

     I had to buy a lot of extra clothing this pay and I'll need some to celebrate the fourth of July so I won't send you any money this pay.

     I'll continue sending the money to you and you can bank it and if the occasion arises that I need some I'll let you know.

     So pops working at the poor house, he always said he would get their some day (not that I wish he does)

     Tell Fat to go ahead pay the lodge dues and I'll send it to him latter. (If it isn't too much trouble.)

     What's wrong with Harold? always getting into trouble, he ought to take it a little easy. I hope he's O.K. by now.

     My foot is slowly healing, all of the infection is gone but it is still sore. I think I'll be able to go swimming on the fourth. Are you going any place over the fourth? How did pop & Dave like the ball game? Wish I could have been with them.

     This past week my marks in school went up considerably. I hope it continues, tomorrow, thursday is examination day and I am a little shaky. Radio Theory is subject that worries me right now. Don't forget to write, tell pop to write and Lucille also

Your son
Wilson

[Postmark is Jacksonville, Fla., June 26, 1941, 8:30 AM, Naval Air Sta.]
Mrs. Erlene Lineaweaver
240 E Cumberland St.
Avon Penna.

[Return Address:]
W.C. Lineaweaver
U.S. Naval Air Station
Jacksonville Florida
Trade School Brks #2

Wilson C. Lineaweaver

July 5th, 1941

Dear Mother & Family:

Well! The fourth of July is gone until another year and I had a swell time, I hope all of you enjoyed yourself as I did.

I spent the whole day at the beach, my leg is completly healed so I went in swimming and in the evening went dancing. They also had a large display of fire works here. Did you see any fire works?

This is Saturday night and I would like to go to town but can't. I have the duty, just my luck.

Most of the fellows that live in the south got leave of four days to go home, because of the distance to Lebanon it was impossible for me to get leave. Maybe by Christmas Ill be stationed up north and will be able to get leave.

How is everything at home, is Harold off the injured list? Is Pop, Jim & Lucille still working? I thought pop was going to write to me? So until I hear from you Ill remain

Your son
Wilson

[Postmark is Jacksonville, Fla., July ?, 1941, 8:30 AM, Naval Air Sta.]
Mrs. Erlene Lineaweaver
1240 E Cumberland St
Avon Penna.

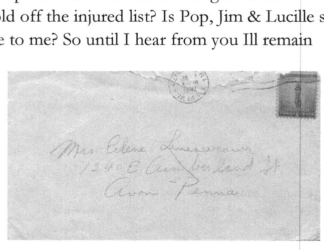

[No return address on envelope.]

Wilson C. Lineaweaver

July 6th 1941 *[July 6th was a Sunday.]*

Dear Mother:

This is a very urgent letter and I hope that you will comply with my wish.

I need ten dollars and I need it bad. I must have it before Sat. Payday is the next Sat. so I will return the money.

If you don't want to disturb the money in bank perhaps you can borrow it from Dave. In a week I'll return it.

I know you will do this for me and to make sure that I get it by Sat. send it as soon as you possibly can

I am feeling fine & hope everyone in the family feels the same.

I don't want you worrying about me being in trouble or something like that, its just that the fourth was quite a drain on my pocket book and I want to see a certain little lass Sat. night bad (you know how it is)

Your son
Chas.

You know mom, they all call me Charles down here
Send the letter Air mail and cash.

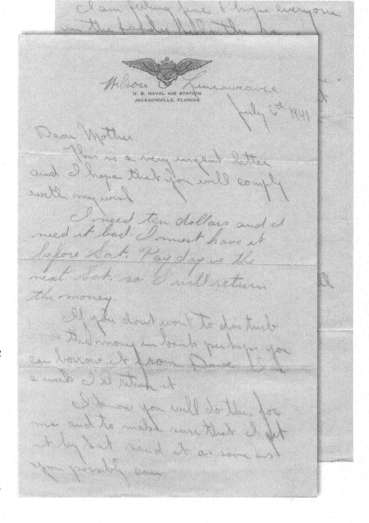

[Postmark is Jacksonville, Fla., July 6, 1941, 3 PM, West Bay Annex.]
Mrs. Erlene Lineaweaver
1240 E Cumberland St.
Avon Penna.   AIR MAIL

[No return address on envelope.]

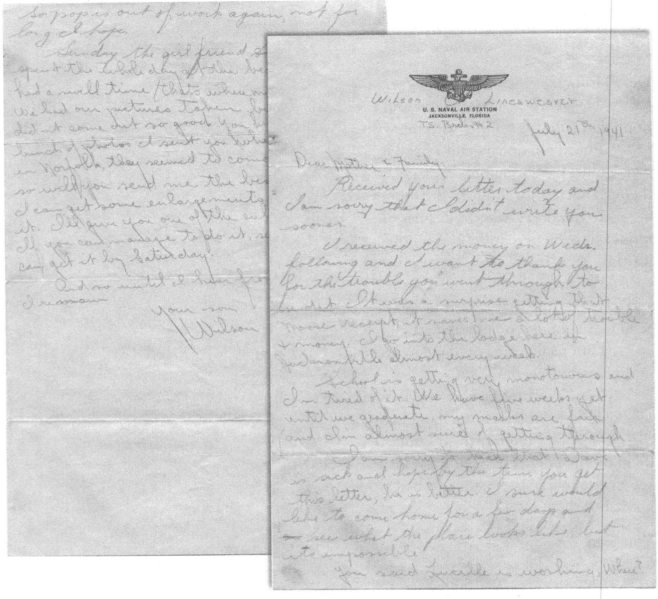

So papers out of work again, not for
long I hope.

Sunday the girl friend &
spent the whole day at the bea[ch]
had a swell time (that's where [we]
We had our pictures taken fo[r]
did not come out so good. You [got a]
bunch of photos I sent you to[o] wh[en]
in Norfolk, they seemed to come [out]
so will you send me the be[st]
I can get some enlargements [of]
it. I'll give you one of the e[nlargements]
if you can manage to do it, s[o I]
can get it by Saturday.

And so until I hear fr[om you]
I remain

your son
Wilson

Wilson Lineaweaver
U. S. NAVAL AIR STATION
JACKSONVILLE, FLORIDA
T.S. Bldg. #2   July 21st, 1941

Dear Mother & Family,

Received your letter today and
I am sorry that I didn't write you
sooner

I received the money on Weds.
following and I want to thank you
for the trouble you went through to
[sen]d it. It was a surprise getting that
Morse receipt, it saved me a lot of trouble
& money. I go into the lodge here in
Jacksonville almost every week.

School is getting very monotonous and
I'm tired of it. We have five weeks yet
until we graduate, my marks are fair
(and I'm almost sure of getting through

I am sorry to hear that [Wayne]
is sick and hope by the time you get
this letter, he is better I sure would
like to come home for a few days and
see what the place looks like, but
it's impossible

You said Lucille is working Where?

Mrs. E. Lineaweaver
1240 E. Cumberland St.
Avon, Penna.

[Postmark is Jacksonville, Fla.
July 22, 1941, 8:30 AM, Naval Air Sta.]
Mrs. E. Lineaweaver
1240 E. Cumberland St.
Avon, Penna.

[No return address on envelope.]

Wilson C. Lineaweaver, T.S. Brck. #2

July 21th 1941

Dear Mother & Family:

Received your letter today and I am sorry that I didn't write you sooner.

I received the money on Weds. following and I want to thank you for the trouble you went through to send it. It was a surprise getting that Moose receipt, it saves me a lot of trouble & money. I go into the lodge here in Jacksonville almost every week.

School is getting very monotonous and I am tired of it. We have five weeks yet until we graduate, my marks are fair (and I'm almost sure of getting through.

I am sorry to hear that Dave is sick and hope by the time you get this letter, he is better. I sure would like to come home for a few days and see what the place looks like, but its impossible

You said Lucille is working, where? So pop is out of work again, not for long I hope.

Sunday the girl friend & myself spent the whole day at the beach and had a swell time (thats where my money goes) We had our pictures taken but they didn't come out so good. You know that bunch of photos I sent you when I was in Norfolk, they seemed to come pretty good so will you send me the best one so I can get some enlargements made from it. I'll give you one of the enlargements. If you can manage to do it, send it so I can get it by Saturday.

And so until I hear from you I remain

Your son
Wilson

"...Lucille is working..."

Wilson's sister Lucille was babysitting her cousin Pearl's son in Cleona (PA). Pearl was a daughter of Aunt Eva (Haag) Clemens and was married to Ralph Lehman. Pearl and Ralph had a son, Ralph Jr., age 8 in the summer of 1941, and he had a disability which Lucille remembered may have been epilepsy. Lucille lived with the Lehman family during the week and came home to 1240 E. Cumberland Street on the weekends. She was paid 10 cents a day / 50 cents a week. Ralph Jr. died at age 22 in 1955.

W. C. LINEAWEAVER
U. S. NAVAL AIR STATION
JACKSONVILLE, FLORIDA
TRADE SCHOOL, BRCK. #2

JULY 25TH 1941

DEAR MOTHER;
        OUR GENEROUS INSTRUCTORS HAVE GIVEN US
A PERIOD OFF TONIGHT TO WRITE LETTERS SO I'LL
ATTEMPT TO WRITE YOU A LETTER ON MY TYPEWRITER,
        I HOPE YOU RECEIVED THE LETTER I SENT THE
OTHER DAY, IT WAS A HURRIED LETTER HAVING ONLY
ABOUT FIVE MINUTES TO WRITE IT IN AS I GUESS
YOU NOTICED, WE HAVE VERY LITTLE TIME TO DO
ANYTHING EXCEPT WEEK ENDS AND THOSE I SPEND
IN JACKSONVILLE, THEY KEEP US ON THE GO ALL THE
TIME.
        I HOPE I GET THAT PICTURE SOON SO I CAN GET
SOME ENLARGEMENTS MADE, I DO HOPE YOU PICK THE
BEST ONE.
        WE HAD A LOT OF RAIN DOWN HERE, PRACTALLY
EVERY DAY, IT LASTS ABOUT AN HOUR AND THEN
GETS HOT AS H--- AND I DO MEAN HOT.
        HOW IS DAVE? BETTER I HOPE, AND THE KIDS,
ARE THEY STILL GETTING INTO TROUBLE? I GOT
A LETTER FROM LUCILLE YESTERDAY, IT WAS POST-
MARKED CLEONA, IS SHE WORKING UP THERE? SHE
ASKED ABOUT THE PRESENT I PROMISED TO SENT HER,
WELL, TELL HER THAT AS YET I AM STILL FINANCIALLY
EMBARRASSED BUT PERHAPS IN THE FUTURE I'LL BE
ABLE TO.
        YOU WILL HAVE TO EXCUSE MISTAKES IN
TYPING BECAUSE I'M STILL LOUSY BUT HOPE TO
LEARN.
        THE BELL IS ABOUT TO RING SO I GUESS I'LL
HAVE TO CLOSE
        HOPING TO HEAR FROM YOU SOON I REMAIN YOUR
SON

                                WILSON
P. S. WHY DOESN'T DAD WRITE ME

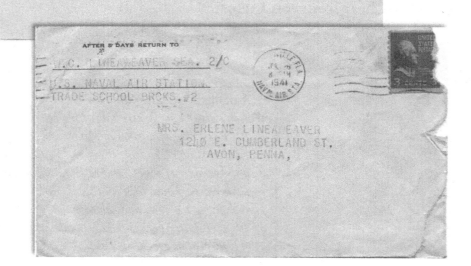

AFTER 5 DAYS RETURN TO
W.C. LINEAWEAVER SEA. 2/C
U.S. NAVAL AIR STATION
TRADE SCHOOL BRCKS. #2

                MRS. ERLENE LINEAWEAVER
                1240 E. CUMBERLAND ST.
                AVON, PENNA,

W. C. Lineaweaver
U. S. Naval Air Station
Jacksonville, Florida
Trade School, Brck.#2

July 25th 1941

Dear Mother;

Our generous instructors have given us a period off tonight to write letters so I'll attempt to write you a letter on my typewriter,

I hope you received the letter I sent the other day, it was a hurried letter having only about five minutes to write it in as I guess you noticed. We have very little time to do anything except week ends and those I spend in Jacksonville, they keep us on the go all the time.

I hope I get that picture soon so I can get some enlargements made, I do hope you pick the best one.

We had a lot of rain down here, practically every day, it lasts about an hour and then gets hot as h--- and I do mean hot.

How is Dave? Better I hope, and the kids, are they still getting into trouble? I got a letter from Lucille yesterday. It was post-marked Cleona, is she working up there? She asked about the present I promised to sent her, well, tell her that as yet I am still financially embarrassed but perhaps in the future I'll be able to.

You will have to excuse mistakes in typing because I'm still lousy but hope to learn.

The bell is about to ring so I guess I'll have to close

Hoping to hear from you soon I remain your son

Wilson

P. S. Why doesn't dad write me

[Postmark is Jacksonville, Fla., July 26, 1941, 8:30 AM, Naval Air Sta.]
Mrs. Erlene Lineaweaver
1240 E. Cumberland St.
Avon, Penna.

[Return Address:]
W.C. Lineaweaver Sea. 2/c
U.S. Naval Air Station
Trade School Brcks.#2

Iceland, or Alaska. that's why
I'm going to try to get [...]
here.

Pretty soon the kid[...]
trotting back to school. W[...]
they start I finish and [...]
will be the end of school da[...]
I go out and put into prac[...]
I learned here in school[...]

Radio is very interest[...]
I must say, hard. I [...]
take years of practical [...]
and studying to become [...]
qualified radio man. b[...]
am going to strive for [...]
day you'll want me to fi[...]
radio.

I hope everyone is h[...]
happy. Is Dave O.K. by [...]
while I write this lette[...]
wondering what pop is c[...]
about, there usually is s[...]
wrong with him.

Are you still working [...]
Your son [...]
Wilso[...]

W.C. Lineaweaver
U. S. Air Station
Jacksonville, Fla.
T.S. Brcks #2

July 29, 1941

Dear Mother:

Enclosed are the pictures
that I am returning to you. If I
would have known that you were
going to chase all over the place
collecting them I wouldn't have sent
for them. Thanks for the trouble.

Yet quite four more weeks of
school is remaining and I am glad
its almost over with. after graduation
we are sent all over the place I
am going to try and stay here at
the air station. but its not what
you want its what they decide to
do.

I imagine its a little warm
at this time around home. It's
a good thing your not down here.
you would really suffer. I guess
when winter comes they will
send back north to freeze. Say

W.C. Lineaweaver
U.S. Air Station
Jacksonville, Fla.
T.S. Brcks #2

July 29, 1941

Dear Mother:

Enclosed are the pictures that I am returning to you. If I would have known that you were going to chase all over the place collecting them I wouldn't have sent for them. Thanks for the trouble.

Not quite four more weeks of school is remaining and I am glad its almost over with. After graduation we are sent all over the place. I am going to try and stay here at the air Station, but its not what you want its what they decide to do.

I imagine its a little warm at this time around home. It a good thing your not down here, you would really suffer. I guess when winter comes they will send back north to freeze. Say Iceland, or Alaska. thats why I'm going to try to get stationed here.

Pretty soon the kids will be trotting back to school Well! when they start I finish and I guess it will be the end of school days for me. I go out and put into practice what I learned here in school.

Radio is very interesting and I must say, hard. It will take years of practical work and studying to become a qualified radioman, but I am going to strive for it. Some day you'll want me to fix your radio.

I hope everyone is healthy & happy. Is Dave O.K. by now? and while I write this letter I'm wondering what pop is complaining about, there usually is something wrong with him.

Are you still working? Write soon

Your son
Wilson

[Postmark is Jacksonville, Fla., July 30, 1941, 8:30 AM, Naval Air Sta.]
Mrs. Erlene Lineaweaver
1240 E. Cumberland St.
Avon Penna.

[Return Address:]
W.C. Lineaweaver Sea 2/c
U.S. Naval Air Station
T.S. Brcks #2
Jacksonville, Fla.

Porpoise at Marine Studios, Marineland, Florida

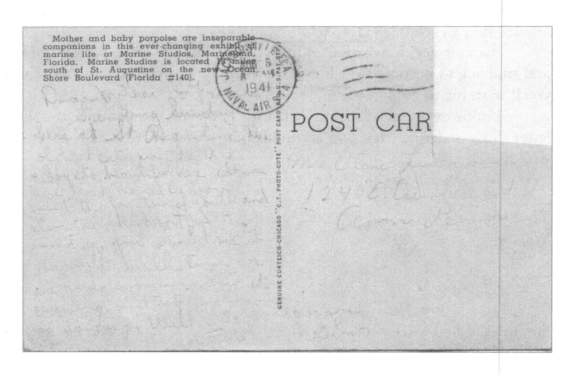

Mother and baby porpoise are inseparable companions in this ever-changing exhibit of marine life at Marine Studios, Marineland, Florida. Marine Studios is located 18 miles south of St. Augustine on the new Ocean Shore Boulevard (Florida #140).

POST CAR

[Postcard - Postmark is Jacksonville, Fla., Aug. 6, 1941, 8:30 AM, Naval Air Sta.]
Mrs Erlene Lineaweaver
1240 E. Cumberland St
Avon Penna

Dear Mother & Family
    Spending Sunday here at St. Augustine, the oldest city in the U.S. & boy its beautiful here. It was here that Peonce De-Leon found the fountain of youth and also the oldest fort in the country, you should see it Having a swell time, we are going swimming now, its evening, and later will go dancing. Will write later.

Your son
Wilson

[The Sunday preceding the August 6th postmark, was Sunday, August 3rd, 1941.]

must have heard it, its the oldest
city in the U.S. and it was ____ that
Ponce De Leon ___ked for the ___
of youth

I got your letter Satur___
afternoon and was glad to ____
Did you get the pictures I
sent?

The date set for grad___ is
the 23rd of this month and I'll be
glad its just about over with. ___
going to have a graduation ___ we
are going to broadcast over a co___
___ hook up. Dont forget to ____
(Saturday the 23rd) [N.B.C.]

Dont forget to write ___
didn't get that letter pop was going
write me? Are you still wor___
Hope everyone is in the bes___
_____ Tell everyone _____

Your son
Wilson

Write soon

U.S. NAVAL AIR STATION
JACKSONVILLE, FLORIDA
Wilson ___ Lineaweaver Sea 2/c
T.S. Brk. #2

August 5, 1941

Dear Mother,
I filled out a post card
when I was at Marineland, but
forgot to mail it so as soon as I got
back I mailed it. I hope you got it.

We had a swell time at St.
Augustine & Marineland Sunday, I
wish you could ____ ____ _____
Perhaps you saw pictures in the movies
of the fish here at Marineland. They
often take pictures here. The fish are
in large aquariums and you look through
glass port holes at them. You should see
them, the funiest & ugliest looking ____
I never new creatures like that existed.

The scenery is beautiful down
here, for about twenty miles we
rode along the ocean. St. Augustine
is the prettiest city I've ever seen, for

Mrs. Alva Lineaweaver
1240 E. Cumberland St.
Avon, Penna

Wilson C. Lineaweaver Sea. 2/c
T.S. Brcks #2

August 5, 1941

Dear Mother:

I filled out a post card when I was at Marineland, but forgot to mail it so as soon as I got back I mailed it, I hope you got it.

We had a swell time at St. Augustine & Marineland Sunday. I wish you could have been with me. Perhaps you seen pictures in the movies of the fish here at marineland. They often take pictures here. The fish are in large aquariums and you look through glass port holes at them. You should see them, the funniest & ugliest looking things, I never new creatures like that existed.

The scenery is beautiful down here, for about twenty miles we rode along the ocean. St. Augustine is the prettiest city Ive ever seen, You must have heard of it, its the oldest city in the U.S. and it was here that Ponce De Leon serched for the fountain of youth

I got your letter Saturday afternoon and was glad to here from you. Did you get the pictures that I sent?

The date set for graduation is the 23rd of this month and boy I'm glad its just about over with. We are going to have a graduation dance and are going to broadcast over a coast to coast Hook up, Don't forget to listen! (Saturday N.B.C. the 23rd)

Don't forget to write and I didn't get that letter pop was going to write me? Are you still working? Hope everyone is in the best of health, take care of yourselves.

Your son
Wilson

Write soon

[Postmark is Jacksonville, Fla., Aug. 6, 1941, 8:30 AM, Naval Air Sta.]   *[No Return Address]*
Mrs Erlene Lineaweaver
1240 E. Cumberland St.
Avon Penna

thing for me to do because they
might have kicked me out of
school (into the mess hall) and
only a week to graduation.
learned my lesson. A friend of
mine is doing 15 days in the
just for loaning his liberty
another sailor.

I thought that new
was being built back of
someplace, crossing fenced
the way pop said in his le
must be right out front.
is it to be completed?

One thing I would li
when I'm going to be sent
that remains to be seen.

And so with a happy
I'll close hoping everyone
in the best of health

Your son
Wil

P.S. I also want to thank dad
writing, keep it up.

Wilson Lineaweaver
U.S. NAVAL AIR STATION
JACKSONVILLE, FLORIDA
T.S. Bcks #2

August 15, 1941

Dear Mother & Family
Well I finally got a letter from
Dad and I also got your letter last
week. I was glad to hear from you

We have one more week to go
and most of our examinations are
over with. My marks weren't so hot
but not bad enough to keep me from
graduating but one consolation is that
the rest of the fellows in my class
didn't do any better, they were tough

I'm up to my old tricks
again, playing hooky but you can't
get away with it the navy. I ducked
out of night class, went to the show
here at the station and got caught but
because of my good record they didn't
do anything, that was a break and
I don't think I'll play hooky
anymore. That was a very foolish

Mrs C. Lineaweaver
1340 E. Cumberland St.
Avon, Penna.

Wilson C Lineaweaver
T.S. Brcks #2

August 15, 1941

Dear Mother, & Family:

Well I finally got a letter from Dad and I also got your letter last week. I was glad to here from you

We have one more week to go and most of our examination are over with. My marks wasn't so hot but not bad enough to keep me from graduating but one consolation is that the rest of the fellows in my class didn't do any better. They were tough.

I'm up to my old tricks again, playing hooky, but you can't get away with it the navy. I ducked out of night class, went to the show here at the station and got caught, but because of my good record they didn't do anything. that was a break and I don't think I'll play hooky anymore. That was a very foolish thing for me to do because they might have kicked me out of school (into the mess hall) and with only a week to graduation. Ive learned my lesson. A friend of mine is doing 15 days in the brig just for loaning his liberty card to another sailor.

I thought that new bridge was being built back of the church someplace, crossing Lehman St., but the way pop said in his letter, it must be right out front. How near is it to be completed?

One thing I would like to know is where I'm going to be sent, but that remains to be seen.

And so with a happy cheerio I'll close hoping everyone is in the best of health

Your son
Wilson

P.S. I also want to thank dad for writing, keep it up.

[Postmark is Jacksonville, Fla., Aug. 16, 1941, 8:30 AM, Naval Air Sta.]
Mrs E. Lineaweaver
1240 E. Cumberland St.
Avon Penna.

[Return Address:]
W.C. Lineaweaver
U.S. Naval Air Station
Jacksonville, Florida
T.S. Brcks #2

and a few other things and Saturday
we have our dance.

Maybe you know the U. S.
is a new ship. So my first
is a brand new one; I hope
like it and I hope I don't g
sick. Will let you know
how I make out. I beli
will go to Norfolk and wa
for to be commissioned.

You'll be hearing from

Your son
Wilson

U. S. NAVAL AIR STATION
JACKSONVILLE, FLORIDA
F.S. Bar #2

Wilson Lineaweaver

August 20, 1941

Dear Mother & Family

This is probably the last
letter that you'll receive from Florida
because next week I leave to
be stationed on the U.S.S. Hornet,
a new Aircraft carrier that is
going to be commissioned soon. I
don't know so much about it, only
that I leave next week. I will
let you know where it'll be later

Please don't send any more
letters to this address and as soon
as I get situated I'll write

Its pretty tough leaving
Jacksonville just when I was
starting to like it here, but thats
the way you get around.

We don't do much in school
this last week but practice code

Mrs. E. Lineaweaver
1240 E. Amberhurst St.
Avon, Penna

Wilson C Lineaweaver
T.S. Brcks #2

August 20, 1941

Dear Mother & Family

This is probably the last letter that you will receive from Florida because next week I leave to be stationed on the U.S.S. Hornet, a new Aircraft carrier that is going to be commissioned soon. I don't know so much about it, only that I leave next week. I will let you know whats what later.

Please don't send anymore letters to this address and as soon as I get situated I'll write.

Its pretty tough leaving Jacksonville just when I was starting to like it here, but thats the U.S. Navy, you get around.

We don't do much in school this last week but practice code and a few other things and Saturday we have our dance.

Maybe you know the U.S.S. Hornet is a new ship. So my first ship is a brand new one, I hope I like it and I hope I don't get sea sick. Will let you know later how I make out. I believe we will go to Norfolk and wait for her to be commissioned.

You'll be hearing from me soon

Your son
Wilson

[Postmark is Jacksonville, Fla., Aug. 20, 1941, 8:30 AM, Naval Air Sta.]
Mrs E. Lineaweaver
1240 E. Cumberland St
Avon Penna

[Return Address:]
W.C. Lineaweaver Sea 2/c
U.S. Naval Air Station
Jacksonville, Florida
T.S. Brcks #2

Graduation from Class 4 Aviation Radio School, Jacksonville, Florida.

Wilson C. Lineaweaver

On group photo, next page, Wilson is in the back row, 6th from left.

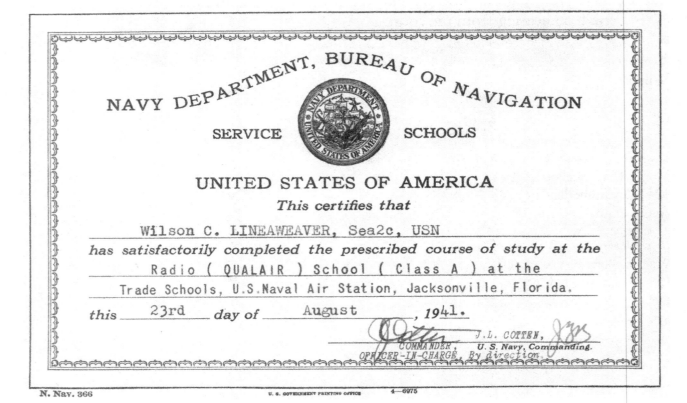

NAVY DEPARTMENT, BUREAU OF NAVIGATION

SERVICE   SCHOOLS

UNITED STATES OF AMERICA

This certifies that

Wilson C. LINEAWEAVER, Sea2c, USN

has satisfactorily completed the prescribed course of study at the
Radio (QUALAIR) School (Class A) at the
Trade Schools, U.S.Naval Air Station, Jacksonville, Florida.

this ___23rd___ *day of* ___August___ , 1941.

J.L. COTTEN,
COMMANDER, U.S. Navy, Commanding.
OFFICER-IN-CHARGE, By direction

N. Nav. 366   U. S. GOVERNMENT PRINTING OFFICE   4—6975

Aviation Radio School Graduation, Jacksonville, Florida, August 23, 1941. Wilson is 6ᵗʰ from left in the back row.

pictures are yours.

And so until I hear from all of
you. Irawaw

Your son
Wilson

I'll send a picture of my graduating
class later on because I can't
well get it in this envelope.

U. S. NAVAL AIR STATION
NORFOLK, VIRGINIA
Operations

W. C. ___ ___weaver

Sept. 2, 1941

Dear Parents:

Got back OK Monday night
a tired sailor. It was a long and
monotonous trip, a very slow train. I
arrived at the base here about 10:00 PM

I want to thank you a lot for
washing and pressing my clothing and boy I
was glad for that lunch you sent along. I
guess it will be a long time till I'll be
able to come home again. Don't forget to
write me, all of you.

Enclosed is some pictures we had
taken in Florida, one of myself and
the other with two ship-mates of mine.
What do you think of the pose. Also
enclosed is my diploma that I got
at graduation. Please put it away with
the rest of my papers and things. The

Mr. & Mrs. Robt. Zineaweaver
1240 E. Cumberland St.
Avon, Penna.

W.C. Lineaweaver
Operations

Sept. 2, 1941

Dear Parents:

Got back O.K. Monday night a tired sailor. It was a long and monotonous trip, a very slow train. I arrived at the base here about 10:00 P.M.

I want to thank you a lot for washing and pressing my clothing and boy I was glad for that lunch you sent along. I guess it will be a long time till I'll be able to come home again. Don't forget to write me, all of you.

Enclosed is some pictures we had taken in Florida, one of myself and the other with two ship mates of mine. What do you think of the pose. Also enclosed is my diploma that I got at graduation, Please put it away with the rest of my papers and things. The pictures are yours.

And so until I hear from all of you I reamain

Your son
Wilson

Ill sent a picture of my graduation class later on because I can't very well get it in this envelope

-----

[Postmark is Norfolk Va., Sep. 3, 1941, 12:30 PM]
Mr. & Mrs. Robt. Lineaweaver
1240 E. Cumberland St.
Avon, Penna.

[Return Address:]
W.C. Lineaweaver
U.S. Naval Air Station
Operations
Norfolk, Va.

my ship to call me, but I
don't think it will last
long.

I may get another c[...]
come home before going [...]
the thing that makes it so [...]
that I'm here on tempor[...]
and may be called any da[...]
a definite date is set, I'm g[...]
leave

Don't forget to write [...]
also want to thank you [...]
my clothes the last time [...]
home. Hoping to hear fr[...]
of you soon I remain

Your son
Wilm[...]

U. S. NAVAL AIR STATION
NORFOLK, VIRGINIA
Operations

W. C. Lineaweaver

Sept 17, 1941

Dear Mother & Family:

I received your letter last
week and am sorry I didn't answer
sooner If you can, Why don't you
write more often, That is if you can
find time and tell the others to write
too. I would like to keep up with
the happenings around home and a
letter every now and then sorta peps
you up and makes you feel that you're
not forgotten.

This temporary duty here at the
Air Station is sorta getting me down,
being very inactive and doing odd
jobs around the place waiting for

W. C. Lineaweaver
U. S. Naval Air Stat[...]
Operations (Land [...]
Norfolk, Va.

NORFOLK
SEP 17
11 AM
1941
VA.

UNITED STATES POSTAGE
3 CENTS 3

BUY
DEFENSE
BONDS AND STAMPS

Mr & Mrs Robt. Lineaweaver
1240 E. Cumberland St.
Avon, Penna.

W.C. Lineaweaver
Operations

Sept 17, 1941

Dear Mother & Family:

I received your letter last week and am sorry I didn't answer sooner. If you can, why don't you write more often, that is if you can find time and tell the others to write too. I would like to keep up with the happenings around home and a letter every now and then sorta peps you up and makes you feel that your not forgotten.

This temporary duty here at the Air Station is sorta getting me down, being very inactive and doing odd jobs around the place waiting for my ship to call me, but I don't think it will last very long.

I may get another chance to come home before going to sea, but the thing that makes it so hard is that Im here on temporary duty and may be called any day. If a definite date is set, I may get leave.

Don't forget to write and I also want to thank you for cleaning my clothes the last time I was home. Hoping to hear from all of you soon I remain

Your son
Wilson

[Postmark is Norfolk Va., Sep. 17, 1941, 11:30 AM]
Mr. & Mrs. Robt. Lineaweaver
1240 E. Cumberland St.
Avon Penna.

[Return Address:]
W.C. Lineaweaver
U.S. Naval Air Station
Operations (Land Plane Hanger)
Norfolk, Va.

Hornet is about ready to put to sea
in a week or so, I'm still here at the
air Station and not knowing when I'll
be called but here's hoping it will be
soon because this is a lousy
city for a sailor. I sure wish I was
back in Jacksonville, the land of
sunshine and beautiful women. When I
pull out of here I'll be a happy sailor
I never hit this port again

So the kids go back to school
soon, that means the epidemic of
paralisis is just about over and that's
good news. Tell Lucille to be a good girl
and she won't get sick

Take care of yourself and give
my regards to Dave, Pat + Connie, tell
pop to write and all the kids to be
good boys and girls and to study hard
when they go to school

Tell Dave I'll send his check as
soon as I can manage

Your son
Wilson

W.C. Lineweaver
U.S. NAVAL AIR STATION
NORFOLK, VIRGINIA
Operations (Land Plane Hangar)

Sept 24th 1941

Dear Mother + Family:
        I received your letter yesterday
but I didn't get the letter you said
Lucille was sending.
        So pop finally got a job, I'm
glad and I hope he likes it and I
also hope that Jim gets in at the
_____ Steel. This morning I
misplaced my tooth brush + powder and
I feel lost without them, if you could
manage would you send me a brush
and powder as soon as you can. (Denbre)
        About that graduation letter, I'll
send it as soon as I get something
to send it in, an envelope is too small.
I'm glad you like the pictures I sent but
I wouldn't get others made from it
because I'll be sending others from
time to time.
        Although my ship the U.S.S.

To everybody:
        What do you think of her, pretty
classy eh!
        Will be home soon

Wilson

Don't ruin this picture, save it

Mrs. Eilene L. _____
_____
Avon, Penna.

W. C. Lineaweaver
Operations (Land Plane Hanger)

Sept 24th, 1941

Dear Mother & Family:

I received your letter yesterday but I didnt get the letter you said Lucille was sending.

So pop finally got a job, I'm glad and I hope he likes it and I also hope that Jim gets in at the Bethleham Steel. This morning I misplaced my tooth brush & powder and I feel lost without them, if you could manage would you send me a brush and powder as soon as you can. (Danke)

About that graduation letter, I'll send it as soon as I get something to send it in, an envelope is too small. Im glad you like the pictures I sent but I wouldn't get others made from it because I'll be sending others from time to time.

Although my ship the U.S.S. Hornet is about ready to put to sea in a week or so, I'm still here at the Air Station and not knowing when I'll be called but here's hoping it will be soon because this is a lousy liberty city for a sailor. I sure wish I was back in Jacksonville, the land of sunshine and beautiful women. When I pull out of here I'll be a happy sailor if I never hit this port again.

So the kids go back to school soon, that means the epedemic of Infitile paralisis is just about over and that's good news. Tell Lucille to be a good girl and she won't get sick

Take care of yourself and give my regards to Dave, Fat & Company. Tell pop to write and all the kids to be good boys and girls and to study hard when they go to school.

Tell Dave I'll send his dollar as soon as I can manage

Your son
Wilson

[Postmark is Norfolk Va., Sep. 24, 1941, 4 PM]
Mrs. Erlene Lineaweaver
1240 E Cumberland St
Avon, Penna.

[No Return Address]

Hi Everybody:
What do you think of her, pretty classy eh!
Will be home soon
Wilson
Don't ruin this picture, save it

(Author no longer has the picture mentioned here.)

want to take a radio course, that will cost about sixty dollars.

How is every body at home I hope. I am doing pretty good wish I could get some action to sea. Tell Pat I'm doing a lot practicing bowling and when I come home I'll challenge him to a few games and beat him.

How do the kids like school. Tell Lucille that when I come home I'll have to give her a spanking for quitting school, it was a very foolish thing to do.

Hoping to hear from you soon and thanks again for the cake. I'll close

your loving son
Wilson

W. C. Lineaweaver
U. S. NAVAL AIR STATION
NORFOLK, VIRGINIA
Operations

Oct. 3rd, 1941

Dear Mother:

Sorry I didn't write as soon as I received your package but I just couldn't get around to it.

It was a surprise getting that large package, the cake was the best I've ever eaten and it was perfect, just like you sent it. I guess it was packed real good because the others that you sent usually were smashed.

With the five dollars enclosed I want you to give Dave the buck I owe him and for your trouble take a dollar and see a show or something, than you can put the other three in bank for me. I wish I could get rated soon so I could really save some money and I

Mrs. C. Lineaweaver
1240 E Cumberland St.
Avon, Penna.

W.C. Lineaweaver
Operations

Oct. 3rd, 1941

Dear Mother:

Sorry I didn't write as soon as I received your package but I just couldn't get around to it.

It was a surprise getting that large package, the cake was the best I've ever eaten and it was perfect, just like you sent it. I guess it was packed real good because the others that you sent were usually smashed.

With the five dollars enclosed I want you to give Dave the buck I owe him and for your trouble take a dollar and see a show or some thing, than you can put the other three in bank for me. I wish I could get rated soon so I could really save some money and I want to take a radio course, that will cost about sixty dollars.

How is every body at home, fine I hope. I am doing pretty good but I wish I could get some action and go to sea. Tell Fat I'm doing a lot of practising bowling and when I come home I'll challenge him to a few games and beat him.

How do the kids like school? Tell Lucille that when I come home I'll have to give her a spanking for quiting school, it was a very foolish thing to do.

Hoping to hear from you soon and thanks again for the cake etc. I'll close

Your loving son
Wilson

[Postmark is Norfolk Va., Oct. 3, 1941, 4 PM]
Mrs. E. Lineaweaver
1240 E. Cumberland St.
Avon, Penna.

[Return Address:]
W.C. Lineaweaver
U.S. Naval Air Station
Operations
Norfolk, Va.

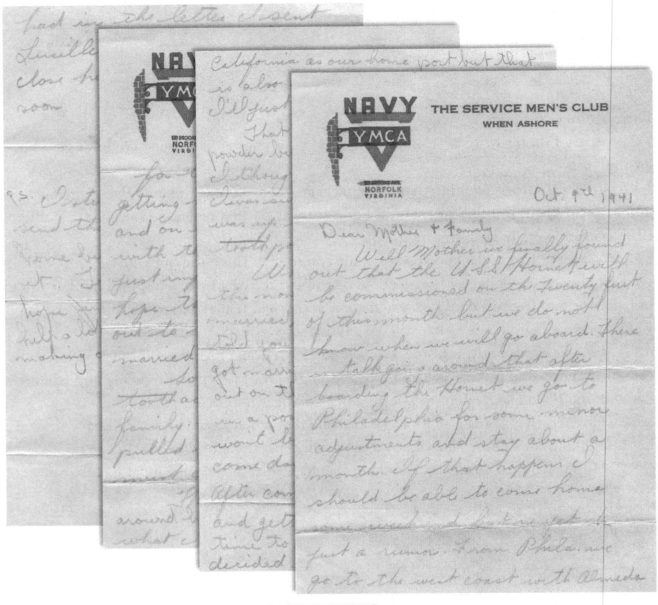

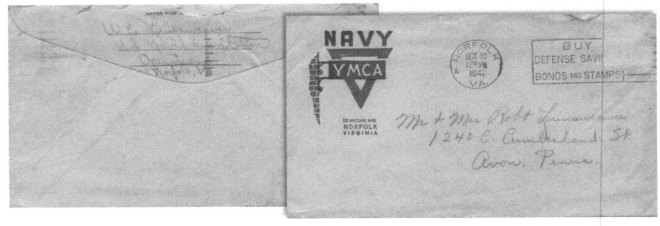

NAVY YMCA
NORFOLK VIRGINIA

THE SERVICE MEN'S CLUB
WHEN ASHORE

Oct. 9th 1941

Dear Mother & Family

Well Mother we finally found out that the U.S.S. Hornet will be commissioned on the twenty first of this month but we do not know when we will go aboard. There is talk going around that after boarding the Hornet we go to Philadelphia for some minor adjustments and stay about a month. If that happens, I should be able to come home _____ but no just a rumor. From Phila. we go to the west coast with Almeda

NAVY YMCA
NORFOLK VIRGINIA

NORFOLK
OCT 10
12ᴾᴹ
1941
VA.

BUY
DEFENSE SAVIN
BONDS ᴬᴺᴰ STAMPS

Mr + Mrs Robt Linaweaver
1240 E. Cumberland St
Avon, Penna.

Oct. 9ᵗʰ 1941

Dear Mother & Family,

Well Mother we finally found out that the U.S.S. Hornet will be commissioned on the Twenty first of this month but we do not know when we will go aboard. There is talk going around that after boarding the Hornet we go to Philadelphia for some minor adjustments and stay about a month. If that happens I should be able to come home some weekend but as yet its just at rumor. From Phila. We go to the west coast with Almeda California as our home port but that is also a rumor and not definite so I'll just have to wait and find out.

That word danke is not a tooth powder but German meaning thanks, I thought you new that and I was surprised to hear that you was up town looking for danke tooth powder.

Where does Lucille get all this nonsense about me being married, I guess I would have told you and dad if I would have got married. You can straighten her out on that because as yet I'm not in a position to get married and won't be for six years but I did come darn close to hanging myself. After coming north a month ago and getting away from her I had time to think it over and I decided that it would be better for both of us to forget about getting married, being in the navy and on the go all the time and with the money I'm making its just impossible to get married. I hope this straightens things out to those who think I'm married.

Sorry to hear about the toothache epidemic in the family. The sooner you get them pulled the better because they must come out sometime.

There isn't much news around here to tell you besides what already told you are had in the letter I sent Lucille so I think Ill close hoping to hear from you soon

Your son
Chas.

P.S. I still didn't find means to send that graduation picture home but I promise you'll get it. Tell pop to write and I hope Jim gets a job soon that will help a lot. Hows Fat and Dave making out.

[Postmark is Norfolk, Va., Oct. 10, 1941, 12:30 PM]
Mr. & Mrs Robt Lineaweaver
1240 E. Cumberland St.
Avon, Penna.

[Return Address:]
W.C. Lineaweaver
U.S. Naval Air Station
Operations
Norfolk, Va.

start being a sailor soon.

What did Dave say when you sent him the buck? I'll bet he th___ wasn't going to get it.

Well! I haven't much more because there's very little acti___ here so I'll close hoping to hear ___ you soon. I want you to know ___ in good health and feeling fine

your son
Wilson

W. C. Lineaweaver
U. S. NAVAL AIR STATION
NORFOLK, VIRGINIA
Operations

Oct 16th 1941

Dear Mother & Family:

I received your letter yesterday and was very glad to hear from you. I'm glad to hear that everyone is O.K. in the family and I'm glad to hear that dad is still working. How does he like his work and by the way how big a salary does he draw? Working for jews I don't he makes out so hot.

How does Jim like it as a boot black? I think he should have stayed in the C.C.C.'s he would be much better off. Do you think he'll get in at the Bethlehem Stell, with all these men being drafted I should think it would be pretty easy.

Monday the U.S.S. Hornet is going to be commissioned, Sec. of the Navy Knox will be there to speak but as yet I haven't got any orders to go aboard although I think that I'll

---

NORFOLK
OCT 16
12 PM
1941
VA

DEFEN___
BONDS___

Mrs. Eilene Lineaweaver
1240 E. Cumberland St.
Avon, Penna.

W.C. Lineaweaver
Operations

Oct 16th, 1941

Dear Mother & Family:

I received your letter yesterday and was very glad to hear from you. I'm glad to hear that everyone is O.K. in the family and I'm glad to hear that dad is still working. How does he like his work and by the way how big a salary does he draw? Working for jews I don't think he makes out so hot.

How does Jim like it as a boot black? I think he should have stayed in the CCC's he would be much better off. Do you think he'll get in at the Bethleham Steel, with all these men being drafted I should think it would be pretty easy.

Monday the U.S.S. Hornet is going to be commissioned, Sec. of the Navy Knox will be there to speak but as yet I haven't got any orders to go aboard although I think that I'll start being a sailor soon.

What did Dave say when you gave him the buck? I'll bet he thought he wasn't going to get it.

Well! I haven't much more to say because there's very little action around here so I'll close hoping to hear from you soon. I want you to know that I'm in good health and feeling fine

Your son,
Wilson

[Postmark is Norfolk, Va., Oct. 16, 1941, 12:30 PM]
Mrs Erlene Lineaweaver
1240 E. Cumberland St.
Avon, Penna.

[Return Address:]
W.C. Lineaweaver
Operations (L.P.H.)
U.S. Naval Air Station
Norfolk, Va.

USS *Hornet* (CV-8) Commissioning Ceremony Program

(Size of original program is 8½" x 5¾")

U.S.S. HORNET

USS *Hornet* (CV-8) Commissioning Ceremony Program

U.S.S. HORNET • COMMISSIONING CEREMONY

U. S. S. HORNET

❖

KEEL LAID 25 SEPTEMBER, 1939

SHIP LAUNCHED 14 DECEMBER, 1940

SPONSOR, MRS. FRANK KNOX

COMMISSIONED 20 OCTOBER, 1941

REAR ADMIRAL M. H. SIMONS, U. S. N.
Commandant Fifth Naval District

CAPTAIN MARC A. MITSCHER, U. S. N.
Commanding Officer

U.S.S. HORNET • COMMISSIONING CEREMONY

COMMISSIONING CEREMONY

(a) Prospective Executive Officer orders "Attention" on the bugle, and reports to Prospective Commanding Officer "All hands up and aft, Sir".

(b) Prospective Commanding Officer reports ready to Commandant.

(c) Commandant requests permission of the Secretary of the Navy to proceed with commissioning.

(d) Commandant asks Chaplain to proceed with Invocation.

(e) Chaplain gives Invocation.

(f) Chief of Staff reads commissioning directive.

(g) Commandant directs that the ship be commissioned.

(h) Prospective Commanding Officer directs the Prospective Executive Officer to conduct the ceremony.

(i) Prospective Executive Officer orders, "Divisions right and left face", then to band, "Sound off". Marine Guard presents arms, band plays National Anthem, National Ensign, Jack, and Commission Pennant are hoisted together. Officers and men not in ranks render hand salute.

(j) Commanding Officer reads his orders and accepts ship.

(k) Commission Pennant is lowered and Senior Personal Flag on board is hoisted, and honors (except gun salute) rendered.

(l) Commanding Officer directs Executive Officer to "set the Watch".

(m) Executive Officer sets watch and calls Guard of the Day, then directs Navigator to take the first watch as Officer-of-the-Deck.

(n) Commandant makes address; introduces the Secretary of the Navy.

(o) The Secretary of the Navy makes address.

(p) Presentation of gifts or trophies.

(q) Commanding Officer replies.

(r) Navigator reports to Executive Officer that watch has been set.

(s) Executive Officer reports to Commanding Officer that watch has been set.

(t) Commanding Officer orders "Pipe Down".

U.S.S. HORNET • COMMISSIONING CEREMONY

The U. S. S. Hornet, seventh ship of her name in the United States Navy, has been bequeathed a glorious heritage and worthy traditions by her illustrious predecessors.

The first Hornet was a ten gun sloop engaged in the hazardous duty of guarding the Delaware Capes in 1777.

The second Hornet, also a ten gun sloop, served with Commodore Rodgers' Squadron during the Tripolitan War in the Mediterranean.

Perhaps the most famous of the proud line was the third Hornet, a brig-rigged sloop of war. She fought in the War of 1812 under command of James Lawrence. She successfully blockaded Bahia Harbor, captured the "Resolution", sank the "Peacock", overwhelmed the "Penguin", and escaped capture by the "Cornwallis".

The fourth Hornet, a five gun schooner, was used as a dispatch vessel between 1813 and 1820.

The fifth Hornet, and the first steam propelled namesake, was an iron, side-wheel steamer. She saw action during the Civil War, and later was ordered to duty in Cuban waters.

The sixth vessel, a converted yacht, was a dispatch vessel in the Spanish-American War. Her record of operations on the Coast of Cuba upheld and added to the highest tradition of the service.

National Archives 80-G-651852

Flight deck view during commissioning ceremony,
October 20, 1941.

and radio work because our whole
squadron is new and in training, _____
care so much for dive bombing _____
do nothing about it. They just _____
that the show is just about _____
to start up on the hangar de_____
I'll finish this letter latter.

This is the following morning _____
everything packed and am standing _____
be transferred any minute. The show _____
night was good just it was a little _____
sitting on the metal deck and ta_____
sea air.

Now that I'm going back _____
Air Station I don't think I'll _____
coming back aboard ship until _____
year when they bring all squad_____
aboard. Its a swell ship and p_____
big. Did you see pictures in the _____
of the Hornet when she was comi_____
Sec. of the Navy Knox spoke and C_____
Mitscher took over command of t_____
Will write again soon. Use the new_____
                              your son
                                Wilson

Wilson C Lineaweaver
VB-8
U.S. Naval Air Station
Norfolk, Va

Oct. 22th, 1941

Dear Mother & Family;
          I am writing this letter aboard
the U.S.S. Hornet anchored in Hampden
Roads, I arrived this morning and
to-morrow I leave already back to the
Air Station at Norfolk to join bombing
eight, one of the Hornet squadrons. This
is permanent duty while the two
months we in operations was temporary
duty.
          I'll be with my squadron at
the Air Station until it is taken aboard
ship so send all letters to the above
address. Now that I am on permanent
duty I have a chance maybe to get a
leave so don't be surprised if I pop
in
          We will do quite a bit of flying

W. C. Lineaweaver
VB-8
U.S. Naval Air Station
Norfolk, Va.

NORFOLK
OCT 24
8:30 PM
1941
VA.

Mrs Eilene Lineaweaver
1240 E. Cumberland St.
Avon Penna.

156

Wilson C Lineaweaver
VB-8
U.S. Naval Air Station
Norfolk, Va.

Oct. 22th, 1941

Dear Mother & Family:

I am writing this letter aboard the U.S.S. Hornet anchored in Hampden Roads, I arrived this morning and tomorrow I leave already back to the Air Station at Norfolk to join bombing eight, one of the Hornet squadrons. This is permanent duty while the two months with operations was temporary duty.

I'll be with my squadron at the Air Station until it is taken aboard ship so send all letters to the above address. Now that I am on permanent duty I have a chance maybe to get a leave so don't be surprised if I pop in

We will do quite a bit of flying and radio work because our whole squadron is new and in training, I don't care so much for dive bombing but I can't do nothing about it. They just anounced that the show is just about ready to start up on the hangar deck so I'll finish this letter latter.

This is the following morning, I have everything packed and am standing by to be transferred any minute. The show last night was good just it was a little cold sitting on the metal deck and the night sea air.

Now that I'm going back to the Air Station I don't think I'll be coming back aboard ship until next year when they bring all squadrons aboard. It's a swell ship and plenty big. Did you see pictures in the paper of the Hornet when she was commissioned. Sec. of the Navy Knox spoke and Captain Mitschner took over command of the ship. Will write again soon. Use the new address

Your son
Wilson

[Postmark is Norfolk, Va., Oct. 24, 1941, 8:30 PM]
Mrs Erlene Lineaweaver
1240 E. Cumberland St.
Avon Penna.

[Return Address:]
W.C. Lineaweaver
VB-8
U.S. Naval Air Station
Norfolk, Va.

training and you never finished.

I do a lot of flying
having at least two hops
at first it was exciting
it is work.

On the 5th of November
whole squadron will take
Columbia, S.C. to take part
Army maneuvers, we come
the beginning of Dec. and
that I'm almost sure of
leave. If I don't I'm sure
come home for xmas or New Y

We will be flying pract
all the time during war games
I should get a lot of experince

Your son
W
Please write before I leave f
maneuvers. Tell the rest th
Take care of yourself and I'll see

NAVY YMCA
130 BROOKS AVE.
NORFOLK
VIRGINIA

THE SERVICE MEN'S CLUB
WHEN ASHORE

W.C. Lineaweaver
VB-8
U.S. Naval Air Station
Norfolk, Va

Oct. 30th 1941

Dear Mother & Family
Well how are you? Fine I
hope because I am the same. Your
letter arrived the other day and I
was glad to hear from you.

I was held aboard ship a
few days longer but here I am,
back at the Air Station. It was
swell aboard ship and I liked it
a lot. By the beginning of next
year I go back with my whole
squadron

You asked in your last letter
if I must train again, I'll tell
you, in the navy your always

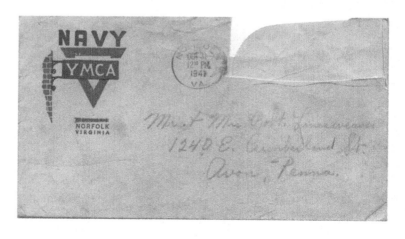

NAVY YMCA
NORFOLK
VIRGINIA

Mr. & Mrs. Wr. Lineaweaver
124 E. Cumberland St.
Avon, Penna.

W.C. Lineaweaver
VB-8
U.S. Naval Air Station
Norfolk, Va.

Oct. 30th, 1941

Dear Mother & Family:

Well how are you? Fine I hope because I am the same. Your letter arrived the other day and I was glad to hear from you.

I was held aboard ship a few days longer but here I am, back at the Air Station. It was swell aboard ship and I liked it a lot, by the beginning of next year I go back with my whole squadron

You asked in your last letter if I must train again, I'll tell you, in the navy your always training and your never finished.

I do a lot of flying lately having at least two hops a day, at first it was exciting but now it is work.

On the 5th of November our whole squadron will take off for Columbia, S.C. to take part in Army maneuvers, we come back the beginning of Dec. and after that I'm almost sure of getting leave. If I don't I'm sure to come home for Xmas or New Years.

We will be flying practially all the time during war games and I should get a lot of experience.

Your son
Wilson

Please write before I leave for maneuvers. Tell the rest to write Take care of yourself and Ill be seeing you soon

-----

[Postmark is Norfolk, Va., Oct. 31, 1941, 12:30 PM]
Mr. & Mrs. Robt. Lineaweaver
1240 E. Cumberland St.
Avon, Penna.

[No Return Address]

W. C. Luneaweaver
VB-8
U.S. Naval Air Station
Norfolk, Va.

Nov. 20th 1941

Dear Parents & Family,

Arrived here at the Air Station safe and sound about ten O'clock Wedn. evening. I read stories and slept all the way down and I was plenty tired when I hit my bunk last night.

Today we are celebrating Thanksgiving, there is no working today and that's a break for me. I just finished eating the biggest ___ meal I ever experienced in the navy. We had seventeen different things including Turkey, ham, three kinds of pie, ice cream, stuffin, cranberry sauce, celery and a lot of trimmings.

Well I think I'll go out and play a little football so I'll close hoping to hear from all of you soon.

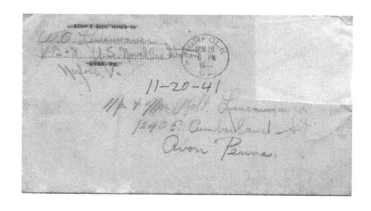

11-20-41

Mr. & Mrs. W. C. Luneaweaver
1240 E. Cumberland St
Avon, Penna.

W.C. Lineaweaver
VB-8
U.S. Naval Air Station
Norfolk, Va.

Nov. 20th, 1941

Dear Parents & Family:

Arrived here at the Air Station safe and sound about ten Oclock Weds. evening. I read stories and slept all the way down and I was plenty tired when I hit my bunk last night

Today we are celebrating Thanksgiving, there is no working today and thats a break for me. I just finished eating the biggest meal I ever experienced in the navy. We had Seventeen different things including Turkey, ham, three kinds of pie, ice cream, stuffin, cranberry sauce, celery and a lot of trimmings.

Well! I think I'll go out and play a little football so I'll close hoping to hear from all of you soon.

Your son
Wilson

[Postmark is Norfolk, Va., Nov. 20, 1941, 6 PM]
Mr. & Mrs. Robt. Lineaweaver
1240 E. Cumberland St.
Avon Penna.

[Return Address:]
W.C. Lineaweaver
VB-8   U.S. Naval Air Station
Norfolk, Va.

RETURNS TO DUTY

Seaman First Class Wilson Charles Lineaweaver, of this city, returned to the Naval Air Station at Norfolk, Virginia, this morning after having spent a 10-day furlough in this city as the guest of his parents, Mr. and Mrs. Robert Lineaweaver, 1240 East Cumberland Street.

This appeared in *the Lebanon Daily News*, Lebanon, PA, on Wednesday, November 19, 1941.

Carolina and will be back next week
but I have plenty of work,
spare parts (We may go aboard
soon) and building signal box
a lot of other odds and ends.
beginning to like radio work
can't learn to like flying, I
just have to like it.

Tell Dave, Fat and their
that I asked about them and
Lucille to watch her blood press
was nice of Mrs. Wolf to bring
into the station, I never say
if I knew her address I'd write
thank her.

Christmas is still quite a
will just be another day for m
I think I'll be at sea but a
you and the rest of family be
be better off so that all of
enjoy Christmas. Maybe I'll
to come home

Give Dave & Fat my
address if they decide to send any
Xmas presents (just a hint)

W. C. Lumeaweaver
VB-5
U. S. Naval Air Station
Norfolk, Va.

Nov. 28th 1941

Dear Mother & Family,
    I received your letter today and
was glad to hear from you. Wish I
could come home and help eat the
ducks Jim won. Did the kids get their
football?
    When I got back here from home
I was expecting to get paid but payday
was Thanksgiving so the men got paid
the day before, that means I'll have to
wait till next payday to get some money.
I need about two dollars to get a haircut,
and my blues cleaned and I also need
cigarettes and a few other things so if
you can manage it I would appreciate it
if you would send me some money as soon
as possible, then payday I'll return it
    My squadron is still in South

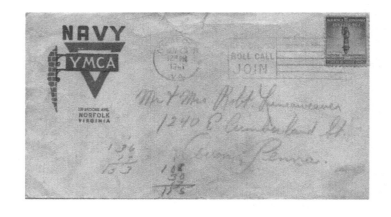

W.C. Lineaweaver
VB-8
U.S. Naval Air Station
Norfolk, Va.

Nov. 28th, 1941

Dear Mother & Family:

I received your letter today and was glad to hear from you. Wish I could come home and help eat the ducks Jim won. Did the kids get their football?

When I got back here from home I was expecting to get paid, but payday was Thanksgiving so the men got paid the day before, that means I'll have to wait till next payday to get some money. I need about two dollars to get a haircut, and my blues cleaned and I also need cigarettes and a few other things so if you can manage I would appreciate it if you would send me some money as soon as possible, then payday I'll return it.

My squadron is still in South Carolina and will be back next week but I have plenty of work. packing spare parts (We may go aboard the Hornet soon) and building signal boxes and a lot of other odds and ends. I am beginning to like radio work but can't learn to like flying, I guess I'll just have to like it.

Tell Dave, Fat and their families that I asked about them and tell Lucille to watch her blood pressure. It was nice of Mrs. Wolf to bring you into the station, I never expected you, if I knew her address I'd write and thank her.

Christmas is still quite a way off and will just be another day for me and I think I'll be at sea but I hope you and the rest of the family by then will be better off so that all of you can enjoy Christmas. Maybe I'll be able to come home.

Give Dave & Fat my address if they decide to send any Xmas presents (just a hint)

Hoping to hear from you soon

Your son
Wilson

[Postmark is Norfolk, Va., Nov. 28, 1941, 12:30 PM]
Mr & Mrs Robt. Lineaweaver
1240 E. Cumberland St.
Avon, Penna.

[No Return Address]

(First page, partially obscured)

carefree are now serious and really mean business.

There is a lot of activity here ... are things I can't even tell you ... or anybody else. I can only say ... my time here at Norfolk is over ... I will still try to send letters ... every chance available.

It's a funny thing we ... it was coming but now that it ... it seems impossible almost incre...

There will be no leaves the ... definite so it will be a long time ... I see you all again if ever. Pl... write, if I'm not here the lett... follow me.

Hoping you wish me luck ... other sailors as well. I'll ... remaining

Your loving so...

Wilson

I had a good time in Washing... sight seeing. I seen many of th... that I always wanted to see

(Second page)

Monday Dec 8th

Dear Parents

We have just heard the President's speech to Congress and shortly later the Declaration of War by Congress. It's hard to believe that the actual thing is here. I was in a car coming from Washington D.C. where I spent the week end when the driver snap the radio on and I first heard of the attack on the Hawaii Islands, at first I thought it was another Orson Wells broadcast like the one that scared us a few years ago but it wasn't long until I realized that this was the real thing.

State Police picked me up in Richmond, Va. and I was sent with other sailors rounded up in that area back to Norfolk in a special Greyhound bus.

Things have changed here you can just feel it. All the sailors usually

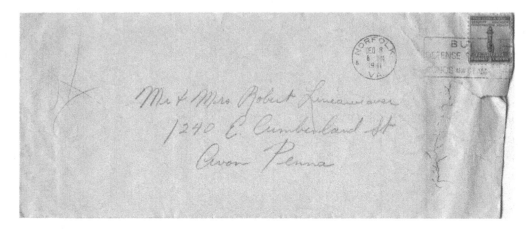

Mr & Mrs Robert Lineaweaver
1240 E. Cumberland St
Avon Penna

Monday Dec 8th

Dear Parents

  We have just heard the Presidents speech to Congress and shortly later the Declaration of War by Congress. Its hard to beleive that the actual thing is here. I was in a car coming from Washington D.C. where I spent the week end when the driver snap the radio on and I first heard of the attack on the Hawaii Islands, at first I thought it was another Orson Wells broadcast like the one that scared us a few years ago but it wasn't long until I realized that this was the real thing.

  State Police picked me up in Richmond, Va. and I was sent with other sailors rounded up in that area back to Norfolk in a special Greyhound bus.

  Things have changed here, you can just feel it, all the sailors usully carefree are now serious and really mean business.

  There is a lot of activity here but those are things I can't even tell you about are anybody else. I can only say that my time here at Norfolk is over. I will still try to send letters and will at every chance available

  Its a funny thing we all knew it was coming but now that it is here it seems impossible almost incredible

  There will be no leaves that is definite so it will be a long time until I see you all again if ever. Please write, if I'm not here the letters will follow me.

  Hoping you wish me luck and the other sailors as well I'll close remaining

Your loving son
Wilson

[Postmark is Norfolk, Va., Dec. 8, 1941, 8 PM]
Mr & Mrs. Robert Lineaweaver
1240 E. Cumberland St
Avon Penna.

[No Return Address]

Lebanon Daily News, Lebanon, PA, Monday, December 8, 1941, Front Page

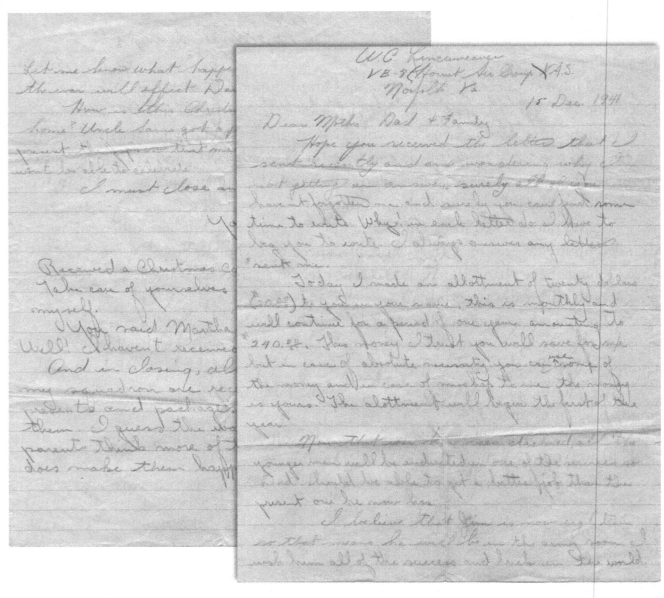

W.C. Linceweaver
VB-8 (front Air Group) N.A.S.
Norfolk, Va.

15 Dec. 1941

Dear Mother, Dad + Family

Hope you received the letter that I
sent recently and am wondering why I'm
not getting an answer, surely you
haven't forgotten me and surely you can find some
time to write. Why, in each letter do I have to
beg you to write. I always answer any letter
sent me.

Today I made an allotment of twenty dollars
($20.00) to you in your name, this is monthly and
will continue for a period of one year, amounting to
$240.00. This money I trust you will save for me
but in case of absolute necessity you can use some of
the money and in case I mother I have the money
is yours. The allotment will begin the first the
year.

Now that _____ _____ _____ _____ the
younger men will be inducted in one of the service at
well should be able to get a better job than the
present one he now has.

I believe that Jim is now eighteen
is that mean he will be in the army soon I
wish him all of the success and luck in the world.

[left letter page, partially obscured:]

Let me know what happ___
the war will affect Da___

How is this Christ___
home? Uncle Sam got a __
present t____ ____ that m___
won't be able to celebrate

I must close an___

Y___

Received a Christmas ca___
Take care of yourselves ___
myself.

You said Martha ___
Well! I haven't received ___

And in closing, al___
my squadron are rec___
presents and packages ___
them. I guess the ___
parents think more of ___
does make them happ___

From_____
132 MA_____
Norfolk, Va._____

[postmark:] NORFOLK DEC 16 3 PM 1941

[stamp:] DEFENSE BONDS AND STAMPS

Mr + Mrs. Robt. Linceweaver
1240 C. Cumberland St.
Avon, Penna.

W.C. Lineaweaver
VB-8 (Hornet Air Group) N.A.S
Norfolk, Va.

15 Dec. 1941

Dear Mother Dad & Family

Hope you received the letter that I sent recently and am wondering why I'm not getting an answer, surely all of you havent forgotten me and surely you can find some time to write. Why! in each letter do I have to beg you to write. I always answer any letters sent me.

Today I made an allottment of twenty dollars ($20.00) to you in your name, this is monthly and will continue for a period of one year amounting to $240.00. This money I trust you will save for me but in case of absolute necessity you can use some of the money and in case of misshap to me the money is yours. The alottment will begin the first of the year.

Now that war has been declared, all the younger men will be inducted in one of the services so Dad should be able to get a better job than the present one he now has.

I believe that Jim is now eighteen so that means he will be in the army soon. I wish him all the success and luck in the world. Let me know what happens to him and whether the war will effect Dave and Fat.

How is this Christmas going to be at home? Uncle Sam got a peach of a Christmas present, the Japs so that means that a lot of sailors wont be able to celebrate

I must close and go on watch

Your loving son
Wilson

Received a Christmas card from Lucille, Thanks!
Take care of yourselves and I'll try to myself.
You said Martha was going to write Well! I haven't received a letter from her yet.

And in closing, all the other men in my squadron are receiving wonderful presents and packages, you should see them. I guess the war has made the parents think more of their sons. It sure does make them happy.

[Postmark is Norfolk, Va., Dec. 16, 1941, 3 PM]
Mr & Mrs Robt. Lineaweaver
1240 E. Cumberland St
Avon, Penna.

[Return Address:]
W.C. Lineaweaver
138 N.A.S.
Norfolk, Va.

Censoring of letters began shortly after the bombing of Pearl Harbor. These pages are from the Don Schroeder Collection. Wilson served on the *Sangamon* in 1943, and Don was a quartermaster on the Sangamon in 1944. The first of Wilson's letters showing a naval censor stamp is dated January 1, 1942, and a letter showing censor cuts is dated May 30, 1942.

U.S.S. SANGAMON (CVE26)

EXAMPLES OF CENSORSHIP VIOLATIONS

1. Using both sides of paper.

2. Failing to sign full family name and initials at end of letter.

3. Sealing envelope (except when enclosures might be lost, if left unsealed).

4. Using X's either at the end of a letter or in the letter. Any other markings.

5. Omitting return address on envelope, including rate, branch of service, and ship or U.S. Navy. Exception: 3¢ mail.

6. Mailing picture postcards which reveal location of ship.

7. Revealing the location of the ship:

   (a) "We're back at the same old island".
   (b) "I saw Bill Bones the other day", where correspondent knows Bill Bones' location.
   (c) "You can guess where I am by reading the papers".
   (d) "Your guess was better than the others where I am".
   (e) "We see many flying fish daily".
   (f) "It's Tuesday where I am, but Monday by you".
   (g) "I havn't seen a white woman in six months".
   (h) "We go ashore, but all we can get is a couple of beers and maybe a swim".

8. Revealing the movement or prospective movement of the ship:

   (a) "Just got into port after three weeks underway".
   (b) "This will be my last letter to you for a long time".
   (c) "Don't worry about me in the next few weeks".
   (d) "Expect to be in port for another week".
   (e) "We will arrive at Mare Island in early August".

9. Revealing the location, movements, or identity of any other ship, naval or military force:

   (a) "The old Manley is still in and out of Pearl".
   (b) "Jim Bottom is in a Seebee unit on Guadalcanal".
   (c) "I saw Dick Leaders and his squadron at Manns Island".
   (d) "You rang the bell in regard to Joe Slocomb and where he is".

10. Detailed discussion of the weather.

11. Revealing the routine or employment of this ship, or any other military unit of the United Nation".

ENCLOSURE (A)-(1)

(a) "We do nothing but anti-submarine patroiling".
(b) "Today we launched planes five times, all for combat air patrol and then strikes".
(c) "Poor old Copahee does nothing but ferry planes".
(d) "Victorious, British carrier, is operating with the Big E and a New Jersey class battleship, training for big future operations".
(e) "We are in the Fifth Fleet, under Spruance".

12. Revealing the effect of enemy operations, or casualties to personnel or materiel suffered by the United States or her Allies, previous to the official publication of such information.

(a) "We caught a fish, and not a bullet was fired at the plane that dropped it".
(b) "Suwannee collided with us a few weeks ago".
(c) "Four pilots were lost from our squadrons this month".
(d) "I'll give you all the dope on our fire".

13. Criticism of equipment, appearance, physical conditions or morale of the collective or individual armed forces of the U.S. or her allies.

(a) "The soldiers on the transports are a crummy looking lot".
(b) "Our planes are no damn good against the Japs".
(c) "I don't like this ship or the way the Navy is run".

14. Discussion of weapons, installations, plans, of the forces of the U.S. or her Allies.

(a) "Our newest radar is magical".
(b) "We have some secret weapons, too. For instance, we have a 5" shell that will............".

15. Use of indirect language, double meanings, code words or phrases, or answers to correspondents' questions to convey prohibited information. This is a much more serious offense than plain statement, because it shows deliberate intent to to evade censorship.

16. Any statement which is apparently meaningless.

17. Letters to "Pen Pals".

The above is not a complete list; it only covers a few of the more common violations.

ENCLOSURE (A)-(2)

[Postmark is U.S. Navy, Jan. 2, 1942,
with "Passed by Naval Censor" stamp]
Mr & Mrs Robert Lineaweaver
1240 E. Cumberland St.
Avon, Penna.

[No return address, or was written on now missing flap.]

W. C. Lineaweaver
VB-8 U.S. S. Hornet
c/o P.M. New York N.Y.

Jan. 1st, 1942

Dear Parents & Family:

Sorry that I didn't write all of you sooner but this is war and we are all too busy to write, are too tired but in the future I'll find time to write more oftner.

Address all letters to me with the above address. Care of the postmaster New York N.Y. and I'll receive them but it may take some time and address the letters in ink because the mail is handled often and pencil writing becomes blurred

I thought for sure that you would send me a package for Christmas and I thought you said Martha was going to send something. If the Fire Company sent me a present I didn't receive it. The reason I didn't send any Christmas presents was that I was financially embarrassed as usual but if I'm still around next Christmas I hope to do better.

The allotment of twenty dollars that I started is now in affect and you should get the first check the latter part of this month or the beginning of February. Please take care of it for me.

How was the christmas at home? Did the kids get many presents and how did Dave and Fat including their families make out. Write and let me know because I'm curious to find out.

Is everybody still working at home? When will Jim get called in the Army?

Hoping to hear from all of you soon and that all of you are in the best of health. I'll close remaining

Your loving son
Wilson

Don't forget to use the new and correct address from now on. Use it always until you hear different. Perhaps you did send me a package and I didn't receive it, in fact I'm sure you did, I was looking for it since Christmas and still am. If you haven't send one as yet why don't bother.

Give the others my address in case they want to write me.

I am feeling fine and in good health plus the best of spirit. "Write soon!" Have pop write me too, Its about as hard to get him to write as it is to win this war.

Dad write me a few lines occasionally.
He could spare a few of the ——
spends sleeping on the couch ——
listening to the radio.

The allotment that I started
into effect the first of Jan. so you
be getting the first check soon. ——
know when it arrives.

There is nothing more I ——
about but I want you to know ——
am feeling fine and in good heal——
like the life aboard ship and ——
out fine. I expect to get my ——
soon

Waiting to hear from ——
you soon I remain

Your loving ——
Wilso——

W.C. Lineaweaver
UNITED STATES SHIP HORNET
% P.M. New York N.Y.

24, Jan. 1942

Dear Mother + Family:

This evening I received two letters
from you dated Jan 4, and Dec 27. I was
very glad to hear from you, it was a
long time since I received your last
letter. I sent a letter previous to this
one and hope you received it.

About those Christmas packages, as
yet I haven't received any and at this
late date I don't expect to. I can't
imagine what happened to them. Please
don't bother sending any more package
at the present because it takes too long
for it to reach me and they are handled
often ruining and spoiling the contents.

I imagine the kids have a lot
of fun playing in the snow and I'm
glad everything is going along O.K. Jim
and Dad working. by the way, why doesn't

Mrs Colene Lineaweaver
1240 C. Cumberland St.
Avon, Penna.

U.S.
JAN
29
1942
NAVY

PASSED BY NAVAL CENSOR

W.C. Lineaweaver
c/o P.M. New York N.Y.

24, Jan. 1942

Dear Mother & Family:

This evening I received two letters from you dated Jan 4, and Dec. 27. I was very glad to hear from you, it was a long time since I received your last letter. I sent a letter previous to this one and hope you received it.

About those Christmas packages, as yet I haven't received any and at this late date I don't expect to. I can't imagine what happened to them. Please don't bother sending any more package. at the present because it takes too long for it to reach me and they are handled often ruining and spoiling the contents.

I imagine the kids have a lot of fun playing in the snow and I'm glad everything is going along O.K. Jim and Dad working, by the way, why doesn't Dad write me a few lines occasionally. He could spare a few of the minutes he spends sleeping on the couch are listening to the radio.

The allotment that I started went into effect the first of Jan. so you should be getting the first check soon. Leave me know when it arrives.

There is nothing more I can write about but I want you to know that I am feeling fine and in good health. I like the life aboard ship and am making out fine. I expect to get my next rate soon

Waiting to hear from all of you soon I remain

Your loving son
Wilson

[Postmark is U.S. Navy, Jan. 29, 1942, with "Passed by Naval Censor" stamp]
Mrs. Erlene Lineaweaver
1240 E. Cumberland St.
Avon, Penna.

[No return address, or was written on now missing flap.]

if not let me know

I also want you to k—
during all the—at sea I did—
sea sick once although I wa—
it any moment

Write soon!

Your son
Wilson

Wilson C. Sineaweaver
U.S. UNITED STATES SHIP HORNET
c/o P.M. New York, N.Y.

2. Feb. 1942

Dear Mother:

Now that I'm in Norfolk for a short time I have more time to myself so I can write oftener. While at sea I received two letters from you and also sent a few hoping you got them.

There is very little that I can write concerning my doings and where I've been because of the strict naval censor but I can say that I'm allright and doing fine. Life at sea isn't so hard but under war conditions its plenty tough. I guess that's to be expected.

I guess you know, that is if you received my previous letters that I didn't get the package you sent. I can't figure what happened to it.

I hope to hear from you soon and I'm wondering if you got the check from the Government

Mr. & Mrs. Robert Sineaweaver
1240 E. Cumberland St.
Anon, Penna.

Wilson C Lineaweaver
VB-8 c/o P.M. New York, N.Y.

2. Feb. 1942

Dear Mother:

Now that I'm in Norfolk for a short time I have more time to myself so I can write oftener. While at sea I received two letters from you and also sent a few hoping you got them.

There is very little that I can write concerning my doings and where I've been because of the strict naval censor but I can say that I'm allright and doing fine. Life at sea isn't so hard but under war conditions its plenty tough. I guess thats to be expected.

I guess you know, that is if you received my previous letters that I didn't get the package you sent. I can't figure what happened to it.

I hope to hear from you soon and I'm wondering if you got the first check from the government If not let me know.

I also want you to know that during all the time at sea I didn't get sea sick once although I was expecting it any moment

Write soon!

Your son
Wilson

[Postmark is Norfolk, Va., Feb. 3, 1942, 8:30 PM]
Mr & Mrs. Robert Lineaweaver
1240 E. Cumberland St.
Avon Penna.

[No Return Address]

get the chance I'll mail it to
you so ple...
for me
for you

Write...
if you got...
the allott...

I was...
pop and...
write often...
is the only...
this sailor...
consistent...

Wait...
soon I...

#3

carrying and it was pitch
dark, so...
we jump...
in front...
chute ea...
wires an...
on the s...
hit hard...
that I...
but I sur...
the good...
feet. It...
I will ne...
I live a...
chute thi...
out and...
as a reme...

everyone is getting along
just fine a...
health

Last...
my first p...
in from...
just before...
ran out of...
and mysel...
pilot hurt...
and I hur...
am O.K.,...
from the e...

The...
make a fo...
because o...

#2

W.C. Limaweaver
VB-8 U.S.S. Hornet
c/o P.M. New York N.Y.

8th Feb, 1942

Dear Parents & Family,
This is Sunday afternoon
and I am writing this letter
from Washington D.C. at a
friends house where I've been
spending the weekend and have
been enjoying myself immensly
I received Dads letter
Friday and one from mother
previously and I was sure glad
to hear from you
I'm also glad to hear that

Mr & Mrs Robt Limaweaver
1210 E. Cumberland St
Avon Penna.

W. C. Lineaweaver
VB-8 U.S.S. Hornet
c/o P.M. New York N.Y.

8ᵗʰ Feb, 1942

Dear Parents & Family.

This is Sunday afternoon and I am writing this letter from Washington D.C. at a friends house where I've been spending the weekend and have been enjoying myself immensly

I received Dads letter Friday and one from mother previously and I was sure glad to hear from you

Im also glad to hear that everyone is getting along just fine and everyone in good health

Last Thursday night I had my first parachute jump. Coming in from patrol we got lost and just before reaching the field we ran out of gas forcing the pilot and myself to bail out. The pilot hurt his back upon landing and I hurt my leg slightly but am O.K., only a little shaky from the experience.

The reason we couldnt make a forced landing was because of the bombs we were carrying and it was pitch dark, so when the motor cut we jumped. I landed right in front of a house, my chute caught on electric wires and I hit the porch on the second bounce. I hit hard and it was dark so that I couldn't see anything but I sure was glad to feel the good earth beneath my feet. It is an experience that I will never forget as long as I live and I have the small chute that pulls the large one out and Im going to keep it as a rememberance. When I get the chance I'll mail it to you so please take care of it for me

Write soon and let me know if you got any money as yet from the allotment I started

I was sure glad to hear from pop and I like all of you to write oftener. It seems as if Mother is the only one that hasn't forgot this sailor and I am glad for her consistent letters.

Waiting to hear from you soon I remain

Your loving son
Wilson

[Postmark is Washington, D.C.4, Feb. 9, 1942, 1:30 AM]   *[No Return Address]*
Mr & Mrs Robt. Lineaweaver
1240 E. Cumberland St
Avon Penna.

to do something to help but all I
can do is express my sympathy
hope Dad doesn't take it so

That parachute jump was an
experience and I can be proud of
I didn't have a joy reception
for me when I landed.

So you finally got a letter
my allotment. I went up to the
office to see about it, something
up so its a month late.

How is everything at home
is Jim working and how is Dad
How are the kids making out in
won't be long until they finish and
hope they must never go through
must

Well I guess I must
know there is very little I can
about, nothing what we do or
you can understand why so
hear from you I remain

All of you write
me a few lines.

Your son
Wils

W. C. Limaweaver, V B-9
c/o P.M. New York, N.Y.

UNITED STATES SHIP HORNET

22 February, 1942

Dear Parents:

About four days ago I gave a
letter to a friend who was going
ashore to mail for me but he
didn't remember if he mailed it or
lost it, so I'm going to try
again.

I received mothers letter
yesterday and I'm sorry to hear
that you are laid up in bed. I hope
it isn't serious and that your up and
around soon. It is a good thing that
you have Lucille around to do the work
and keep things running. The two kids
must be getting big so their not so much
trouble and Dot can help a lot too. I
would like a chance to come home for
a while but the things are going it
will be a long time I fear.

I was sorry to hear about Uncle
George and I know it must be pretty
tough for Dad. I sure would like to

178

W.C. Lineaweaver VB-8
c/o P.M. New York, N.Y.

22, February, 1942

Dear Parents:

About four days ago I gave a letter to a friend who was going ashore to mail for me but he can't remember if he mailed it or lost it, so I'm going to try again.

I received mothers letter yesterday and I'm sorry to hear that you are laid up in bed. I hope it isn't serious and that your up and around soon. It is a good thing that you have Lucille around to do the work and keep things running. The two kids must be getting big so their not so much trouble and Dot can help a lot too. I would like a chance to come home for a while but the way things are going it will be a long time if ever.

I was sorry to hear about Uncle George and I know it must be pretty tough for Dad. I sure would like to to do something to help but all I can do is express my sympthy and hope Dad doesn't take it so hard.

That parachute jump was quite an experience and I can be thankful that I didn't have a Jap reception waiting for me when I landed.

So you finally got a letter concerning my allotment. I went up to the disbursing office to see about it, something was screwed up so its a month late.

How is everything at home? Where is Jim working and how is Dads work? How are the kids making out in school? it won't be long until they finish another year. I hope they must never go through what I must.

Well! I guess I must close, you know there is very little I can write about, nothing we do or have done, you can understand why. So until I hear from you I remain

Your son
Wilson

All of you write me a few lines.

[Postmark is Norfolk, Va., Feb. 22, 1942, 6:30 PM]
Mr & Mrs. Robert Lineaweaver
1240 E. Cumberland St
Avon Penna.

[No Return Address]

"...sorry to hear about Uncle George..."
Wilson's Uncle George Lineaweaver was age 50 in 1942 and unemployed. He was a younger brother (there were 13 siblings) of Wilson's father, Robert. George and Robert's parents were Joseph and Ellen Lineaweaver. Wilson's grandparents, Joseph and Ellen, did not get along and lived in separate parts of the same house. On February 8, 1942, an argument arose between George and his father Joseph over heat not being allowed to migrate from Joseph's part of the house to Ellen's part of the house, as well as other ill treatment of Ellen by Joseph. The argument resulted in Joseph shooting his son George twice with a .38 caliber pistol, hitting him in the chest and the abdomen. George then went home to bed. He did not go to the hospital until the following morning where he died on February 9, 1942. Joseph, at the age of 83, died on Aug. 26, 1943, in the Eastern State Penitentiary in Philadelphia.

me may be long in coming due
to war conditions so if [you] [don't]
receive any letters for a while
think I'm not writing and d[on't]
[think] you forget to write me also.

There isn't much mor[e]
[to write] about but I know there are a [lot of]
things happening around hom[e that]
would interest me so write a[nd tell]
me about them. Try and ge[t Dad]
and Fat or Martha to writ[e]
Lucille, Dot, the kids and [tell]
both of you write me often. Y[our letters]
will find me someplace in the [world]
sometime. Being awful tire[d I can]
just about hold my eyes open [so]

Your loving [son]
W.[C.]

W. C. Linnenwever
UNITED STATES SHIP HORNET
VB-9 ℅ PM. New York, N.Y.

Feb 26th 1942

Dear Parents & Family,

I finally got an evening off
and after washing all my clothing
and bathed myself I have a few
minutes before teps when the lights go
off and I have to turn into my bunk,
so I'll write you a few lines to let
you know that I am all right and in
good health and I'm hoping that it
is the same at home and that you
are out of bed and up and around. You
know, your last letter you were laid
up in bed so I hope by the time you
get this letter you are out of bed and in
good health.

I sent a letter a few days
ago hoping you got it and am
waiting for an answer. Letters from

Mr. & Mrs. Robert Linnenwever
1240 E. Cumberland St
Avon, Penn[a]

W.C. Lineaweaver VB-8
c/o P.M. New York, N.Y.

Feb 26th 1942

Dear Parents & Family:

I finally got an evening off and after washing all my clothing and bathed myself I have a few minutes before taps when the lights go off and I have to turn into my bunk, so I'll write you a few lines to let you know that I am all right and in good health and I'm hoping that it is the same at home and that you are out of bed and up and around. You know, your last letter you were laid up in bed so I hope by the time you get this letter you are out of bed and in good health.

I sent a letter a few days ago hoping you got it and am waiting for an answer. Letters from me may be long in coming due to war conditions so if you don't receive any letters for a while don't think I'm not writing and don't all of you forget to write me also.

There isn't much more to write about but I know there are a lot of things happening around home that would interest me so write and tell me about them. Try and get Dave and Fat or Martha to write, have Jim, Lucille, Dot, the kids and above all both of you write me often. Your letters will find me someplace in this world some time. Being awful tired and can just about hold my eyes open I'll close.

Your loving son
Wilson

[Postmark is Norfolk, Va., Feb. 2?, 1942, 4:30 PM]
Mr. & Mrs. Robert Lineaweaver
1240 E. Cumberland St.
Avon, Penna.

[No Return Address]

Don't forget to have Dad, the kids and even Dave & Fat write me, I know you haven't forgotten me and will write often

Wishing every one back home lots of luck and with lots of love I rema

Your son

Wilson

Excuse the writing

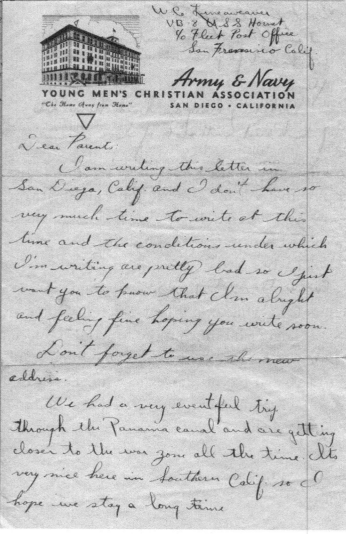

W C Lineaweaver
VB-8 U S S Hornet
% Fleet Post Office
San Francisco Calif

Army & Navy
YOUNG MEN'S CHRISTIAN ASSOCIATION
SAN DIEGO • CALIFORNIA
"The Home Away from Home"

Dear Parent:

I am writing this letter in San Diego, Calif. and I don't have so very much time to write at this time and the conditions under which I'm writing are pretty bad so I just want you to know that I'm alright and feeling fine hoping you write soon.

Don't forget to use the new address.

We had a very eventful trip through the Panama canal and are getting closer to the war zone all the time. Its very nice here in Southern Calif. so I hope we stay a long time

CORRESPONDENCE ROOM
Army & Navy
YOUNG MEN'S CHRISTIAN ASSOCIATION
SAN DIEGO, CALIFORNIA

SAN DIEGO
MAR 21
7 PM
1942
CALIF.

BUY
DEFENSE SAVINGS
BONDS AND STAMPS

3 CENTS

Mr & Mrs Robert Lineaweaver
1240 C Cumberland St
Cimon Penna.

W.C. Lineaweaver
VB-8 U.S.S. Hornet
c/o Fleet Post Office
San Francisco Calif.

[No date on letter; March 21, 1942 is the postmark date.]

Dear Parents:

I am writing this letter in San Diego, Calif. And I don't have so very much time to write at this time and the conditions under which I'm writing are pretty bad so I just want you to know that Im alright and feeling fine hoping you write soon.

Don't forget to use the new address.

We had a very eventful try through the Panama canal and are getting closer to the war zone all the time. Its very nice here in Southern Calif. So I hope we stay a long time Don't forget to have Dad, the kids and even Dave & Fat write me, I know you haven't forgotten me and will write often

Wishing every one back home lots of luck and with lots of love I remain

Your son

Wilson

Excuse the writing

[Postmark is San Diego, Calif., Mar. 21, 1942, 7:30 PM]
Mr & Mrs Robert Lineaweaver
1240 E Cumberland St.
Avon Penna.

[No Return Address]

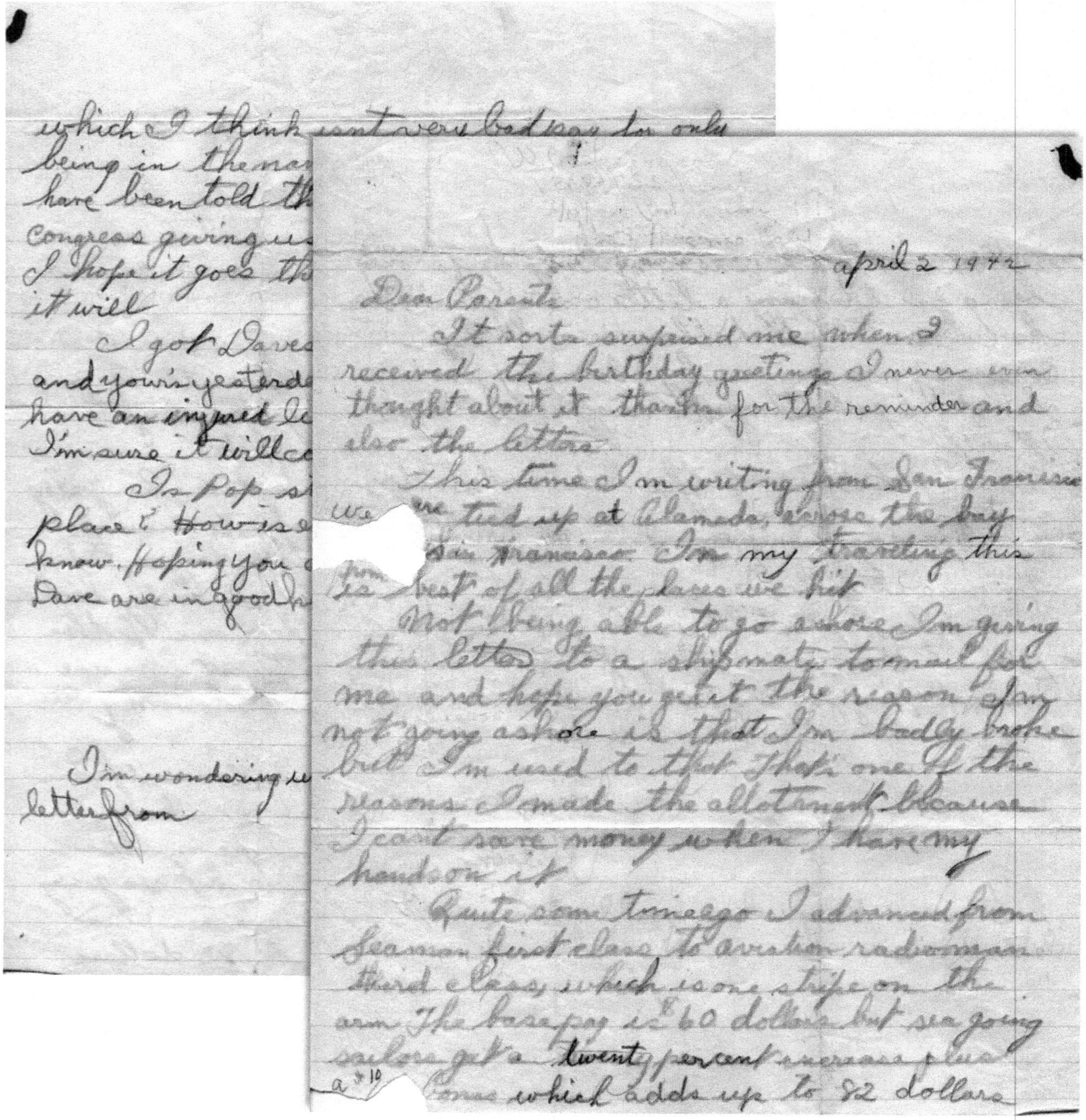

which I think isnt very bad pay tu only
being in the navy
have been told th
Congress giving us
I hope it goes th
it will

I got Daves
and your's yesterd
have an injured le
I'm sure it will c

Is Pop st
place? How is e
know. Hoping you a
Dave are in good h

I'm wondering w
letter from

---

april 2 1942

Dear Parents

It sorta surprised me when I
received the birthday greetings I never even
thought about it thanks for the reminder and
also the letters

This time I'm writing from San Francisco
we are tied up at Alameda, across the bay
from San Francisco I'm my traveling this
is best of all the places we hit

Not being able to go ashore, I'm giving
this letter to a shipmate to mail for
me and hope you get it the reason of my
not going ashore is that I'm badly broke
but I'm used to that That's one of the
reasons I made the allotment because
I cant save money when I have my
hands on it

Quite some time ago I advanced from
Seaman first class to aviation radioman
third class, which is one stripe on the
arm The base pay is 60 dollars but sea going
sailors get a twenty percent increase plus
a *10 bonus which adds up to 82 dollars

[No envelope remains with this letter.]

April 2 1942

Dear Parents:

It sorta surprised me when I received the birthday greetings I never even thought about it. thanks for the reminder and also the letters.

This time I'm writing from San Franisco. We are tied up at Alameda, across the bay from San Francisco. In my traveling this is best of all the places we hit

Not being able to go ashore I'm giving this letter to a shipmate to mail for me and hope you get it. the reason I'm not going ashore is that I'm badly broke but I'm used to that. That's one of the reasons I made the allotment because I can't save money when I have my hands on it

Quite some time ago I advanced from Seaman first class to aviation radioman third class, which is one stripe on the arm. The base pay is $60 dollars but sea going sailors get a twenty percent increase plus a $10 bonus which adds up to 82 dollars which I think isn't very bad pay for only being in the navy a little over a year. We have been told that there is a bill in congress giving us a big base pay increase. I hope it goes through. The officers think it will

I got Daves & the kids cards today and your's yesterday. I am sorry that you have an injured leg, Don't work so hard I'm sure it will come around alright.

Is Pop still working at the same place? How is everything at home? Let me know. Hoping you and Dad plus the kids Fat & Dave are in good health I'll close

You loving son
Wilson

I'm wondering where you'll get my next letter from.

This is the card, shown actual size, for Wilson's crossing of the 180th Meridian (International Date Line) on April 14, 1942, in Latitude 40° North, on board on the USS *Hornet* (VB-8). (The back side of the card is blank.)

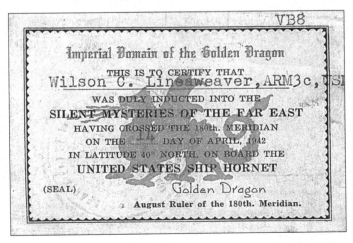

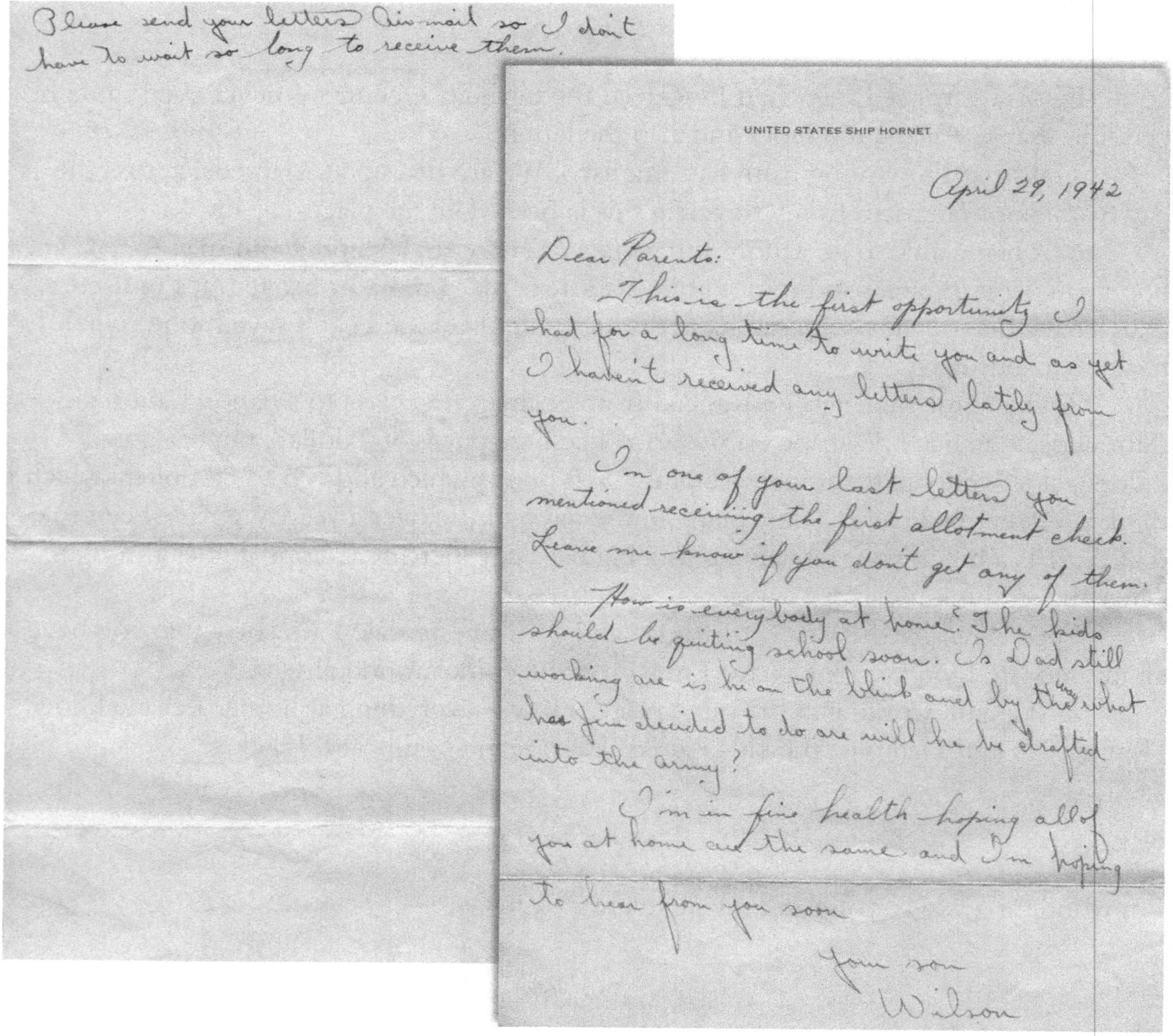

Please send your letters Air-mail so I don't have to wait so long to receive them.

UNITED STATES SHIP HORNET

April 29, 1942

Dear Parents:

This is the first opportunity I had for a long time to write you and as yet I haven't received any letters lately from you.

In one of your last letters you mentioned receiving the first allotment check. Leave me know if you don't get any of them.

How is everybody at home? The kids should be quitting school soon. Is Dad still working or is he on the blink and by the way what has Jim decided to do or will he be drafted into the army?

I'm in fine health hoping all of you at home are the same and I'm hoping to hear from you soon

Your son
Wilson

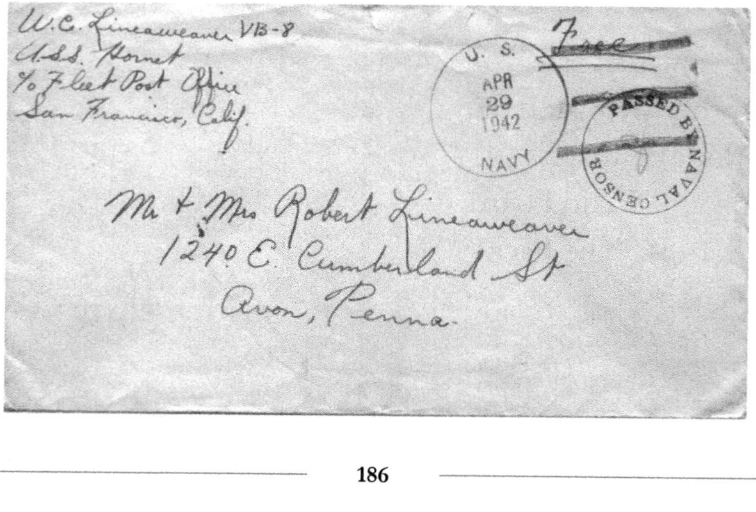

W.C. Lineaweaver VB-8
U.S.S. Hornet
% Fleet Post Office
San Francisco, Calif.

Free

U.S.
APR
29
1942
NAVY

PASSED BY NAVAL CENSOR

Mr. & Mrs. Robert Lineaweaver
1240 E. Cumberland St
Avon, Penna.

April 29, 1942

Dear Parents:

This is the first opportunity I had for a long time to write you and as yet I haven't received any letters lately from you.

In one of your last letters you mentioned receiving the first allotment check. Leave me know if you don't get any of them. How is everybody at home? The kids should be quiting school soon. Is Dad still working are is he on the blink and by the way what has Jim decided to do are will he be drafted into the army?

I'm in fine health hoping all of you at home are the same and Im hoping to hear from you soon

Your son
Wilson

Please send your letters Air mail so I don't have to wait so long to receive them.

[Postmark is U.S. Navy Apr. 29, 1942, with a "Passed By Naval Censor" stamp.]
Mr & Mrs Robert Lineaweaver
1240 E. Cumberland St
Avon, Penna.

[Return Address:]
W.C. Lineaweaver VB-8
U.S.S. Hornet
c/o Fleet Post Office
San Francisco, Calif.

This is Wilson's Dog Tag. This style of tag was typically only made in 1942, so he likely would have had a set of dog tags made at a later date. The front side shows his name of Wilson C. Lineaweaver, his ID number of 2583224, blood type A, tetanus shot in January of 1942, and USN for U.S. Navy. The back side has an impression of his thumb print. Actual size is 1 ½" x 1 ¼".

Telegram reads: DEAR PARENTS SORRY I COULDNT WRITE SOONER AM OK LETTER WILL FOLLOW SOON WRITE SON= WILSON C. LINEAWEAVER.

The scenery here on the Islands
is beautiful but the [...]
lousy. We are only allowed [...]
until six o'clock in the eve[...]
other day I was in Honolu[...]
couldn't find anything to [...]

Don't forget to send your [...]
mail from now on and above [...]
forget to write.

I guess I told you i[...]
letter that I was advance[...]
to third class petty office[...]
considerable increase in p[...]
now, financially, I'm g[...]
fine.

Hoping everyone at [...]
the best of health and [...]
impatiently to hear the n[...]
close, remaining.

Your loving [...]
Wilson
A R [...]

W. C. Lineaweaver AR M 3/c
C.A.S.U. #1
% Fleet Post Office
Pearl Harbor T.H.

May 2, 1942

Dear Parents:

I have not received a letter
from any of you for a long time,
perhaps it is due to slowness in
distributing mail to the fleet.

Just a few days ago I was transferred to Carrier Aircraft Servicing
unit here at Pearl Harbor for
advanced radio and gunnery training.
After this training I think I'll
return to one of the ships in the
fleet.

Don't forget to use the
above address from now on instead
of the former and also send them
Air mail so they come out by
Clipper plane, and I won't have to
wait months for your letters.

W. C. Lineaweaver AR M 3/c
C.A.S.U. #1
% Fleet Post Office
Pearl Harbor T.H.

VIA AIR MAIL

NAVY
May 2, 1942

PASSED BY [...] CENSOR

Mr. & Mrs. Robert Lineaweaver
1240 E. Cumberland St.
Avon, Penna.

W.C. Lineaweaver ARM 3/c
C.A.S.U. #1
c/o Fleet Post Office
Pearl Harbor T.H.

May 2, 1942

Dear Parents:

I have not received a letter from any of you for a long time, perhaps it is due to slowness in distributing mail to the fleet.

Just a few days ago I was transferred to Carrier Aircraft Servicing unit here at Pearl Harbor for advanced radio and gunnery training. After this training I think I'll return to one of the ships in the fleet.

Don't forget to use the above address from now on instead of the former and also send them Air mail so they come out by Clipper plane, and I won't have to wait months for your letters.

The scenery here on the Islands is <u>beautiful</u> but the liberty is lousy. We are only allowed liberty up until six o clock in the evening. The other day I was in Honolula but just couldn't find anything to do.

Don't forget to send your letters air mail from now on and above all don't forget to write.

I guess I told you in a previous letter that I was advanced in rating to third class petty officer with a considerable increase in pay. Right now, financially, I'm getting along fine.

Hoping everyone at home is in the best of health and waiting impatiently to hear the news I'll close, remaining.

Your loving son
Wilson Charles Lineaweaver
ARM 3/c

[Postmark has been mostly torn off of envelope; has a "Passed By Naval Censor" stamp.]
Mr. & Mrs. Robert Lineaweaver
1240 E. Cumberland St.
Avon, Penna.

[Return Address:]
W.C. Lineaweaver ARM 3/c
C.A.S.U. #1
c/o Fleet Post Office
Pearl Harbor T.H.

May 11th, 1942

Dear Parents:

This being the first chance
I've had for a long time, I'm
dropping these few lines to let
you know that I am still
kicking and in good health and
waiting impatiently to hear about
all of you and the news from
home. The last letter I received
from you was dated early in
April and I also got your
birthday greetings, so you can
see how long I've been waiting to
hear from you.

I am hoping you received
the mother's day greetings I sent and
also the letter.

Reminding you to use my
new address and send your mail
airmail I'll close

Your loving son
Wilson Charles Lineaweaver AM3/c
My new address→ C.A.S.U. #1
%o Fleet Post Master
Pearl Harbor T.H.

Mr & Mrs Robert Lineaweaver
1240 E. Cumberland St.
Avon, Penna.

PASSED BY NAVAL CENSOR

May 11th, 1942

Dear Parents:

This being the first chance Ive had for a long time, I'm dropping these few lines to let you know that I am still kicking and in good health and waiting impatiently to hear about all of you and the news from home. The last letter I received from you was dated early in April and I also got your birthday greetings, so you can see how long I've been waiting to hear from you.

I am hoping you received the mother's day greetings I sent and also the letter.

Reminding you to use my new address and send your mail airmail I'll close

Your loving son
Wilson Charles Lineaweaver, ARM 3/c
My new address   CAS.U. #1
                    c/o Fleet Post Master
                    Pearl Harbor T.H.

[Postmark is U.S. Navy, May 13, 1942, AM, with a "Passed By Naval Censor" stamp.]
Mr & Mrs Robert Lineaweaver
1240 E. Cumberland St.
Avon, Penna.

[No return address remains on the envelope.]

five years since I first left home
only being there occasionly during
that period.

How is Dave and Pat includ
their families prospering. Tell
I asked about them and con
them to write a few lines. H
fick mate out few in school and
good health Lucille quit did'nt sh
think being away from home th
they have just about forgot me
did they?

I would like to sen
one of you some little gift f
Hawaii but this is war and a
space is reserved for essential t
but as soon as they lift the
restriction you can expect some t

How is Dads work? Hop
don't have to work too hard and
dot and Lucille growing up, your
should ease up considerably.

Well! I guess it's time
say aloha, hoping to hear fro
soon I remain as ever
Your loving son
Nelson
Send your letters air mail. Do you get them

May 16, 1942

Dear Mother & Dad:
Taking a few moments off
from school I decided to write
a few lines leaving you know
that as yet I'm still alright
but a little grieved that I
haven't heard from you since
th early part of March. Could
there be any thing wrong?

Enclosed are a few pictures
we had taken while on liberty in
Honolulu. The chap posing with me
is a fellow radioman, a former
Dartmouth University graduate
who missed out on a commission
in the navy because of bad teeth.
He hails from Boston and his
name is Woodman

The war seems to be getting
nowhere fast and it seems that it
will be a long time before I get
a chance to come home again. I
sure would like to see the old
town, I imagine I won't even
know the place. It is almost

Mr. & Mrs. Robert Lindweaver
1240 E. Cumberland St.
Avon, Penna.

May 16, 1942

Dear Mother & Dad:

Taking a few moments off from school I decided to write a few lines leaving you know that as yet Im still alright but a little grieved that I haven't heard from you since the early part of March. Could there be anything wrong?

Enclosed are a few pictures we had taken while on liberty in Honolulu. The chap posing with me is a fellow radioman, a former Dartmouth University graduate who missed out on a commission in the navy because of bad teeth. He hails from Boston and his name is Woodman.

The war seems to be getting no where fast and it seems that it will be a long time before I get a chance to come home again. I sure would like to see the old town, I imagine I won't even know the place. It is almost five years since I first left home only being there occasionly during that period.

How is Dave and Fat including there families prospering. Tell them I asked about them and convince them to write a few lines. Hope the kids made out fine in school and are in good health. Lucille quit didn't she? I think being away from home this long they have just about forgot me, are did they?

I would like to send each of you some little gift from Hawaii but this is war and all space is reserved for essential things, but as soon as they lift the restriction you can expect some thing.

How is Dads work? Hope he don't have to work too hard and with Dot and Lucille growing up, your work should ease up considerably.

Well! I guess it's time to say aloha, hoping to hear from you soon I remain as ever

Your loving son
Wilson

Send your letters air mail. Do you get the monthly allotment?

[Postmark is U.S. Navy, May 19, 1942, AM, with a "Passed By Naval Censor" stamp.]
Mr. & Mrs. Robert Lineaweaver
1240 E. Cumberland St.
Avon, Penna.

[No return address remains on the envelope.]

most humorous and tickled me
immensly. I guess they would be
glad t...
some ...
Dot is ...
and ...
Jake ...
with ...
did ...

prow ...
a lo...

will ...
close ...

was in
he can
go thro...

must ...
does h...
his car
or two ...

waya ...
Fat ha...
still wa...
I guess ...
big. D...
Rodney ...

so long. Lately I'ved been~~d~~ moved
around frequently so if you use the
address ...
future.

letter a...
to book ...
which ...
forgive m...
and I ...
occasion...
it I ...

You al...
to the ...
an avi...
with ...
going to ...

libeties ...
at the ...
The ...
wish g...

I wrot...
I also ...
from o...

May 30th 1942

Dear Mother & Dad:
　　　After not hearing from you since
the early part of March I thought
perhaps there was something wrong, but
today after being at sea for long
periods I received about twenty
letters. About five or six from you, and
one from Lucille, one from Nathan & Harold
and another from Martha & Fat & others.
　　　It sure was pleasing after about
2½ months and I was glad to hear
that everything was allright and going
along fine. Everyone working and
and in good health is good news. Sorry
to hear that Dads work is uncomfortable
... thing about
... self and
... t to com ...
...icken dinner followed
...next day by chicken mood
as only you can make it. This ...
will be soon.
　　　In your letters you asked quite
a few questions which I will try and
answer asking a few myself. I ...
expect answers in the very

[This letter is written on both sides of the paper with information cut out by censors.]

May 30th 1942

Dear Mother & Dad:

After not hearing from you since the early part of March I thought perhaps there was something wrong, but today after being at sea for long periods I received about twenty letters. About five or six from you, and one from Lucille, one from Nathan & Harold and another from Martha & Fat. & others.

It sure was pleasing after about 2 ½ months and I was glad to hear that everything was allright and going along fine. Every one working and in good health is good news. Sorry to hear that Dads work is uncomfortable *[information here cut out by censor]* chicken dinner followed the next day chicken noodle *[information here cut out by censor]* as only you can make it. This *[information here cut out by censor]* will be soon.

In your letters you asked quite a few questions which I will try and answer asking a few myself *[information here cut out by censor]* expect answers in the very *[information here cut out by censor]* future.

I left a few mates read Lucille's letter and took quite a ribbing for trying to hook my kid sister of two dollars which I completely over looked. Please forgive me and accept my humble apology and I vow that when the first occasion arises so that I can send it I will.

There is very little I can tell you about what Ive been doing due to the naval censor. I am still an aviation radioman and gunner with most of my time at sea and going to advanced schools.

Last month I had a few liberties in *[information here cut out by censor]* at the *[information here cut out by censor]* The *[information here cut out by censor]* are sure *[information here cut out by censor]* wish you could see the *[information here cut out by censor]*.

Did you receive the recent letters I wrote and the one with the pictures? I also want you to send your letters from now on airmail so they come *[information here cut out by censor]* and I don't have to wait so long. Lately I'ved been moved around frequently so if you use the address at the end of this letter, your letters will find me sometime. Did you receive the telegram I sent from *[information here cut out by censor]* and you didn't let me know if you got the telegram I sent a long time ago from San Francisco.

I expected to hear that Jim was in the army but am glad if he can stay out and don't have to go through this.

So Dave has good work, he must be floating in dough but what does he do about gas and tires for his car? I guess he has a different car or two since the last one I seen.

The letter from Martha & Fat was a surprise. I imagine by now Fat has some good war job or is he still working at the same place and I guess Billy must be getting pretty big. Do you think Id know him or Rodney?

Harold & Nathans letters were most humorous and tickled me immensely. I guess they would be glad to see me again and maybe get some show money. From your letters Dot is staying at Martha's helping them, and Lucille is still tending *[information here cut out by censor]* Jake and Harold I guess are finished with this years school term. How did they make? Did they pass?

Will write soon again and will wait impatiently to hear from you Ill close remaining

Your loving son
Wilson

[No envelope remains with this letter.]

Wilson Charles Lineaweaver ARM 3/c
C.A.S.U. #1
c/o Fleet Post Office
Pearl Harbor, T.H.

forgives me for making her wait
so long.

Tell Jim if he gets drafted
and has to go in the army, the
going may be tough but make a
good soldier and I will try and make
a good sailor out of myself.

I'm closing I want you to
know that if anything should
happen to me, the money in the bank
and all property of mine will be
yours to do with as you please.

Your loving son

Wilson C. Linaweaver
C A S U #1
% Fleet Post Office
Pearl Harbor T.H.

Write soon

June 13th 1942

Dear Mother:

Just received a few of your
most welcomed letters and I
sure was glad to hear the home
news. The reason I haven't
been getting your letters is that
I have been at sea for long
periods and moving around but
they finally catch up some
time.

So I am once again an
uncle, you forgot to tell me
my new niece's name and tell
Dave not to forget the cigars.

I am glad to hear that
everyone is working and everything
going along swell. Take care of
yourselves.

You know I plum forgot
about Dads birthday so tell him
that as soon as I get home we'll
go down and have a few beers on
me to celebrate.

And you know I forgot all
about the money I owed Lucille so
enclosed you will find 3.00 which
I hope repays her and that she

W.C. Linaweaver 1 S M. 3/c
C A S U #1
% Fleet Post Office
Pearl Harbor T.H.

JUN 15 A.M. 1942
NAV

PASSED BY NAVY

Mr. + Mrs. Robert Linaweaver
12 40 E. Cumberland St
Avon Penna.

June 13th 1942

Dear Mother:

Just received a few of your most welcomed letters and I sure was glad to hear the home news. The reason I haven't been getting your letters is that I have been at sea for long periods and moving around but they finally catch up some time.

So I am once again an uncle, you forgot to tell me my new neice's name and tell Dave not to forget the cigars. *[Carol Anne Lineaweaver, born May 10, 1942.]*

I am glad to hear that everyone is working and everything going along swell. Take care of yourselves.

You know I plum forgot about Dads birthday so tell him that as soon as I get home we'll go down and have a few beers <u>on me</u> to celebrate.

And you know I forgot all about the money I owed Lucille so enclosed you will find $3.00 which I hope repays her and that she forgives me for making her wait so long.

Tell Jim if he gets drafted and has to go in the army, the going may be tough but make a good soldier and I will try and make a good sailor out of myself.

In closing I want you to know that if anything should happen to me, the money in bank and all property of mine will be yours to do with as you please.

Your loving son
Wilson C. Lineaweaver ARM 3/c
CASU #1
c/o Fleet Post Office
Pearl Harbor T.H.

<u>Write Soon</u>

[Postmark is U.S. Navy, June 15, 1942, AM, with a "Passed By Naval Censor" stamp.]
Mr. & Mrs. Robert Lineaweaver
1240 E. Cumberland St
Avon, Penna.

[Return Address:]
W.C. Lineaweaver ARM. 3/c
CASU #1
c/o Fleet Post Office
Pearl Harbor T.H.

working hard most of the time but
this is war and I'm not complaining
because I sure want to do my
part.

It's hard to say when I'll
ever get a chance to come home but
I think of you often and perhaps some
day I'll walk in and surprise you.

Your loving son
Wilson

Write often

Don't forget to use the new
or rather the old one.

Wilson C. Lineaweaver ARM 3/c
VB-8 U.S.S Hornet
℅ Postmaster
San Francisco, Calif.

June 18th, 1942

Dear Mother & Dad:
Lately I have been receiving
many of your letters, some dated
months ago and some recently. I was
sure glad to hear from you. Try and get
Dad to write me every now and then.
I'm sure he can find a few spare
moments. A few days ago I sent you
a letter containing the money I owed
Lucille, hope you received it OK. and
please let me know.

Have you been getting the allotment
every month? I've been thinking
about increasing it to about thirty
five dollars so when this increase
takes effect continue the same way
as always.

So Dave's the father of a little
girl. How are they doing and did they
name it yet? Tell him to write also.
Lately I've been very busy and

W.C. Lineaweaver ARM 3/c
VB-8 U.S.S. Hornet
℅ Postmaster
San Francisco, Calif.

June 19 1942

Mr & Mrs Robert Lineaweaver
1240 E. Cumberland St.
Avon, Penna.

Wilson C Lineaweaver ARM 3/c
VB-8 USS Hornet
San Francisco, Calif.

June 18th, 1942

Dear Mother & Dad:

Lately I have been receiving many of your letters, some dated months ago and some recently. I was sure glad to hear from you. Try and get Dad to write me every now and then, I'm sure he can find a few spare moments. A few days ago I sent you a letter containing the money I owed Lucille, hope you received it O.K. and please let me know.

Have you been getting the allotment every month? Ive been thinking about increasing it to about thirty five dollars so when this increase takes effect continue the same way as always.

So Dave's the father of a little girl. How are they doing and did they name it yet? Tell him to write also.

Lately Ive been very busy and working hard most of the time but this is war and I'm not complaining because I sure want to do my part.

Its hard to say when I'll ever get a chance to come home but I think of you often and perhaps some day I'll walk in and surprise you.

Your loving son
Wilson

<u>Write often</u>
Dont forget to use the new <u>address</u> or rather the old one.

[Postmark is missing; envelope has a "Passed By Naval Censor" stamp.]
Mr & Mrs Robert Lineaweaver
1240 E. Cumberland St
Avon, Penna.

[Return Address:]
W.C. Lineaweaver ARM 3/c
VB-8 U.S.S. Hornet
c/o Postmaster
San Francisco, Calif.

no additional you [illegible] we can write to each other.

Will be expecting to [hear] from you soon

Your loving [son]

Wilson

W.C. Lineaweaver ARM3/c
VB-8 U.S.S. Hornet
℅ Fleet Post Master
San Francisco, Calif.

June 25th 1942

Dear Mother:

Have not heard from you lately, but I guess its due to mail mix-up and I hope you received my previous letter.

Enclosed is a money order for $50.00 which I want you to bank for me. Please let me know if you receive it and I'm wondering how much I have in bank by this time. Did [Kuhl] get the $300 I sent a few weeks ago?

I am still kicking and in good health. hope y all of you are the same.

I imagine by this [time] [Jim] in the Army [illegible]

W.C. Lineaweaver ARM3/c
VB-8 U.S.S. Hornet
℅ Fleet Postmaster
San Francisco, Calif.

Mrs. Arlene Lineaweaver
1240 E. Cumberland St.
Avon Penna.

PASSED BY NAVAL CENSOR

W.C. Lineaweaver A.R.M. 3/c
VB-8 USS Hornet
c/o Fleet Post Master
San Francisco, Calif.

June 25th 1942

Dear Mother:

Have not heard from you lately but I guess its due to mail mix up and I hope you received my previous letter.

Enclosed is a money order for $50.00 which I want you to bank for me. Please let me know if you receive it and I'm wondering how much I have in bank by this time? Did Lucille get the $3.00 I sent a few weeks ago?

I am still kicking and in good health hoping all of you are the same.

I imagine by this time Jim's in the Army. If he is send me his address or give him mine so we can write to each other.

Will be expecting to hear from you soon

Your loving son
Wilson

[Postmark is U.S. Navy, June 28, 1942, with a "Passed By Naval Censor" stamp.]
Mrs. Erlene Lineaweaver
1240 E. Cumberland St.
Avon Penna.

[Return Address:]
W.C. Lineaweaver ARM 3/c
VB-8 USS Hornet
c/o Fleet Postmaster
San Francisco, Calif.

USS *Hornet* CV-8; Crewmen of VB-8, July 1942

Front Row (left to right)

ARM2/c Kilmer (KIA at Santa Cruz), ARM2/c Moore, ARM3/c Ferguson, ARM3/c Leach, ARM3/c Brougton, ARM1/c Stuart (lost Aug.1942), **ARM3/c McLean**, ARM3/c Tereskerz, ARM3/c Berthold, **ARM3/c Lineaweaver**, unknown.

Second Row

ENS Grant (KIA at Santa Cruz), ENS Carter, ENS Fisher, ENS Gee, ENS Adams, LCDR Tucker (C.O. - lost Aug 1942), ENS Auman, ENS Wood, ENS Barrett, **ENS King**, unknown.

Back Row

ARM1/c Riley, ENS Friesz, ARM1/c Rider, LT Bates, ARM3/c Quillin, ENS White, ARM1/c Woods, LT Lynch, CPO McCoy, ARM1/c Jackson, ENS Nickerson, ARM1/c Canfield, LT Vose, ENS Cason, ENS Christofferson, ARM2/c Poorman, ARM3/c Wells.

Photo and Identifications from Clayton Fisher via www.johngreaveart.ca/ hornetmen.htm

USS *Hornet* CV-8; Crewmen of VB-8, July 1942

Front Row (left to right)

Ensigns Cason, Grant (KIA at Santa Cruz), Gee, Adams, Barrett, Nickerson, **King** *[Joe W. King, 1917-1963, was Wilson's Pilot]*, Carter, and Fisher.

Back Row

Ensigns Friesz, White, Christofferson, LT Lynch, LCDR Tucker (lost August 1942), LCDR Vose, LT Bates, Ensigns Auman and Woods.

"We lost our C.O. LCDR Tucker and his gunner ARM1/c Stuart on their first flight after leaving Pearl Harbor for the South Pacific in August of 1942. They had a fire in the cockpit and both of them bailed out successfully but we didn't have individual life rafts in the "chute packs" in 1942, so they didn't have a life raft. You had to ditch the SBD which had a two-man life raft stowed behind the rear seat. We searched for them but it was like looking for a needle in a haystack! ENS Grant and his gunner, ARM2/c Kilmer were shot out of formation and killed at Santa Cruz. We had a pilot named Bebas killed practicing dive bombing shortly after Midway. ENS Friesz became a test pilot after the war and was killed test flying aircraft." - Clay Fisher, 2002*

Photo and Identifications from Clayton Fisher via www.johngreaveart.ca/hornetmen.htm

met recently is very nice but I don't think
there is anything serious between us. Save the
pictures for me.

Tell all the _____
and I'll bet they _____
found all that mon__
Glad to hear that _____
school OK. keep it _____
Carole ann, that _____
glad to hear that _____
and I imagine he _____
around, you can't _____
it you said. What _____
the same as before.

All of you _____
and do not worry a_____
to hear from you I _____

W. C. Luneaweaver ARM 3/c
VB-8 U.S.S. Hornet
% Fleet Post Master
San Francisco, Calif

July 8, ____

Dear Mother & Dad:

Writing a few lines to leave you know
that I am still allright and in good health
hoping all of you are the same. I also received
a few of your letters lately and was glad to
hear from you. Since your letters are sent air
mail it doesn't take so long for me to rec__
them, thanks for complying.

I can't understand why the others
won't write me, keep after them.

Enclosed is the new pay bill which was
just passed, perhaps you have seen it in the papers
but I cut it out anyway for you. I have it
marked at my pay and pay grade. Added to
that I get 20% plus 50 % for flight pay which
amounts to 148 ºº which I think is darn good
considering that I'm not in this navy very long,
but wait till that income tax man comes around,
I'll be a sick boy.

Enclosed also are a few pictures we had
taken, hope you like, I don't. I had about six
sticks of chewing gum in my mouth so don't think
I'm chewing tobacco. The girl friend who

W.C. Lineaweaver ARM 3/c
VB-8 USS Hornet
c/o Fleet Post Master
San Francisco, Calif.

July 8, 1942

Dear Mother & Dad:

Writing a few lines to leave you know that I am still allright and in good health hoping all of you are the same. I also received a few of your letters lately and was glad to hear from you. Since your letters are sent air mail it doesn't take so long for me to receive them, thanks for complying.

I can't understand why the others won't write me, keep after them.

Enclosed is the new pay bill which was just passed, perhaps you have seen it in the papers but I cut it out anyway for you. I have it marked at my pay and pay grade. Added to that I get 20% plus 50% for flight pay which amounts to $140.00 which I think is darn good considering that I'm not in this navy very long, but wait till that income tax man comes around, I'll be a sick boy.

Enclosed also is a few pictures we had taken, hope you like them, I don't. I had about five sticks of chewing gum in my mouth so don't think I'm chewing tobacco. The girl friend who I met recently is very nice but I don't think there is anything serious between us. Save the pictures for me.

Tell all the kids I think of them often and I'll bet they were a happy bunch when they found all that money. Did they have to return it? I'm glad to hear that they all got through this year's school O.K. keep it up. So Daves baby is named Carole Ann, that sure is a pretty name and am glad to hear that they are making out allright and I imagine he misses driving his car around, you can't go very far on three gallons of gas a week. What kind of work does Dad do? the same as before.

All of you take good care of yourselves and do not worry about me. Waiting impatiently to hear from you I remain

Your loving son
Wilson

[No envelope remains with this letter.]

Note: There is no indication on the money order message of the amount Wilson sent home.
The July 25th letter states that $50.00 was sent. This was to be deposited in his bank account at home.

Form 3300C

WESTERN UNION
[...]CK SERVICE | LOW RATES

MONEY ORDER MESSAGE

Money Sent by Telegraph and Cable to all the World

R. B. WHITE
PRESIDENT

NEWCOMB CARLTON
CHAIRMAN OF THE BOARD

J. C. WILLEVER
FIRST VICE-PRESIDENT

LEBANON PENNA   JULY 12TH-42   193

OFFICE   DATE

No. PAF126

To   MRS ERLENE LINEAWEAVER

MR., MRS. OR MISS

1240 EAST CUMBERLAND ST

ADDRESS

TRANSIT TIME OF THIS
MONEY ORDER
MINUTES

The Money Order paid you herewith is from _____ WILSON LINEAWEAVER

NAME

at   HONOLULU   and included the following message:

PLACE

DEAR MOTHER AM ALRIGHT HOPE YOU ARE THE SAME YOUR LOVING SON

THE WESTERN UNION TELEGRAPH COMPANY

WESTERN UNION
MONEY ORDER

No. PAF126

To   MRS ERLENE LINEAWEAVER

MR., MRS. OR MISS

1240 EAST CUMBERLAND ST

July 25, 1942

Dear Mother & Dad:

Just a few lines to leave you know that I am still allright and in good health hoping all of you are the same.

Have not received any letters from you recently and am wondering what is wrong. I also have not received Lucille's letter which you said she sent.

I also sent another fifty dollars the other week hoping you received it and please let me know. Hope Dads work is still good and I'm still waiting for a letter from him.

It sure was a surprise hearing that Jim plans to get married. I don't think I know the girl but I wish him all the luck in the world and hope he doesn't get drafted. Is he still working?

Waiting to hear from you I remain

Your loving son
Wilson

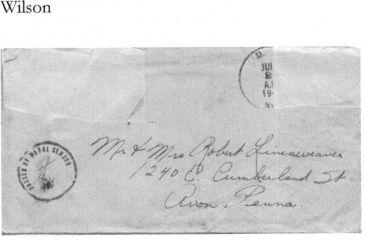

[Postmark is partially missing, with a "Passed By Naval Censor" stamp.]

Mr & Mrs Robert Lineaweaver
1240 E. Cumberland St
Avon Penna.

[No return address remains on the envelope.]

James Luther Lineaweaver and
Elizabeth Jane (Betty) Hartman
were married on August, 1, 1942 at Lebanon, Pa.

⚓ AUGUST 1, 1942 ⚓

Wilson's
Pay Card

ComCarPac—7-26-42—2M.

CARRIERS, PACIFIC FLEET

8/1 /42   -rles

LINEAWEAVER, Wilson Cha-

258 32 24 Pay No. C- 339

ARM3c   78.00
Avia. 46.80
Sea & FSD 15.60
MAQ (W) at 1.15 . .
Allotments:
Erline Lineaweaver 20.

Money Drawn During Quarter	
Date	Amount
8/15/42	37 00/XX
10/1/42	119 00/XX
11/13/42	120 X

Aug 6, 1942

Dear Mother & Dad:

This afternoon I received your letter dated July 30, and was sure glad to hear from you. As yet I haven't received the letter you said Lucille sent or from the rest.

I guess by this time Jim is married and I wish him luck not excluding his wife. I don't recall ever meeting her or having heard of her. Is she nice?

About the money you asked about, you know darn well its O.K. with me. Take as much as you need, get the best and don't worry about paying it back. The other day I sent fifty more by cable-gram, write and leave me know if you receive it O.K.

Tell the kids I think of them often ? and tell that old man of mine to take one night off, stay away from the fire hall and write me a long letter. You also asked if I'm getting heavier, Well! I weigh about 150 lbs, I don't think there is much change although I may be a little heavier.

Your loving son
Wilson C Lineaweaver
VB-8 USS Hornet, c/o Fleet Postmaster, San Francisco, Calif.

[A note written at the bottom says "Received 24 of aug"]

[Postmark is U.S. Navy, Aug 7, 1942, with a "Passed By Naval Censor" stamp.]
Mr & Mrs. Robert Lineaweaver
1240 E. Cumberland St.
Avon Penna.

[No return address remains on the envelope]

This is a two-sided program for a Community Victory Club event at the Pleasant Hill neighborhood of Lebanon, PA. The back side lists the men from the community in the service. Actual size is 5 ½" x 8 ½".

BUY DEFENSE BONDS

COMMUNITY VICTORY CLUB
PLEASANT HILL

SATURDAY EVENING, AUGUST 8, 1942

ST. JOHN'S U. B. CHURCH

...— v ...—

PROGRAM

W. W. "Tiny" Parry, Master of Ceremonies

SINGING---America

My Country! 'tis of thee,
Sweet land of liberty,
Of thee I sing;
Land where my fathers died,
Land of the pilgrim's pride!
From every mountain side,
Let freedom ring.

Our father's God, to thee,
Author of liberty,
To thee we sing;
Long may our land be bright
With freedom's holy light;
Protect us by thy might,
Great God, our King.

INVOCATION - - - Rev. J. E. Keene, Pastor St. John's U. B. Church

VOCAL SOLO - - - - - - - - Cyril Hetrick

SPEAKER - - - J. M. Hall, Post Chaplain of Indiantown Gap

SINGING---God Bless America

God bless America, land that I love,
Stand beside her and guide her
Through the night, with the light from above
¶From the mountain, to the prairie,
To the ocean white with foam,
God bless America, my home, sweet home.
(¶ Repeat)

MUSIC - - - - - Veterans of Foreign Wars Drum Corps

SINGING---The Star Spangled Banner

Oh, say can you see by the dawn's early light,
What so proudly we hailed at the twilight's last gleaming?
Whose broad stripes and bright stars thro' the perilous fight
O'er the ramparts we watched were so gallantly streaming,
While the rocket's red glare, the bombs bursting in air,
Gave proof thro' the night that our flag was still there.
Oh, say, does that Star Spangled Banner yet wave
O'er the land of the free and the home of the brave.

BUY DEFENSE BONDS

(OVER)

BUY DEFENSE BONDS

Baylor, Walter L. J., Maj.	McGee, Warren, Pvt.
Brener, Victor P., Corp.	Mumford, Robt. E., Pvt.
Boltz, Geo. W., Pvt.	Parkes, Sterling, Pvt.
Boyer, Raymond, Pvt.	Putt, Clayton, Corp.
Bombgardner, Floyd D., Corp.	Rank, Harry, Corp.
Clements, Lester C., Pvt.	Ream, Joseph, Pvt.
Cox, Wm., Pvt. 1st Class	Shaak, Warren S. S., Pvt.
Ditt, Arthur, 1st Lt.	Schaeffer, Elam, Pvt. 1st Class
Ditzler, Russel, Pvt.	Sheffy, Richard, Corp.
Elliott, Richard	Sheffy, Warren, Pvt. 1st Class
Funk, Harold, Corp.	Sholly, Richard, Pvt.
Gettle, James, 2nd Class Seaman	Simmers, Richard, Staff Sgt.
Gloss, Kenneth, Pvt.	Smith, David, Pvt.
Heagy, Chester, Pvt.	Smith, Elmer, Corp.
Klepper, John H. Jr., Pvt. 1st Class	Spangler, Donald, Corp.
Kreiser, Ray K., Pvt.	Spitler, Aloysius, Pvt.
Kreiser, Wm. E., Pvt.	Stoudt, Eden, Pvt.
Kulovich, Adam, Pvt.	Stoudt, Elmer, Pvt.
Lane, Eden R., Pvt.	Swalm, John, Pvt.
Lineweaver, Wilson, 3rd Class Pt. Off.	Thiel, John, Corp.
McElwee, Chas., Pvt. 1st Class	Trinic, Michel J., Sgt.
McElwee, Warren R., Sgt.	Vucetic, Geo., Sgt.
McElwee, Quenton L., Pvt.	Walters, Cheston, Pvt.,
McGee, Harry, Pvt.	Young, Chas. R., Sgt.
McGee, Nestor M., Pvt.	Young, Wm., Pvt.

Yountz, Allie

BUY DEFENSE BONDS

Note: There is no indication on the money order message of the amount Wilson sent home.

Form 3300C

WESTERN UNION

QUICK SERVICE   LOW RATES

MONEY ORDER MESSAGE

Money Sent by Telegraph and Cable to all the World

R. B. WHITE
PRESIDENT

NEWCOMB CARLTON
CHAIRMAN OF THE BOARD

J. C. WILLEVER
FIRST VICE-PRESIDENT

LEBANON PENNA   AUGUST 16   19342

OFFICE   DATE

No. PD60

To   MRS ERLINE LINEAWEAVER

MR., MRS. OR MISS

1240 E CUMBERLAND STREET   AVON PENNA

ADDRESS

TRANSIT TIME OF THIS
MONEY ORDER

MINUTES

The Money Order paid you herewith is from   WILSON C LINEAWEAVER

NAME

at   HONOLULU HI   and included the following message:

PLACE

AM ALRIGHT LETTER FOLLOWING WRITE   YOUR LOVING SON

THE WESTERN UNION TELEGRAPH COMPANY

WESTERN UNION
MONEY ORDER

No. PD60

To   MRS ERLINE LINEAWEAVER

MR., MRS. OR MISS

1240 E CUMBERLAND STREET   AVON PENNA

from high school the same time he died

How's Jim and married life. How's he's making out O.K. Tell Fat plus families howdy for me and the kids I think of them often. Poor Fat must have to work hard not being to write but I guess he'll get around one of these years. The last one ___ me was in Jacksonville, over a year ___ If I recall right the kids must ___ go to school the other day, time ___ on. Dot must be going to jr. high ___

Not having written for a long ___ still can't find much to write ab___ censored in what I say so I ___ close ___ wishing all of you h___ and happiness and remain in___

Your loving son
Wilson

excuse the ~~sloppy~~ sloppy writing

Wilson C. Lineaweaver ARM⅓
VB-2 U.S.S. Hornet
℅ Fleet Postmaster
San Francisco, Calif.

Sept. 10, 1942
Rec'vd 28

Dear Mother:

I am sorry that I couldn't write sooner because under certain conditions and being at war the occasions we may seldom but I do write every time its possible, that does not mean I don't think of all of you when unable to write.

Hope you and the rest are in good health and by this time you should have new teeth, hope their O.K. I am still alright and in fair health, have a cold but they can't keep me down or from fighting.

Don't think if I have a chance to come home until we set the rising sun which I'm hoping will be soon.

Met a fellow the other day who has been with me for quite some time and never knew he was from Lebanon. His name is Soliday and lives on Canal St. Have you ever heard of him? We have some good times chatting about home and some of the things we use to do. He knows Pat pretty well, graduati'd

Rec'vd 28

SEP
10
A.M.
1942
NAVY

Mr. & Mrs. Robert Lineaweaver
1240 E. Cumberland St
Avon, Penna.

PASSED BY
NAVAL CENSOR

Wilson C. Lineaweaver ARM 3/c
VB-8 USS Hornet
c/o Fleet Postmaster
San Francisco, Calif.

Sept. 10, 1942 *[A note written here says "Received 28"]*

Dear Mother:

I am sorry that I couldn't write sooner because under certain conditions and being at war the occasions are very seldom but I do write every time its possible, that doesn't mean I don't think of all of you when unable to write.

Hope you and the rest are in good health and by this time you should have new teeth, hope their O.K. I am still alright and in fair health, have a cold but that can't keep me down or from fighting.

Don't think I'll have a chance to come home until we set the rising sun which I'm hoping will be soon.

Met a fellow the other day who has been with me for quite some time and never knew he was from Lebanon. His name is Soliday and lives on Canal St. Have you ever heard of him? We have some good times chatting about home and some of the things we use to do. He knows fat pretty well, graduated from high school the same time he did.

Hows Jim and married life? Hope he's making out O.K. Tell Fat & Dave plus families howdy for me and tell the kids I think of them often. Poor Dad must have to work hard not being able to write but I guess he'll get around to it one of these years. The last one he sent me was in Jacksonville, over a year ago. If I recall right the kids must have gone to school the other day, time marches on. Dot must be going to jr. high this year.

Not having written for a long time I still can't find much to write about being censored in what I say so Ill close wishing all of you health and happiness and remaining

Your loving son
Wilson

excuse the sloppy writing

[Postmark, partially missing, is U.S. Navy, Sep 10, 1942, AM, with a "Passed By Naval Censor" stamp.]
Mr. & Mrs. Robert Lineaweaver
1240 E. Cumberland St
Avon, Penna.

[No return address remains on the envelope.]

All Rooms and Compartments Fitted With Flash Clothing, Gas Masks, Life Jackets,
Steel Helmets, Ventilation - Proof Ventilators and Other Inconveniences

THE HORNET'S NEST

Looking Over the Blue Pacific

American Plan

Conveniently Located
Near Jap Extensions

Fite M. Lykell,
Manager

Oct. 1st, 1942

Dear Mother & family.

I received a few of your letters today, also Dad's, Lucille's, Dave's and one from Jim and boy it made me feel good to sit down and read them. Thanks. I don't think I'll have time to answer all of them so I'll write all I have to say in this letter and perhaps I'll write Jim a letter.

This morning I increased my allotment to $50.∞ The first increased check will probably arrive in November. Hope by this time your mouth is all fixed up and as I said before don't worry about repaying me, forget it. I would like to know how much you used as I said before, if anything should happen to me why the money is yours. Tell Lucille I would like to send what she asked for but I'm sorry, it just can't be arranged as yet.

How does Dave feel about the increase in his family, pretty proud. I'll bet Rodney is big and I'll bet Dot, Nat & Harold are getting big. I don't think I'll know them when I get back.

Is Dad & Lucille still working at the same place? Why can't Dad get something better and you should have a better home to live in. If Dad still thinks about farming have him look around for a small farm that's selling at a good price. I'm seriously thinking about investing my money in a farm and have him run it for me (Think it over pop).

How is every body making out on the rations "Mom", do you have enough, such as sugar etc. I know its pretty tough on Dave, only three gallons of gas a week.

Music furnished continuously by Hornet Air Group and Anti-Aircraft Batteries
Modern toilet facilities suspended without notice

RATES: Sea. 2c. to Admiral

And Mother don't bo[...]
not that I wouldn't ca[...]
it finally gets to me t[...]

So Nat is a little
scared of the water, tell[...]
he'll have to get over bei[...]
of water in the navy.

In closing I wis[...]
good health and think[...]
home. Write often

See close-up of printed letterhead on page following transcription of this letter.

[Postmark is dated Oct. 6, 1942, but is too light for legibility, with "Passed by Naval Censor" stamp.]

Mrs & Mrs Robert Lineaweaver
1240 E. Cumberland St.
Avon, Penna.

[No Return Address; Received in Lebanon, PA, Oct. 21.]

1942

Mrs & Mrs Robert Lineaweaver
1240 E. Cumberland St.
Avon, Penna.

Received Oct 21st

Oct.1st, 1942

Dear Mother & Family.

I received a few of your letters today, also Dad's, Lucille's Daves and one from Jim and boy it made me feel good to sit down and read them. Thanks. I don't think I'll have time to answer all of them so I'll write all I have to say in this letter and perhaps I'll write Jim a letter.

This morning I increased my allottment to $50.00. The first increased check will probably arrive in November. Hope by this time your mouth is all fixed up and as I said before don't worry about repaying me, forget it. I would like would like to know how much you used and as I said before, if anything should happen to me why the money is yours. Tell Lucille I would like to send what she asked for but Im sorry, it just can't be arranged as yet.

How does Dave feel about the increase in his family, pretty proud. I'll bet Rodney is big and I'll bet Dot, Nat & Harold are getting big. I don't think I'll know them when I get back.

Is Dad & Lucille still working at the same places? Why can't Dad get something better and you should have a better home to live in. If Dad still thinks about farming have him look around for a small farm thats selling at a good price. Im seriously thinking about investing my money in a farm and have him run it for me (Think it over pop)

How is every body making out on the rations "Mom", do you have enough, such as sugar etc. I know its pretty tough on Dave, only three gallons of gas a week.

And mother don't bother to send me any packages, its not not that I wouldn't care for them but it takes so long till it finally gets to me that the things would spoil.

So Nat is a little water dog but whats wrong with Harold, scared of the water, tell him if he expects to be a sailor some day he'll have to get over being scared, because you do see quite a bit of water in the navy.

In closing I want you to know that I'm still in good health and I think of you often. Hope some day to come home. Write often

Your loving son
Wilson

All Rooms and Compartments Fitted With Flash Clothing, Gas Masks, Life Jackets,
Steel Helmets, Ventilation - Proof Ventilators and Other Inconveniences

THE HORNET'S NEST

Looking Over the Blue Pacific

Conveniently Located
Near Jap Extensions

American Plan

Fite M. Lykell,
Manager

Dear Mother & Family,

do you have enough, such as sugar etc. I know its pretty tough on Dave, only three gallons of gas a week.

Music furnished continuously by Hornet Air Group and Anti-Aircraft Batteries
Modern toilet facilities suspended without notice

RATES: Sea. 2c. to Admiral

[Actual size of letter is 8" x 10 3/8". Complete letter is on previous page.]

This is from a photocopy of a letter from Wilson to his brother Jim. Location of the original letter and envelope is unknown.

Oct. 1st 1942

Dear Jim: & Wife

It was quite a surprise hearing from you, but being married is the biggest and making 75 cents an hour at the Textile is another but after all thats all this world is and I do mean it.

Well! I wish you lots of luck in your war (I guess you can call it that) and I sure will need it in mine. I don't think I know your wife, if you want to send a couple pictures. Tell Fat & Martha that I'm sorry not writing them but hope to get around to it soon.

Shortstop and batting .500 (Hot stuff) I guess McKiney is still working at the Textile. Is he playing ball too?

Mother said in her last letter that you lost a lot of weight lately, I guess that can be expected when you get married, you know, worries and all that. I sure would like the chance to come back there and loose a little weight too.

Excuse the writing, I have to conserve space and the stationary is the best I could bum. I didnt like that crack about admiral and girls, there just isn't any, I mean girls.

Take it easy Jim and tell the Mrs. I'd like to have the chance of meeting her. Write if you can find time. Tell the rest that I'm still O.K.

Your brother
Charles

[This is a program for a Service Flag Dedication at the Pleasant Hill neighborhood of Lebanon, PA.]

BUY WAR BONDS AND STAMPS

NEVERSINK FIRE COMPANY No. 1, PLEASANT HILL

DEDICATION OF SERVICE FLAG
Sunday, October 11th, 1942 at 2:30 p. m.

PROGRAM

SINGING—"America"   CHORISTER, MR. WAYNE MILLER

1st Stanza	Last Stanza
My Country! 'tis of thee,	Our father's God, to thee,
Sweet land of liberty,	Author of liberty,
Of thee I sing;	To thee we sing;
Land where my fathers died,	Long may our land be bright
Land of the pilgrim's pride!	With freedom's holy light;
From every mountain side,	Protect us by thy might,
Let freedom ring.	Great God, our King.

INVOCATION   MR. J. A. BIEVER

MUSIC   AMERICAN LEGION DRUM & BUGLE CORPS, WM. H. BOLLMAN POST No. 158

SPEAKER   REV. J. E. KEENE
Pastor St. John's U. B. Church

SINGING—"God Bless America"

God bless America, land that I love,
Stand beside her and guide her
Through the night, with the light from above
¶From the mountain, to the prairie,
To the ocean white with foam,
God bless America, my home, sweet home.
(¶ Repeat)

MUSIC   AMERICAN LEGION DRUM & BUGLE CORPS, WM. H. BOLLMAN POST No. 158

ROLL CALL OF MEMBERS IN THE ARMED FORCES OF THE UNITED STATES

Rank	Name	Present Location
Lt. Col.	WALTER L. J. BAYLER	Solomon Islands
Corp.	VICTOR P. BIEVER	England
Pvt.	GEORGE W. BOLTZ	unknown
Pvt.	CLYDE BOLTZ	Fort Eustis, Va.
Pvt.	RAYMOND A. BOYER	Fort Bliss, Texas
Pvt.	LESTER C. CLEMENTS	Pacific Area
Pvt.	STERLING A. CLEMENTS	Fort Belvoir, Va.
Corp.	RUSSELL DEITZLER	Camp Livingston, La.
Pvt.	MARK E. DENGLER	England
Pvt.	HARRISON A. DOUGHTY	New Cumberland, Pa.
Pvt.	CLIFFORD FOX	Washington State
Pvt.	EARNEST N. FOX	England
Corp.	HAROLD FUNK	Alaska
Pvt.	KENNETH A. GLOSS	Morris Field, Charlotte, N.C.
Pvt.	CHESTER B. HEAGY	Indiantown Gap, Pa.
Pvt.	LERRAINE K. HEAGY	Fort Eustis, Va.
Seaman	ANDREW F. KULBY	U.S.N.
Pvt.	ADAM KULOVICH	unknown
Pvt.	ELI KULOVICH	unknwon
Seaman 1st Class	WILSON C. LINEWEAVER	Pacific Coast
Pvt. 1st Class	CHARLES M. McELWEE	Washington, D.C.
Pvt.	QUENTIN McELWEE	Panama
Sgt.	WARREN R. McELWEE	Puerto Rico
Tech. Sgt.	HARRY S. RANK	Camp Livingston, La.
Pvt. 1st Class	ELAM A. SCHAEFFER	Australia
Pvt. 1st Class	WARREN SHEFFY	Camp Shelby, Miss
Pvt.	LLOYD A. SNELL	Fort Belvoir, Va.
Pvt.	GEORGE VUCETIC	Tennessee
Sgt.	CHARLES YOUNG	East Indies
Corp.	ALFRED R. YANTZ	Hawaiian Islands

UNFURLING OF SERVICE FLAG

SINGING—"The Star Spangled Banner"

Oh, say can you see by the dawn's early light,
What so proudly we hailed at the twilight's last gleaming?
Whose broad stripes and bright stars thro' the perilous fight
O'er the ramparts we watched were so gallantly streaming.
While the rocket's red glare, the bombs bursting in air,
Gave proof thro' the night that our flag was still there.
Oh, say, does that Star Spangler Banner yet wave
O'er the land of the free and the home of the brave.

In case of rain, will be held indoors, at the Fire Hall.

Collect Your Scrap to Beat the Jap

The South Pacific Battle of Santa Cruz was fought on October 26, 1942, as part of the Guadalcanal Campaign that stretched from August 1942 to February 1943. John B. Lundstrum includes a detailed account of the Santa Cruz battle in his book *The First Team and the Guadalcanal Campaign*[11]. During the battle, Wilson Lineaweaver was in an SBD piloted by Lieutenant (junior grade) Joe W. King. There were three waves of U.S. air attacks on October 26th in search of the Japanese fleet. Two were launched from the *USS Hornet* and one from the *USS Enterprise*. King and Lineaweaver were part of the second strike from the *Hornet* which included six SBDs from squadron VB-8 and led by Lt. John J. Lynch. Each of these six SBDs were armed with a 1,000 pound bomb.

Between the hours of 0926 and 0931, Lynch's dive bombers attacked the Japanese heavy cruiser *Chikuma*. Two 1,000 lb. bombs hit the ship and demolished the bridge. One bomb was a VS-8 bomb and one bomb was from the VB-8. The VB-8 bomb exploded on the port side of the bridge and knocked out the main battery directors. Lundstrum does not identify which plane from VB-8 dropped this bomb, but in the next pages' *Lebanon Daily News* article of January 30, 1943, Sterling Soliday says Wilson (who was part of VB-8 and the second wave attack) dropped a 1,000 lb. bomb on one of the two Jap carriers sunk in the battle. Actually, no Japanese ships were sunk in the Battle of Santa Cruz, but the carriers *Shōkaku* and *Zuihō* and the heavy cruiser *Chikuma* were badly damaged. If Wilson and his pilot Joe King dropped a bomb that hit a ship, it's likely, but could not be verified, that the bomb would have hit the *Chikuma*. In air battles, it was difficult to determine who shot down which plane, and which bomb hit its target.

On the way back to the *Hornet*, the second strike group, which was by now in several smaller groups, was told to go to the carrier *Enterprise* to land because the *Hornet* was badly damaged and actually later sank. This second group then encountered a strike group from the Japanese *Junyō*. During this air battle, Lundstrum writes: "Teammates Lt. (jg) J. Clark Barrett and Lt. (jg) Joe W. King gave their radiomen, William Berthold, ARM3c, and Wilson C. Lineaweaver, ARM3c, shots at a dive bomber, later declared a kill."[12]

Lundstrum also says that Sam McLean, one of Wilson's best friends and whose letters are included in this book, and Sam's pilot Forrester Auman, were part of the first wave of attackers on October 26th.[13] They are credited with shooting down a Japanese torpedo plane that morning.

Pictures of the crewmen of Squadron VB-8 can be seen at the beginning of Wilson's July 1942 letters.

---

[11] Lundstrom, John B. *The First Team and the Guadalcanal Campaign: Naval Fighter Combat from August to November 1942.* Annapolis, MD: Naval Institute Press, 1994.
[12] Ibid. 144.
[13] Ibid. 429.

Lebanon Sailor Tells Of Sinking Of Hornet

This newspaper article mentions Wilson and appeared in the Lebanon Daily News *on Wednesday, January 30, 1943.*

Petty Officer First Class Sterling Soliday, of the U. S. Navy, was a member of the crew of U. S. S. Hornet, Navy aircraft carrier, sunk in the Solomon Islands area on October 26, 1942. On a recent week-end visit to his parents, Mr. and Mrs. Grant L. Soliday, of 122 Canal Street, this city, the young bluejacket, who was among those who went "over the side" of the giant carrier in the Pacific Ocean, told a graphic story of that particular battle and others in which the Hornet figured. He told the story to a NEWS reporter in an exclusive interview and with questioning also unfolded some of his personal experiences as a U. S. Navy fighting man.

It might be proper to note that Petty Officer Soliday enlisted in the Navy in 1935, shortly after graduating from Lebanon High School in the 1935 class, and entered the service with the idea of making a career of the Navy. He still clings to that intention. On his recent week-eend visit he was accompanied by his wife, the former Florence Boltz, of this city, who is making her home with her husband in New York at present while he is awaiting his next assignment to duty.

The story of the battle which ultimately cost the Hornet, as well as some of the Lebanon bluejackets, will be unfolded in the following article as developed from the recent interview.

Petty Soliday began his narrative in this manner:

"I was below decks when the Hornet moved into the Gaudalcanal area about nine o'clock the morning of October 26, because as an engineer my job is to work with the operating machinery and during battle it was special work to look after the fuel oil. The first Jap bomb struck directly above me but I managed to stay on my feet because I was intent on the job I was doing at the time. Some of the men were tossed around some and then the Japs began dropping aerial torpedoes

STERLING SOLIDAY

that landed fore and aft on the topside, and they did pretty much damage. Fumes and smoke from the exploding bombs then began filtering below decks and the

(Continued on Page Three)

(Continued from Page One)

fumes overcame many of the men. It got in our eyes and lungs and almost choked most of us. We could hear the explosions above us and anti-aircraft guns going, but we were all trapped below because of the damage and could not get out for about two hours.

By that time the men were really suffering from the thick smoke and choking fumes and somebody finally found that we could get out by crawling up a cable trunk. About three hundred of us got up on deck that way, but we were so sick from the smoke and so nearly overcome that we simply laid out on the deck gasping for breath and trying to inhale all the fresh air possible.

We laid there for some time regaining our breath and then watched the actual battle itself as none of us were in much shape to do anything else.

While watching the aerial fighting and the bombs dropping, I saw one big bomb come down and hit the water not more than twelve feet away from the Hornet. Expecting a terrific concussion from the explosion, I set myself to wait, but was surprised to feel only a dull thud and then see muddy water and foam gushing up where the bomb went down.

Shortly after that a torpedo struck somewhere on the deck and the force of that explosion sent me scooting across the deck on my stomach and I was powerless to stop myself. It was a funny feeling to go sliding across there like going over a bowling alley, but I finally managed to come to a stop and move back to watch the action."

At that stage of the story, the young navy man interrupted his narrative to recount what to him was one of the many sights he never expects to forget. During the battle while so many of the men were still feeling the effects of the fumes they inhaled below decks, someone found the ship's ice cream and the word spread quickly. In less time than it takes to tell it, the man dug into the ice cream and went back to the deck to watch the progress of the battle while eating the tasty delicacy with the same composure as most folks would at a summer picnic.

"Here's something not many Lebanon people know and I think you might be interested in it yourself. A Lebanon fellow, Petty Officer 2nd Class Wilson Lineaweaver, was one of our bombardiers on the Hornet and he was the lad who dropped a 1000-pound bomb square on the deck of the one of the two Jap carriers we sank in that battle."

-Sterling Soliday

A remarkable part of that aside is that all the while Jap bombers and torpedo planes were dumping their lethal loads from overhead and many of them were finding their target on the Hornet's deck.

Petty Officer Soliday also noted that he took in the courageous fighting of our own planes battling the Japs over the sea battle and took occasion to comment that our planes were knocking the Japs down all over the place. Asked if many crashed on the Hornet's deck as the earlier stories indicated, he replied that he saw a number of flaming Jap planes crash on the spacious deck of the big carrier.

"Most of them were blazing when they came down, though, but some burst into flames when their gasoline caught fire when they crashed," he said. He then told how the fire-fighting men aboard the Hornet quickly went to work to extinguish the blazing Jap planes before they did too much fire damage to the ship.

"Did you see any of the Jap pilots or bomber crews?" he was asked. "Yes, I did," he replied. "I could see their heads in the planes that flew pretty low, but the ones I saw real close were the best ones. They were dead. They were the pilots of the planes that crashed on our deck, but most of them were so badly burned it was hard to recognize them as people. There were a few, however, not too badly burned that looked fairly young."

Asked if he knew that one story circulated after the battle in which the Hornet was lost told that the pilot of one Jap plane was a woman, he said he'd heard the tale but personally couldn't vouch for it.

Resuming the narrative of the battle, the Lebanon bluejacket told of a lull in the fight about three hours after it started, and during that lull he was one of many members of the crew to go below to try to get the ship's machinery going again.

During that lull, a U. S. destroyer came alongside to remove the most badly wounded, mostly those struck by flying shrapnel from exploding bombs.

He then told that after about two to three hours of desperate efforts to get the big ship's power machinery into working order the Jap planes came again along about four o'clock in the afternoon. When that second bombing squadron came over the Hornet was by that time almost helpless with it's machinery out of commission and the big carrier was merely afloat and drifting. About that same time, the general terse order to abandon the ship went out, and Soliday was among the many crew members who went over the side, leaving their big ship to the mercy of the waves and the Jap bombers.

Even then, however, anti-aircraft gunners were at their stations and the ship's ack-ack bullets were flying thick and fast at the overhead attackers.

He digressed from his general narrative at that juncture to recall a happening that still gives him the shudders but will always stand out in his memory as something, almost unbelievable in the way of human endurance, courage, and complete forgetfulness of pain in the heat of a battle.

He told of seeing a gunner remove a red-hot gun barrel from an anti-aircraft gun with his bare hands, toss the overheated barrel to one side and with badly burned hands replace it in the gun structure with a fresh, cool barrel. Never noticing that his hands were seared almost to the bone, this same Navy gunner promptly resumed firing at enemy planes and was still working his gun when he was killed at his post.

Taking to the water, Petty Officer Soliday told of being dressed only in his customary working clothes at the time, but also took occasion to mention that all of the men removed their shoes before going overboard. He explained that they were told to do so. They, of course, had donned their life packets some time before the "abandon ship" order came.

One little amusing note in connection with leaving his floating home and all his worldly possessions such as extra clothing, money, and other belongings one would acquire after a year aboard the same vessel, was the fact that the Lebanon bluejacket, for some reason or other, had only the key to his parents' home on Canal Street, this city, in his possession at the time. He said he remembered picking it up so he could get in the house if he ever got home at night, and the recollection of the incident brought a hearty laugh from the sailor and the assembled members of his family who sat in on the interview last Sunday afternoon at 122 Canal Street.

When the crew members and officers of the Hornet finally quit the ship many of the men took to large life rafts while many of them remained in the water floating about as they were buoyed up by their life jackets. The Lebanon bluejacket was among those who preferred to remain in the water.

He explained that preferment by revealing that Jap planes repeatedly flew low to strafe men on board the rafts and he thought his chances were better out in the water. He added that some of the men were wounded by machine gun bullets during those raft-strafing sorties by the Japs.

While floating about in the water, repeated bombing from the big Jap planes kept up and the waters around the floating survivors were continually churning and gushing upwards from the explosions. Asked if the concussions bothered them, the local sailor replied that they finally got accustomed to the jarring and thudding, but recalled that for a matter of about three or four weeks thereafter, most of them suffered constant pains in their backs, an aftermath of the constant concussions.

During that stay in the water, a matter of about three hours, Petty Officer Soliday now recalls laughingly seeing the amazing sight of two of his fellow-survivors floating about on their life jackets, one reading a magazine as calmly as if he were sitting in a comfortable chair in a library, and still another deciphering a water-soaked letter from his wife. Both men appeared oblivious to their surroundings and seemed unconscious of the fact that bombs were continually bursting all around them.

Toward dusk of that day, still another Jap bombing expedition came out over the survivors, dropping death-dealing explosives, and, according to the local sailor, they seemed to be making a special effort to concentrate on the Hornet. He smiled with recollection after that remark and added: "They had cause to remember us, too, because the Hornet's planes and anti-aircraft guns gave them plenty to remember."

Following that bombing raid, a destroyer hove into the area to pick up the survivors from the rafts and those afloat on life jackets and the Lebanon sailor was among those rescued from the sea by that warship.

It was the same destroyer and a sister ship of the same type that was later ordered to remain behind to attend the final sinking of the Hornet. That order came after the Jap fleet fled the scene and the main body of the U. S. Navy force was preparing to return to an appointed rendezvous.

Shells and torpedoes were fired into the Hornet by the destroyers and when the work of sinking the massive carrier was completed, the two warships had still another task to perform. Although darkness hid their moves to some extent, their job was to serve as a decoy to lure any Jap planes away from the main body of the U. S. task force by taking a different route. In that, the destroyers apparently succeeded as about ten o'clock that night the Jap planes (this time believed to be land-based planes) came after the two speedy warships and a running fight began that lasted until about three o'clock the following morning. The warships finally lost the Jap planes about that time in the morning but in luring the attackers from the rest of the force succeeded in their mission.

In spiriting the enemy away, however, the two ships became widely separated from the balance of the force and remained separated for several days before returning to the appointed rendezvous. It was then that the Lebanonian and his mates attended a two-hour mass funeral for those who gave up their lives in the bloody battles recently won.

Because of the crowded condition of the rescue ships, many of the men, wounded and shocked, were removed and placed aboard the heavy cruiser Northampton, a ship that was to meet it's fate not too long thereafter.

The Northampton, however, took the Hornet survivors to a prepared rest camp before putting back out to sea to get into the action at Guadalcanal on November 13-15 when both the Juneau and Northampton were lost.

After some time in the island rest camp somewhere in the South Pacific, survivors of the Hornet and other ships were brought back to California, landing in the "States" on November 18. Petty Officer Soliday was in that group and at that time he was granted a 38-day rest furlough and arrived in Lebanon on November 26 to spend the time with his parents. At that time, however, the Lebanon bluejacket was non-committal as to his experiences and never breathed a word about the loss of the Hornet or the battles in which he was engaged. Since then, however, the Navy Department has officially announced the results of those various engagements, and he consented to talk to a NEWS reporter.

Coming to the close of an interesting narrative, told in a straight forward manner without any attempt to dramatize his experiences, and with certainly no effort to create an impression upon his listeners, the local naval hero, suddenly recalled something of importance to him.

He sat up quickly, as though the thought struck him like a bolt and said:

"Here's something not many Lebanon people know and I think you might be interested in it yourself. A Lebanon fellow, Petty Officer 2nd Class Wilson Lineaweaver, was one of our bombardiers on the Hornet and he was the lad who dropped a 1000-pound bomb square on the deck of the one of the two Jap carriers we sank in that battle. Maybe Lebanon people would like to know that."

Lineaweaver and Soliday saw plenty of each other in their life aboard the Hornet as they were members of the crew which put the big carrier into commission on October 20, 1941, and served with the ship through its creditable career of one year and six days.

At the close of the interview, the Lebanon seaman was asked if the morale of the men was high and what their reactions were after coming out of battle. He answered that after a time there is a decided reaction of nervousness mostly, but that the spirit of the men is great and all of them are anxious to get into the scraps. He added that all of them naturally expressed regret at losing their ship as they all become attached to their big warships of the fleet after serving on them a year or more, but noted, rather proudly, that while the Hornet was lost, but "she paid for herself, alright."

Quizzed as to that latter statement he then revealed that he was in action aplenty since the Hornet first steamed down into the Pacific war zone last August and with few lulls had been in and around the action almost continually since then. It was during that recollection that he spoke proudly of the Hornet plane crews and boasted of their heroic conquests and achievements. He then noted that none of the planes were on board when the ship went down as all of them were in the air fighting when the bombs were landing on the decks. They refuelled on another carrier, he remembered, as the Japs seemed to concentrate plenty on the Hornet.

Recalling some of the action he saw, the young bluejacket then said, rather sadly: "I saw four of our carriers go down now. We were in the Coral Sea when the Lexington went down and at Midway when the Yorktown got it. We were in it when the Wasp went down in the Solomons, and then, of course, my own ship got it at Guadalcanal." Adding: "A fellow loses a lot of close friends and pals in something like this and you hate to leave your own ship, but in cases like those there's nothing you can do about it."

In commenting upon some of his observances, he mentioned that the Jap Zeros don't seem to be able to take any punishment at all and frequently burst into flames or seem to come apart in the air. On the other hand, he recalled seeing many U. S. planes return full of bullet holes but flying like new ships.

Before readying himself to return to his present base, the young sailor admitted that he was getting ready to report to a new ship soon but was not willing to mention anything more about it. He also added, that in addition to the action in the Coral Sea, Midway, the Solomons and Guadalcanal, he might sometime be permitted to reveal one other big adventure by the Hornet but until it is announced, (possibly after the war), that big escapade in the creditable career of the big carrier is a closed book to all save those who were on it and those whose business it is to know.

"...one other big adventure..." Sterling Soliday's reference to a big adventure in the last paragraph of the above article, may be referring to the famous Doolittle Raid. See "The Doolittle Raid" in the anecdotes chapter.

[This is a citation signed by Frank Knox that Wilson received for his part in the Battle of Santa Cruz. The newspaper account, published before the family received this citation, states his citation was signed by Admiral F. W. Halsey. Also see his letters dated January 31, 1943, February 3, 1943, February 5, 1943, and November 10, 1943.]

THE SECRETARY OF THE NAVY

WASHINGTON

The President of the United States takes pleasure in presenting the AIR MEDAL to

WILSON C. LINEAWEAVER, AVIATION RADIOMAN FIRST CLASS
UNITED STATES NAVY

for service as set forth in the following

CITATION:

"For meritorious achievement while participating in aerial flight as radioman and rear seat gunner in a scout bomber of the U.S.S. HORNET Air Group during action against enemy Japanese forces near Santa Cruz Islands, October 26, 1942. Coolly and effectively performing his task in the face of strong enemy fighter opposition and extremely heavy anti-aircraft fire, LINEAWEAVER, by his skill and gallant devotion to duty, contributed in a large measure to the success of the attack by our forces on the enemy. His courageous conduct throughout the engagement reflects great credit upon the United States Naval Service."

For the President,

Frank Knox

Secretary of the Navy.

[Envelope Wilson used to send the citation home. Postmark is Alameda, Calif., March 28, 1943, 10:30 PM.

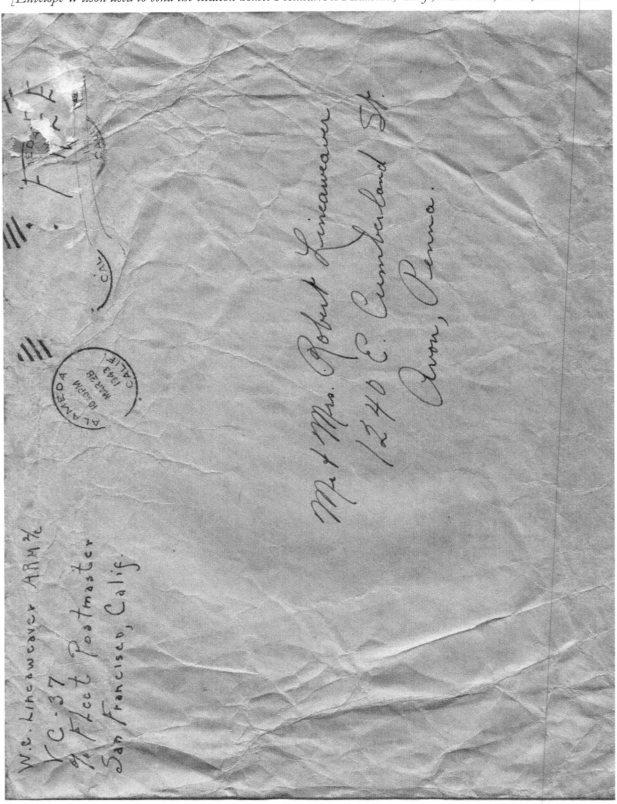

TWELVE NAVY AIRMEN GIVEN MEDALS FOR HEROIC ACTIONS

ALAMEDA, Jan. 30.—Twelve heroes, who fought in the Pacific theaters of war, received decorations and citations today in ceremonies at the U.S. Naval Air Station. The awards were presented by Rear Admiral W. K. Harrill of the Fleet Air Detachment.

One award, the Distinguished Flying Cross, for Lieut. J. E. Breeding of McMinnville, Ore., was made posthumously and was presented to his mother, Mrs. Lelah Breeding, Breeding, who "showed extraordinary heroism and achievement in aerial flight as commander of a patrol plane in action against enemy Japanese forces during the Aleutian Islands campaign, June 1 to 15, 1942, was recently killed in a plane crash off the Oregon coast.

OTHERS HONORED

For the same campaign, during which bullet-ridden patrol planes were used as bombers and "every flight was a flight that the crew should not have returned from," Lieut. (j.g.) J. J. Schmauss, 24, Lake City, Minn., received the Distinguished Flying Cross; W. E. Forland, aviation radioman first class, 24, Seattle, a Citation for Air Medal; and T. T. Tull, aviation radioman second class, 32, Omaha, Wash., Citation for Air Medal.

Lieut. J. J. Lynch, 31, La Jolla, was decorated for two heroic actions. He received the Distinguished Flying Cross for sinking a Jap submarine while piloting a bombing plane during operations in the Solomons on September 6 and was given a citation for Air Medal for a direct hit on a Japanese heavy cruiser during action near Santa Cruz Islands on October 26.

ATTACK UNDER FIRE

For coolly attacking a Jap task force while under fire from enemy aircraft and fighter planes, Lieut. (j.g.) E. R. Hanson, 25, Burlington, Iowa, torpedo plane pilot, and Ensign W. R. Grady, 22, El Paso, Texas, received the Navy Cross.

Distinguished Flying Cross and citation for Air Medal were presented to Lieut. (j.g.) W. C. Presley, 26, of Los Angeles, for separate actions. As pilot of a fighting squadron, he maintained a position over the invasion fleet during the battle of Midway and assured an unopposed approach for dive bombers. During the Solomon Islands campaign, he followed the enemy dive bombers down through anti-aircraft fire from his own ships to press home his attack.

E. E. Robinson, chief boatswain's mate, San Diego, was given a citation for "heroically requesting that he be allowed to return to the U.S.S. Yorktown to assist in her salvage, knowing full well the ship's precarious condition."

AIDED IN ATTACK

G. D. Stokely, aviation radioman first class, 29, Newport, Tenn., as fire control director of a striking force of planes, aided in fighting off prolonged attacks by enemy fighters near Santa Cruz Islands and not only contributed to the destruction of 15 fighters, but to the success of the attack on a large Jap carrier. For this he received the Navy Cross.

During the same battle, as radioman and rear seat gunner of a scout bomber, J. H. Honeycutt, aviation radioman second class, 25, of Thomasville, N.C., aided in the destruction of at least 15 enemy fighters and received the Citation for Air Medal.

Two Citations for Air Medals went to W. H. Berthold, aviation radioman second class, 21, of Detroit, Mich. As radioman and free machine gunner in an airplane of a bombing squadron, he participated in the bombing and strafing attack on fleeing enemy light forces in the face of heavy anti-aircraft fire during the battle of Midway.

As radioman and rear seat gunner of a scout bomber during aerial action near Santa Cruz Islands, Berthold "in the face of strong enemy fighter opposition and extremely heavy anti-aircraft fire, coolly and effectively performed his task."

W. C. Lineaweaver, aviation radioman second class, 23, Lebanon, Pa., was given the Citation for Air Medal for performing his task in the same way during the same battle.

Excellent Results

Was the comment of 675 Westley when they rented their room in the second day of advertising.

Left: Newspaper article that appeared in the *Oakland Tribune*, Oakland, CA, on January 31, 1943, page 10.

Right: Newspaper article that appeared on the front page of the *Lebanon Daily News*, Lebanon, PA, on January 30, 1943.

CITED FOR BRAVERY

WILSON C. LINEAWEAVER

LOCAL SAILOR WINS CITATION FOR BRAVERY

Petty Officer W. S. Lineaweaver Is Decorated Today

Wilson C. Lineaweaver, petty officer 2nd class, U. S. Navy, of Lebanon, Pa., is one of twelve naval officers and enlisted men who received decorations and citations for bravery at the U. S. Naval Air Station at Alameda, California, today. The honors were bestowed on the men who saw action in the Pacific theatres of war, and it is known that the Lebanon native recently returned to the states from the terrific fighting in the Solomon Islands area.

As a matter of record, Petty Officer Sterling Soliday, of Lebanon, who recently graphically described the sinking of the U.S.S. Hornet in the battle of Guadalcanal on on October 26, last, informed a NEWS reporter that Lineaweaver is a bombardier on a Navy bombing plane and was serving aboard the Hornet when the big aircraft carrier went down.

Soliday also revealed the information that Lineaweaver dropped a 100-pound bomb squarely on the deck of one of two Jap carriers that were sunk in that battle.

The Lebanon naval hero is the son of Mr. and Mrs. Robert Lineaweaver, of 1240 East Cumberland Street, and some years ago was active in local tennis circles, participating several times in the NEWS county tennis tournament.

National Archives 80-G-395284

Personnel at the Naval Air Station in Alameda, CA, who received medals and awards on January 30, 1943. Left to Right: J.J. Lynch, W.C. Bresley, J.G. Hanson, J.J. Schmaus, W.R. Grady, E.E. Robinson, G.D. Stokley, W.E. Foreland, J.H. Honeycutt, W.H. Berthold, T.H. Hull, **W.C. Lineaweaver**.

FURTHER DATA ON AIR MEDAL AWARD RECEIVED

Further information on the award given to Wilson C. Lineaweaver, who is a petty officer, second class, in the U. S. Navy, has been received here today.

According to an official dispatch from Alameda, Calif., Lineaweaver, whose home is at 1240 East Cumberland Street, this city, received a citation for the air medal, for "heroism as a rear seat gunner of a scout bomber in air fights against Jap naval forces October 23, near the Santa Cruz Islands."

Above: Newspaper clipping that appeared in the *Lebanon Daily News*, Lebanon, PA, on February 1, 1943, page 8.

Right: Newspaper clipping that appeared in the *Lebanon Daily News*, Lebanon, PA, on February 10, 1943, page 2. *Note: this does not appear to be the citation on the previous page.*

SENDS NAVY CITATION HOME TO HIS PARENTS

Mr. and Mrs. Robert Lineaweaver, of 1240 East Cumberland St., recently received citation which was given their son, Petty Officer Second Class Wilson Lineaweaver on January 30, during impressive rites conducted at the United States Naval Air Station at Alameda, California. The young navyman, was one of twelve men to be honored for their services during action in the South Pacific war zones.

The citation which was signed by W. F. Halsey, Admiral of the United States Navy, reads as follows:

"For distinguished service and meritorious achievement in the line of his profession as radioman and rear seat gunner of a scout bomber during the aerial action against Japanese naval forces on October 26, 1942, near Santa Cruz Islands. Lineaweaver, in the face of strong enemy fighter opposition and extremely heavy anti-aircraft fire, coolly and effectively performed his task, contributing largely to the success of the attack upon the enemy. His courageous conduct was in keeping with the highest traditons of the Naval Service."

Nov 11, 1942

Dear Parents:

    It has been a long time since I have had the opportunity to write you and I hope you receive this letter soon. Not being able to write you during the previous months I want you to know that I have been alright, times have been hectic but I pulled through and right now I'm still alive and in good health hoping your the same at home.

    Will write again soon because I am very busy. Just wanted all of you know that I'm still O.K.

Your loving son
Wilson

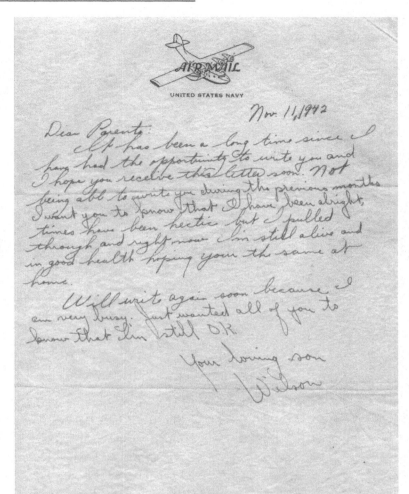

[Postmark is U.S. Navy, Nov. 11, 1942, P.M. with a "Passed By Naval Censor" stamp.]
Mr. & Mrs. Robert Lineaweaver
1240 E. Cumberland St.
Avon, Penna.

[Return Address:]
W.C. Lineaweaver
VB-8 USS Hornet
c/o Fleet Postmaster
San Francisco, Calif.

Serving in Pacific

nov 19 1942

Among the Lebanon County servicemen on duty "somewhere in the Pacific" is Seaman Third Class Wilson C. Lineaweaver, pictured above. He is the son of Mr. and Mrs. Robert Lineaweaver, of 1240 East Cumberland Street, who recently received welcomed news that their son is well and enjoying navy life.

Seaman Lineaweaver graduated from the Lebanon High School in 1937 and following his graduation served for three years as a member of the Civilian Conservation Corps, stationed at Waynesboro, Pennsylvania. In January, 1941, he enlisted in the Navy and was assigned to Norfolk, Virginia, for basic training. He continued his course of study at Jacksonville, Florida, and later returned to Virginia, where he embarked on foreign duty.

Newspaper clipping that appeared in the *Lebanon Daily News*, Lebanon, PA, on November 21, 1942.

Left: Wilson Lineaweaver; Right: Chester "Chet" Behney. The picture above was taken at Avon, PA, when Wilson was on leave in December 1942. The 'new' Route 422 / Avon Bridge is in the background, and he is facing his parent's house at 1240 East Cumberland Street, which is behind the photographer. Chet Behney was a neighbor and in 1946 married Wilson's sister Lucille.

Returns to Duties

After enjoying a thirty-day furlough greeting relatives and friends, Petty Officer Second Class Wilson Charles Lineaweaver, shown above, left this city on Thursday to resume his duties at Alameda, California.

Petty Officer Lineaweaver is the son of Mr. and Mrs. Robert Lineaweaver, of 1240 East Cumberland Street. He entered the armed forces in January, 1941, training at Norfolk, Virginia and Jacksonville, Florida. Prior to his visit home, he was engaged on active duty "somewhere" in the Solomons. He graduated from the Lebanon High School in 1937 and served with the C.C.C. camp in Waynesboro.

Newspaper clipping that appeared in a Lebanon, PA, newspaper on Jan. 2, 1943.

Jan 4th 1943 [*January 4th was a Monday*]

Dear Mother:

    Arrived in Oakland Monday morning O.K.. Was sick so I slept most of the way across and boy was that monotonous.

    Sorry I had to leave the depot when you arrived, wish I could have spent more time with you.

    This letter is to let you know that I got back O.K. and as soon as I get stationed & settled down I'll write

Your loving son
Wilson

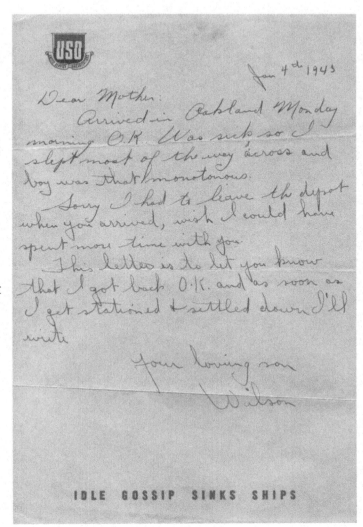

IDLE GOSSIP SINKS SHIPS

[*Postmark is U.S. Navy, Jan. 4, 1943, 2:30 PM*]
Mr & Mrs. Robert Lineaweaver
1240 E. Cumberland St.
Avon, Penna.

[*Return Address:*]
W. C. Lineaweaver ARM 2/c
U.S.N.

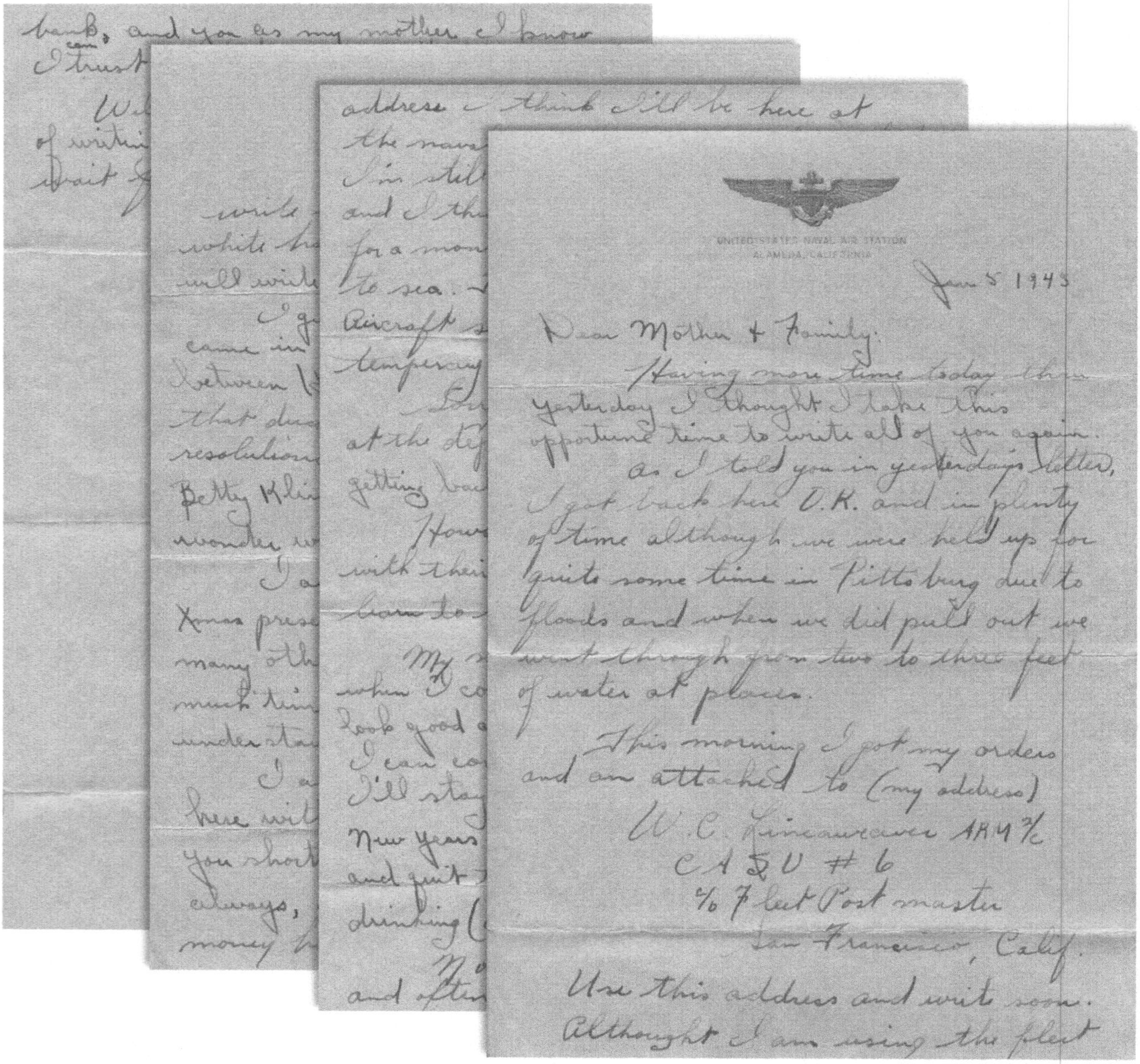

UNITED STATES NAVAL AIR STATION
ALAMEDA, CALIFORNIA

Jan 5 1943

Dear Mother & Family:

Having more time today than yesterday I thought I take this opportune time to write all of you again.

As I told you in yesterday's letter, I got back here O.K. and in plenty of time although we were held up for quite some time in Pittsburg due to floods and when we did pull out we went through from two to three feet of water at places.

This morning I got my orders and am attached to (my address)

W.C. Lineaweaver ARM 2/c
CASU #6
% Fleet Postmaster
San Francisco, Calif.

Use this address and writ soon. Allthought I am using the fleet

[Postmark is U.S. Navy, Jan. 6, 1943, 2:30 PM]
Mr & Mrs Robert Lineaweaver
1240 E. Cumberland St
Avon, Penna

[Return Address:]
W.C. Lineaweaver ARM 2/c
CASU #6
c/o Fleet Postmaster
San Francisco, Calif

Jan 5, 1943

Dear Mother & Family:

Having more time today than yesterday I thought I take this opportune time to write all of you again.

As I told you in yesterday's letter, I got back here O.K. and in plenty of time although we were held up for quite some time in Pittsburg due to floods and when we did pull out we went through from two to three feet of water at places.

This morning I got my orders and am attached to (my address)

W.C. Lineaweaver ARM 2/c, CASU #6

c/o Fleet Postmaster, San Francisco, Calif.

Use this address and write soon. Althought I am using the fleet address I think I'll be here at the naval air station for awhile, but I'm still attached to Carriers Pacific and I think they will keep me here for a month or two before sending me to sea. The C.A.S.U. means "Carrier Aircraft service unit, This is only temperary.

Sorry I couldn't spend more time at the depot but I was worried about getting back on time.

Hows the two kids making out with their erector set? I hope they learn to like it and get interested in it.

My mom! you sure surprised me when I come home because you sure look good and I hope in the near future I can come home again and this time I'll stay at home more. One of my New Years resolutions was to settle down and quit this wild running around and drinking (I mean it)

Now don't forget to write me and often, send fats address, so I write them. Did you give Billy his white hat? I have Daves address and will write him soon, tell them to write.

I guess you know the new year came in with me asleep on the train between Harrisburg & Pittsburg (wasn't that ducky) so I made all of my resolutions when I woke. I had promised Betty Kline to come down to Reading, I wonder what she thinks.

I am sorry I didn't buy more Xmas presents like for Fat & family an many others but I just couldn't find much time to shop, so I'm sure they understand.

I also have my bank book out here with me and will send it to you shortly and we will continue as always, I will continue to send money home as always for you to bank, and you as my mother I know I can trust to take care of it for me.

Well! I'm sorta running out of writing material so I'll close and wait for your answer

Your loving son
Wilson

Jan 6th 1943

Dear Mother:

Enclosed is my bank book and following will be some money to bank for me also that allottment

And mother, you and pop and the kids take care of yourself, I may be home soon

Your loving son
Wilson

Would of wrote more but Im busy working (and I do mean working) Please write Tell pop to write & the kids this also includes Dot & Lucille. Send Fats & Jims address. I have Daves and already wrote him

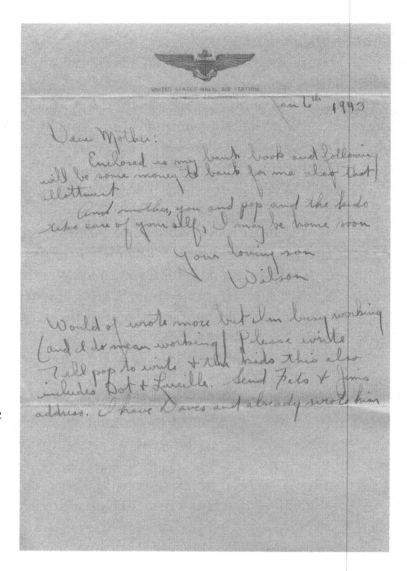

[Postmark is U.S. Navy, Jan. 6, 1943, ?:30 PM]
Mrs ErleneLineaweaver
1240 E Cumberland St.
Avon, Penna.

[No return address remains on the envelope.]

Jan 6th 1943

Dear Mother:

Enclosed is a hundred dollar money order which I want you to put in bank for me. This morning I sent you my bank book which may arrive later than this letter which I'm sending airmail so hold on to this until the bank book arrives, then put it in bank.

You will still get my allotment check.

Take care of my money for me and if anything arises you may have to send me some

I remain as ever
Your loving son
Wilson

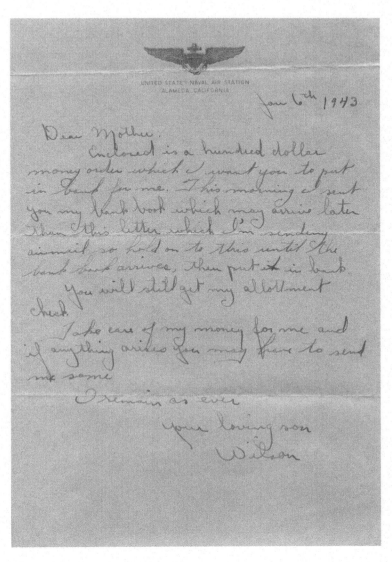

[Postmark is U.S. Navy, Jan. 8, 1943, 4:30 PM]
Mrs. Erlene Lineaweaver
1240 E. Cumberland St.
Avon, Penna.

[Return Address:]
W.C. Lineaweaver A.R.M. 2/c
CASU #6
c/o Fleet Postmaster
San Francisco, Calif.

a lot. Liberty is swell with all of these
cities around the bay to go to, but as
yet I have it gotten around and
I don't think I will. I'm g[...]
a good boy and stay home, [...]
one of my new years resolution[...]

Tell Jake if he doesn't [...]
on his schooling, why the nex[...]
I come home I'll have to t[...]
ers. I think he can do be[...]
tried and forgot all that non[...]
and Dot you finish school y[...]
and make the best of it.

Now don't forget to wri[...]
until I hear from you I rema[...]
            your brother
                Wilson

UNITED STATES NAVAL AIR STATION
ALAMEDA, CALIFORNIA

Jan. 6th, 1943

Dear Sis:
    This evening just before bed time
I have a few moments so I've decided
to write you a few lines

    Sorry I didn't have more time
to say good bye to you, Mom & the rest
and besides I was pretty sick. I
guess you think I'm a dickens of a brother.

    Hope you liked your xmas present
and be a good girl, help Mom & pop but
whenever you can. Think twice and
you'll find that their both swell.

    Drop me a few lines every now
and then with some news from the
old town.

    This is a very nice air station
here at Alameda just across the bay
from San Francisco with the large
Oakland bridge spanning the bay.
Out further is the massive Golden
Gate bridge and before it is Alcatraz
island which you have heard about

W.C. Lineaweaver ARM 3/c
CASU #6
℅ Fleet Postmaster
San Francisco, Calif.

Free

U.S.
JAN 18
4 30 PM
1943
NAVY

Miss Dorthy Lineaweaver
1240 E. Cumberland St.
Avon, Penna

Jan. 6th, 1943

Dear Sis:

This evening just before bed time I have a few moments so I've decided to write you a few lines

Sorry I didn't have more time to say good bye to you, Mom & the rest and besides I was pretty sick. I guess you think I'm a dickens of a brother.

Hope you liked your Xmas present and be a good girl, help Mom & pop out whenever you can. Think twice and you'll find that their both swell.

Drop me a few lines every now and then with some news from the old town.

This is a very nice Air Station here at Alameda just across the bay from San Francisco with the large Oakland bridge spanning the bay. Out further is the massive Golden Gate bridge and before it is Alcatraz island which you have heard about a lot. Liberty is swell with all of these cities around the bay to go to, but as yet I haven't gotten around and in fact I don't think I will. I'm going to be a good boy and stay home, which was one of my new years resolutions.

Tell Jake if he doesn't brush up on his schooling, why the next time I come home I'll have to box his ears. I think he can do better if he tried and forgot all that nonsense and Dot, you finish school yourself and make the best of it.

Now don't forget to write and until I hear from you I remain

Your brother
Wilson

[Postmark is U.S. Navy, Jan. 8, 1943, 4:30 PM]
Miss Dorothy Lineaweaver
1240 E. Cumberland St.
Avon, Penna

[Return Address:]
W.C. Lineaweaver ARM 2/c
CASU #6
c/o Fleet Postmaster
San Francisco, Calif

I had a punch on your last board and
I'm wondering if I won. Did I? or did you
kids win again as usual.

You kids be good boys and [I] [hope]
to see you again sometime. En[closed]
is a half to each, see a movie a[nd have]
a plate of ice cream on me

     Your sailor bro[ther]
     Wilo

While flying today I thoug[ht of you]
two playing with planes and [how you]
would like to fly. Well it isn't [what...]

UNITED STATES NAVAL AIR STATION

          Jan 7th 1943

Dear Brothers:
    Since either one of you keep going
down to the post office a couple of times
a day looking for mail from me, I'm
surprising you.

    Thanks for coming all the way out
to the station to see me off. I guess you
was wondering what was wrong with me,
well I was sick, thats why I didn't
say very much. Its fun arriving but its
a tough job to say good bye specially
times like this.

    Why don't you two kids starting
this new year be good boys, be good to
mom, help her out and above all forget
all your baby notions and study hard
in school, don't be lazy because some
day it will help out alot, believe me.

    How are you two kids making out
with your erector set, building anything.
Both of you write me and let me know,
also how your making out in school
and what you do. I'd enjoy hearing.

Nathan & Harold Lineaweaver
1240 C. Cumberland St.
Avon, Penna.

Jan 7th 1943

Dear Brothers:

Since either one of you keep going down to the post office a couple of times a day looking for mail from me, I'm surprising you.

Thanks for coming all the way out to the station to see me off. I guess you was wondering what was wrong with me, well I was sick, thats why I didn't say very much. Its fun arriving but its a tough job to say goodbye specially times like this.

Why don't you two kids starting this new year be good boys, be good to mom, help her out and above all forget all your baby notions and study hard in school, don't be lazy because some day it will help out alot, believe me.

How are you two kids making out with your erector set, building anything. Both of you write me and let me know, also how your making out in school and what you do. Id enjoy hearing.

I had a punch on your last board and Im wondering if I won. Did I? or did you kids win again as usual.

You kids be good boys and I hope to see you again sometime. Enclosed is a half to each, see a movie and have a plate of ice cream on me

Your sailor brother
Wils

While flying today I thought of you two playing with planes and how you would like to fly, Well it isn't fun

-----

[Postmark is U.S. Navy, Jan. 8, 1943, 4:30 PM]
Nathan & Harold Lineaweaver
1240 E. Cumberland St.
Avon, Penna

[No return address remains on the envelope.]

dog gone war is going to last? Soon
I hope, before they have a chance to
send me back out there. Fate has been
kind to me so you and I have to keep
peps it up.
        Until I hear from you I
remain
                your loving son
                        Wilson

UNITED STATES NAVAL AIR STATION
ALAMEDA CALIFORNIA

Jan. 8ᵃ, 1943

Dear Father:
        Just a few lines to let you know
that I am still thinking of you and hope
during this coming year things will be
better for you and the rest. I also hope
you can get out of that sweat shop where
your working and get a better job.
        I had a swell time on Xmas
day and I know you did too. Your
bowling was getting better when I left, so
keep at it and maybe you'll be some
competition the next time I get home.
        Are you going to get your teeth pulled?
I believe it would do you a lot of good
because it sure made Mom look 100%
better and I'll bet she feels a lot better.
        Take care of yourself pop and I
hope soon I can come home to see all
of you
        Don't forget to write me and often.
How long do you think this

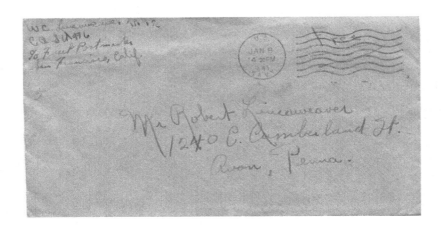

W.C. Lineaweaver ___
CA ____
℅ Fleet Postmaster
San Francisco, Calif.

Mr. Robert Lineaweaver
1240 E. Cumberland St.
Avon, Penna.

Jan. 8th, 1943

Dear Father:

Just a few lines to let you know that I'm still thinking of you and hope during this coming year things will be better for you and the rest. I also hope you can get out of that sweatshop where your working and get a better job.

I had a swell time on Xmas day and I know you did too. Your bowling was getting better when I left, so keep at it and maybe you'll be some competition the next time I get home.

Are you going to get your teeth pulled? I believe it would do you a lot of good because it sure made "mom" looks 100% better and I'll bet she feels a lot better.

Take care of yourself pop and I hope soon I can come home to see all of you.

Don't forget to write me and often.

How long do you think this dog gone war is going to last? Soon I hope, before they have a chance to send me back out there. Fate has been kind to me so far and I hope it keeps up.

Until I hear from you I remain

Your loving son
Wilson

[Postmark is U.S. Navy, Jan. 8, 1943, 4:30 PM]
Mr Robert Lineaweaver
1240 E. Cumberland St.
Avon, Penna.

[Return Address:]
W.C. Lineaweaver ARM 2/c
CASU #6
c/o Fleet Postmaster
San Francisco, Calif.

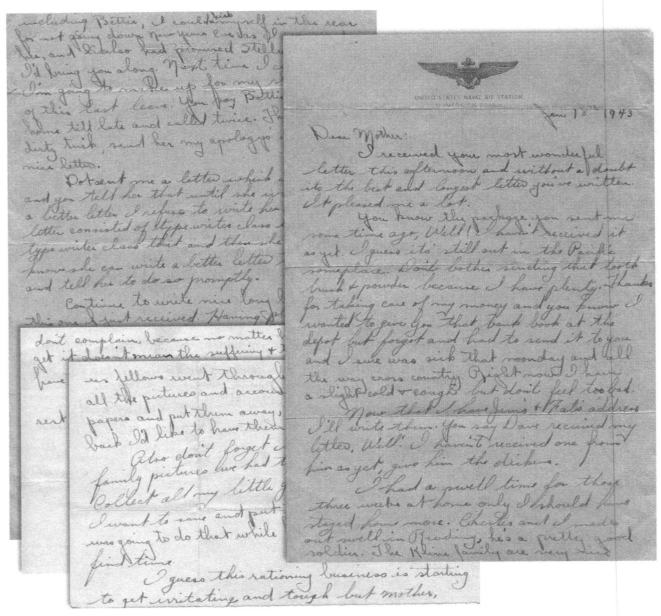

including Bettie, I could smile myself in the rear
for not going down New Years Eve has Jo
like, and Kaiser had promised Stella
I'd bring you along. Next time I am
I'm going to make up for my sid
of this last leave. You say Bettie
home till late and called twice. If
dirty trick, send her my apology's —
nice letter.

Dot sent me a letter which —
and you tell her that until she wr —
a better letter I refuse to write her
letter consisted of type writer class
type writer class that and then she
know she can write a better letter
and tell her to do so promptly.

Continue to write nice long
this one I just received. Having
don't complain, because no matter
get it doesn't mean the suffering +
have us fellows went through
all the pictures and accous
papers and put them away,
back I'd like to have them

Also don't forget a
family pictures we had t
Collect all my little g
I want to save and put
was going to do that while
find time

I guess this rationing business is starting
to get irritating and tough but mother,

UNITED STATES NAVAL AIR STATION
ALAMEDA, CALIFORNIA

Jan 18 1943

Dear Mother:

I received your most wonderful
letter this afternoon and without a doubt
its the best and longest letter you've written.
It pleased me a lot.

You know the package you sent me
some time ago, Well I haven't received it
as yet I guess its still out in the Pacific
someplace. Don't bother sending that tooth
brush & powder because I have plenty. Thanks
for taking care of my money and you know I
wanted to give you that bank book at the
depot but forgot and had to send it to you
and I sure was sick that noonday and all
the way cross country. Right now I have
a slight cold & cough but don't feel too bad.

Now that I have Jim's & Pat's address
I'll write them. You say Dave received my
letter. Well I haven't received one from
him as yet, give him the dickens.

I had a swell time for those
three weeks at home only I should have
stayed home more. Charles and I made
out swell in Reading, he's a pretty good
soldier. The Kline family are very nice

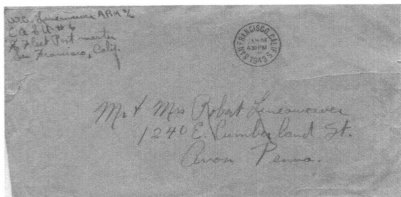

W.C. Lineaweaver ARM 2/c
CASU #6
c/o Fleet Postmaster
San Francisco, Calif.

SAN FRANCISCO CALIF.
JAN 19
4:30 PM
1943

Mr & Mrs Robert Lineaweaver
1240 E. Cumberland St.
Avon Penna.

[Postmark is San Francisco, Calif., Jan. 19, 1943, 4:30 PM]

Mr & Mrs Robert Lineaweaver
1240 E. Cumberland St.
Avon, Penna.

[Return Address:]

W.C. Lineaweaver ARM 2/c
CASU #6
c/o Fleet Postmaster
San Francisco, Calif.

Jan 18th 1943

Dear Mother:

I received your most wonderful letter this afternoon and without a doubt its the best and longest letter you've written. It pleased me a lot.

You know the package you sent me some time ago, Well! I haven't received it as yet. I guess it's still out in the Pacific someplace. Don't bother sending that tooth brush & powder because I have plenty. Thanks for taking care of my money and you know I wanted to give you that bank book at the depot but forgot and had to send it to you and I sure was sick that noonday and all the way cross country. Right now I have a slight cold & cough but don't feel too bad.

Now that I have Jim's & Fat's address I'll write them. You say Dave received my letter, Well! I haven't received one from him as yet, give him the dickens.

I had a swell time for those three weeks at home only I should have stayed home more. Chester and I made out swell in Reading, he's a pretty good soldier. The Kline family are very nice including Bettie, I could kick myself in the rear for not going down New Years Eve as I promised her, and I also had promised Stella that I'd bring you along. Next time I come home I'm going to make up for my shortcomings of this last leave. You say Bettie stayed home till late and called twice. That was a dirty trick, send her my apology's with a nice letter.

Dot sent me a letter which I got today and you tell her that until she writes me a better letter I refuse to write her. Her letter consisted of typewriter class this and typewriter class that and then she close. I know she can write a better letter than that and tell her to do so promptly.

Continue to write nice long letters like this one I just received. Having plenty of spare time and in a writing mood, I'll do the same. Have Jim & Betty and Fat & Mots write also.

Glad to hear that things are going along swell at home and hope Lucille will be up and around soon. Give the kids my regards and tell that armchair politician Pop of mine to write

Well! They finally announced the Hornet including other ships that was with us as sunk. The newspaper stories were pretty straight so you can realize the hell us fellows went through. I hope you cut out all the pictures and accounts that were in the papers and put them away, one day when I come back I'd like to have them.

Also don't forget I want one of the family pictures we had taken when I was home. Collect all of my little gadgets and paper's, things I want to save and put them away together. I was going to do that while home but just couldn't find time.

I guess this rationing business is starting to get irritating and tough but mother, don't complain, because no matter how tough it does get it doesn't near the suffering & type of life we have to go through. Remember that!

I'll be waiting to hear from you & the rest

Your loving son
Wilson

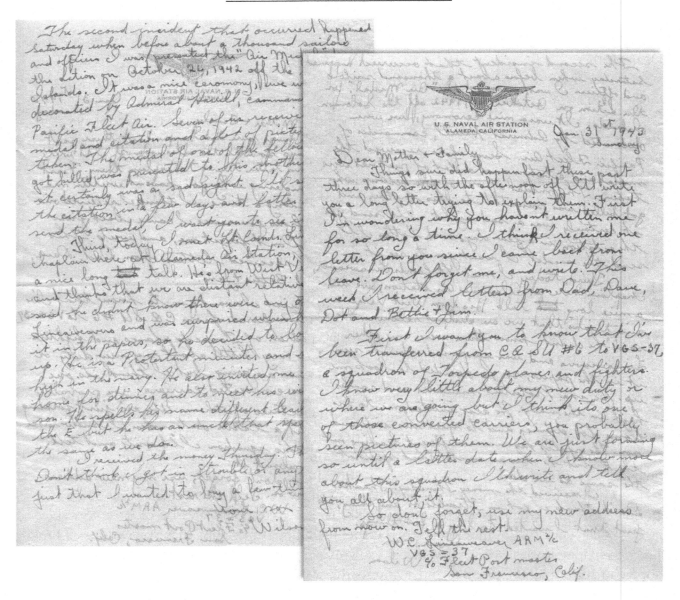

U. S. NAVAL AIR STATION
ALAMEDA CALIFORNIA

Jan 31st 1943
Sunday

Dear Mother & Family

Things sure did happen fast these past three days so with the afternoon off I'll write you a long letter trying to explain them. First I'm wondering why you haven't written me for so long a time. I think I received one letter from you since I came back from leave. Don't forget me, and write. This week I received letters from Dad, Dave, Dot and Bettie & Jim.

First I want you to know that I've been transferred from CASU #6 to VGS-37, a squadron of Torpedo planes and fighters. I know very little about my new duty or where we are going but I think its one of those converted carriers, you probably seen pictures of them. We are just forming so until a latter date when I know more about this squadron I'll write and tell you all about it.

So don't forget, use my new address from now on. Tell the rest.

W.C. Lineaweaver ARM 2/c
VGS-37
% Fleet Post master
San Francisco, Calif.

[Postmark is U.S. Navy, Feb. 2, 1943, 2:30 PM]

Mr & Mrs Robert Lineaweaver
1240 E. Cumberland St.
Avon, Penna.

[Return Address:]
W.C. Lineaweaver ARM 2/c
VGS-37
c/o Fleet Postmaster
San Francisco, Calif

Jan 31ˢᵗ 1943 Sunday

Dear Mother & Family

Things sure did happen fast these past three days so with the afternoon off I'll write you a long letter trying to explain them. First I'm wondering why you haven't written me for so long a time. I think I received one letter from you since I came back from leave. Don't forget me, and write. This week I received letters from Dad, Dave, Dot and Bettie & Jim.

First I want you to know that I've been transferred from CASU #6 to VGS-37, a squadron of Torpedo planes and fighters. I know very little about my new duty or where we are going but I think its one of those converted carriers, you probably seen pictures of them. We are just forming so until a latter date when I know more about this squadron I'll write and tell you all about it.

So don't forget, use my new address from now on. Tell the rest.

W.C. Lineaweaver ARM 2/c
VGS-37
c/o Fleet Postmaster
San Francisco, Calif.

The second incident that occurred happened Saturday when before about a thousand sailors and officers I was presented the "Air Medal", for the action on October 26, 1942 off the Solomon Islands. It was a nice ceromony, we were decorated by Admiral Harrill, cammander of Pacific Fleet Air. Seven of us received the medal and citation and a lot of pictures were taken. The medal of one of the fellows who got killed was presented to his mother and it certainly was a sad sight. I'll send you the citation in a few days and latter I'll send the medal, I want you to see it.

Third, today I met Lt. Comdr. Linaweaver, chaplain here at Alameda Air Station, we had a nice long talk. He's from West Virginia and thinks that we are distant relatives. He said he didn't know there were any other Lineaweavers and was surprised when he seen it in the papers, so he decided to look me up. He is a Protestant minister and ranks high in the navy. He also invited me to his home for dinner and to meet his wife and son. He spells his name different leaving out the E but he has an uncle that spells it the same as we do.

I received the money Thursday. Thanks. Don't think I got in trouble or anything, its just that I wanted to buy a few things.

Your son
Wilson

> *A $50.00 Western Union Money Order was sent to Wilson on January 25, 1943. Charge for the money order was $3.37.*

Jan 31ˢᵗ 1943

Dear Mots & Fat:

Just a few lines to let you know I'm still thinking of you and sorry I didn't write sooner.

I should have seen more of you over my leave but, Well! its one of those things, I had a lot of running around to get out of my system. I'm still smoking the pipe, its swell and there still a little tobacco left. Thanks a million and it was the nicest present I received. Sorry I didn't return the favor.

I know mother brings her letters in to have you read them so there's little that's new I can write about. Enclosed is a copy of the citation that I received if you care to have it. The original I sent to mother.

I know both of you can find some spare moments so why not drop me a few lines every now and then.

Don't forget to use my new address. In this squadron we are going to have torpedoe planes, what a change from dive bombing.

Hoping to hear from you soon I remain

Your brother & brother-in-law
Wilson

[Postmark is San Francisco, Calif., Feb. 5, 1943, 10:30 PM]
Mr & Mrs Mahlon Lineaweaver
239 S. 10ᵗʰ St.
Lebanon Penna.

[Return Address:]
W.C. Lineaweaver ARM 2/c
VGS-37
c/o Fleet Postmaster
San Francisco, Calif.

Feb. 3rd, 1943

Dear Mother:

As I told you in my last letter about receiving the "Air Medal", Well enclosed is the citation. I want you to put it away with the rest of my things and treasure it.

I've told you very little about what we actually did that one day because I didn't care to talk about it or worry you. Now with some spare moments I'll try to enlighten you.

This medal was given to me for the days action in which we got sunk. My former shipmate and fellow Hornet sailor Soliday, also of Lebanon as you know has already described it. Betty sent me the clippings out of the "News". My squadron also was officially credited with shooting down fifteen Enemy Zero fighters alone not counting the other types of planes and also many hits on enemy ships.

I also received a few commendations for other occasions.

You may if you want to, show this citation to friends and relatives or better yet, put it in the paper. That would save a lot of time and trouble.

I'm sitting here trying to write a nice long letter but failed, but hope I put across to you what I wanted to.

Don't forget I'm waiting impatiently to hear from you

Your loving son
Wilson

Will write again soon
Will send the medal latter so you can see it.

[Postmark is U.S. Navy, Feb. 4, 1943, 2:30 PM]
Mr & Mrs Robert Lineaweaver
1240 E. Cumberland St.
Avon, Penna.

[Return Address:]
W.C. Lineaweaver
VGS-37
c/o Fleet Postmaster
San Francisco, Calif

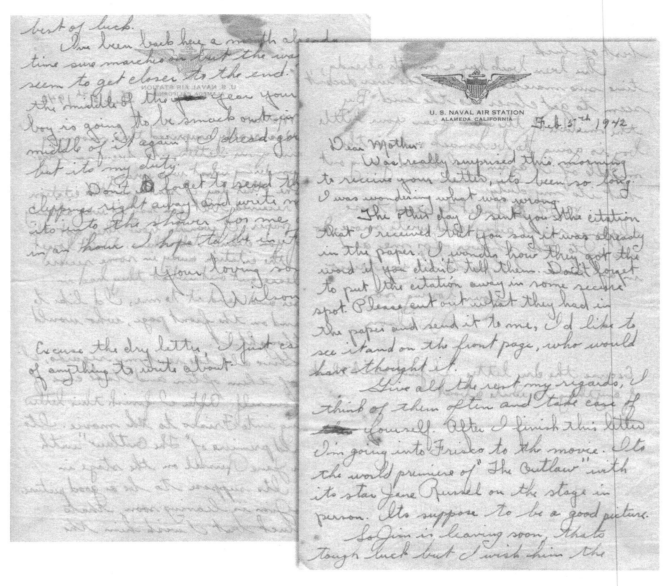

best of luck.

    I've been back here a month already time sure marches on but the war ... seem to get closer to the end. ... the middle of the ... year your boy is going to be smack out in the middle of it again. I dread going but its my duty.

    Don't forget to send the clippings right away and write ... into into the shower for me in an hour. I hope to be ... Your loving son

...

Excuse the dry letter, I just can't ... of anything to write about.

U. S. NAVAL AIR STATION
ALAMEDA, CALIFORNIA   Feb 5th 1942

Dear Mother

    Was really surprised this morning to receive your letter, its been so long I was wondering what was wrong.

    The other day I sent you the citation that I received but you say it was already in the paper. I wonder how they got the word if you didn't tell them. Don't forget to put the citation away in some secure spot. Please cut out what they had in the paper and send it to me, I'd like to see it and on the front page, who would have thought it.

    Give all the rest my regards, I think of them often and take care of yourself. After I finish this letter I'm going into Frisco to the movie. Its the world premiere of "The Outlaw" with its star Jane Russel on the stage in person. Its suppose to be a good picture.

    So Jim is leaving soon, Thats tough luck but I wish him the

W. C. Lineaweaver
VGS-37,
c/o Fleet Post master
San Francisco Calif.

VIA AIR MAIL

SAN FRANCISCO CALIF. FEB 5 1943

Mr & Mrs Robert Lineaweaver
1240 E. Cumberland St.
Avon Penna.

Feb. 5th, 1942 *[1943]*

Dear Mother:

Was really surprised this morning to receive your letter, its been so long. I was wondering what was wrong.

The other day I sent you the citation that I received but you say it was already in the paper. I wonder how they got the word if you didn't tell them. Don't forget to put the citation away in some secure spot. Please cut out what they had in the paper and send it to me, Id like to see it and on the front page, who would have thought it.

Give all the rest my regards, I think of them often and take care of yourself. After I finish this letter I'm going into Frisco to the movie. Its the world premiere of "The Outlaw" with its star Jane Russel on the stage in person. Its suppose to be a good picture.

So Jim is leaving soon, thats tough luck but I wish him the best of luck.

Ive been back here a month already, time sure marches on but the war doesn't seem to get closer to the end. By the middle of the year your little boy is going to be smack out in the middle of it again. I dread going out but its my duty.

Don't forget to send those clippings right away and write more. So its into the shower for me and in an hour I hope to be in Frisco.

Your loving son
Wilson

Excuse the dry letter, I just can't think of anything to write about.

[Postmark is San Francisco, Calif., Feb. 5, 1943, 10:30 PM]
Mr & Mrs Robert Lineaweaver
1240 E. Cumberland St.
Avon Penna.

[Return Address:]
W.C. Lineaweaver
VGS-37
c/o Fleet Postmaster
San Francisco, Calif.

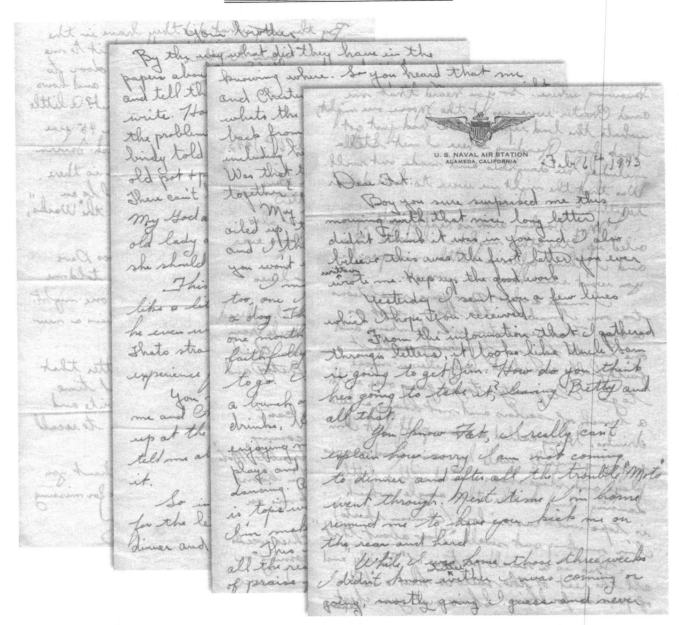

U.S. NAVAL AIR STATION
ALAMEDA, CALIFORNIA

Feb 6th 1943

Dear Fat:

Boy you sure surprised me this morning with that nice long letter. I sure didn't think it was in you and I also believe this was the first letter you ever wrote me. Keep up the good work.

Yesterday I sent you a few lines which I hope you received.

From the information that I gathered through letters, it looks like Uncle Sam is going to get Jim. How do you think hes going to take it, leaving Betty and all that.

You know Fat, I really can't explain how sorry I am not coming to dinner and after all the trouble "Mom" went through. Next time I'm home remind me to have you kick me on the rear and hard.

While I was home those three weeks I didn't know whether I was coming or going, mostly going I guess and never

VIA AIR MAIL

Mr Mahlon Lineaweaver
239 South 10th St.
Lebanon Penna.

[Postmark is U.S. Navy, Feb. 10, 1943, 4:30 PM, having been returned for postage]
Mr Mahlon Lineaweaver
239 South 10th St.
Lebanon Penna.

[Return Address:]
W.C. Lineaweaver
VGS-37
c/o Fleet Postmaster
San Francisco, Calif

Feb. 6th, 1943

Dear Fat:

Boy you sure surprised me this morning with that nice long letter, I didn't think it was in you and I also believe this was the first letter you ever wrote me. Keep up the good work

Yesterday I sent you a few lines which I hope you received.

From the information that I gathered through letters, it looks like Uncle Sam is going to get Jim. How do you think he's going to take it,? leaving Betty and all that.

You know Fat, I really can't explain how sorry I am not coming to dinner and after all the trouble "Mots" went through. Next time I'm home remind me to have you kick me on the rear and hard

While I was home those three weeks I didn't know whether I was coming or going, mostly going I guess and never knowing where. So you heard that me and Chester were up at the Moose one night, whats the bad reports. We had just got back from Reading where I met Stella including her daughters and made out swell. Was that the night we were to have dinner together?

My bowling arm is really getting oiled up, the other night I bowled 186 and I think after a little more practice you won't even have me worried.

I made a few New Year's resolutions too, one I made on the train, sick as a dog. That resolution was drinking and one month has gone by already with it faithfully carried out. Only eleven more to go. Its pretty tough going over with a bunch of sailors and not having a few drinks, being called a cream puff but I'm enjoying myself swell by seeing good movies plays and stage shows mixed with a little dancing. And on the other angle which is tops with us sailors (I mean skirts) I'm making out swell. "How about that."

This is a swell picture of "Billy" and all the rest of the sailors had a lot of praise for him. Shove out your chest papa.

By the way what did they have in the papers about me? Why not send it to me and tell that soldier to be next door to write. Hows everything out home and hows the problem girl (Lucille) making out? A little birdy told me she was seeing a 45 year old pot & pan scrubber at the Wash. Tavern. There can't be any truth in that or is there. My God at sixteen, why she'll be an old lady at twenty. Get her in the "Wacks", she should make out swell.

This is a good one, How does Dave like a little walking? Someone told me he even walked up to the show one night. Thats strange for Dave and I believe a new experience for him.

You mentioned in your letter that me and Chester had a wonderful time up at the "Moose" one night, write and tell me about it, I can't seem to recall it.

So in closing I want to thank you for the letter & picture, apologize for missing dinner and will write again soon

Your brother
Wilson

doesn't get very cold.

How's Pop and the rest of the family
I hope Aunt Eva recovers quick. It
of you to help her out and tell
asked about her.

I'm making out swell in
squadron and am in good health
all of you are the same.

Your loving
Wilson

[second page]

U. S. NAVAL AIR STATION
ALAMEDA, CALIFORNIA

Feb. 10th, 1943

Dear Mother:

This morning I got a whole stack
of old mail addressed to the Hornet including
many of your letters dating as far back as
October. Another letter was from Rev. Keene,
which had enclosed a small bible and
prayers. Also there were Christmas cards, one
was from Aunt Eva. But dog gone it that
package still hasn't caught up with me.

I guess you were surprised to see
my picture on the front page, it even
surprised me.

Got a letter from Jim this morning
and I suppose Uncle Sam will have him
soon. I also received one of yours dated
Jan 29th and after finishing this letter I
think I'll write Fat a few lines because
believe it or not he finally broke down
and wrote me a nice long letter.

The weather around here is usally
nice but with quite a bit of rain. It

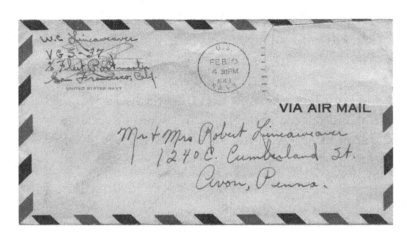

W. C. Linaweaver
VGS-37
% Fleet Postmaster
San Francisco, Calif.
UNITED STATES NAVY

U.S.
FEB 10
4 30PM
K43
NAVY

VIA AIR MAIL

Mr & Mrs Robert Linaweaver
1240 C. Cumberland St.
Avon, Penna.

Feb. 10th, 1943

Dear Mother:

This morning I got a whole stack of old mail addressed to the Hornet including many of your letters dating as far back as October. Another letter was from Rev. Keene, which had enclosed a small bible and prayers. Also there were Christmas cards, one was from Aunt Eva. But dog gone it that package still hasn't caught up with me.

I guess you were surprised to see my picture on the front page, it even surprised me.

Got a letter from Jim this morning and I suppose Uncle Sam will have him soon. I also received one of yours dated Jan 29th and after finishing this letter I think I'll write Fat a few lines because believe it or not he finally broke down and wrote me a nice long letter.

The weather around here is usally nice but with quite a bit of rain. It doesn't get very cold.

Hows Pop and the rest of the family and I hope Aunt Eva recovers quick. Its nice of you to help her out and tell her I asked about her.

I'm making out swell in my new squadron and am in good health hoping all of you are the same.

Your loving son
Wilson

[Postmark is U.S. Navy, Feb. 10, 1943, 4:30 PM]
Mr & Mrs Robert Lineaweaver
1240 E. Cumberland St.
Avon, Penna.

[Return Address:]
W.C. Lineaweaver
VGS-37
c/o Fleet Postmaster
San Francisco, Calif.

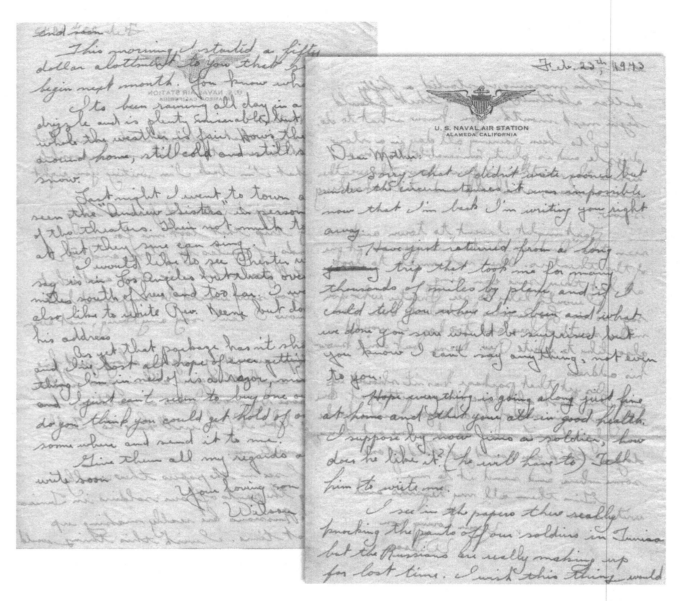

Mr & Mrs Robert Lineaweaver
1240 E. Cumberland St.
Avon Penna.

[Return Address:]
W.C. Lineaweaver
VGS-37
c/o Fleet Postmaster
San Francisco, Calif.

Feb. 23ʰ, 1943

Dear Mother:

Sorry that I didn't write sooner but under the circumstances it was impossible, now that I'm back I'm writing you right away.

Have just returned from a long trip that took me for many thousands of miles by plane and if I could tell you where I've been and what we done you sure would be surprised but you know I can't say anything, not even to you.

Hope everything is going along just fine at home and that your all in good health. I suppose by now Jims a soldier, how does he like it? (he will have to) Tell him to write me.

I see in the papers there really knocking the pants off our soldiers in Tunisa but the Russians are really making up for lost time. I wish this thing would end soon

This morning I started a fifty dollar allotment to you that should begin next month. You know what to do.

Its been raining all day in a slow drizzle and is plenty miserable, but on a whole the weather is fair. How's the weather around home, still cold and still shoveling snow.

Last night I went to town and seen the "Andrew Sisters" in person at one of the theaters. Their not much to look at but they sure can sing.

I would like to see Chester who you say is in Los Angeles but thats over 500 miles south of here and too far. I would also like to write Rev. Keene but don't know his address

As yet that package hasn't showed up and I've lost all hope of ever getting it. One thing I'm in need of is a razor, mine broke and I just can't seem to buy one out here, do you think you could get hold of one some where and send it to me.

Give them all my regards and write soon

Your loving son
Wilson

[Note: Attempts to locate information about the "long trip" mentioned in this letter were unsuccessful.]

reminder

What do you know, I'm a school boy again. This time its Bomadiers school but it only lasts two hours a day. I believe I've spent half of my time in navy going to school.

We had a few nice days this week but its raining again as usual. On days it reminds you of London, drizzly and misty.

Has Dad got a better job yet, if he doesn't he should.

Take care of yourself mom and all the rest my regards. Will write soon

You loving son

Wilson

A girl out here wants to give me her for a birthday present, how about that.

March 3rd 1943

U. S. NAVAL AIR STATION
ALAMEDA, CALIFORNIA

Dear Mother:

Received your letter this morning and was very glad to hear from you and I'm glad to hear that every one is well and happy. Tell Nathan I was glad to hear from him also.

Its too bad Jim had to leave, hows Bettie making out? As yet I haven't heard from him, perhaps he doesn't have my address so when you write him, give him my address

I'm still at the Naval Air Station Alameda and hope to stay here for many more months. I'm also beginning to like it here and have had quite a few good times

Don't forget to send me that razor and you know, I have a birthday coming up in a few weeks. Just a

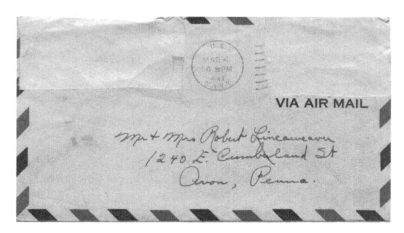

VIA AIR MAIL

Mr & Mrs Robert Lineaweaver
1240 E. Cumberland St
Avon, Penna.

March 3rd, 1943

Dear Mother:

Received your letter this morning and was very glad to hear from you and I'm glad to hear that everyone is well and happy. Tell Nathan I was glad to hear from him also.

Its too bad Jim had to leave, hows Bettie making out? As yet I haven't heard from him, perhaps he doesn't have my address so when you write him, give him my address

I'm still at the Naval Air Station Alameda and hope to stay here for many more months. I'm also beginning to like it here and have had quite a few good times

Don't forget to send me that razor and you know, I have a birthday coming up in a few weeks. Just a reminder.

What do you know, I'm a school boy again. This time its Bomadier school but it only lasts two hours a day. I believe I've spent half of my time in the navy going to school

We had a few nice days this past week but its raining again as usual. Some days it reminds you of London, drizzling and misty.

Has Dad got a better job yet? If he doesn't he should.

Take care of yourself mom and give all the rest my regards. Will write soon

Your loving son
Wilson

A girl out here wants to give me herself for a birthday present, how about that

-----

[Postmark is U.S. Navy, March 4, 1943, 4:30 PM]
Mr & Mrs Robert Lineaweaver
1240 E. Cumberland St
Avon, Penna.

[No return address remains on the envelope.]

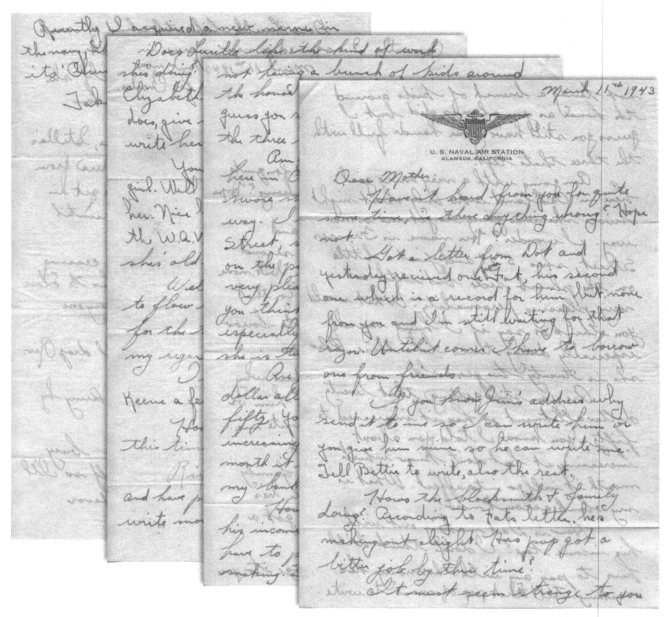

U. S. NAVAL AIR STATION
ALAMEDA, CALIFORNIA

March 11th 1943

Dear Mother:

Have not heard from you for quite some time, is there anything wrong? Hope not.

Got a letter from Dot and yesterday received one Fat, his second one which is a record for him but none from you and I'm still waiting for that razor. Until it comes I have to borrow one from friends.

If you know Jim's address why send it to me so I can write him or you give him mine so he can write me. Tell Bettie to write, also the rest.

Hows the blacksmith & family doing? According to Fats letter he's making out alright. Has pap got a better job by this time? It must seem strange to you

VIA AIR MAIL

Mr & Mrs Robert Lineaweaver
1240 E. Cumberland St.
Avon Penna.

[Postmark is U.S. Navy, March 12, 1943, 2:30 PM]
Mr & Mrs Robert Lineaweaver
1240 E. Cumberland St.
Avon Penna.

[No return address remains on the envelope.]

March 11th 1943

Dear Mother:

Haven't heard from you for quite some time, is there anything wrong? Hope not.

Got a letter from Dot and yesterday recieved one from Fat, his second one which is a record for him but none from you and I'm still waiting for that razor. Until it comes I have to borrow one from friends.

If you know Jim's address why send it to me so I can write him or you give him mine so he can write me. Tell Bettie to write, also the rest.

Hows the blacksmith & family doing? According to Fats letter, he's making out alright. Has pop got a better job by this time?

It must seem strange to you not having a bunch of kids around the house as you always did but I guess you still have your hands full with the three thats left.

Am going with a very nice girl here in Oakland who only last night swore she was going to get me some way. I wonder? Her name is Frances Street, she's 5'2" and just a little on the plumb side but with a very pleasing personality. What would you think or say if I hung myself especially during times like these. Also she is twenty two years old.

Are you still getting that twenty dollar allotment or has it increased to fifty. You know I told you about increasing it but don't know which month it will go into effect. What is my bank account now?

How is Dad making out with his income tax? I don't think he'll have to pay any with the money he's making. Tell that pop of mine to write.

Does Lucille like the kind of work she's doing? Does she stay over at Elizabethtown all the time? If she does, give me her address so I can write her.

You remember Bettie Kline, Stella's girl. Well I'm still getting letters from her. Nice letters. She's trying to get in the W.A.V.E.S. but has to wait until she's old enough.

Well Mother! words are ceasing to flow so I think I'll have to close for the time being . Give everyone my regards.

In the near future I'll drop Rev. Keene a few lines.

How does Jim like the Army by this time?

Right now I'm not so busy and have plenty time to myself so I'll write more if you return the favor

Your loving son
Wilson

Recently I acquired a new name in the navy, it used to be Charles but now it's Chuck and old nickname for Charles.

Take care of yourself.

[Left letter page]

1943

I still haven't filed my income
tax returns, just can't find time to
do it. Do you have to pay any?

You asked about my work,
you know darn well I just can't
love it although I can say that I
just don't like torpedo planes &
wish I could get out and go
flying.

Liberty here is darn good
& the time I go into Oakland
the "Andrew Sisters" the other
week and tonight I am taking
girl friend to hear Tommy Dorsey
I've seen a number of good
in San Francisco.

Take it easy Pat, don't
too hard and continue writing.

Your Brother

Give Mots & Billy & the Mots &
my regards
That was a swell
picture of Billy

In the navy
Charles or

[Right letter page — U.S. NAVAL AIR STATION, ALAMEDA, CALIFORNIA]

March 12th 1943

Dear Pat:

Received your letter yesterday
and the surprise was so great I just
had to answer immediately. I have

Glad to hear that all of you
are O.K. and that you got an increase
in pay. You deserve it.

Have you heard from Jim as yet?
I'm wondering how he's making out
and if he likes the army by this
time. How's Bettie making out and
what is she doing while he's gone?

So your bowling is pretty good.
Well it will have to be, because
when I get back I'll show you
some real competition. Me and the
girl I'm going with out here bowl
& step she bowls high for a girl and
I consistently get close to 200. How
about that.

[Envelope]

W.E. Lineaweaver ARM 3/c
VGS-37
% Fleet Post ma
San Francisco,

OAKLAND
MAR 12
4 PM
1943
CALIF.

FREE
RED CROSS
WAR FUND

Mr & Mrs Mahlon Lineaweaver
239 S 10th St.
Lebanon Penna

March 12th 1943

Dear Fat:

Recieved your letter yesterday and the surprise was so great I just had to answer imediately.

Glad to hear that all of you are O.K. and that you got an increase in pay, you deserve it.

Have you heard from Jim as yet? I'm wondering how he's making out and if he likes the army by this time. Hows Bettie making out and what is she doing while he's gone?

So your bowling is pretty good Well! it will have to be, because when I get back I'll show you some real competition. Me and the girl I'm going with out here bowl often, she bowls high for a girl and I consistantly get close to 200. How about that.

I still haven't filed my income tax returns, just can't find time to do it. Do you have to pay any?

You asked about my work, Well you know darn well I just cant talk about it although I can say this, I just don't like torpedoe planes and wish I could get out and quit flying.

Liberty here is darn good, most of the time I go into Oakland. Seen the "Andrew Sisters" the other week and tonight I am taking my girl friend to hear Tommy Dorsey, also Ive seen a number of good plays in San Francisco.

Take it easy Fat, don't work too hard and continue writing

Your Brother
Wilson   (In the navy its Charles or chuck)

Give Mots & Billy & The Nogles my regards
That was a swell picture of Billy

[Postmark is Oakland, Calif., March 12, 1943, 4:30 PM]
Mr & Mrs Mahlon Lineaweaver
239 S 10th St.
Lebanon Penna

[Return Address:]
W.C. Lineaweaver ARM 2/c
VGS 37, c/o Fleet Postmaster
San Francisco, Calif

recieved your letter this morning.
If martha sent me a razor too, _____
recieved it as yet.

Almost got married Mom, we _____
date set and everything, Frances even _____
wedding presents but a few days ago _____
got cold feet and called it off. N_____
I don't like the girl, its just that _____
can't see getting married at a time _____
this with me probably going to _____
soon. She says she'll wait ____

Has the allotment increa_____
50% dollars a month yet, ther_____
that much out of my pay.

Haven't got any letters from _____
or yet so I think I'll writ_____
in the very near future.

I am doing lots of flying lat_____
plenty work.

Will write again soon. Give _____
my love _____
P.S. Use VC-37 instead   Your loving son
of VG5-37. They changed   Wilson
the letters. Don't forget.

March 27th 1943

U. S. NAVAL AIR STATION
ALAMEDA, CALIFORNIA

Dear Mother
  I knew that I could count on
you complying with my wishes. The money
arrived here O.K. Thanks! Please don't
think that I'm in trouble or the likes,
its just that I'm afraid that in
the near future I'll be going to sea
again, so as long as I am here in the
states I'm going to enjoy myself.

  Sorry that I had to put you
through all the trouble, so thanks
again.

  I feel like a heel not writing
you but will try hard not to forget
from now on.

  The razor arrived and it sure
is swell, I like it a lot. Give
uncle Horace my thanks. Also I

W. C. Lineaweaver
VC-37
7or Fleet Postmaster
San Francisco, Calif.
UNITED STATES NAVY

U.S.
MAR 29
12 30PM
1943
NAVY

VIA AIR MAIL

Mr & Mrs Robert Lineaweaver
1240 E. Cumberland St
Avon Penna.

March 27th 1943

Dear Mother

I knew that I could count on you complying with my wishes. The money arrived here O.K. Thanks! Please don't think that I'm in trouble or the likes, its just that I'm afraid that in the near future I'll be going to sea again, so as long as Im here in the states I'm going to enjoy myself.

Sorry that I had to put you through all the trouble so thanks again.

I feel like a heel not writing you but will try hard not to forget from now on.

The razor arrived and it sure is swell, I like it a lot. Give uncle Horace my thanks. Also I recieved your letter this morning. If martha sent me a razor too, I haven't recieved it as yet.

Almost got married Mom, we had the date set and everything, Frances even got wedding presents but a few days ago I got cold feet and called it off. Not that I don't like the girl, its just that I can't see getting married at a time like this with me probably going to sea soon. She says she'll wait.

Has the allotment increased to 50.00 dollars a month yet, there taking that much out of my pay.

Haven't got any letters from Jim as yet so I think I'll write him in the very near future.

I am doing lots of flying lately and plenty work.

Will write again soon. Give everyone my love

Your loving son
Wilson

P.S. use VC-37 instead of VGS-37. They changed the letters   Don't forget.

[Postmark is U.S. Navy, March 29, 1943, 12:30 PM]
Mr & Mrs Robert Lineaweaver
1240 E. Cumberland St
Avon Penna.

[Return Address:]
W.C. Lineaweaver
VC-37
c/o Fleet Postmaster
San Francisco, Calif.

On March 25, 1943, $75.00 was sent to Wilson by Western Union. Money order charges were $3.99.

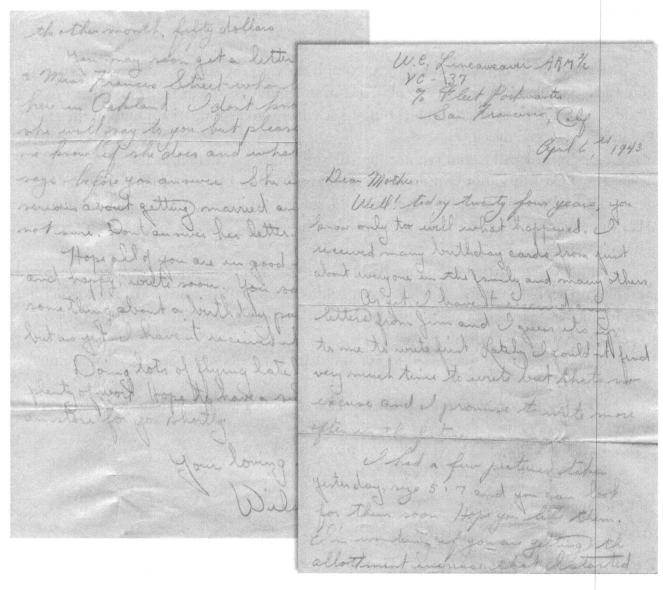

th other month, fifty dollars

You may soon get a letter
a Miss Frances Street who
her in Oakland. I don't know
she will nay to you but please
me know if she does and what
say before you answer. She is
serious about getting married an
not sure. Don't answer her letter

Hope all of you are in good
and happy, write soon. You sa
something about a birthday pa
but as yet I haven't received it

Doing lots of flying late
plenty of work. Hope to have a su
in store for you shortly.

Your loving
Will

W.C. Lineaweaver ARM⅔
VC-137
℅ Fleet Postmaster
San Francisco, Calif

April 6, 1943

Dear Mother,
Well! today twenty four years, you
know only too well what happened. I
received many birthday cards from just
about everyone in the family and many others.
As yet I have not received a
letter from Jim and I guess it's up
to me to write first. Lately I couldn't find
very much time to write but that's no
excuse and I promise to write more
often in the future

I had a few pictures taken
yesterday, size 5 x 7 and you can look
for them soon. Hope you like them.
I'm wondering if you are getting the
allotment increase that I started

W.C. Lineaweaver
VC-
℅ Fleet Postmaster
San Francisco Calif.
UNITED STATES NAVY

VIA AIR MAIL

Mr & Mrs Robert Lineaweaver
1240 E. Cumberland St.
Avon Penna.

W.C. Lineaweaver ARM 2/c
VC-37
c/o Fleet Postmaster
San Francisco, Calif.

April 6th, 1943

Dear Mother:

Well! today twenty four years, you know only too well what happened. I received many birthday cards from just about everyone in the family and many others.

As yet I haven't received any letters from Jim and I guess its up to me to write first. Lately I couldn't find very much time to write but thats no excuse and I promise to write more often in the future.

I had a few pictures taken yesterday, size 5 x 7 and you can look for them soon. Hope you like them. I'm wondering if you are getting the allottment increase that I started the other month, fifty dollars.

You may soon get a letter from a Miss Frances Street who lives here in Oakland. I don't know what she will say to you but please let me know if she does and what she says before you answer. She is very serious about getting married and I'm not sure. Don't answer her letter. Thanks.

Hope all of you are in good health and happy, write soon. You said something about a birthday package but as yet I haven't received it.

Doing lots of flying lately with plenty of work. Hope to have a surprise in store for you shortly.

Your loving son
Wilson

[Postmark is U.S. Navy, April 8, 1943, 2:30 PM]
Mr & Mrs Robert Lineaweaver
1240 E. Cumberland St.
Avon Penna.

[Return Address:]
W.C. Lineaweaver
VC-37
c/o Fleet Postmaster
San Francisco, Calif

Courtesy of Suzanne Frazier

Wilson

NOTE: *This letter was not written by Wilson, but by his good friend Sam McClean.*

he was still here in Calif we wrote to one another. not
often ✗ But often enough to let each other know that
mew is alright. wh
person I looked up w

He has a suff
in it as he is. It will
think millions of it.

please for giv
know that you are a
Best wishes to you
to be with your so

God bless you

S.P. McLean a RM 3/c
VS - 67
c/o Fleet post master
San Francisco
Calif.

S.P.
Care of
Care

We used to go up on the flight deck while we were a-
board ship and talk about the stars and get in friendly arguments about which o were which and th
talk about flying and
to us and we would al
and our familys. W
about them a great m

Some of our arg
which is a great topic
if That is all we did
many night aboard s
were standing by to

I learned more a
have from a study
plant and the coal m
your little and cities
still come back to o
it was all over.

Wilson has d
more than he will e
of but he is a grea

He has sunk
been through. He
a toughing liked
That way.

when he got
I know that he
than I. He desen

He and I a
much to my sorro

S.P. McLean

Dear Mrs. Lineaweaver:
I guess you will be surprised to get a letter from
a strange person, but I really don't feel strange or as a
stranger writing to you. you see I have known your son
Wilson Charles or "chuck" as we call him for a long
time. By some strange thing or way we joined the
Navy on the same day and at the same time. with only
a few minutes difference. although I am from Tenn.
and he from Pa. We went to Norfolk Va. to the same
station. I saw "chuck". If you will alow me to call him
that; quite a few times in the first eight weeks of our
Navy life. We then went to Jacksonville Fla. to Radio
School and from there to VB-8 aboard the V.S.S. Hornet.
We grew to be great friends by that time. greater than
most men or boys in the navy do. We made our Rate
at the same time. went into battles together and in
general were together quite a lot.

We saw our first battle against our
enemy on board the Hornet when we went to Tokyo.
I guess you have read about that and I know that chuck
will tell you many intresting things about where
he has been and and what he saw has seen.

Mrs. Lineaweaver; "chuck" loves you and his
family as I love mine. and that is next to the greatest
love I have. only our Lord above deserves as much
love and more. He has talked of you all has shown
me pictures of his Bro and sister. It is great to hear
him talk.

"chuck" is well educated and speaks well
which shows that he had a grand home and family.

[Postmark is Oakland, Calif., April 26, 1943, 10:00 AM]
Mrs E. Lineaweaver
1240 E. Cumberland St.
Lebdon Pa.

[Return Address:]
S.P. McLean
VS-67
c/o Fleet Postmaster
San Francisco, Calif

S.P. McLean

Dear Mrs. Lineaweaver:

 I guess you will be supprised to get a letter from a strange person but I really don't feal strange or as a stranger writing to you. You see I have known your son Wilson Charles or "Chuck" as we call him for a long time. By some strange thing or way we joined the Navy on the same day and at the same time. with only a few minutes difference. Although I am from Tenn. and he from Pa. we went to Norfolk Va. to the same station. I saw "Chuck", if you will allow me to call him that?, quite a few times in the first eight weeks of our Navy life. We then went to Jacksonville Fla to Radio School and from there to VB-8 aboard the USS Hornet. We grew to be great friends by that time. Greater than most men or boys in the navy do. We made our rates at the same time. Went in to battles to gether and in general were to gether quite a lot.

 We saw our first battle against our enmey on board the Hornet when we went to Tokyo. I guess you have read about that and I know that "Chuck" will tell you many intresting things about where he has been and what he has seen.

 Mrs. Lineaweaver! "Chuck" loves you and his family as I love mine. and that is next to the greatest love I have. only our Lord above dserves as much love and more. He has talked of you all has shown me pictures of his Bro and Sister. It is great to hear him talk.

 "Chuck" is well educated and speaks well which shows that he had a grand home and family.

 We used to go up on the flight deck while we were aboard ship and talk a bout the stars and get in friendly arguments about which ones were which and then we would talk about flying and radio and all the things interesting to us and we would always end up by talking about home and our family's. We are both proud of them and talked about them a great many times.

 Some of our arguments were about the civil war which is a great topic in the navy. It must seam to you as if that is all we did was argue but there were many many night aboard ship when it was to hot to sleep or we were standing by to fly and all our talks were educational.

 I learend more about Pa. from him then I would have from a study book in months. About the Hershy plant and the coal mines and what you grow and about your cattle and cities. It was all very interesting but we still come back to our parents and Bro and Sisters before it was all over.

 Wilson has done great things for his country. More than he will ever tell you or could think of but he is a great man. Take it from his ship mate.

 He has sunk ships made raids on islands and been through Hell and high water. and he is still a laughing likable guy. and he will always be that way.

 When he got his medal and I heard of it, I know that he or you or any one was more proud than I. He deserved it and more to.

 He and I ar in different Squadrons now. Much to my sorrow. but when I was in Seattle and he was still here in Calif we wrote to one another. Not often but often enough to let each other know that we were alright. When I came back to Calif the first person I looked up was "Chuck".

 He has a supprise for you and I am as much interested in it as he is. It will be a present and I know that you will think millions of it.

 Please for give the long letter. Again I say that I know that you are all swell and I don't feal as a stranger. Best wishes to you on the fine Easter. Glad that I got to be with your son.

 God Bless you.

Yours Truly
S.P. Mc

S.P. McLean ARM 2/c
VS-67
c/o Fleet Post Master
San Francisco Calif.

Samuel P. McLean was born in 1922 in Lawrenceburg, TN. He met Wilson in the Navy and they became close friends. Until 1974 when he had a heart attack, Sam was the Director of Housing at Middle Tennessee State University. Sam passed away in 1990 in Murfreesboro, TN, and is buried there in Evergreen Cemetery. He was married three times and had one son and one adopted daughter. Sam's widow, Pam, said the students at MTSU loved him as he was always there for them. He had a heart of gold and was a true friend to many.

⚓ _____ ⚓

going with her but I would like to
know what she said in her letter

The time is drawing near
I'll soon be back out home
only this war would end. I
so now, at my last f
g

Write me and how did all
Dave, Pat & families making
think Pat will be drafted? g
a letter but as yet haven't
answer.

Give every one my reg
send in all the news from a
and I'm writing impatiently
you

Your loving

If you need some money
I have it for some useful
in my bankroll

Louisville Date. It's las
we knew I got the cockage

UNITED STATES NAVY

April 26th 1943

Dear Mother

Once again I'm here late in
writing you that I promised not to do
again. Your letters have been very slow too.

How is everything at home? O.K. and
I do hope you get another place to live
and get away from that hole where your
at now. Where Pat lives would be just
fine and it will be close for Dick to
go to work and the kids to go to
school. By the way are the kids in
better health by this time.

Yesterday I went to Easter service
and they were fine. The church that I
went to was Lutheran at a small town
called Lodi, California where the people
are just about 10% German.

Did you get a letter from Frances?
Well marriage is out and I have stopped

April 26th, 1943

Dear Mother

Once again I've been late in writing you but hope it doesn't happen again. Your letters have been very few too.

How is everything at home? O.K. and I do hope you get another place to live and get away from that hole where your at now. Where Fat lives would be just fine and it would be close for Dad to go to work and the kids to go to school. By the way are the kids in better health by this time.

Yesterday I went to Easter services and they were fine. The church that I went to was Lutheran at a small town called Lodi, California where the people are just about 100% German.

Did you get a letter from Frances? Well! marriage is out and I have stoped going with her but I would like to know what she said in her letter.

The time is drawing very short and I'll soon be back out there again. If only this war would end. The way it looks now, it may last for many more years.

Write me and have Dad write too. Hows Dave, Fat & families making out. Do you think Fat will be drafted? I wrote Jim a letter but as yet haven't recieved an answer.

Give every one my regards and send me all the news from around home and I'm waiting impatiently to hear from you.

Your loving son
Wilson

If you need some money why go ahead but use it for some useful purpose. How is my bank roll

I recieved "Dots" letter last week and you know I got the package.

[Postmark is U.S. Navy, April 27, 1943, 12:30 PM]
Mr & Mrs Robert Lineaweaver
1240 E. Cumberland St.
Avon, Penna.

[Return Address:]
W.C. Lineaweaver ARM 2/c
VC-37
c/o Fleet Postmaster
San Francisco, Calif.

April 28th 1943

Dear Mother.

It has been quite a long time since I've written you and I'm very sorry. I wrote Jim a letter but he doesn't seem to be able to find time to answer, so I'll try again. How is he making out?

They have us working plenty hard and were doing lots of flying but I'm not complaining as long as they keep me in the states.

Next month I go up for first class petty officer and I hope I make it. It will mean wearing three stripes instead of two that I have now and will also mean a nice increase in pay. You know I'm in the navy about 2 ½ years already, how time flies.

Did you get a letter from Frances yet? Let me know what she had to say. I stoped going with her so don't answer her letter. Sammy McLean said he was going to write you, Did he?

This navy life is getting very monotonous and I'm tired of it and wish to get out but thats impossible, so please Mother write often, that helps some and have the rest write too.

Hoping your all in the best of health and happy I'll close remaining

Your loving son
Wilson

[Postmark is U.S. Navy, May 1, 1943, 3 PM]
Mr & Mrs Robert Lineaweaver
1240 E. Cumberland St
Avon, Penna.

[Return Address:]
W.C. Lineaweaver ARM 2/c
VC-37   c/o Fleet Postmaster
San Francisco, Calif.

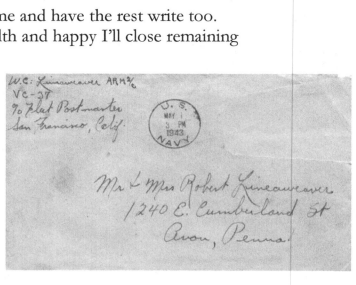

Telegram reads: PLEASE SEND $50 IMMEDIATELY AM OK LETTER FOLLOWING YOUR LOVING SON= WILSON.

that he is going to be a daddy. He's a better
man than I thought he was. So wish him
lots of luck and his
over seas.

        Will write ag___
to Alameda. Expecting
and hoping you lik___
remaining

P.S. You can give th___
Fat or to whom you___

W.C. Lineaweaver ARM ½
VC-37
℅ Fleet Postmaster
San Francisco, Calif

May 10th, 1943

Dear Mother:

        Hope you recieved and like your Mothers Day
gift, knowing you haven't any good pictures of me
I thought they would be a present to you. Please
let me know if you recieved them O.K. or were
they bent or broke? Did you get them before
Mothers Day ?,

        Am writing this letter from a small town
inland from San Francisco some 100 miles, the
name being Lodi and the people are just about
100% German. I am on a few days special liberty
and am having a swell time and will return
back to the air station tomorrow.

        Have not heard from you recently so
please write and give me all the news from
home and you know mother, I finally got a
letter from Jim and was I surprised to hear

W.C. Lineaweaver ARM ½
VC-37
℅ Fleet Postmaster
San Francisco, Calif

LODI. CALIF MAY 10 6-PM 1943

FREE

Mr & Mrs. Robert Lineaweaver
1240 E. Cumberland St.
Avon, Penna.

W.C. Lineaweaver ARM 2/c
VC-37
c/o Fleet Postmaster
San Francisco, Calif

May 10th, 1943

Dear Mother:

Hope you recieved and like your Mothers Day gift, knowing you haven't any good pictures of me I thought they would be a fitting present to you. Please let me know if you recieved them O.K. or were they bent or broke? Did you get them before Mothers Day?

Am writing this letter from a small town inland from San Francisco some 100 miles, the name being Lodi and the people are just about 100% German. I am on a few days special liberty and am having a swell time and will return back to the air station tomorrow.

Have not heard from you recently so please write and give me all the news from home and you know mother, I finally got a letter from Jim and was I surprised to hear that he is going to be a daddy. He's a better man than I thought he was. I wish him lots of luck and hope he doesn't have to go over seas.

Will write again as soon as I get back to Alameda. Expecting to hear from you soon and hoping you like the pictures I'll close remaining

Your loving son
Wilson

P.S. You can give the other pictures to Dave & Fat or to whom you wish.

[Postmark is Lodi, Calif., May 10, 1943, 6 PM]
Mr & Mrs. Robert Lineaweaver
1240 E. Cumberland St.
Avon, Penna.

[Return Address:]
W.C. Lineaweaver ARM 1/c
VC-37
c/o Fleet Postmaster
San Francisco, Calif

are out of school so you have your handsfull
You say Lucille is sticking to ?
at Elizabethtown, thats swell a?
she does good. Have her write me ?
to drop a few lines if he can spar?
time.

By this time Dave shoul?
to walking. I guess it was a har?
him. I'll bet the little girl is ?
big. When you drop in to Dave's ?
tell him and his family that ?
about them.

I expect to be her at ?
a short time and then to sea ?
I sure dread going.

Had three days off over M?
and spent them with a girl fr?
sure had a swell time.

Sorry to bother you so often ?
but things cost so much and the ?
it really costs and the near futur?
able to spend any.

Take care of yourself and ?
Your lovin?
W?

June 2nd 1943

Dear Mother:
Its about time I get around to writing
you. As I mentioned in the telegram about
leaving, Well! we left. I'm still in Calif.
a little south of Frisco, between Frisco and
Los Angeles at Monterey.

Its very nice here although the
living conditions aren't so hot because this
is a new place but will improve as time
goes by. This area is a well known summer
resort and is really pretty country. The
view from our dormitory overlooks Monterey
bay and is really beautiful. Also the
weather here is perfect compared to Frisco
where it is usually raining and foggy.

Hope you and the rest are in good health
and getting along swell. I'm also glad Dad
got a better job and is out of that sweat shop.
Hope you get a better house to live in Keep
trying and some day something will pop up.

Well! I guess by this time the kids

W.C. Lineaweaver
VC-37
c/o Fleet Postmaster
San Francisco, Calif.

FREE

Mr + Mrs Robert Lineaweaver
1240 E Cumberland St.
Avon, Penna.

June 2nd 1943

Dear Mother:

Its about time I get around to writing you. As I mentioned in the telegram about leaving, Well! we left. I'm still in Calif. a little south of Frisco, between Frisco and Los Angeles at Monterey.

Its very nice here although the living conditions aren't so hot because this is a new place but will improve as time goes by. This area is a well known summer resort and is really pretty country. The view from our dormitory overlooks Monterey bay and is really beautiful. Also the weather here is perfect compared to Frisco where it is usually raining and foggy.

Hope you and the rest are in good health and getting along swell. I'm also glad Dad got a better job and is out of that sweat shop. Hope you get a better house to live in. Keep trying and someday something will pop up.

Well! I guess by this time the kids are out of school so you have your hands full You say Lucille is sticking to her job over at Elizabethtown, thats swell and I hope she does good. Have her write me and tell pop to drop a few lines if he can spare some of his time.

By this time Dave should be used to walking. I guess it was a hard job for him. I'll bet the little girl is really getting big. When you drop in to Dave's place, why tell him and his family that I asked about them.

I expect to be here at Montery only a short time and then to sea again and I sure dread going.

Had three days off over Memorial day and spent them with a girl friend and we sure had a swell time.

Sorry to bother you so often about money but things cost so much and to have a good time it really costs and the near future I won't be able to spend any.

Take care of yourself and write me

Your loving son
Wilson

[Postmark is Monterey, Calif., June 4, 1943, 8 AM]
Mr & Mrs Robert Lineaweaver
1240 E Cumberland St.
Avon, Penna.

[Return Address:]
W.C. Lineaweaver
VC-37
c/o Fleet Postmaster
San Francisco, Calif.

Well! I have about two and half years in
the navy, time sure flies. Doesn't ——— that ————
and its almost a half year since I ———
Am getting to like this part of the ———
and believe if I ever do settle klown
out here

Did you get any more lett———
You know I almost married that ———
why should I get married and ———
miserable when by staying sin———
make lots happy.

Will be going to sea with———
month or two and I dread it. T———
will give me a little leave before ———
but not enough to come home ———
do I think I'll spend it with ———
friends in Lodi (they have a swee———
if I get more than fifteen days ———

Waiting to hear from you wit———
and I will write again soon I re———
Your lovi———
W———

June 7th 1943

Dear Mother & Family.

Having a little spare time at the present.
I think its fitting to drop you a few lines
seeing that I have been very lax lately in
my correspondence with you.

Got a letter from Jim this morning
and was glad to hear from him. He explained
how tough army training is and expressed his
wish to be in the navy with me. Wish he
could have got in the navy

How is everyone at home? Fine I hope
I'll bet Pop sure looks funny with his new
glasses. I imagine the kids are by this
time on their summer vacation and you
must have your hands full Are they getting big?
They haven't written me for a long time, either has
Pat or Dave. Looks like I'm the forgotten
sailor.

By the way, when are you getting out of
that dump you live in now and find something
more livable? I don't think I could stand
living in the place you are. Surely you must be
able to find a place somewhere in Lebanon.

W.C. Lineaweaver
VC-37
7 Fleet Postmaster
San Francisco Calif.

MONTEREY, CALIF.
JUN 8
1943

FREE

Mr & Mrs Robert Lineaweaver
1240 C. Cumberland St.
Avon Penna.

June 7th 1943

Dear Mother & Family.

Having a little spare time at the present. I think its fitting to drop you a few lines seeing that I have been very lax lately in my correspondence with you.

Got a letter from Jim this morning and was glad to hear from him. He explained how tough army training is and expressed his wish to be in the navy with me. Wish he could have got in the navy

How is every one at home? Fine I hope I'll bet Pop sure looks funny with his new glasses. I imagine the kids are by this time on their summer vacation and you must have your hands full. Are they getting big? They haven't written me for a long time, either has Fat or Dave. Looks like I'm the forgotten sailor.

By the way, when are you getting out of that dump you live in now and find something more livable? I don't think I could stand living in the place you are. Surely you must be able to find a place somewhere in Lebanon.

Well! I have about two and half years in the navy, time sure flies. Doesn't seem that long and its almost a half year since I've been home Am getting to like this part of the country, Calif. and believe if I ever do settle down it will be out here

Did you get any more letters from Frances? You know I almost married that girl but why should I get married and make one miserable when by staying single I can make lots happy.

Will be going to sea within the next month or two and I dread it. Perhaps they will give me a little leave before going to sea but not enough to come home. If they do I think I'll spend it with some German friends in Lodi (they have a swell daughter) but if I get more than fifteen days I'll be home.

Waiting to hear from you with all the news and I will write again soon I remain

Your loving son
Wilson

[Postmark is Monterey, Calif., June 8, 1943, 8 AM]
Mr & Mrs Robert Lineaweaver
1240 E. Cumberland St.
Avon Penna.

[Return Address:]
W.C. Lineaweaver
VC-37
c/o Fleet Postmaster
San Francisco Calif.

much I like tennis

Have put on quite a bit of weight
weigh about 155 at present. Yo[u]
noticed in the pictures I sent th[at]
on more weight. By the way ho[w]
like them and what does Pat t[hink]
of them? Personally I think they [ ]

Would like to hear from [you]
and soon. Am wondering how eve[ryone]
making out.

I could get 10 days l[eave]
going to sea again but that ju[st]
enough to come home so I'll [stay]
here where I am.

And Mother, I'm wonderi[ng how]
likes the walking for a change [ ]
ration business. Do you get e[verything]
what you want?

Give every one my reg[ards]
of all of you often and it won['t be]
until it'll be right out in the [ ]
war once again. Things are brewi[ng]

Your l[oving son]

June 13th, 1942

Dear Mother

Here it is Sunday evening and nothing to
do down in this neck of the country so I've
decided to write you although I haven't heard
from you for quite some time.

While at Alameda I had very little
time to write, their was always plenty to do
and I did it. Here at Monterey there is very
little to do so I catch up on my letter
writing.

Am still doing the same type of work,
flying every day and I'm getting tired of it. I
haven't made another promotion as yet but
think I will next month.

Perhaps you and the rest have been
wondering just what type of plane I fly in. They
are called T.B.F.'s or torpedo bombers, you
must have seen pictures of them. They are
nick-named "Avenger" and are made by Grumman.

I was pretty wild after returning to the
states but have finally settled down. Don't
go out very much in fact this is the tenth day
in a row that I stayed in. When I have
time off I play tennis and you know how

W.R. Luneaweaver ARM³/c
VC-37
℅ Fleet Postmaster
San Francisco, Calif.

FREE

MONTEREY, CALIF
JUN 14
1943

Mr. & Mrs. Robert Luneaweaver
1240 E. Cumberland St.
Avon, Penna.

June 13th, 1942 *[1943]*

Dear Mother

Here it is Sunday evening and nothing to do down in this neck of the country so I've decided to write you although I haven't heard from you for quite sometime

While at Alameda I had very little time to write, their was always plenty to do and I did it. Here at Monterey there is very little to do so I catch up on my letter writing.

Am still doing the same type of work, flying every day and I'm getting tired of it. I haven't made another promotion as yet but think I will next month.

Perhaps you and the rest have been wondering just what type of plane I fly in. They are called T.B.F.'s or torpedo bombers, you must have seen pictures of them. They are nicknamed "Avenger" and are made by Grumman.

I was pretty wild after returning to the states but have finally settled down. Don't go out very much in fact this is the tenth day in a row that I stayed in. When I have time off I play tennis and you know how much I like tennis

Have put on quite a bit of weight, weigh about 155 at present. You say you noticed in the pictures I sent that I had put on more weight. By the way how do you like them and what does Fat & Dave think of them? Personally I think they stink.

Would like to hear from you Mother and soon. Am wondering how every body is making out.

I could get 10 days leave before going to sea again but that just isn't enough to come home so I'll just sit here where I am.

And Mother, I'm wondering how Dave likes the walking for a change and all that ration business. Do you get enough of what you want?

Give every one my regards, I think of all of you often and it won't be long until I'll be right out in the thick of this war once again. Things are brewing.

Your loving son
Wilson

[Postmark is Monterey, Calif., June 14, 1943, 3 PM]
Mr & Mrs Robert Lineaweaver
1240 E. Cumberland St.
Avon, Penna.

[Return Address:]
W.C. Lineaweaver ARM 2/c
VC-37
c/o Fleet Postmaster
San Francisco, Calif.

Telegraph reads: DEAR MOTHER HAVE 10 DAYS LEAVE CANNOT COME HOME SEND $100.00 IMMEDIATELY CARE POSTAL TELEGRAPH= WILSON.

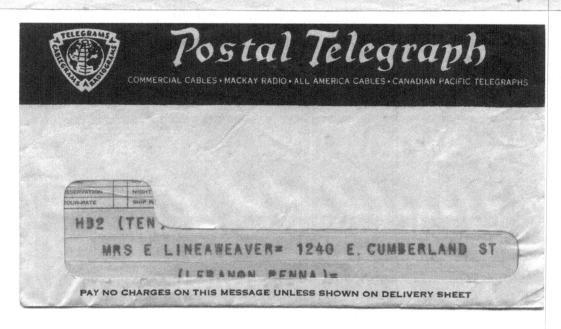

This is the receipt for the money sent to Wilson.

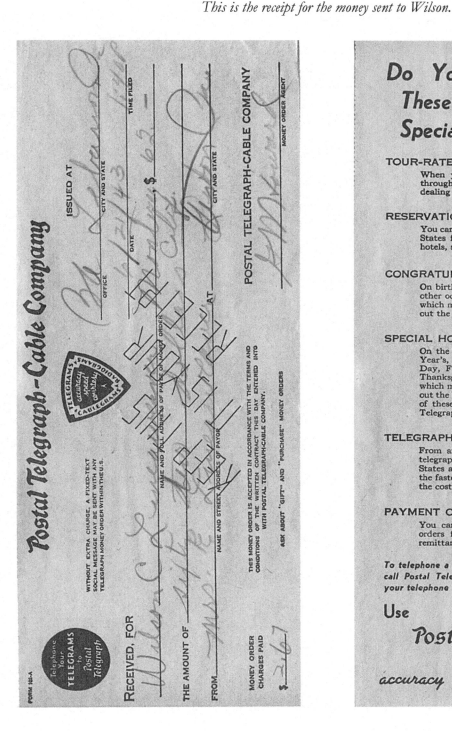

by this time their both black from
the sun.

This is really pretty country
Monterey. Before the war this was
summer resort. It doesn't get
most of the time there's a cool

So Dave done it again, a
He sure can't stick to one.

Give everyone my regards
leave I'll drop you a few line
you know if I'm enjoying my
I hope I do. It will feel goo
free and on my own ..

                    Your son
                    Wilso

June 23rd 1943

Dear Mother:
        Recieved your most welcomed letter
this morning and I was very glad to hear
from you.
        Tomorrow I start on a ten day
leave but I'm unable to come home. We
are not allowed east of the Mississippi and
if we were, ten days wouldn't be enough
time. It took nine days the last time
for travelling.
        I'll spend my ten days here
in Calif. visiting different parts. Will
probably spend a few days at Yosemite
park. Thanks for sending the money, I hate
to put you to all that trouble but I
figure its going to cost plenty.
        Sorry to hear that Harold has
a bad case of poison Ivy. He better watch
where he plays around. Do the two kids
do much swimming? I imagine that

Mr & Mrs Robert Kinsaweaver
1240 E. Cumberland St.
Avon, Penna.

June 23rd, 1943

Dear Mother:

Recieved your most welcomed letter this morning and I was very glad to hear from you.

Tomorrow I start on a ten day leave but I'm unable to come home. We are not allowed east of the Mississippi and if we were, ten days wouldn't be enough time. It took nine days the last time for travelling.

I'll spend my ten days here in Calif. visiting different parts. Will probably spend a few days at Yosemite park. Thank for sending the money, I hate to put you to all that trouble but I figure its going to cost plenty.

Sorry to hear that Harold has a bad case of poison Ivy. He better watch where he plays around. Do the two kids do much swimming? I imagine that by this time their both black from the sun.

This is really pretty country here around Monterey. Before the war this was a famous summer resort. It doesn't get too hot, most of the time there's a cool sea breeze.

So Dave done it again, another car. He sure can't stick to one.

Give everyone my regards. While on leave I'll drop you a few lines to let you know if I'm enjoying myself and I hope I do. It will feel good to be free and on my own.

Your son
Wilson

[Postmark is U.S. Navy, June 23, 1943, P.M.]
Mr & Mrs Robert Lineaweaver
1240 E. Cumberland St.
Avon, Penna.

[No Return Address]

> *A Western Union Telegram dated June 26, 1943 reads:*
> DEAR MOTHER. RECEIVED MONEY OK THANKS HAVE 10 DAYS LEAVE UNABLE TO COME HOME MAKING OUT WELL LOVE = WILSON

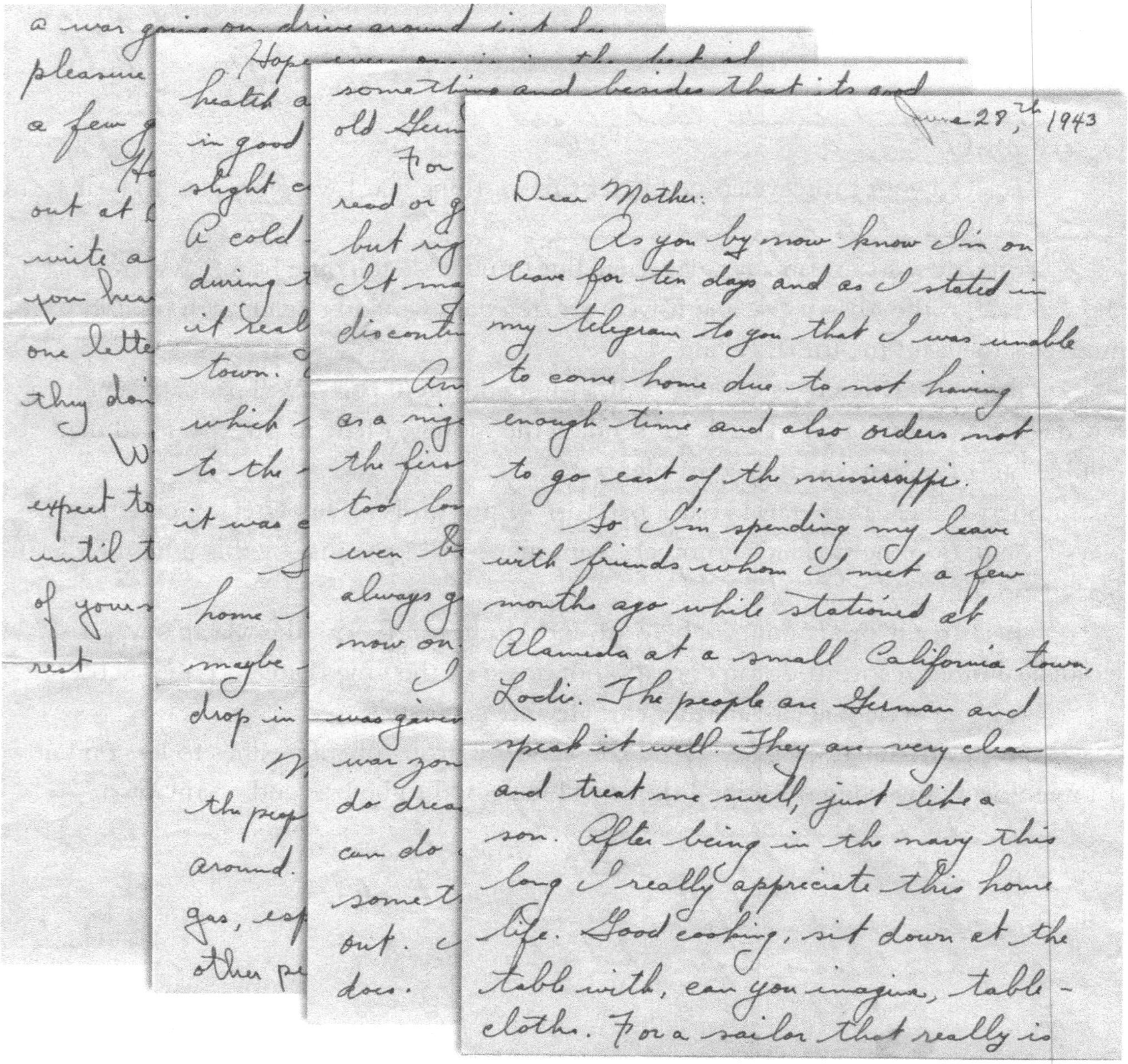

June 28th, 1943

Dear Mother:

As you by now know I'm on leave for ten days and as I stated in my telegram to you that I was unable to come home due to not having enough time and also orders not to go east of the mississippi.

So I'm spending my leave with friends whom I met a few months ago while stationed at Alameda at a small California town, Lodi. The people are German and speak it well. They are very clean and treat me swell, just like a son. After being in the navy this long I really appreciate this home life. Good cooking, sit down at the table with, can you imagine, table-cloth. For a sailor that really is

LODI, CALIF. JUN 29 12-M 1943

Mr. & Mrs. Robert Lineaweaver
1240 E. Cumberland St.
Avon, Penna.

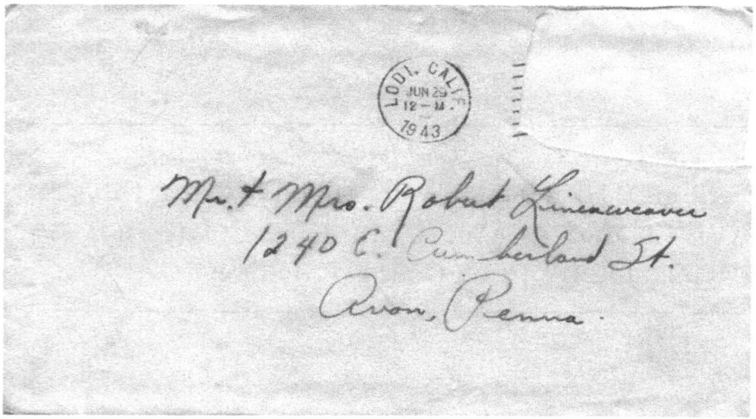

[Postmark is Lodi, Calif., June 29, 1943, 12-M]
Mr. & Mrs. Robert Lineaweaver
1240 E. Cumberland St.
Avon, Penna.

[No Return Address]

June 28th, 1943

Dear Mother:

As you by now know I'm on leave for ten days and as I stated in my telegram to you that I was unable to come home due to not having enough time and also orders not to go east of the mississippi.

So I'm spending my leave with friends whom I met a few months ago while stationed at Alameda at a small California town, Lodi. The people are German and speak it well. They are very clean and treat me swell, just like a son. After being in the navy this long I really appreciate this home life. Good cooking, sit down at the table with, can you imagine, tablecloths. For a sailor that really is something and besides that its good old German meals.

For recreation I lay around and read or go out to the lake swimming but right now I have a sore ear. It may be from the water so I'll discontinue for a while.

Am beginning to get as black as a niger from the sun. Last month, the first day out in the sun I stayed too long and boy did I get sore, even blistered then pealed. I'm always going to take it easy from now on.

I also expect that this leave was given because we're going into the war zone again and soon. I sure do dread it but there's nothing I can do about it but pray that something happens before we ship out. I still have hopes that it does.

Hope every one is in the best of health and making out swell. Am in good health myself other than a slight cold which I can't get rid of. A cold is really miserable especially during this hot weather and boy! it really is hot at this inland town. I guess its due to the mountains which block all the wind. Went to the movie this afternoon because it was cool their.

Sorry I was unable to come home because I sure wanted to but maybe sometime in the future I'll drop in like before, I hope.

Managed to get some gas for the people here so they could drive me around. They sure are stingy with the gas, especially after seeing all the other people who don't even know their's a war going on, drive around just for pleasure and then give a sailor just a few gallons.

How are the two girls making out at Elizabethtown? Get them to write along with the rest of you. Do you hear from Jim often? I only got one letter in the last few months. Hope they don't ship him across right away.

When I get back to Monterey I'll expect to find some letters from you so until then I'll close. Take care of yourself and give my regards to the rest

Your loving son
Wilson

It could have been a lot worse. Some of the men who came back with ... how am ... a long time ago.

I still have hope ... won't say anything to ...

Still doing lots ... few close ones again bu ... luck is still holding o ... who I've come to kno ... say the same, in fact ...

Take care of your ... my two big draft dodg ... I hope. I imagine Dave ... a lot of walking lat ... mother.

You'll be hearing ... I remain.

Tell dad his letter could it ... have been any shorter, I get ... from him and then its only a ... Glad he got a better job and I'm ... he likes his work.

July 7th 1943

Dear Mother:

Have just returned from my ten days leave and had a wonderful time. Spent most of my time with friends whom I told you about before at Lodi, Calif. They treated me swell and anything I wanted they gave me.

Wrote you a letter from Lodi and also sent a telegram from Merced which I hope you recieved.

Upon arrival back here at Monterey, one of your letters was waiting for me. Also one from Dad and Jim. It was good to hear from you.

Jim didn't have very much to say so I'm wondering how he's making out. Is he beginning to like Army life? Do you think they'll ship him across soon? I hope not for yours and Bettie's sake. How soon is the blessed event to come off?

Sorry I was unable to come home but they were my Captains orders and even at that, they didn't give me enough days. I won't have another chance now for a long time. We are expecting to go Jap hunting once again, any day now. Wish me luck, I'll need it.

I've had seven months back in the states and forty days leave, so I'm not complaining.

[Postmark is Monterey, Calif., July 14, 1943, 9 AM]
Mr & Mrs. Robert Lineaweaver
1240 E Cumberland St.
Avon, Penna.

[No Return Address]

July 7th, 1943

Dear Mother:

Have just returned from my ten days leave and had a wonderful time. Spent most of my time with friends whom I told you about before at Lodi, Calif. They treated me swell and anything I wanted they gave me.

Wrote you a letter from Lodi and also sent a telegram from Merced which I hope you recieved.

Upon arrival back here at Monterey, one of your letters was waiting for me. Also one from Dad and Jim. It was good to hear from you.

Jim didn't have very much to say so I'm wondering how he's making out. Is he beginning to like Army life? Do you think they'll ship him across soon? I hope not for your's and Bettie's sake. How soon is the blessed event to come off?

Sorry I was unable to come home but they were my Captains orders and even at that, they didn't give me enough days. I won't have another chance now for a long time. We are expecting to go Jap hunting once again, any day now. Wish me luck, I'll need it.

Ive had seven months back in the states and forty days leave, so Im not complaining. It could have been a lot worse. Some of the men who came back with me have gone out again a long time ago.

I still have hopes for something better but I won't say anything to you until it happen, if ever.

Still doing lots of flying and had quite a few close ones again but I'm still kicking and my luck is still holding out. Many of my shipmates who I've come to know so far in the navy can't say the same, in fact they can't say anything.

Take care of yourselves and write often. Hows my two big draft dodging brothers making out? Swell I hope. I imagine Dave must be losing weight doing a lot of walking lately. Give them my regards mother.

You'll be hearing again from me soon, until then I remain.

Your loving son
Wilson

Tell dad his letter couldn't have been any shorter, I get one a year from him and then its only a paragraph. Glad he got a better Job and I'm also glad he likes his work.

July 27th, 1943

Dear Mother & Family,

Received your letter this morning and was very glad to hear from you. Glad that everyone is alright and in good health. I'm just fine. California is beginning to agree with me. Getting a little heavier but thats because I do very little physical work and drink quite a bit of beer.

Give my congratulation to Fat & Mots. A baby girl. That makes him even with Dave and in less time. So Jim & Bettie are expecting theirs in October. Guess Bettie will have a tough time, she's so small

Got a letter from Jim yesterday and have just answered it. He's complaining about the Infantry but I told him that regardless how tough it is it's not as tough as across and if they keep him in the states he shouldn't complain.

Lucille is home again but now Dot is over at Elizabethtown. What does

[Postmark is Monterey, Calif., July 28, 1943, 9 AM]
Mr & Mrs Robert Lineaweaver
1240 E. Cumberland St.
Avon, Penna.

[No Return Address]

Mr & Mrs Robert Lineaweaver
1240 E. Cumberland St.
Avon, Penna.

July 27th, 1943

Dear Mother & Family.

Recieved your letter this morning and was very glad to hear from you. Glad that every one is alright and in good health. I'm just fine. California is beginning to agree with me. Getting a little heavier but thats because I do very little physical work and drink quite a bit of beer.

Give my congradulation to Fat & Mots. A baby girl. *[Linda Anne Lineaweaver, born July 19, 1943.]* That makes him even with Dave and in less time. So Jim and Bettie are expecting theirs in October. Guess Bettie will have a tough time, she's so small

Got a letter from Jim yesterday and have just answered it. He's complaining about the Infantry but I told him that regardless how tough it is it's not as tough as across and if they keep him in the states he shouldn't complain.

Lucille is home again but now Dot is over at Elizabethtown. What does Dot do over there and I'll bet Lucille doesn't like her new job. By the way, what does she do?

Sorry that I was unable to come home on leave. Its just one of those things. Will be going hunting again real soon. Wish this thing would end soon, am beginning to get tired of it. If I have done my part already, I'll have to go out and do more. Most of the fellows that came back with me are already out so how can I complain.

Will be promoted to Petty officer 1st class (ARM 1/c) the first of August. There is only one more advancement that I can get, then I'm done. I believe I did fairly good for myself since I came in the navy. What do you think? Its funny Jim can't advance himself.

Would like to write Fat & Mots a letter but lost their address so I guess I'll write it to you and you can give it to them if I get around to writing.

So you got the phone, quite a surprise. Well Lucille is always full of them. Whats the phone number? Before I pull out I may phone you. How would you like that and it most likely will be collect.

You know the picture you had enclosed in you last letter. The Hoffman's. Didnt they live just below the school house out on the hill. I believe that I used to play with them when I was a kid. Too bad about James Gettle. He was on the U.S.S. Juneau and you know what. He probably was sailing along side of me for months before they got sunk and I never knew it until I came home and talked to his brother Chas. Wish I could of seen him and had a talk with him. He certainly was a swell fellow. This time when I go out I'll have to get a few for him.

Now I'm flying with the Captain of my squadron and am leading flight radioman and gunner with lots of responseability. Hope me and my boys can give them hell when we go out and which will be soon. Wish I could tell you more but you know I can't. As soon as we go aboard our carrier, letters will be censored again so I won't even be able to tell you this much.

Wish me luck.

Don't forget to continue writing, letters sure do help a lot when your out like that. Most of the time their slow but they finally catch up with me.

Whats new around Lebanon and Pleasant Hill. Guess by this time the Army or the navy has all the younger fellows that are fit for service. None of the boys in the service from Pleasant Hill have been killed other than Jimmie Gettle has their? How are the others making out.

Get the others to write me a few lines Mother. Think I'll send home some stamps so they can.

Glad pop likes his new job and hope you get a better home soon and closer to pops work. Can't begin to figure where the place is that he's working. Well Lebanon is beginning to be a strange place to me. It must be over six years since Ive left their Almost three years in the CCC's and now almost three years in the navy. Time sure is marching on. Will be twenty five next birthday.

Sorry I forgot your birthday which is to day. All I can say is Congradulations and hope there are many more and all happy. Don't work too hard and I hope to see all of you when this is over.

How old are the kids now? Just can't keep track of them. Don't suppose Jake and Harold know me anymore. They've seen so little of me.

What did S.P. McLean have to say when he wrote you? I ran around with him for almost two years. He is now out in the South Western Pacific someplace. Left a few months ago.

I recieve quite a bit of mail from friends here in California. More than I do from my own family and friends back home. One soldier in Alaska writes me. A few sailors at sea and some on islands write also. So I get quite a few letters but would like to get more from home. Seems funny with all the spare time people have, they can't sit down and use a few of them moments to drop a line.

This I guess is one of the longest letters I've ever written you. Hope it doesn't bore you. You see I was just in a writing mood.

All of you take good care of yourselves and keep the home fires burning.

Your loving son
Wilson

Telegraph reads: MOTHER PLEASE SEND FIFTY DOLLARS IMMEDIATELY CARE POSTAL LOVE= WILSON.

Postal Telegraph

STANDARD TIME INDICATED

RECEIVED AT

TELEPHONE YOUR TELEGRAMS TO POSTAL TELEGRAPH

Mackay Radio   All America Cables
Commercial Cables   Canadian Pacific Telegraphs

THIS IS A FULL RATE TELEGRAM, CABLE-GRAM OR RADIOGRAM UNLESS OTHERWISE INDICATED BY SYMBOL IN THE PREAMBLE OR IN THE ADDRESS OF THE MESSAGE. SYMBOLS DESIGNATING SERVICE SELECTED ARE OUTLINED IN THE COMPANY'S TARIFFS ON HAND AT EACH OFFICE AND ON FILE WITH REGULATORY AUTHORITIES.

Form HB3 (TEN) 9NL= MONTEREY CALIF JULY 28 1943=

MRS ERLINE LINEAWEAVER= 1240E CUMBERLAND ST   JUL 29 AM 9 08

(LEBANON PENNA)=

MOTHER PLEASE SEND FIFTY DOLLARS IMMEDIATLY CARE POSTAL

LOVE=

WILSON.

Postal Telegraph-Cable Company

FORM 102-A

Telephone Your TELEGRAMS to Postal Telegraph

WITHOUT EXTRA CHARGE, A FIXED-TEXT SOCIAL MESSAGE MAY BE SENT WITH ANY TELEGRAM MONEY ORDER WITHIN THE U.S.

TELEGRAMS accuracy speed courtesy CABLEGRAMS RADIOGRAMS

ISSUED AT

OFFICE   CITY AND STATE

DATE   TIME FILED

RECEIVED FOR

NAME AND FULL ADDRESS OF PAYEE OF MONEY ORDER

THE AMOUNT OF

FROM

NAME AND STREET ADDRESS OF PAYOR   AT   CITY AND STATE

MONEY ORDER CHARGES PAID

$

THIS MONEY ORDER IS ACCEPTED IN ACCORDANCE WITH THE TERMS AND CONDITIONS OF THE WRITTEN CONTRACT THIS DAY ENTERED INTO WITH POSTAL TELEGRAPH-CABLE COMPANY.

ASK ABOUT "GIFT" AND "PURCHASE" MONEY ORDERS

POSTAL TELEGRAPH-CABLE COMPANY

MONEY ORDER AGENT

[Note: This letter was written by Wilson's good friend Sam McLean to Wilson's mother.]

again I must say that I appreciated you
letter very ~~
I want you to
I think
his Family.
Take care
lip for you

only Mather can Cook.

I Know y
son, as "chuck
he happy unle
him.
do much
that air planes
him away fr
wants those
I Know very C
I am over
fit and like
thing out of th
go to and see
seen a couple
Yet n
that more th
to it from b
from my mai
me all abou
and about the
Many eggs th

S. P. McLean

Dear Mrs Lineaweaver;
I was very very glad and very proud to get your
letter. I appreciated it more then you will
ever know.
I wrote Wilson the other day. In fact one
day before I received your letter. But right away
I set down and wrote him a gain and told him
I received a letter from you.
It was to bad that "chuck" didn't get to
come home while he had his ten day leave
but he couldn't have gotten cross country and
back in that time.
We use to talk about you and his brothers
and sisters and Father very much. And I think
he enjoyed his leave home at X mas more
than any thing he had ever done. He is very
proud of all of you and who wouldn't he.
I have three Brothers in the service too.
We are all in Different countrys. And like
James we had all rather be home with
our loved ones more then off some where.
We all look foward very much to coming
home and sitting down to a meal cooked as

S P McLean AR
VS-67
70 Fleet post
San Francisc
Ca

[Postmark is U.S. Navy, July 30, PM, with a "Passed by Naval Censor" stamp]
Mrs E. Lineaweaver
1240 E. Cumberland St.
avon, Pa.

[Return Address:]
S P McLean ARM 2/c
VS-67
c/o Fleet post office
San Francisco Calif

S.P. McLean

Dear Mrs. Lineaweaver:

I was very very glad and very proud to get your Letter. I appreciated it more than you will know.

I wrote Wilson the other day. In fact one day before I receaved your letter. But right away I set down and wrote him again and told him I receaved a Letter from you.

It was to bad that "Chuck" didn't get to come home while he had his ten day Leave but he couldn't have gotten cross country and back in that time.

He use to talk about you and his brothers and Sisters and Father very much. And I think he enjoyed his leave home at Xmas more than any thing he had ever done. He is very proud of all of you and who wouldn't be.

I have three Brothers in the Service too. We are all in Different countrys. And Like James we had all rather be home with our loved ones more then off somewhere. We all Look foward very much to coming home and sitting down to a meal cooked as only Mother can cook.

I Know you are very busy. With a grand son, as "Chuck" describes him, you wouldn't be happy unless you were doing something for him.

As much as Wilson told his young brothers that air planes aren't fun you couldn't get him away from them for any thing. He wants those two to be something big. He is. I Know Very Big and very Swell.

I am over seas again now. In a nice out fit and like it as much as I could like any thing out of the States. We have movies to go to and see some good pictures. Also have even seen a couple of Movie Stars.

Get mail pretty often and enjoy that more than any thing else. Look foward to it from day to day. I receaved a Letter from My Mother also to day. They tell me all about the Neighbors and my friends and about the chickens and farm and how many eggs they get every day. I enjoy it all.

Again I must say that I appreciated you Letter very very much and when you get time I want you to write again.

I think a Lot of Wilson. And of all his Family. And you uspecially.

Take care of your self. Keep a stiff upper lip for you boys. "God Bless You."

Love
S.P. McLean

S P McLean ARM 2/c
VS-67   c/o Fleet post office
San Francisco Calif.

This is a newspaper clipping that appeared in the Lebanon Daily News, *Lebanon, PA, on Tuesday, September 28, 1943.*
Wilson references this in his October 25, 1943 letter.

TUESDAY EVENING, SEPT. 28, 1943

LOCAL BROTHERS IN SERVICE

Mr. and Mrs. Robert Lineaweaver, of 1240 East Cumberland Street, are the parents of two sons serving as nephews of Uncle Sam. They are Private James Luther Lineaweaver, left, of the United States Army and Petty Officer First Class Wilson Lineaweaver, of the United States Navy.

The former entered the service in February, 1943, and received his basic training at Fort Jackson, S. C., where he qualified as a sharpshooter. He later trained at Camp Gordon, Ga., and at present is serving at Camp Campbell, Ky.

Private Lineaweaver's wife, the former Elizabeth Hartman, is residing at 243 South Tenth Street. He was employed as a screen printer at the Textile Printing and Finishing plant, Spruce and Mifflin Streets, before his call to duty. The local soldier is also known as a former caddy at the Lebanon Country Club.

According to recent word received by the parents from their son, Wilson, who has been stationed at a naval air base in California since the first of the year, he recently was promoted to his present rank and at the time of writing was expecting an assignment to sea duty. While at sea, the young navy man serves as leading flight wireless man and gunner on an aircraft carrier based plane. On January 30, 1943, Officer Lineaweaver was the recipient of a citation and was decorated for bravery, after his return from seeing action in the Pacific theatres of war. He was cited for the bombing of a Jap cruiser. The young navy man enlisted in January, 1941, and prior to that served in the C.C.C. in Waynesboro. His parents recently received the medal which was presented to their son in California.

Aug. 9th, 1943

Dear Fat & Mots.

A little late but congradulations anyway, rather late then never. So you did it again, that gives you quite a family and makes me once again a proud uncle.

Perhaps your wondering why I don't return the favor and make you an uncle. Maybe I have, who knows whats running around in this world.

Would have written sooner but didn't know your address. Mother sent your new one. You wouldn't. By the way when are you going to break down and drop me a few lines.

Not much news out this way. Was rated again to first class, thats three stripes. There still flying my rear off. One consolations is that I'm back in dive bombers and have nothing to do with torpedoe planes which I've been flying these past 6 months. Will be going to see in the very near future

At the present I'm stationed at Monterey a famous old California summer resort and I'm making out fine.

Don't forget to write and give me all the news. Hows things at home. Hows everybody making out.

Your brother & brother-in-law
Wilson

W.C. Lineaweaver ARM 1/c
VC-37, c/o Fleet Postmaster
San Francisco, Calif.

[Postmark is Fort Bragg, Calif., Aug. 11, 1943, 8 PM]
Mr & Mrs Mahlon Lineaweaver
439 Walnut St.
Lebanon, Penna   -   *[No Return Address]*

fly. I'm glad that Jim is getting the
chance to come home. Got a [letter]
from him this morning. He [writes]
fairly regular although he [hasn't]
much to say.

Not much news out [here than I]
told you in my last letter. [I]
was promoted to petty offic[er]
(Aviation radioman 1st class) [can't go]
much further. Still going to [be here for a]
very near future unless somet[hing comes]
up to change things. Still f[eeling fine all the]
time and I'm getting very sic[k]

Give every one my regards [and think]
of you often. Will be wait[ing for]
your letter.

Your lo[ving son]
Wi[lliam]

Aug 9th 1943

Dear Mother
Thanks for the nice long letter
that I recieved the other day, I was very
glad to hear from you.

Glad to hear that everything is
just fine at home and that every body
is in good health.

So Dad likes his work, thats fine.
He's also making better pay, so you
should'nt be having any financial
difficulties.

Take care of yourself mother and
don't work too hard. Your in the position
now where you can take it easy and
watch others do the work. All the kids
are getting big. Won't even know them
when I see them next time.

Its seven ~~days~~ months now
since I was home last, time sure does

FORT BRAGG CALIF
AUG 11
8-PM
1943

Mr & Mrs Robert Linaweaver
1240 E. Cumberland St.
Avon, Penna.

Aug 9th 1943

Dear Mother

Thanks for the nice long letter that I recieved the other day, I was very glad to hear from you.

Glad to hear that everything is just fine at home and that everybody is in good health.

So Dad likes his work, thats fine. He's also making better pay so you shouldn't be having any financial difficulties.

Take care of yourself mother and don't work too hard. Your in the position now where you can take it easy and watch others do the work. All the kids are getting big. Won't even know them when I see them next time.

Its seven months now since I was home last, time sure does fly. I'm glad that Jim is getting the chance to come home. Got a letter from him this morning. He writes fairly regular although he never has much to say.

Not much news out this way. I told you in my last letter that I was promoted to petty officer 1st class (Aviation radioman 1st class.) Can't go much further. Still going to sea in the very near future unless something comes up to change things. Still flying all the time and I'm getting very sick of it.

Give every one my regards. I think of you often. Will be waiting for your letter.

Your loving son
Wilson

[Postmark is Fort Bragg, Calif., Aug. 11, 1943, 8 PM]
Mr & Mrs Robert Lineaweaver
1240 E. Cumberland St.
Avon, Penna.

[No Return Address]

Still haven't got any letters from back
there other than yours. Whats wr— I & t
a letter to Fat & Moto the other
congraduleting them on the newce—
haven't received an answer as yet
you read it. Tell Fat I bowled a
the other night. Is he still bowli

Jim and me write each o
He does'nt seem to care much for
guess I cain't blame him much.

Take care of yourself and gi
to Pop and the kids and the rest.
from you soon I close remaini

Your loving s—
Wilson

If I phone you it will probab
in th morning. There are three
in time and night rates are ch

Aug. 18th 1943

Dear Mother & Family:
    Well Mother! We moved again, further
south. The name of this place is Los Alamitos,
located just outside of Long Beach. About 20 mi.
from Los Angeles and 25 mi. from Hollywood. Our
next move will be west, Jap hunting.
    Received your letter dated Aug 12th this
morning and was glad to hear from you. Not
much news out this way to write about so I'll
just rattle on.
    I lost your phone number so if you
send it again I may phone you before going to
sea. I'll call you collect and you can pay for
it out of my money.
    As soon as I get a day off I plan on
going to Hollywood and have a look around
and see what I can see. One thing about
the navy, you sure get around. Can you recall
all the places I've been? After this is over and
I get out of the navy I'll be glad to settle
down on some nice quite farm.
    The kids go back to school next month.
Seems like a century since I've been in school
Time sure marches on.

[Postmark is U.S. Navy, Aug. 19, 1943, AM]
Mr. & Mrs. Robert Lineaweaver
1240 E. Cumberland St.
Avon, Penna.

[Return Address:]
W.C. Lineaweaver ARM 1/c
VC-37
c/o Fleet Postmaster
San Francisco, Calif.

Aug. 18th 1943

Dear Mother & Family:

Well Mother! We moved again, further south. The name of this place is Los Alamitos, located just outside of Long Beach. About 20 mi from Los Angeles and 25 mi. from Hollywood. Our next move will be west, Jap hunting.

Recieved your letter dated Aug 12th this morning and was glad to hear from you. Not much news out this way to write about so I'll just rattle on.

I lost your phone number so if you send it again I may phone you before going to sea. I'll call you collect and you can pay for it out of my money.

As soon as I get a day off I plan on going to Hollywood and have a look around and see what I can see. One thing about the navy, you sure get around. Can you recall all the places I've been? After this is over and I get out of the navy I'll be glad to settle down on some nice quite farm.

The kids go back to school next month. Seems like a century since I've been in school Time sure marches on.

Still haven't got any letters from back there other than yours. Whats wrong? Sent a letter to Fat & Mots the other week congradulating them on the newcomer but haven't recieved an answer as yet. Did they leave you read it. Tell Fat I bowled a 222 game the other night. Is he still bowling.

Jim and me write each other quite often. He doesn't seem to care much for the army. I guess I can't blame him much.

Take care of yourself and give my regards to Pop and the kids and the rest. Hoping to hear from you soon I close remaining

Your loving son
Wilson

If I phone you it will probably be early in the morning. There are three hours difference in time and night rates are cheaper.

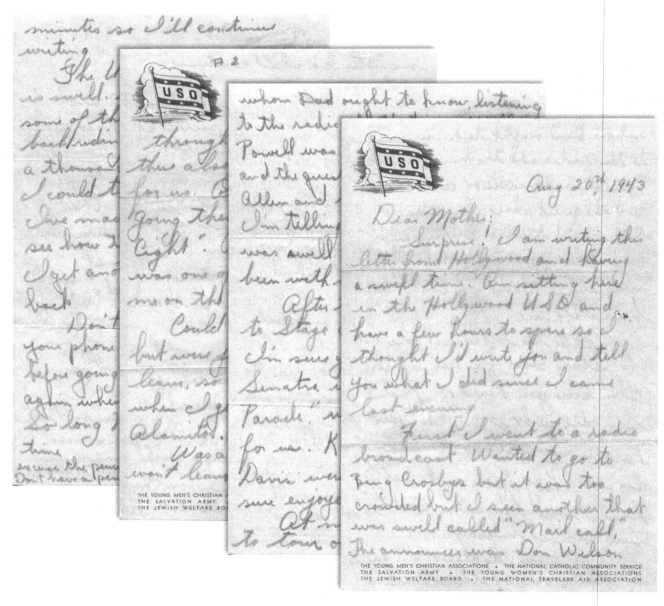

minutes so I'll continue
writing

The U[...]
is swell [...]
some of th[...]
back radi[...]
a thousan[...]
I could t[...]
I've mad[...]
see how [...]
I get and[...]
back.

Don't[...]
your phone[...]
before going[...]
again when[...]
So long [...]
time
excuse the pe[...]
Don't have a pen[...]

through[...]
there al[...]
for us. [...]
going the[...]
Eight". [...]
was one [...]
me on th[...]

Could[...]
but were[...]
leave, so[...]
when I g[...]
Alamitos.[...]

Was a[...]
won't leave[...]

THE YOUNG MEN'S CHRISTIAN [...]
THE SALVATION ARMY
THE JEWISH WELFARE BO[...]

whom Dad ought to know, listening
to the radio[...]
Powell was[...]
and the que[...]
Allen and [...]
I'm telling[...]
was swell.[...]
been with.[...]

After [...]
to Stage [...]
I'm sure[...]
Sinatra [...]
Parade." [...]
for us. K[...]
Davis we[...]
sure enjoy[...]

At [...]
to tour o[...]

Aug. 20th, 1943

Dear Mother;

Surprise! I am writing this
letter from Hollywood and having
a swell time. Am sitting here
in the Hollywood USO and
have a few hours to spare so I
thought I'd write you and tell
you what I did since I came
last evening

First I went to a radio
broadcast. Wanted to go to
Bing Crosbys but it was too
crowded but I seen another that
was swell called "Mail call,"
The announcer was Don Wilson

THE YOUNG MEN'S CHRISTIAN ASSOCIATIONS • THE NATIONAL CATHOLIC COMMUNITY SERVICE
THE SALVATION ARMY • THE YOUNG WOMEN'S CHRISTIAN ASSOCIATIONS
THE JEWISH WELFARE BOARD • THE NATIONAL TRAVELERS AID ASSOCIATION

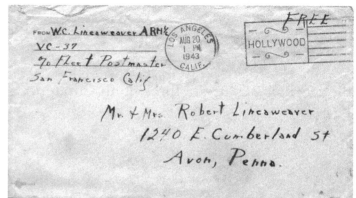

FROM W.C. Lineaweaver ARM½
VC-37
℅ Fleet Postmaster
San Francisco Calif.

FREE

HOLLYWOOD

LOS ANGELES
AUG 20
1 PM
1943
CALIF.

Mr. & Mrs. Robert Lineaweaver
1240 E. Cumberland St
Avon, Penna.

[Postmark is Los Angeles, Calif., Aug. 20, 1943, 1 PM]
Mr. & Mrs. Robert Lineaweaver
1240 E. Cumberland St
Avon, Penna.

[Return Address:]
W.C. Lineaweaver ARM 1/c
VC-37
c/o Fleet Postmaster
San Francisco Calif

Aug 20th, 1943

Dear Mother:

Surprise! I am writing this letter from Hollywood and having a swell time. Am sitting here in the Hollywood U.S.O. and have a few hours to spare so I thought I'd write you and tell you what I did since I came last evening.

First I went to a radio broadcast. Wanted to go to Bing Crosbys but it was too crowded but I seen another that was swell called "Mail call," The announcer was Don Wilson whom dad ought to know, listening to the radio all the time. William Powell was master of cermonies and the guest stars were Gracie Allen and George Burns and I'm telling you the whole show was swell. Wish you could have been with me.

After the broadcast I went to Stage door Canteen which I'm sure you heard of. Frank Sinatra who is on the "Hit Parade." was there to sing for us. Kay Kyser and Betty Davis were here also and I sure enjoyed myself.

At noon to day I'm going to tour one of the studios. through the U.S.O. and there also going to have dinner for us. At the studio were going there shooting "Torpedoe Eight". Remember that was one of the squadrons with me on the U.S.S. Hornet

Could rave on and on Mother but were just about ready to leave, so I'll write again when I get back to Los Alamitos.

Was a false alarm and we won't leave for fifteen more minutes so I'll continue writing

The U.S.O. here in Hollywood is swell. Swimming parties at some of the stars homes. Horse back riding, play, shows and a thousand other thing. Wish I could take them all in but Ive made up my mind to see how they make pictures. If I get another chance I'll come back.

Don't forget. If you send me your phone number I'll call you before going to see. Will write again when I return to Los Alamitos. So long Mother. Having a swell time

Your loving son
Wilson

excuse the pencil. Don't have a pen.
give everyone my love

Telegram reads: DEAR MOTHER PLEASE SEND SOME MONEY AM OK LOVE= WILSON
CARE WESTERNUNION LONGBEACH CALIF.

WESTERN UNION

(29)

CLASS OF SERVICE

This is a full-rate Telegram or Cablegram unless its deferred character is indicated by a suitable symbol above or preceding the address.

A. N. WILLIAMS
PRESIDENT

NEWCOMB CARLTON
CHAIRMAN OF THE BOARD

J. C. WILLEVER
FIRST VICE-PRESIDENT

SYMBOLS

DL=Day Letter
NT=Overnight Telegram
LC=Deferred Cable
NLT=Cable Night Letter
Ship Radiogram

The filing time shown in the date line on telegrams and day letters is STANDARD TIME at point of origin. Time of receipt is STANDARD TIME at point of destination

PAS17 13 4 EXTRA NL=LONGBEACH CLIF AUG 1943 AUG 22 AM 9 34

MRS ERLINE LINEAWEAVER=

1240 E CUMBERLAND ST LEBANON PENN=

DEAR MOTHER PLEASE SEND SOME MONEY AM OK LOVE=

WILSON   CARE WESTERNUNION LONGBEACH CALIF.

WESTERN UNION
TELEGRAM

FORM 1529-OA

The filing time shown in the date

PAS17 1

MRS ERLINE LINEAWEAVER=

1240 E CUMBERLAND ST LEBANON PENN=

Telegraph it!

QUICK AND SAFE.
ECONOMICAL...NO RED TAPE

THE WESTERN UNION TELEGRAPH COMPANY 4178-A

RECEIPT

LEBANON, PA.   AUG 23 1943   19___

OFFICE   DATE

Received from _Mrs Earline Lineweaver_ $45.00

Forty Five _____ Dollars in payment of:

☐ Account for the month of _____ 19___

☒ Telegraphic Money Order

☐ Telegram or Cable   To _1/c Wilson Lineweaver_

☐ Deposit on Collect Telegram   At _Long Beach Cal_
Returnable after 24 hours

☐ Account No. _____   THE WESTERN UNION TELEGRAPH COMPANY
For Remittance

MONEY ORDER
CHARGES PAID $ _5.52_   By _____

Money by
Telegraph and Cable

MONEY ORDERS—Telegraphed throughout the country. Payable during all open hours of Western Union offices during day or night, Sundays or holidays. Easy—Safe—Speedy. No red tape. Message to payee included at small extra cost.

SHOPPING ORDERS—For the purchase and delivery at distant cities of gifts and other articles—including railroad, bus, airplane and theatre tickets. A message may be included.

GIFT ORDERS—Solve the perplexing problem of what to give and combine sense and sentiment. Exchangeable anywhere for the gift most desired. Free sentiment for various occasions with each order.

ASK MANAGER FOR DETAILS

seen then shoot scenes of th new
picture "Ali Babi" and his Forty th__"
Also I seen many stars and it
was quite interesting.

Haven't been doing much
lately for recreation, too busy f
and working.

Glad to hear that Jim h
a chance to come home and I
also glad to hear that things
coming along O.K.

Give everyone my love
I hope to hear from you again soo

Got th money O.K. and I
expect a small package one of the
days. What it will contain I w
you to take good care of

Your loving son
Wilson

Wilson C. Lineaweaver ARM½
VC-37
℅ Fleet Postmaster
San Francisco, Calif.

Sept 2nd, 1943

Dear Mother,

Have a day off today and not
anything to do so I've decided to
answer a few letters. One of your
letters arrived yesterday.

Isn't much I can write about
without revealing things no one
should know but I can say that
this Southern Calif and agrees with
me and th only thing wrong, were
not going to get enough of it.

Hope you recived the letter that
I sent from Hollywood. After
writing you that letter I went
out th "universal studio" and

W.C. Lineaweaver ARM½
VC-37
℅ Fleet Postmaster
San Francisco, Calif

U.S. SEP 2 1943 P.M. NAVY

FREE

Mr & Mrs Robert Lineaweaver
1240 A Cumberland St
Avon, Penna

Wilson C. Lineaweaver ARM 1/c
VC-37
c/o Fleet Postmaster
San Francisco, Calif.

Sept 2nd 1943

Dear Mother:

Have a day off today and not anything to do so I've decided to answer a few letters. One of your letters arrived yesterday.

Isn't much I can write about without revealing things no one should know but I can say that this Southern Calif. sure agrees with me and the only thing wrong, were not going to get enough of it.

Hope you recieved the letter that I sent from Hollywood. After writing you that letter I went out to "universal studio" and seen them shoot scenes of the new picture "Ali Babi" and his Forty thieves". Also I seen many stars and it was quite interesting.

Haven't been doing much lately for recreation, too busy flying and working.

Glad to hear that Jim had a chance to come home and I'm also glad to hear that things are coming along O.K..

Give everyone my love and I hope to hear from you again soon

Got the money O.K. and Mother, expect a small package one of these days. What it will contain I want you to take good care of.

Your loving son
Wilson

[Postmark is U.S. Navy, Sept. 2, 1943, PM]
Mr & Mrs Robert Lineaweaver
1240 E Cumberland St.
Avon, Penna.

[Return Address:]
W.C. Lineaweaver ARM 1/c
VC-37
c/o Fleet Postmaster
San Francisco, Calif.

Leaving California

This was Wilson's last letter before heading out to sea on the USS Sangamon, *it being his second time to the Pacific war zone. The* Sangamon *departed on October 19th from San Diego with Squadron VC-37 onboard. She sailed to the South Pacific island of Espiritu Santo. According to the history of the* Sangamon *by Donald Schroeder, the ship remained there for a short time. Then on November 9th she went out to participate with transport and support groups in a practice landing at Pango Point on Efate Island. On November 13th she left Espiritu Santo again, rendezvoused with Task Force 53 the next day and steamed out. The Central Pacific Offensive began.*

NOTE: *In 1943 Wilson trained in TBF planes for six months. He may have flown in TBF's or SBD's while on the* Sangamon *as both type planes were aboard. No specific record of which plane he flew in could be found.*

them my regards. Seems to me that it
won't be long
fathers. Does
category? They
and not exclu
do better the

Still li
guess houses
keep trying, e

Hope eve
health. Take
and have the

W.C. Lineaw
VC-37
℅ Fleet Post
San Francisco

Glad to hear that you recieved my
medal OK. an
of it for me.

You men
that you had g
paper together
things like t
me or anythi
interest me.

Jim use
but about a
stopped. Wa
did happen?
a new camp
is his wife B
occur as yet?
a few lines

Coming
don't forget to
It must hav
you still got t
month?

Hows f
Tell them I a

Oct 25th 1943

Dear Parents.

It has been a long time since I've
heard from you and I must admit that I
have been lax myself. But now I have
plenty of spare time so you'll recieve my
letters more frequently.

You got the phone call as I promised.
Were you surprised? I could hear you very
plain but every now and then you were cut off.
The reason it was so early in the morning, I
waited for night rates which are cheaper and
the lines are not so busy. There also was a
difference in time of three hours so there
wasn't much choice but to get you up at
that early hour.

Many of the things that I wanted to
say I forgot at the time. Did the two
kids come down or did they sleep on? By
the way how old are Nate and Harold
getting to be. I keep forgetting Lucille
must be about seventeen and Dot about
fifteen. Are they all getting big.

[Postmark is U.S. Navy, Nov. 8, 1943, 6 PM,
with a "Passed By Naval Censor" Stamp]
Mr & Mrs Robert Lineaweaver
1240 E. Cumberland St
Avon, Penna.

[Return Address:]
W.C. Lineaweaver ARM 1/c U.S.N.
VC-37
c/o Fleet Postmaster
San Francisco, Calif.

Oct 25th 1943

Dear Parents.

It has been a long time since I've heard from you and I must admit that I have been lax myself. But now I have plenty of spare time so you'll recieve my letters more frequently.

You got the phone call as I promised. Were you surprised? I could hear you very plain but every now and then you were cut off. The reason it was so early in the morning, I waited for night rates which are cheaper and the lines are not so busy. There also was a difference in time of three hours so there wasn't much choice but to get you up at that early hour.

Many of the things that I wanted to say I forgot at the time. Did the two kids come down or did they sleep on? By the way how old are Nate and Harold getting to be. I keep forgetting. Lucille must be about seventeen and Dot about fifteen. Are they all getting big.

Glad to hear that you recieved my medal O.K. and I know you'll take care of it for me.

You mentioned in one of your letters that you had Jims and my picture in the paper together. Mother! Why don't you cut things like that out and send them to me or anything else that you think would interest me. I sure would appreciate it.

Jim used to write me quite regular but about a month and a half ago he stopped. Was he shipped across or what did happen? Last I heard he was in a new camp somewhere in Kentucky. How is his wife Bettie? Did the big event occur as yet? Ask Bettie to drop me a few lines if she finds time.

Coming back to that phone call again, don't forget to pay for it out of my money. It must have been pretty expensive. Do you still get the allotment checks every month?

Hows fat, Dave and families doing? Tell them I asked about them and give them my regards. Seems to me that it won't be long before they start drafting fathers. Does Fat and Dave come in that category? They sure would make good soldiers and not excluding "pop," I think he could do better than most of these fatheads.

Still living at the same dump? I guess houses are hard to get but if you keep trying, eventually you'll succeed.

Hope everyone is in the best of health. Take care of yourself. Write often and have the others write too.

Your loving son
Wilson

W.C. Lineaweaver ARM 1/c U.S.N.
VC-37
c/o Fleet Postmaster
San Francisco Calif.

"Crossing The Line" Ceremony

The "Crossing the Line" ceremony is for sailors crossing the equator for the first time. It is organized around "Neptune's Court". Sailors are either Shellbacks, those that have previously crossed the equator, or Pollywogs, those that have not. The initiation ceremony includes a royal chaplain, royal baby, barber, dentist, doctor, and others. "King Neptune", who at times is played by the captain, 'comes aboard' and takes temporary command of the ship. The royal baby is a fat guy wearing only a diaper. Pollywogs are put through a series of tasks, including kissing the royal baby's belly, lying on your back while the royal chaplain blesses you with a purple dye that does not wash off, the royal painter puts paint in your hair which makes it necessary for the royal barber to shave your head. The royal dentist gives a shot of foul tasting Novocain. After completion of the initiation, Pollywogs are given a certificate declaring their new status as Shellback.

According to his military file from the National Archives, Wilson qualified as a Shellback on October 27, 1943, while onboard the USS *Sangamon* CVE-26. See his letter dated June 29, 1944, where he references these photos that he sent home. Nine of the twelve photos that he sent home are on these two pages. (Wilson was not aboard the USS *Hornet* when it crossed the equator in 1942, but was on temporary duty at Pearl Harbor.)

Donald Schroeder of Manitowoc, WI, was a Quartermaster on the *Sangamon* in 1944. In 2016 he was able to identify two of the men on these photos. Left is Lt. Cdr. Leonard O. Fox, Executive Officer. Right is B. G. Levine, QM3c (the royal chaplain).

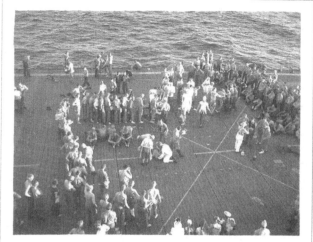

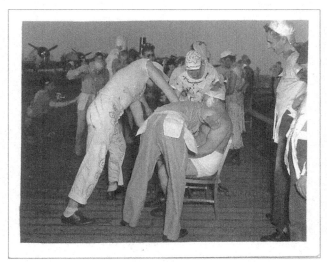

In one of your letters you said Jim
was coming ho[me]
he? Hows Jim
I'd hear from h[im]
from Dave and F[...]
to write them

What's ne[w]
the country, pleas[e]
anything happen[...]
I know making [...]
my regards to [...]
I'll be writing [...]

W.C. Lineaweaver
VC-37
% Fleet Postm[aster]
San Francisco, [Calif.]

Nov. 10th 1943

Rec'd Dec. 2

Dear Mother & Family:

Recieved two of your letters recently
and was very glad to hear from you and
home. Am happy and glad to know that
every little thing is alright.

Concerning the medal that I sent
you a few months ago. This is what I
would like you to have done for me. Take
the medal to some jeweler that has an
engraver and have him engrave on the
back of it these words:

"Presented to: W.C. Lineaweaver ARM1/c
Battle of Santa Cruz Oct. 26, 1942.

Have the engraver put this on the
back of the medal as he sees fit and
Mother, whoever does the job, see that
he does a good job. I feel sure that you
will do this for me so I'll thank you
now for the trouble I'm putting you to.

About all I can say about myself
is that I'm getting along swell and am
still in good health. It is almost a
year now since I've been home. Time sure
marches on. Things sure were changed the
last time when I came home, guess it
will be more so next time.

[Postmark is U.S. Navy, Nov. 1943
with a "Passed By Naval Censor" Stamp]
Mr & Mrs. Robert Lineaweaver
1240 E. Cumberland St.
Avon Penna.

[Return Address:]
W.C. Lineaweaver ARM 1/c U.S.N.
VC-37
c/o Fleet Postmaster
San Francisco, Calif.

Nov. 10ᵗʰ 1943 *[A note added says "Rec Dec 2"]*

Dear Mother & Family:

Recieved two of your letters recently and was very glad to hear from you and home. Am happy and glad to know that every little thing is alright.

Concerning the medal that I sent you a few months ago. This is what I would like you to have done for me. Take the medal to some jeweler that has an engraver and have him engrave on the back of it these words:

Presented to W. C. Lineaweaver ARM 1/c   Battle of Santa Cruz   Oct. 26, 1942.

Have the engraver put this on the back of the medal as he sees fit and Mother, whoever does the job, see that he does a good job. I feel sure that you will do this for me so I'll thank you now for the trouble I'm putting you to.

About all I can say about myself is that I'm getting along swell and am still in good health. It is almost a year now since I've been home. Time sure marches on. Things sure were changed the last time when I came home, guess it will be more so next time.

In one of your letters you said Jim was coming home for a few days. Did he? Hows Jim getting along? Thought I'd hear from him but no soap. Same from Dave and Fat. Guess I'll have to write them first so they write me.

Whats new around that part of the country, please keep me informed if anything happens. How are the fellows that I know making out in the service? Give my regards to the kids and friends and I'll be writing again soon

Your son
Wilson

W. C. Lineaweaver ARM 1/c U.S.N.
VC-37
c/o Fleet Postmaster
San Francisco, Calif.

mother and dad think about it?

How is th...
there still man...
about sailors, do...
home?

Take care...
gal and when you...
Its very pleasi...

Enclosed is a litt...
keep for a souven...

Dec 10th 1943

Dear Susie:

It was very nice of you writing me and I was glad to hear from you. I must apologize to you and the rest for not sending xmas presents, you see I'm not able too but I can wish you a very enjoyable Christmas hoping you get many of the things you want.

It is true that just about the only enjoyments we have is letter reading and sometimes we go for long periods at sea without even recieving letters. It makes you feel good hearing news from back home.

So you now going to high school and you like it. I'm glad to hear that and hope you make the best out of it. Are you going to Leb. High? Working some nights aloo ought to give you the money for school clothing.

It also was surprising to hear that Lucille is planning to get married. Hope she knows what she's doing. What does

---

W.C. Lineaweaver ARM1/c U.S.N.
Air Group 37
% Fleet Postmaster
San Francisco, Calif.

[postmark BELL, CALIF DEC 24 1 PM 1943]

Miss Dorothy Lineaweaver
1240 E. Cumberland St.
Avon, Penna.

[Postmark is Bell, Calif., Dec. 24, 1943, 1 PM]
Miss Dorothy Lineaweaver
1240 E. Cumberland St.
Avon, Penna.

[Return Address:]
W.C. Lineaweaver ARM 1/c U.S.N.
Air Group 37
c/o Fleet Postmaster
San Francisco, Calif.

Dec 10th 1943 *[Note that this letter is postmarked Dec. 24.]*

Dear Susie:

It was very nice of you writing me and I was glad to hear from you. I must apologize to you and the rest for not sending Xmas presents, you see I'm not able to but I can wish you a very enjoyable Christmas hoping you get many of the things you want.

It is true that just about the only enjoyments we have is letter reading and sometimes we go for long periods at sea without even recieving letters. It makes you feel good hearing news from back home.

So your now going to high school and you like it. I'm glad to hear that and hope you make the best out of it. Are you going to Leb. High? Working some nights also ought to give you the money for school clothing.

It also was surprising to hear that Lucille is planning to get married. Hope she knows what she's doing. What does mother and dad think about it?

How is the old city of Lebanon? Is there still many soldiers around? How about sailors, do you see many around home?

Take care of yourself and be a good gal and when you find time, drop me a letter. Its very pleasing hearing from you.

Your brother,
Wilson

Enclosed is a Hawaiian dollar you can keep for a souvenier

Battle of Tarawa

The time between the previous letter dated November 10, 1943, and this next letter dated December 10, 1943, the Sangamon *rendezvoused with Task Force 53 on November 14th. On November 20th they arrived in the Gilbert Islands to support the assault on Tarawa. The bloody battle of Tarawa was November 20-23. Wilson participated in the taking of Tarawa by providing air support to the landing Marines (see his letter dated December 13, 1943). Tarawa is an atoll in the Gilbert Islands that had a Japanese air base on the islet of Betio. Though the Americans were victorious, over 1,000 Marines were killed. The Japanese suffered nearly 4,700 deaths. The campaign for the taking of the Gilbert and Marshall Islands lasted from November 1943 to February 1944, and was needed for establishing airfields and naval bases that would allow air and naval support for upcoming operations across the Central Pacific. According to the history of the* Sangamon *by Donald Schroeder, after the assault on Tarawa, the* Sangamon's *planes continued providing air support through December 6th. Sent out were combat air patrols and anti-submarine patrols for both the target area and carrier group. Also, searches and hunter-killer flights were launched regularly, and sorties were at times carried out at the request of troops ashore. The ship left the Tarawa area on December 7th to return to the States for alterations, arriving in San Diego on December 20th.*

do not expect anything and as usual
I'll expect noth[...]
it would be usele[...]
here. You know wha[...]
There isn't m[...]
write about other t[...]
interest you, besid[...]
anyway. By reading[...]
more than I can [...]
Excuse this [...]
so very little in [...]
practice.
How is everyt[...]
everyone in good h[...]
as well as can [...]
in good health h[...]
Will be [...]
look for the follo[...]
remain

W.C. Lineaweaver [...]
VC-37
%o Fleet Postm[...]
San Francisco,

Dec 11th 1943

Dear Mother:

Last year at this time I was home on thirty days leave, what a difference this year. Guess I can't complain though, think of the million of other boys who will miss Christmas too and the boys who will never even see another. So all in all I consider myself lucky just being able to write you and hope that next Christmas will be different and I'll be home with this long bloody mess over with.

It has been a long time since I've heard from you but that, I imagine, is not your fault. Some times its hard for the mailman to get too me so, when he does I'll have quite a bit of letter reading to do and I'll know more to write about.

In another letter following this one I'm sending $250.00 for you to bank for me. Please do that for me and let me know if you recieved the money O.K.

With Christmas drawing near I wish I was in a position to send home some presents but I'm not so please

---

W.C. Lineaweaver ARM½ USN
VC-37
%o Fleet Postmaster
San Francisco, Calif

Dec.
13
1943

Mr & Mrs Robert Lineaweaver
1240 E. Cumberland St.
Avon, Penna.

PASSED BY NAVAL CENSOR

[Postmark is missing,
has a "Passed By Naval Censor" Stamp]
Mr & Mrs Robert Lineaweaver
1240 E. Cumberland St.
Avon, Penna.

[Return Address:]
W.C. Lineaweaver ARM 1/c USN
VC-37
c/o Fleet Postmaster
San Francisco, Calif.

Dec 11th 1943

Dear Mother:

Last year at this time I was home on thirty days leave, what a difference this year. Guess I can't complain though, think of the millions of other boys who will miss Christmas too and the boys who will never even see another. So all in all I consider myself lucky just being able to write you and hope that next Christmas will be different and I'll be home with this long bloody mess over with.

It has been a long time since Ive heard from you but that, I imagine, is not your fault. Sometimes its hard for the mailman to get too me so, when he does I'll have quite a bit of letter reading to do and I'll know more to write about.

In another letter following this one I'm sending $250.00 for you to bank for me. Please do that for me and let me know if you recieved the money O.K.

With Christmas drawing near I wish I was in a position to send home some presents but I'm not so please do not expect anything and as usual I'll expect nothing from home because it would be useless to send anything out here. You know what happened last year.

There isn't much more that I can write about other than war and that wouldn't interest you, besides I can't write about it anyway. By reading the papers you can learn more than I can tell.

Excuse this scribbling mother, I do so very little writing that I'm out of practice.

How is everything at home? and is everyone in good health? I'm getting along as well as can be expected and I'm still in good health hoping all of you are too.

Will be writing again soon and look for the following letter until then I remain

Your son,
Wilson

W. C. Lineaweaver ARM 1/c U.S.N.
VC-37
c/o Fleet Postmaster
San Francisco, Calif

Dec 12th 1943
[A note added says "Dec 18"]

Dear Mother:

Enclosed is $250.00 in postal money orders that I want you to cash and bank for me. As soon as you bank the money please write letting me know you recieved the money O.K.

Thanks a lot mother and I know you will comply with my wishes.

Hoping to hear from you soon I remain

Your son,
Wilson

Date 18

Dec 12th 1943

Dear Mother:
Enclosed is $250.00/xx in postal money orders that I want you to cash and bank for me. As soon as you bank the money please write letting me know you recieved the money O.K.
Thanks a lot mother and I know you will comply with my wishes.
Hoping to hear from you soon I remain

Your son,
Wilson

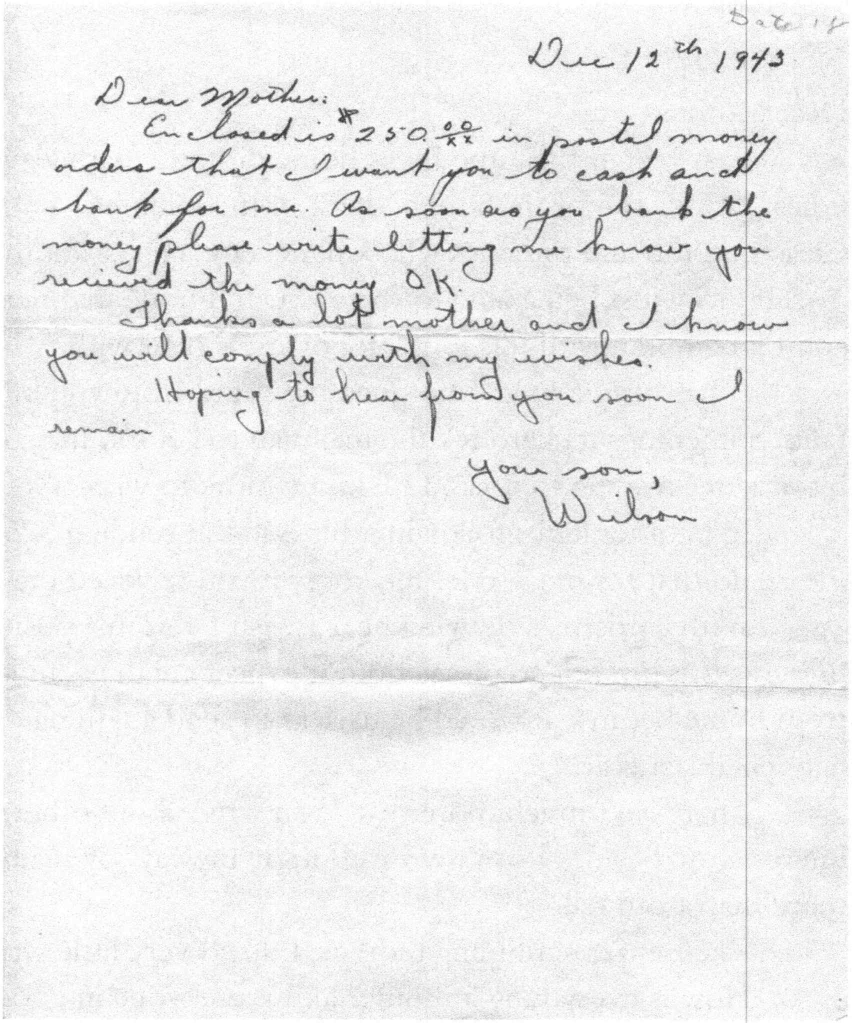

Dec 25, 1943

Dear Mother

Under the conditions I'm writing this will not be much of a letter.

I'm writing this letter for your son as he is not feeling very well at the moment. I know you want to know what has happened so I will try to make it as pleasant as possible.

Your son was injured by a trailer and is in the hospital with a broken pelvic bone. It is not too serious but will be here for some time.

He hopes you have had a very nice Christmas and wishes he was with you on this Christmas Day.

He wants you to write him here at the hospital his address is
U. S. Naval Hospital
Bldg 5 Ward 2
San Diego, Calif.

I am a friend of one of the boys in your sons squadron and we came up to see him. There is nothing to worry about and your son said he would write to you in a day or two.

May I as well as his friend Humphrey Lane express our best wishes to you for the New Year.

Your son by Louise Miklovic
Your son
Wilson

[Postmark is San Diego, Calif., Dec. 26, 1943, 12 M]
Mrs. Erline Lineaweaver
1240 E. Cumberland
Lebanon, Penna.

[Return Address:]
W.C. Lineaweaver ARM 1/c
Bldg 5   Ward 2
U.S. Naval Hospital
San Diego, Calif.

time and then were included in the taking
of the Gilbert Islands I
_____ of the island where we
covered marine landings Pe___
read about_ in the papers We
Gilberts about 21 days and th__
Harbor and ___ here

As yet I haven't heard wh___
the money I sent Hope you did
got my _____ packages as ye___
one mother

When you write use th__

U S Naval Hospi___
Building #5 Ward
San Diego C___

will write again soon

You lo___

U___

Dec 31st 1943

Dear Mother
        Laying here on my back with pain running
through me is quite a handicap to write
you this letter so I hope you bear with me
and only hope this is readable
        I arrived in the U.S.A. on Dec 20th and
entered the naval hospital here at San Diego
on the 21st The doctors here told me
very little that whats wrong with me one
thing my pelvis is broke and I think my
leg is also just below the hip The pain is
severe but the doctors say I'll be O.K. in
time so do not worry too much over me.
        The hardest thing for me is laying here
in one spot unable to move but when I
look at all the other _____ dad men around
me and think of what there going through
it makes it easier for me.
        I suppose you are wandering what I
was doing the last 3 or 4 months Well
I am able to tell you now We were down
in the southwest Pacific for some

[Postmark is San Diego, Calif., Jan. 1, 1944, 11 AM]
Mr & Mrs Robert Lineaweaver
1240 E Cumberland St.
Avon, Penna.

[No Return Address]

[It appears that this letter was written by Wilson in a very light penciling, and then may have been overwritten in a darker penciling, perhaps by a family member after receiving the letter.]

Dec. 31st 1943

Dear Mother

Laying here on my back with pain running through me is quite a handicap to write you this letter so I hope you bear with me and only hope this is readable.

I arrived in the U.S.A. on Dec 20th and entered the naval hospital here at San Diego on the 21st. The doctors have told me very little of whats wrong with me one thing my pelvis is broke and I think my leg is also just below the hip The pain is severe but the doctors say I'll be O.K. in time so do not worry too much over me.

The hardest thing for me is laying here in one spot unable to move but when I look at all the other wounded men around me and think of what there going through it makes it easier for me.

I suppose you are wandering what I was doing the last 3 or 4 months. Well I am able to tell you now. We were down in the southwest Pacific for some time and then were included in the taking of the Gilbert Islands. Tarawa was the name of the island where we attacked and covered marine landings Perhaps you have read about it in the papers. We stayed in the Gilberts about 21 days and then went to Pearl Harbor and now here.

As yet I haven't heard whether you received the money I sent Hope you did and I haven't got my xmas package as yet. Did you send one Mother

When you write use this address

US Naval Hospital

Building #5 Ward 2

San Diego, Calif.

Will write again soon

Your loving son
Wilson

and having done exceptionaly good
job we were ordered
to the states for the ___
after a very short stay
East Hadden.

Within the last few ___
have received many of ___
and very glad to hear ___
you and the news ___

The Christmas packages ___
you sent have not ___
as yet, will probably ___
like last year and I ___
will recive them.

I haven't heard ___
few months and I'm
wandering if he is still
States. Glad to hear ___
their baby has finally ___
& doing swell. Guess ___
a proud papa. Next ___
you write Jim remind ___
that his sailor brother ___
like to hear from him. ___
able to be home when ___
baby was born?
Hope everyone are in ___
health and doing fine. ___
of yourself, Mother and ___
write again soon.
Your loving Son – W ___

U.S. Naval Hospital
San Diego, Calif.
Jan. 1, 1944

Dear Mother –
I'm sorry that I haven't
written, lying here on my back
makes writing almost impossible
but one of the nurses stationed
here at the hospital has
volunteered to do so for me.
The extent of my injury is not
fully known as far as I
know I have a fractured
pelvis but very much pain
but please do not worry too
much about me. The Dr.
says I'll be up & around before
I know it.

I guess you've been
wandering what I've been doing
the last month, but as you
know I was unable to tell
you, now I can. We spent
a few months in the South
West Pacific & then were included
in the plans for the taking
of the Gilbert Islands. Our
job was to assist the Marines
landing at Tarawa. Our stay
in that group of islands
lasted twenty one days

[Postmark is San Diego, Calif., Jan. 2, 1944,
10:30 AM]
Mrs. Erline Lineaweaver
1240 East Cumberland St.
Lebanon, Penna.

[Return Address:]
W.C. Lineaweaver ARM 1/c
U.S. Naval Hospital
Bldg 5 - Ward 2
San Diego, Calif.

(Note: This letter was written by a Wave at the hospital as dictated by Wilson.)

U.S. Naval Hospital
San Diego, Calif.
Jan. 1 – 1944

Dear Mother –

I'm sorry that I haven't written, lying here on my back makes writing almost impossible but one of the Waves stationed here at the hospital has volunteered to do so for me. The extent of my injury is not fully known as far as I know I have a fractured pelvis but very much pain but please do not worry too much about me. The Dr. says I'll be up & around before I know it.

I guess you've been wondering what I've been doing the last month, but as you know I was unable to tell you, now I can. We spent a few months in the South West Pacific & then were included in the plans for the taking of the Gilbert Islands. Our job was to assit the Marines landing at Tarawa. Our stay in that group of Islands twenty one days and having done exceptionaly good job we were ordered back to the states for the Holidays after a very short stay at Pearl Harbor.

Within the last few days I have received many of your letters and very glad to hear from you and the news from home

The Christmas packages that you sent have not arrived as yet, will probably be like last year and I never will receive them.

I haven't heard from Jim for months and I'm wondering if he is still in the states. Glad to hear that their baby has finally arrived & doing swell. Guess Jim is a proud papa. Next time you write Jim remind him that his sailor brother would like to hear from him. Was he able to be home when the baby was born? *[James Luther Lineaweaver, Jr., born November 3, 1943.]*

Hope everyone are in good health and doing fine. Take care of yourself, Mother and I'll write again soon.

Your loving Son-
Wilson

Jan. 9, 1944

Dear Mother:

This is Sunday morning, my 19th day here in the hospital and I feel lots better. Most of the pain is gone but lying here in one spot is hard to stand and almost drives me crazy.

Every day I am waiting for a letter from you but in vain. Is anything wrong that you cannot write? I'm sure you have written but probably have used my former address. From now on until I move from the hospital my address will be —

W. C. Lineaweaver A.R.M.
U.S. Naval Hospital
Building 5 Ward 2
San Diego, Calif

Perhaps as my condition improves they may move me to different buildings and wards. This is what

[Postmark is San Diego, Calif., Jan. 10, 1944, 4 PM]
Mr & Mrs. Robert Lineaweaver
1240 E. Cumberland St.
Avon, Penna

[Return Address:]
W. Lineaweaver
U.S. Naval Hosp
San Diego, 34 Calif.

Jan. 9, 1944

Dear Mother:

This is Sunday morning, my 19th day here in the hospital and I feel lots better. Most of the pain is gone but lying here in one spot is hard to stand and almost drives me crazy.

Every day I am waiting for a letter from you but in vain. Is anything wrong that you cannot write? I'm sure you have written but probably have used my former address. From now on until I move from the hospital my address will be --

> W.C. Lineaweaver ARM 1/c
> U.S. Naval Hospital, Building 5 Ward 2
> San Diego, Calif

Perhaps as my condition improves they may move me to different buildings and wards. In that case I'll let you know immediately.

This is a very nice Sunday morning, the sun is shining bright and warm. One of the nurses has promised to push my bed outside so I can get some fresh air and sunshine this afternoon. I'll like that. One of the sailors who I have made friends with brought me a Sunday paper to read. Every one is very nice to me.

The fellows from my squadron also were very good to me because I think they liked me a lot although at times I had to give them some harsh orders. They brought me a radio so the time passes easier for me and let me tell you mother, this radio is a big help. I listen to it all the time and at night it helps me to go to sleep. They also brought lots of cigarettes, magazines and to top everything, a nice bouquet of of flowers. Also numerous other things

Two other sailors by name of Kado and Schley are two ship mates I'll never forget. When real sick and in much pain they cheered me up, washed and fed me when I was helpless. Without them I don't know how I could have managed through the first two weeks.

Well I guess that's enough about myself for a while. Give my regards to all of my brothers and sisters. Have them write and also ask dad to write.

I expect to be O.K. only it will take a long time. My doctor is one of the best bone doctors in the country so please do not worry too much about me. Take care of yourself and don't work too hard. Perhaps when I get well they may leave me come home for a while but its not a promise so I'm just hoping.

Am waiting impatiently to hear from you I remain

Your loving son
Wilson

P.S. Writing in bed so excuse the writing

every day and everyone comments about them.

Realy mother, I can't [wait] to tell you how thankful I am and that you thought so much about me to remember. It helps a lot to go through this ordeal that I must [face]

And mother, I was worried about that money I sent, but now I know its safe in [bank] thanks to you.

As yet I haven't recieved [the] package you sent in Oct, it will catch up with me one of these days. And mother, right now there isn't anything that I need, everyone is so good to me but when I do need something I'll ask you for it.

Well I'll write again soon

Your loving son
Wilson

Jan 10th 1944

Dear Mother:

This morning I recieved your most welcome letters and card, also one from Pat & family. [The] top everything flowers arrived this evening and I must say they are beautiful and smell like perfume. I never bothered much about flowers so I'm pretty ignorant when they concern. That's why I can't tell what kind they are, but as I lay here looking at them and studying them I come to the conclusion that they are the most beautiful thing that I ever cast my eyes upon.

They sit along side my bed on a small table just a foot from my face and they seem to send a cool smelly breeze across my face. The nurse has promise to water them for me

W. [illegible]
U.S. Signal [Corps]
[illegible]
San Diego [illegible]

SAN DIEGO
JAN 11
11 AM
1944
CALIF.

NAVAL [illegible]
BRA[illegible]

Mr & Mrs Robert Lineaweaver
1240 E. Cumberland St
Avon, Penna.

Jan 10th 1944

Dear Mother:

This morning I recieved your most welcome letters and card, also one from Fat & family. To top everything flowers arrived this evening and I must say they are beautiful and smell like perfume. I never bothered much about flowers so I'm pretty ignorant where they concern. That's why I can't tell what kind they are, but as I lay here looking at them and studying them I come to the conclusion that they are the most beautiful thing that I ever cast my eyes upon.

They sit along side my bed on a small table just a foot from my face and they seem to send a cool smelly breeze across my face. The nurse has promise to water them for me every day and every one comments about them.

Realy mother, I can't begin to tell you how thankful I am and that you thought that much about me to remember. It helps a lot to go through this ordeal that I must go.

And mother, I was worried about that money I sent but now I know its safe in bank, thanks to you.

As yet I haven't recieved the package you sent in Oct., it will catch up with me one of these days. And mother, right now there isn't anything that I need, everyone is so good to me but when I do need something I'll ask you for it.

Will write again soon

Your loving son
Wilson

[Postmark is San Diego, Calif., Jan. 11, 1944, 11 AM]
Mr. & Mrs. Robert Lineaweaver
1240 E. Cumberland St.
Avon, Penna.

[Return Address:]
W.C. Lineaweaver ARM 1/c
U.S. Naval Hospital
Building 5 Ward 2
San Diego, Calif.

is lying on my back unable to move.
Also getting on bed pans and wh...
before them if you know what I...
To top everything is to have a ...
wipe my rear (Gad!) I'm com...
helpless. Sometimes I can't ...
any water and you know what they do...
insert a tube and drain me. ...
that ducky.

Well! this is enough abo...
my tough luck. How are you ...
Better I hope than I. Still...
ing? Suppose right now you ...
beat me.

By the way Fat, what's th...
of U.S. getting you? Or Dave ...
Not but you never can tell.

In closing I hope th...
letter finds you, Martha and ...
finds in the best of health...
soon

Your brother
Wilson

Received your card, thanks

Jan. 14th, 1944

Dear Fat & Family:

As I'm sure that by this time
you know my condition there at the
hospital, I won't say much about
it. What I do want to say is
that I am very thankful for the
box of candy that I received
the other day. Although at that
time I was unable to eat them
due to the liquid diet that
I was on. Yesterday my diet
was changed to solid food so
I went to town on the candy.
Again let me thank you for
remembering.

My condition was plenty
serious and I was pretty much
broken up but I feel sure that
now I'm on the road to recovery.
With most of the pain gone,
what I now find almost unbearable

W.C. Lingaweaver AM 2/c
U.S. Naval Hospital
Building 5 Ward 2
San Diego, Calif.

SAN DIEGO
JAN 15
11 AM
1944
CALIF

NAVAL HOS
BRAN

1-14-44

Mr. & Mrs. Mahlon Lingaweaver
439 Walnut St
Lebanon, Penna.

Jan. 14th, 1944

Dear Fat & Family:

As I'm sure that by this time you know my condition here at the hospital, I won't say much about it. What I do want to say is that Im very thankful for the box of candy that I recieved the other day. Although at that time I was unable to eat them due to the liquid diet that I was on. Yesterday my diet was changed to solid food so I went to town on the candy. Again let me thank you for remembering.

My condition was plenty serious and I was pretty much broken up but I feel sure that now I'm on the road to recovery.

With most of the pain gone, what I now find almost unbearable is lying on my back unable to move. Also getting on bed pans and what comes before them if you know what I mean. To top everything is to have a nurse wipe my rear (Gad!) I'm completely helpless. Sometimes I can't pass any water and you know what they do, they insert a tube and drain me. Isn't that ducky.

Well! this is enough about my tough luck. How are you doing? Better I hope than I. Still bowling? Suppose right now you could beat me.

By the way Fat, whats the chances of U.S. getting you? Or Dave? Hope not but you never can tell.

In closing I hope this letter finds you, Martha and the kids in the best of health. Write soon

Your brother
Wilson

Recieved your card, thanks

[Postmark is San Diego, Calif., Jan. 15, 1944, 11 AM]
Mr. & Mrs. Mahlon Lineaweaver
439 Walnut St
Lebanon, Penna.

[Return Address:]
W.C. Lineaweaver ARM 1/c
U.S. Naval Hospital
Building 5 Ward 2
San Diego, Calif.

taking them.

The weather here at San De[igo is]
nice and warm almost the who[le year]
around, but being along the o[cean]
we have mist and damp rains [now]
now and then. One thing it i[s not]
as cold as you have it at home.

Mother, I'd like you to sen[d the]
Lebanon Daily news to me as of[ten as]
you can. I enjoy reading it and [get]
into lots of things that interes[t me.]

My arm gets very tired wr[iting]
and I seem to be very weak so [I]
have to keep my letters short.

Write often and have the [others]
write too. Will be waiting to [hear]
from. I remain

Your loving son
Wilson

Jan. 18th 1944

Dear Mother,

Your letter arrived this morning
and I was very glad to hear from you.
Glad to hear that everything is
getting along well at home and
everyone is in good health.

I am feeling much better today
and am well on the way to recovery. I
have quit taking sleeping pills and dope
and believe it or not, lately I have
been sleeping better. My injurie
occured while on duty and performing
in my work.

You said you received the money I
sent, was it all there? 250.00

I also received your flowers and
package of candy 7 ats box of candy
arrived too. Thanks to all of you.

The fellows from my former outfit
have sent me a nice sterling silver
Identification bracelot with my name
engraved on it and good luck from VC-37.
Was'nt that nice of them. I imagine
they somewhere in the Marshall Islands.
Watch, one of these days we will be

Jan. 18th, 1944

Dear Mother

Your letter arrived this morning and I was very glad to hear from you. Glad to hear that everything is getting along swell at home and every one is in good health.

I am feeling much better today and am well on the way to recovery. I have quit taking sleeping pills and dope and believe it or not, lately I have been sleeping better. My injuries occurred while on duty and performing in my work.

You said you recieved the money I sent, was it all there. $250.00.

I also recieved your flowers and package of candy. Fats box of candy arrived too. Thanks to all of you.

The fellows from my former outfit have sent me a nice sterling silver Identification bracelet with my name engraved on it and good luck from VC-37. Wasn't that nice of them. I imagine there somewhere in the Marshall Islands. Watch, one of these days we will be taking them.

The weather here at San Diego is nice and warm almost the whole year around, but being along the ocean, we have mist and damp rains every now and then. One thing it isn't near as cold as you have it at home.

Mother, I'd like you to send the Lebanon Daily news to me as often as you can. I enjoy reading it and run into lots of things that interest me.

My arm gets very tired writing and I seem to be very weak so I'll have to keep my letters short.

Write often and have the rest write too. Will be waiting to hear from you I remain

Your loving son
Wilson

[Postmark is San Diego, Calif., Jan. 19, 1944, 11 AM]
Mr & Mrs Robert Lineaweaver
1240 E. Cumberland St.
Avon, Penna.

[Return Address:]
W.C. Lineaweaver ARM 1/c
US Naval Hospital
Building 5 Ward 2
San Diego, Calif.

Haven't much more to rattle
on about so [...] [...]
to hear from [...]
wishing you [...]

You [...]

see she is a little older than
me and went [...]
High but we [...]
to talk about [...]
in 35. Perhaps [...]
father use to g[...]
[...] I'm su[...]
Dad. She also [...]
Lebanon pretzels [...]
sent.

Boy mother [...]
surprised the oth[...]
mail boy broug[...]
Uncle Charles [...]
hear from him [...]
lots of cards [...]
recovery.

I haven't r[...]
letter from J[...]
months but y[...]
also got a [...]

Jan. 27, 1944

Dear Mother

Just a few lines Mother to
let you know that I'm feeling
much better. Still have some
pain but not near as severe
as before. I also get pains in
the stomach.

Your papers arrived yesterday
and I enjoyed them very much.
I also read them from beginning
to end running across numerous
articles that interested me. Thanks
a lot.

I had a nice surprise Sunday
a wave from Lebanon stationed here
at the hospital by name of
Mary Folmer came up to see
me. She heard that I was here
from her mother. Although I
didn't know her before, you

W. E. Lineaweaver S1/C
U S Naval Hospital
Bldg 5 Ward 2
San Diego, Calif

SAN DIEGO
JAN 28
11 AM
1944
CALIF.

NAVAL [...]
BR.

1-27-44

Air Mail

Mr + Mrs Robert Lineaweaver
1240 E. Cumberland St.
Avon, Penna.

Jan. 27, 1944

Dear Mother

Just a few lines Mother to let you know that I'm feeling much better. Still have some pain but not near as severe as before. I also get pains in the stomach.

Your papers arrived yesterday and I enjoyed them very much. I also read them from beginning to end running across numerous articles that interested me. Thanks a lot.

I had a nice surprise Sunday, a Wave from Lebanon stationed here at the hospital by name of Mary Folmer came up to see me. She heard that I was here from her mother. Although I didn't know her before, you see she is a little older than me and went to Lebanon Catholic High but we have many things to talk about. She graduated in 35. Perhap you know her, her father use to own the fifth ward hotel. I'm sure Dad knows her Dad. She also brought up some Lebanon pretzels that her mother sent.

Boy Mother! Did I get surprised the other week when the mail boy brought a letter from Uncle Charles. Never expected to hear from him. I also recieved lots of cards wishing me speedy recovery.

I haven't recieved many letters from Jim in the past months but yesterday one arrived. Also got a letter from Mahlon.

Haven't much more to rattle on about so I'll close hoping to hear from you soon and wishing you the best of health.

Your loving son
Wilson.

[Postmark is San Diego, Calif., Jan. 28, 1944, 11 AM]
Mr & Mrs Robert Lineaweaver
1240 E. Cumberland St.
Avon, Penna.

[Return Address:]
W.C. Lineaweaver ARM 1/c
US Naval Hospital
Bldg 5 Ward 2
San Diego, Calif.

Jan. 27, 1944

Hi Jake & Harold.

    I recieved your card and the five sticks of chewing gum the other day, thanks for remembering me. Thought by now you forgot all about me.

    Enclosed is a dollar for you to divide and maybe see a show on me, Hows that?

    Glad to hear that both of you are doing fine in school, Keep up the good work.

    Perhaps I'll be seeing you soon until then I remain

Your sailor brother
Wilson

[Postmark is San Diego, Calif., Jan. 28, 1944, 11 AM]
Nathan & Harold Lineaweaver
1240 E. Cumberland St.
Avon, Penna.

[No return address remains on this envelope.]

At right is a newspaper clipping which appeared on page one of the January 15, 1944 edition of the *Lebanon Daily News*, Lebanon, PA. The article states that Wilson was injured in the Pacific. Instead, he was apparently injured right after arriving in San Diego, CA. Wilson's letter dated December 31, 1943, states that he arrived in the U.S. on December 20, 1943, and entered the Naval Hospital on December 21ˢᵗ. The USS *Sangamon*, which Wilson was on, arrived in San Diego on December 20, 1943.

REPORTED INJURED

Wilson Lineaweaver

LOCAL HERO INJURED IN PACIFIC ACTION

Wilson Lineaweaver Is Now In Calif. Hospital

Petty Officer First Class Wilson Lineaweaver, one of Lebanon County's early World War II heroes, has been confined to the Naval Hospital at San Diego, Calif., since the latter part of December, after being injured while fighting on the Gilbert Islands, it was learned here today.

According to information received by the young sailor's parents, Mr. and Mrs. Robert Lineaweaver, of 1240 East Cumberland Street, Lineaweaver is suffering from a broken pelvis bone and a possible broken leg. Details are meager as to the extent of the injuries or the manner in which they were received. In recent letters received from him, he informed his parents that he spent twenty-one days on the Gilbert Islands out of four months in the South Pacific theatre of war. While serving with the Navy, he was engaged as a wireless operator and gunner.

The Lebanon County sailor is credited with being in the plane which dropped bombs of a Jap aircraft carrier that was sunk in Guadalcanal in October of 1942. At that time he was aboard the U.S.S. Hornet.

In Wilson's letter dated December 25, 1943, it is stated that he was "injured by a trailer". In later years, Wilson's youngest brother Harold related that Wilson was actually injured by a vehicle (pulling a trailer?) that was being driven by the wife of a high ranking officer, perhaps a general. At the time of the newspaper article, news of the war was very limited and censored, so perhaps the family, or news staff, had made some assumptions of Wilson's injury.

Feb 3rd 1944

Dear Mother—

This being a long monotonous afternoon I've decided to write some letters so here goes.

Most of the morning was spent reading the newspapers you sent which arrived early th_____. I noticed by all the names of the men in the service, they are really everybody. It must be almost deserted around Lebanon. How's the chances of them getting Dave & Mahlon?

The way it looks at the present time, this war will last long enough to get Nat & Harold too.

My condition is much better Mother! and I feel

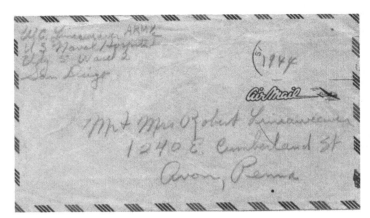

[Postmark is missing]
Mr & Mrs Robert Lineaweaver
1240 E. Cumberland St.
Avon, Penna.

[Return Address:]
W.C. Lineaweaver ARM 1/c
US Naval Hospital
Bldg. 5 Ward 2
San Diego

Feb 3rd, 1944

Dear Mother

This being a long monotonous afternoon I've decided to write some letters so here goes.

Most of the morning was spent reading the newspapers you sent which arrived early this morning. I notice by all the names of the men in the service, they are really getting everybody. It must be almost deserted around Lebanon. Hows the chances of them getting Dave & Mahlon?

The way it looks at the present time, this war will last long enough to get Nat & Harold too.

My condition is much better Mother! and I feel fine. This makes almost seven weeks flat on my back and Boy thats a long time. I'm wondering how much longer it will take.

I get mineral oil twice a day and its just like taking castor oil but the hardest thing for me to stand is the bed pan. Can you imagine going while flat on your back. It's quite a job and then to have someone wipe me (At my age)

Got another letter from Jim and also two old ones from Dot & Betty. Mailed back in Dec. What did Dot do with the Hawaiian dollar that I sent her? I also got Dads letter some time ago.

Hows everything at home, O.K. I hope? From your letters I gather that many improvements have been made to the house your living in. To my estimation they would have to tear that shack down and rebuild it to make any improvement. It must be very cold and hard to heat.

The squadron that I just left is fighting right now in the Marshall Islands. Perhaps I am lucky to be in the hospital but if I had my pick I'd sooner be out there fighting than on my back here useless.

Perhaps in another month or two I may be able to come home but I'm not sure. Some get leave and others just don't. Hope I'm one of the lucky ones.

Tomorrows pay day for me but I can't spend or use the money in any way so I'll send it home to you and have it banked. Be on the lookout for it.

Will be writing again soon

Your son
Wilson

"Men As Well As Ships Need A Haven For Repair"

Built on a 22 acre hilltop in Balboa Park and overlooking San Diego Bay, the United States Naval Hospital at San Diego, California, was commissioned on August 22, 1922. A central administration building flanked with three wards on either end and four other small buildings were built at a cost of over 1.1 million dollars. The first buildings provided bed space for less than 300 patients. Tents were provided for overflow of patients in a center patio. Construction of additional buildings

occurred throughout the 1920's so that by 1929 the entire compound represented an investment of $3,500,000.

By 1941 and the beginning of World War II, the hospital contained 56 buildings with the authorized capacity of 1,424 beds, and was caring for approximately 1,200 patients. In 1944 the U.S. Naval Hospital Corps School for medical training was transferred to the hospital. The last month of the war, August 1945, the hospital cared for an average of 8,096 patients daily. During this war period approximately 172,000 patients were treated; with a peak of 12,068 patients on December 27, 1944. At the height of WWII, as many as 5,000 patients were admitted each month, or an average of about 166 per day.

Due to large numbers of war casualties coming from the Pacific Theater of Operations, the hospital took over most of the buildings in present-day Balboa Park. For instance, 400 beds were placed in the San Diego Museum of Art; the San Diego Natural History Museum was also converted into hospital wards; the Lily Pond became a rehabilitation pool; the Japanese Tea Garden a Red Cross Servicemen's Center; and the House of Pacific Relations

became officers' quarters. San Diego Naval Hospital was one of the largest of several dozen U.S. naval hospitals during WWII. In 1946 after the end of the war, the Balboa Park grounds and buildings were returned to the city.

During the 1980's an entirely new $270 million hospital complex was built north of the original hospital. A 39-acre portion of the original site was then returned to the city of San Diego and restored to Park use.

Photos, clockwise from top: c1950, as the hospital would have looked when Wilson was a patient; North patio; Chief nurse and assistant in 1941; Entrance gate. All photos courtesy of the U.S. Navy Bureau of Medicine and Surgery Historian.

Feb. 4th, 1944

Dear Mother:

Enclosed are two money orders, the sum of $160.00. Please bank this money for me. Thanks.

By the way mother how much does this make in my bank account? Do you still get the allottment check monthly?

Wrote you a letter yesterday, hope you got it O.K. and after you recieve this, write and let me know right away.

Your loving son
Wilson

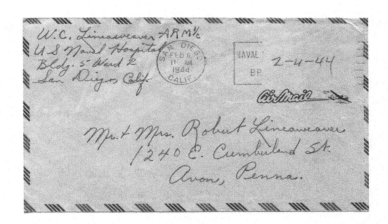

[Postmark is San Diego, Calif., Feb. 6, 1944, 11 AM]
Mr. & Mrs. Robert Lineaweaver
1240 E. Cumberland St.
Avon, Penna.

[Return Address:]
W.C. Lineaweaver ARM 1/c
US Naval Hospital
Bldg. 5 Ward 2
San Diego, Calif.

the squadron I left (VC-37)
is right in the _____
so I can't _____
be glad up in _____
Guess Fate is _____
me and just _____
in that batt_____
I'm concerned, _____
a lot more.

Did you _____
money I sent _____
mention that y_____
letter.

Hoping yo_____
of health, also _____
the family, c_____

yo_____

rather be home. Well who
wouldn't. They _____
of others in the _____
of those day i_____
love but it's _____
off.

My condit_____
improve and _____
forward to th_____
get out of th_____
of April I sh_____
get on my fee_____
before. All t_____
I'm beginning to_____
right. Last _____
clear through _____
time since _____
Only the doc_____
I'll be able _____
he tells me _____

You proba_____
papers about _____
the Marshal_____

Feb. 11th - 44

Dear Mother:

I'm just about due to answer
your letters so here you are. The
newspaper arrived the other day
and I was very glad to recieve
them. Also yours and the boys
valentine arrived.

This morning I managed
to get off a box of valentine
candy to you. Hope you like it
when it gets there. This letter
will most likely beat the
candy. Monday is Valentine Day
so I imagine the candy will
be late. Hope you don't mind
Recently I recieved letters
from Jim and one from Bettie.
They seem to be doing alright.
By his letters Jim doesn't like
the army and would much

Mr. & Mrs Robert. Lineaweaver
1240 E. Cumberland, St.
Avon, Penna.

[Postmark is U.S. Navy, Feb. 21, 1944, 11:30 AM]
Mr. & Mrs Robert . Lineaweaver
1240 E. Cumberland, St.
Avon, Penna.

[No return address remains on this envelope.]

Feb. 11th, -44

Dear Mother:

I'm just about due to answer your letters so here you are. The newspapers arrived the other day and I was very glad to recieve them. Also yours and the boy's valentine arrived.

This morning I managed to get off a box of valentine candy to you. Hope you like it when it gets there. This letter will most likely beat the candy. Monday is Valentine Day so I imagine the candy will be late. Hope you don't mind.

Recently I recieved letters from Jim and one from Bettie. They seem to be doing alright. By his letters Jim doesn't like the army and would much rather be home. Well! who wouldn't. There are millions of others' in the same boat. One of these days it should all be over but it's still a long way off.

My condition is very much improved and I'm sure looking forward to the day when I can get out of this bed. By the first of April I should be able to get on my feet again or maybe before. All the pain is gone and I'm beginning to sleep good at night. Last night I slept clear through for the first time since I'm in the hospital. Only the doctor knows when I'll be able to get up and he tells me very little.

You probably read in the papers about the fighting in the Marshall Islands. Well! the squadron I left (VC-37) is right in the thick of it, so I can't complain to much being laid up in the hospital. Guess fate is taking care of me and just didn't want me in that battle. As far as I'm concerned, I hope I miss a lot more.

Did you get the last money I sent ($60.00)? You didn't mention that you did in your last letter.

Hoping you are in the best of health, also the rest of the family, I'll close

Your loving son
Wilson

Feb 15th 44

Dear Dad:

I'm sorry that I didn't write sooner but rather late than never. Most always all the news out this way, are concerning me I put in my letters to mother so there's very little thats new to write about.

Seems to me that the Tony you mentioned in your letter sounds familiar if he used to be a boss at the Textile Printing in Lebanon.

How do you like your work Dad? Seems to me it does it take much to beat that sweatshop you used to work in. I can't seem to recall the place where you now working. although I must have seen it some time or other. Lebanon

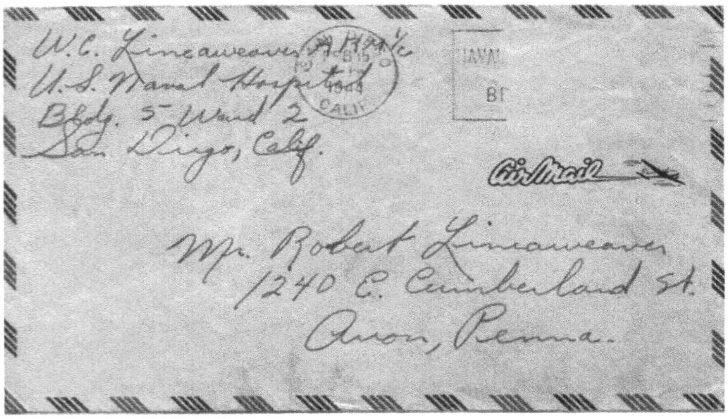

[Postmark is San Diego, Calif., Feb. 15, 1944, 4 PM]

Mr. Robert Lineaweaver
1240 E. Cumberland St.
Avon, Penna.

[Return Address:]

W.C. Lineaweaver ARM 1/c
U.S. Naval Hospital
Bldg. 5 Ward 2
San Diego, Calif.

Feb 15th - 44

Dear Dad:

I'm sorry that I didn't write sooner but rather late than never. Most always all the news out this way, are concerning me I put in my letters to mother so there's very little thats new to write about.

Seems to me that the Tony you mentioned in your letter sounds familiar if he used to be a boss at the Textile Printing in Lebanon.

How do you like your work Dad? Seems to me it doesn't take much to beat that sweatshop you used to work in. I can't seem to recall the place where your now working, although I must have seen it sometime or other. Lebanon is almost a strange city to me. It must be just about seven years since I left.

Hows the bowling coming along? Start getting that arm of yours in shape so that I have some competition when I get home. A 30 day leave isn't promised but I feel sure that it will be given as soon as I am able to stand it.

Heard that you had your teeth pulled and replaced with false ones. Can you still manage to chaw tobacco? I would be glad to finance your teeth if you already don't have them. Let me know.

I am sorry Dad that I was unable to send anything for Christmas. Being at sea and then in the hospital, I was in no position to get anything but I'll make up for it when I get home.

Hows the beer and liquor situation back there? Here on the coast you just can't buy a bottle or get good wiskey over the bar. Beer is scarce and eastern beer is impossible to get.

I remember now that back in your younger days you were laid up with a smashed leg. Wasn't you kicked by a horse? So you know in part what I have to go through. Hardest for me wasn't the pain but laying here in this bed all the time. It dam near drives me buggy. I hope in another month or two to get out of this bed.

Wishing this letter finds you in the best of health I'll close hoping to see you soon.

Your son
Wilson

Feb 15th -44

Dear Mother:

Your letter arrived this morning and I was very glad to hear from you. I will be looking forward for the newspapers within the next few days. Its very nice of you sending them and I enjoy reading them a lot.

Hope everything is still moving along swell at home. Here at the hospital its the same day in and out, very little change in the daily routine. Nothing new happens.

I am feeling fine mother, only I'm beginning to get sore from laying all this time but that can be expected. Every night before the lights go out we get alchohol back rubs then powder put on. That seems to help some. We also get a glass of milk before retireing.

Did the box of candy arrive and in time for Valentines' Day? Hope you enjoyed it. One of the "Waves" working here got and mailed it for me.

Having nothing more for the present I close this letter and attempt to write Jimmie a letter.

Your loving son
Wilson

[Postmark is San Diego, Calif., Feb. 16, 1944, 11 AM]
Mr & Mrs Robert Lineaweaver
1240 E. Cumberland St.
Avon, Penna.

[Return Address:]
W.C. Lineaweaver ARM 1/c
U.S. Naval Hospital
Bldg 5 Ward 2
San Diego, Calif.

Feb. 21st, -44

Dear Mother:

The papers arrived yesterday and I also recieved your letters, but as yet the package has'nt arrived. It's still a little early to expect it though. You haven't mentioned whether that box of candy got there or not. Hope it did!

The weather here in Southern California is nice and warm and sunny most all the time. Last night and today we are getting a little rain but the usual weather is nice. If I was back home right now, in all your winter snow and cold weather, it would probably kill me. I haven't seen any snow since the last time that I was home.

I'm still in bed mother but feeling fine. It sure takes a long time for bones to heal. All my other injuries have healed a long time ago and left only one scar on my right knee.

By the way mother did Dad get the letter I sent him? Give him the word to answer. I also got yours and Aunt Eva's card. Also a letter from your neighbor, Mrs Behney but haven't got around to answer it.

Hoping everything is alright and that you and the rest are in the best of health. I'll close remaining

Your loving son
Wilson

[Postmark is San Diego, Calif., Feb. 22, 1944, 11 AM]
Mr & Mrs Robert Lineaweaver
1240 E. Cumberland St.
Avon, Penna.

[Return Address:]
W.C. Lineaweaver ARM 1/c
U.S. Naval Hospital
Bldg 5 Ward 2
San Diego, Calif.

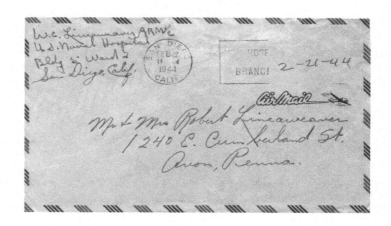

I don't recall much about this Chester only that he's in the army. What do you think about the idea of her making such a venture?

I'm putting on quite a bit of weight since I landed in the hospital. I'm afraid I'll have to get a new uniform or to fit when I get up. I weigh more now then I ever did, about 155 lbs.

Our Navy is really going to town at the present in the Pacific only the rats won't come out and fight. Hope its all over before I have to go out for the third time.

Thanks for everything and thinking of you. I close for the present remaining:

Your loving son
Wilson

Feb. 26th 44

Dear Mother:

Your package arrived in good shape, also the papers and yours and the two kids letters. The papers are always in good condition, not tattered in the least.

Yesterday a letter arrived from Jim. He sure has his troubles, 30 mile marchers. Gad! that would kill me.

Next week X rays will be taken, then I'll know how I'm doing and how soon I'll be able to get up. Today is the 67th day in bed and thats plenty.

Whats this I hear about Lucille going to get married, she's still pretty young isn't she?

W.C. Lineaweaver AR 1/c
U.S. Naval Hospital
Bldg 5 Ward 2
San Diego, Calif.

NAVAL HOS   2-26-44
BRANC

Air Mail

Mr & Mrs Robert Lineaweaver
1240 E. Cumberland St.
Avon, Penna.

Feb. 26th -44

Dear Mother:

Your package arrived in good shape, also the papers and yours and the two kids letters. The papers are always in good condition, not tattered in the least.

Yesterday a letter arrived from Jim. He sure has his troubles, 30 mile marchers. Gad! that would kill me.

Next week Xrays will be taken, then I'll know how I'm doing and how soon I'll be able to get up. Today is the 67th day in bed and thats plenty.

Whats this I hear about Lucille going to get married, she's still pretty young isn't she? I don't recall much about this Chester only that he's in the army. What do you think about the idea of her making such a venture?

I'm putting on quite a bit of weight since I landed in the hospital. I'm afraid I'll have to get a new uniform, one to fit when I get up. I weigh more now than I ever did, about 155 lbs.

Our Navy is really going to town at the present in the Pacific only the rats won't come out and fight. Hope its all over before I have to go out for the third time.

Thanks for everything and thinking of you I close for the present remaining:

Your loving son
Wilson

[Postmark is San Diego, Calif., Feb. 27, 1944, 11 AM]
Mr & Mrs Robert Lineaweaver
1240 E. Cumberland St.
Avon, Penna.

[Return Address:]
W.C. Lineaweaver ARM 1/c
US Naval Hospital
Bldg 5 Ward 2
San Diego, Calif.

guess she done a lousy job.

The weather is nice and warm, just like summer back where you at. Yesterday I was pushed outside and seen a U.S.O. show, it was very enjoyable.

They sure are bringing in the wounded men from overseas. This evening 400 more arrived and the hospital is crowded. It's pathetic. Today is my 75th day in bed.

Nothing new happens here so this is all for now. Thinking of you. Irene xx.

Your loving son
Wilson

March 5th 1944

Dear Mother:

Another week has gone by with no change. Still in this bed. Last Wednesday they took x-rays of me but as yet I haven't heard what the results are. My fingers are crossed and I'm hoping to be up in a wheel chair or crutches this week.

The papers arrive regular and in good shape, also your letters. Tell Dot that I got hers and will write soon. I also recieved letters from Nat & Harold. Up till this time I got letters from everybody but Lucille, is her arm broke?

Glad you liked the candy Mother. I'm sorry that it broke open, you see I had a "Wave" wrap it for me and I

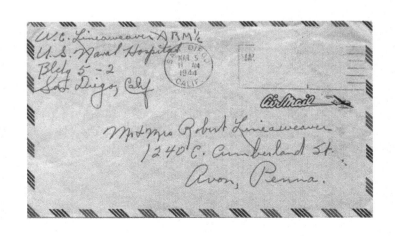

W.C. Lineaweaver A RM ½
U.S. Naval Hospital
Bldg 5 - 2
San Diego, Calif

Air Mail

Mr & Mrs Robert Lineaweaver
1240 E. Cumberland St.
Avon, Penna.

March 5th, 1944

Dear Mother:

Another week has gone by with no change. Still in this bed. Last Wednesday they took Xrays of me but as yet I haven't heard what the results are. My fingers are crossed and I'm hoping to be up in a wheel chair or crutches this week.

The papers arrive regular and in good shape, also your letters. Tell Dot that I got hers and will write soon. I also recieved letters from Nat & Harold. Up till this time I got letters from everybody but Lucille, is her Arm broke?

Glad you liked the candy Mother. I'm sorry that it broke open, you see I had a "Wave" wrap it for me and I guess she done a lousy job.

The weather is nice and warm, just like summer back where your at. Yesterday I was pushed outside and seen a U.S.O. show, it was very enjoyable.

They sure are bringing in the wounded men from overseas. This evening 400 more arrived and the hospital is crowded. Its pathetic. Today is my 75th day in bed.

Nothing new happens here so this is all for now. Thinking of you I remain.

Your loving son
Wilson

[Postmark is San Diego, Calif., March 5, 1944, 11 AM]
Mr & Mrs Robert Lineaweaver
1240 E. Cumberland St.
Avon, Penna.

[Return Address:]
W.C. Lineaweaver ARM 1/c
U.S. Naval Hospital
Bldg 5-2
San Diego, Calif

Yesterday I got the newspapers
and just finished reading them. I
also seen a movie tonight, the
first in a long time. The name
of the picture was "Gung Ho", a
marine war picture. Wasn't bad.

Being pretty tired I'll have
to make this letter short until
later. Wishing all of you the best
of health I close, remaining

Your loving son

Wilson

March 11th -44

Dear Mother:

Well! I have some good news
today. Believe it or not I'm up on
crutches. Its hard getting around and
it seems to me that I have to
learn to walk all over again. As
tough as it is, I'm glad to be up
and know that I'm O.K. and won't
be a cripple.

My first day on crutches and
the score, two blisters, one on each
hand. In a few days my hands
should be tough enough to take
it. Also I get very tired mother but
what can I expect after laying in
bed all that time.

Tomorrow due to crowded conditions here they are going to move
me to another ward. 122 W So
address your letter there. Its still
here at the hospital just its a
ward for men that can get around
and take care of them self.

W.C. Lineaweaver ARMY
U.S. Naval Hospital
Ward 122 W
San Diego Calif.

SAN DIEGO
MAR 12
5:30 PM
1944
CALIF.

Air Mail

Mr & Mrs Robert Lineaweaver
1240 E. Cumberland St.
Avon, Penna.

March 11th - 44

Dear Mother:

Well! I have some good news today. Believe it or not I'm up on crutches. Its hard getting around and it seems to me that I have to learn to walk all over again. As tough as it is, I'm glad to be up and know that I'm O.K. and won't be a cripple.

My first day on crutches and the score, two blisters, one on each hand. In a few days my hands should be tough enough to take it. Also I get very tired mother but what can I expect after laying in bed all that time.

Tomorrow due to crowded conditions here they are going to move me to another ward. 122W. So address your letters there. Its still here at the hospital just its a ward for men that can get around and take care of them self.

Yesterday I got the newspapers and just finished reading them. I also seen a movie tonight, the first in a long time. The name of the picture was "Gung Ho", a marine war picture. Wasn't bad.

Being pretty tired I'll have to make this letter short until later. Wishing all of you the best of health I close, remaining

Your loving son
Wilson

[Postmark is San Diego, Calif., March 12, 1944, 5:30 PM]
Mr & Mrs Robert Lineaweaver
1240 E. Cumberland St.
Avon, Penna.

[Return Address:]
W.C. Lineaweaver ARM 1/c
U.S. Naval Hospital
Ward 122-W
San Diego Calif.

March 27th '44

Dear Mother;

It's been some time since my last letter and I'm very sorry. In the meantime I've received two of yours and the newspapers which was nice of you to send. Also the package that you sent last Oct. as a Xmas present arrived and was in bad shape. Half of the things were missing or weren't fit to eat. I'm sorry that I was unable to enjoy your package but the thought behind it is enough to make me fully appreciate it.

I haven't heard from Jim or any of the others recently. Yesterday there was a surprise waiting me but I was away at the time. Aunt Sarah's boy from Elizabethtown was here. He is now a chief. I remember when he left. I'm sorry that I missed seeing him but he left word that he would come back soon. If I knew what outfit he is in I'd look him up. Aunt Sarah also wrote me a very nice letter.

Also John Sheaffy who is now stationed at Los Alamitos where I was for a short time came down to see me. You remember him, he lives in the ninth house out at Pleasant Hill where we lived.

I'm doing fine mother and getting around swell. Hope all of you at home are in the best of health.

Your loving son
Wilson

W. E. Kneaweaver
US Naval Hospital 122W
UNITED STATES NAVY

SAN DIEGO MAR 28 11 AM 1944 CALIF

NAVAL HOSPITAL BRANCH

FREE

3-27-44

Mr & Mrs Robt. Kneaweaver
1240 E. Cumberland St
Aron, Penna

March 27th -44

Dear Mother:

It's been some time since my last letter and I'm very sorry. In the meantime I've recieved two of yours and the newspapers which were nice of you to send. Also the package that you sent last Oct. as a Xmas present arrived and was in bad shape. Half of the things were missing are weren't fit to eat. I'm sorry that I was unable to enjoy your package but the thought behind it is enough to make me fully appreciate it.

I haven't heard from Jim or any of the others recently. Yes - today there was a surprise waiting me but I was away at the time. Aunt Sarah's boy from Elizabethtown was here. He is now a chief. I remember when he left. I'm sorry that I missed seeing him but he left word that he would come back soon. If I new what outfit he's in I'd look him up. Aunt Sarah also wrote me a very nice letter.

Also John Sheaffy who is now stationed at Los Alamitos where I was for a short time came down to see me. You remember him, he lives in the ninth house out at Pleasant Hill where we lived.

I'm doing fine mother and getting around swell. Hope all of you at home are in the best of health.

Your loving son
Wilson

[Postmark is San Diego, Calif., March 28, 1944, 11 AM]
Mr & Mrs Robt. Lineaweaver
1240 E Cumberland St.
Avon, Penna.

[Return Address:]
W.C. Lineaweaver ARM 1/c
US Naval Hospital 122W

A Western Union Telegram dated April 1, 1944 reads:

LEAVE NOT GRANTED AS YET PLEASE SEND $100 THANKS LOVE = SON.

UNITED STATES NAVY

April 10th 1944

Dear Mother:

Another Easter is over and it was just like another day to me. How was Easter at home? Did you enjoy yourself? Guess you didn't have a ham dinner due to that ration business.

Hope you got the Easter card, I sent it a little late and I'm afraid it did not arrive in time. The flowers arrived on Thursday, my birthday and they are very beautiful but more so yesterday on Easter, they seem to have opened up more. A few of the fellows and nurses had quite some time arguing which were the prettiest and what kind they were. I say the roses were the prettiest but of the five or six kinds its hard to

---

disease, they are all nice and doing fine with a few starting to _____

Right now I'm doing fine ___ able to walk around but _____ quiet a limp and still get _____ a bit of pain through my hip _____ base of my spine. I don't _____ what they are going to do wit___ I couldn't stand the trip ____ all that bouncing around. _____ will be some time until _____ able.

The newspapers arrived ____ I also got a nice long letter ___ Lucille. Did you enjoy your ____ Topton? Take care of your self and I hope to see you so_____ my regards to all the rest.

Your loving ___

Wil___

April 10th, 1944

Dear Mother:

Another Easter is over and it was just like another day to me. How was Easter at home? Did you enjoy yourself? Guess you didn't have a ham dinner due to that ration business.

Hope you got the Easter card, I sent it a little late and I'm afraid it did not arrive in time. The flowers arrived on Thursday, my birthday and they are very beautiful but more so yesterday on Easter, they seem to have opened up more. A few of the fellows and nurse's had quite some time argueing which were the prettiest and what kind they were. I say the rose's were the prettiest but of the five or six kinds its hard to dicide, they are all nice and doing fine with a few starting to droop.

Right now I'm doing fine, I'm able to walk around but I have quiet a limp and still get quiet a bit of pain through my hip to the base of my spine. I don't know what they are going to do with me. I couldn't stand the trip home, all that bouncing around so it will be some time until I'm able.

The newspapers arrived and I also got a nice long letter from Lucille. Did you enjoy your trip to Tapton? Take care of yourself mother and I hope to see you soon. Give my regards to all the rest.

Your loving son
Wilson

[Postmark is San Diego, Calif., April 11, 1944, 11 AM]
Mr & Mrs Robert Lineaweaver
1240 E Cumberland St.
Avon, Penna.

[Return Address:]
W.C. Lineaweaver ARM 1/c
122W
US Naval Hospital
San Diego, Calif.

you can do as you please with
them.

I am doing fine here
at the hospital and feeling
swell. Should be able to
leave the hospital soon.

Hope you like this little
gift mother and I hope to see
you soon. Again let me thank
you for the flowers and everything.
You have been swell to me while
I laid in the hospital.

Give my love & regards
to all the rest. Write often.
Your loving son
Wilson

April 19th, 1944

Dear Mother:

Last evening I sent you
a "Mother's Day" gift, a little
early but sooner early than
never.

The gift is a small locket
and chain which I hope you
will like. Also I included
a set of my wings with the
three stars. Perhaps you
have never seen the wings
I'm allowed to wear or you
may have seen them on some
other enlisted sailor. Anyway
I hope you like them and

W.C. Lineaweaver A.A.M ½c
122 W
U.S. Naval Hospital
San Diego, Calif.

SAN DIEGO
APR 20
11 AM
1944
CALIF.

NAVAL
B

4-19-44

Mr. & Mrs. Robert Lineaweaver
1240 E. Cumberland St
Avon, Penna.

April 19th, 1944

Dear Mother:

Last evening I sent you a "Mother's Day" gift, a little early but sooner early than never.

The gift is a small locket and chain which I hope you will like. Also I included a set of my wings with the three stars. Perhaps you have never seen the wings I'm allowed to wear or you may have seen them on some other enlisted sailor. Anyway I hope you like them and you can do as please with them.

I am doing fine here at the hospital and feeling swell. Should be able to leave the hospital soon.

Hope you like this little gift mother and I hope to see you soon. Again let me thank you for the flowers and everything. You have been swell to me while I laid in the hospital.

Give my love & regards to all the rest. Write often

Your loving son
Wilson

[Postmark is San Diego, Calif., April 20, 1944, 11 AM]
Mr. & Mrs. Robert Lineaweaver
1240 E. Cumberland St
Avon, Penna.

[Return Address:]
W.C. Lineaweaver ARM 1/c
122W
U.S. Naval Hospital
San Diego, Calif

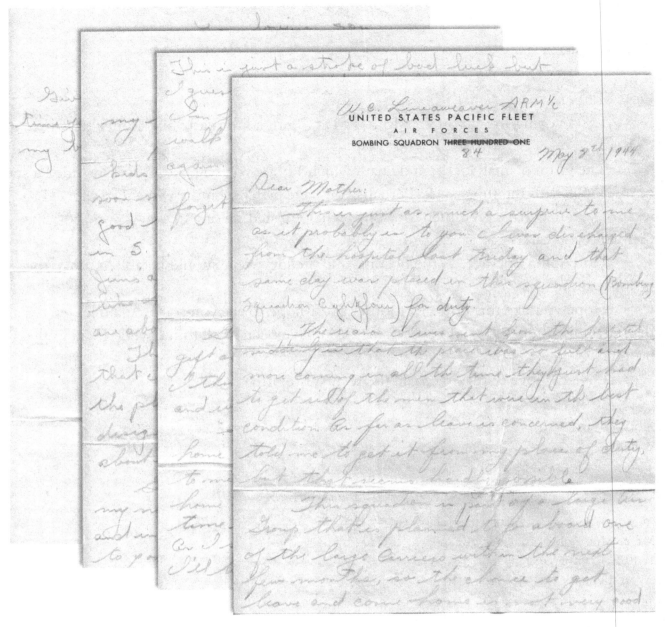

W. C. Lineaweaver ARM½
UNITED STATES PACIFIC FLEET
A I R   F O R C E S
BOMBING SQUADRON THREE HUNDRED ONE
84   May 8th 1944

Dear Mother:

This is just as much a surprise to me as it probably is to you. I was discharged from the hospital last Friday and that same day was placed in this squadron (Bombing Squadron Eighty four) for duty.

The reason I was sent from the hospital instead of you that the place was so full and more coming in all the time, they just had to get rid of the men that were in the best condition. As far as leave is concerned, they told me to get it from my place of duty, but that seems hardly possible.

This squadron is part of a large air group that is planned to go aboard one of the large carriers within the next few months, so the chance to get leave and come home is not very good.

[Postmark is U.S. Navy, May 8, 1944, 5 PM]
Mr & Mrs Robert Lineaweaver
1240 E. Cumberland St
Avon Penna

[Return Address:]
W.C. Lineaweaver ARM
VB 84
c/o F.P.O.
San Francisco Calif.

W.C. Lineaweaver ARM 1/c, United States Pacific Fleet
Air Forces, Bombing Squadron 84

May 8th 1944

Dear Mother:

This is just as much a surprise to me as it probably is to you. I was discharged from the hospital last Friday and that same day was placed in this squadron (Bombing Squadron Eighty four) for duty.

The reason I was sent from the hospital suddenly is that the place was so full and more coming in all the time they just had to get rid of the men that were in the best condition. As far as leave is concerned, they told me to get it from my place of duty, but that seems hardly possible.

This squadron is part of a large Air Group that is planned to go aboard one of the large carriers within the next few months, so the chance to get leave and come home is not very good. This is just a stroke of bad luck but I guess that can't complain too much, I'm just thankful to be able to walk around and know that I'm OK again.

So in writing from now on, don't forget my new address:

W.C. Lineaweaver ARM 1/c
Bombing Squadron 84, c/o Fleet P.O.
San Francisco, Calif.

Glad to hear that you recieved the gift and that you liked it. Personally I think that I could have done better and will the next time.

Sorry that I was unable to come home mother, it was also quite a blow to me because I had planned a trip home and what I would do all the time while laying in the hospital. As I said before, in the next few months I'll be off to sea again, this will make my third trip out in the war zone.

How is everybody at home? The kids ought to be quitting school pretty soon so their happy. Hows dad, in good health I hope. Is Jimmie still in S. Ca. or did they ship him across? Jim's about due to go across and it looks like he'll be right in big things that are about to pop in Europe.

This squadron is the same as others that I have been in just its larger and the planes are the new "Hell Diver" designated SB2C. My work will be about the same.

Give my love to everybody, also my new address. Take care of yourself and in closing with love & happiness to you all I remain

Your loving son
Wilson

Give Jimmie my new address next time you write him. Also the rest of my brothers

1944-1945 Chronology of VB-84 from the National Archives' WWII War Diaries, Record Group 38, Roll 2050, "VB-84"

UNITED STATES PACIFIC FLEET
AIR FORCE
BOMBING SQUADRON EIGHTY-FOUR

CHRONOLOGY

1944

1 May — Squadron commissioned NAS, San Diego, Calif., Lt.Comdr. John Pinkney CONN, Jr., A-V(N), USNR (77719), of Monticello, Mississippi, commanding. Complement: 36 planes, 54 pilots. Started training under ComFairWestCoast.

3 July — Ensign Thomas Benjamin PRITCHARD, Jr., pilot and Richard Allen VICKERS, ARM3c, gunner, killed when plane crashed into sea during training.

23 Aug. — Squadron reorganized. Complement: 24 planes, 36 pilots.

2 Oct. — Arrived US NAAS, Twenty-nine Palms, Calif. for rocket training.

15 Oct. — Returned NAS, San Diego, Calif.

2 Nov. — Boarded USS TAKANIS BAY (CVE89) for carrier landing qualifications.

6 Nov. — Returned NAS, San Diego, Calif.

27 Nov. — Boarded USS RANGER (CV4) for further carrier landing qualifications and group exercises.

2 Dec. — Returned NAS, San Diego, Calif.

19 Dec. — Squadron reorganized. Complement: 15 planes, 24 pilots.

1945

2 Jan. — Boarded USS RANGER (CV4) for night carrier landing qualifications.

3 Jan. — Returned NAS, San Diego, Calif.

18 Jan. — Departed NAS, San Diego, Calif.

19 Jan. — Arrived NAS, Alameda, Calif. and boarded USS BUNKER HILL (CV17).

24 Jan. — Departed Alameda, Calif.

27 Jan. — Arrived Pearl Harbor, T.H.

28 Jan. — Departed Pearl Harbor, T.H.

7 Feb. — Arrived Ulithi.

1944-1945 Chronology of VB-84 from the National Archives' WWII War Diaries, Record Group 38, Roll 2050, "VB-84"

CONFIDENTIAL

10 Feb.   Departed Ulithi.

16 Feb.   Bombed Nakajima Aircraft Assembly Plant, Ota, Japan.

17 Feb.   Bombed Nakajima Tama Aircraft Engine Plant, Tokyo.

19 Feb.   Supported "D" Day landings on Iwo Jima with H-55 and
           Afternoon Strikes.

20 Feb.   Provided morning and afternoon call strikes against
           Japanese positions on Iwo Jima.

25 Feb.   Bombed Nakajima Aircraft Assembly Plant, Koizumi, Japan.

1 March   Bombed installations near Machinato Airfield, Okinawa Jima,
           Nansei Shoto, in morning and installations near Naha Airfield,
           Okinawa, in afternoon.

4 March   Arrived Ulithi.

- CHRONOLOGY -

1945
January

2-5	Aboard USS RANGER (CV-4) for night carrier landing qualifications.
18	Departed NAS, San Diego, California.
19	Arrived NAS, Alameda, California.
23	Boarded USS BUNKER HILL (CV-17).
24	Departed Alameda, California.
27	Arrived Pearl Harbor, T.H.
28	Departed Pearl Harbor, T.H.

February

7	Arrived Ulithi.
10	Departed Ulithi.
16-17	Attacked Aircraft Plants, Airfields and other installations in Tokyo Area.
19-20	Supported "D" Day Landings on Iwo Jima.
25	Attacked Nakajima Aircraft Assembly Plant, Koizumi, Japan.

March

1	Attacked installations on Okinawa Jima.
4	Arrived Ulithi.
14	Departed Ulithi.
18	Strikes against Miyazaki and Omura Airfields, Kyushu.
19	Attack on Fleet Units in Kure Harbor.
23	Strike on pillboxes and installations on Okinawa.
24	Strikes on Pt. Bolo, Chatan, Naha Harbor on Okinawa.

CONFIDENTIAL

- 1 -

1945 Chronology of VB-84 from the National Archives' WWII War Diaries, Record Group 38, Roll 2086, "COM AIR GR 84"

1945
March

24	Lieutenant Commander R.R. Hedrick assumed command, replacing Commander Geo. M. Ottinger, lost in combat.
26-27	Support Strikes on Yontan and Katena Airfields, Okinawa.
28	Strike on Minami Daito Jima.
29	Strike on Tojimbara, Kyushu airfield.
30-31	Support Strikes on Unten Ko, Naha defense positions, and Katina gun installations, on Okinawa.

April

1	Strikes on landing beaches, installations and Yontan Airfield in support of "Love" Day landings of the Marines and the Army on Okinawa.
3-4	Strikes on Ie Shima.
6	Strike on Tokuna Shima Airfield.
7	Strike on Jap Fleet Units in East China Sea.
10 April through 10 May	Strikes, Fighter Sweeps and Supports on Central and Southern Okinawa, Naha Harbor and enemy positions around Naha Town, Okinawa.
27	Lieutenant Commander R.E. Hill succeeded Lieutenant Commander Hedrick as skipper of theFighter Squadron.

May

11	USS BUNKER HILL (CV-17) hit by Japanese Suicide Bombers.
12	Started retirement to Ulithi.
14	Arrived Ulithi.
17	Departed Ulithi.
20	Memorial Services for all Air Group Personnel and Ship's Company lost.
25	Arrived Pearl Harbor, T.H.
28	Departed Pearl Harbor, T.H.

JUNE

3	Arrived NAS, Seattle.

- 2 -

Was just interrupted to check planes
coming in. They'll be going out again soon
so I'll better close for now. Please
write ... know. When I leave for sea again I
... may increase the size of the allotment.
... Haven't heard from any of you for
some ... me for the next few days. I should
... have flew anyway because they gave
... me a harder job on the ground.

UNITED STATES PACIFIC FLEET

AIR FORCES

BOMBING SQUADRON ~~THREE HUNDRED ONE~~
74

May 10th 1944

Dear Mother:

Taking a little time off from work
in this new squadron I decided to write
you a few lines to let you know how
I'm doing.

So far I definitely do not like
this outfit in fact I'm beginning to
dislike the whole navy ... because I'm getting tired of this isle
and the war in general. Believe me, after
this is over and I'm still kicking, but
I come.

Yesterday ... two flights ...
... they ... just ...
last year. I was supposed to fly
again today but my hips and
whole bottom hurt so they grounded

[No envelope remains with this letter.]

May 10th, 1944

Dear Mother:

Taking a little time off from work in this new squadron I decided to write you a few lines to let you know how I'm doing.

So far I definitely do not like this outfit in fact I'm beginning to dislike the whole navy. Possible because I'm getting tired of this life and the war in general. Believe me, after this is over and I'm still kicking, out I come.

Yesterday I flew two flights, being the first time in the air since last year. I was supposed to fly again today but my hips and whole bottom hurt so they grounded me for the next few days. I should have flew anyway because they gave me a harder job on the ground.

Before going to sea again I may telephone you so look for a call in the next 2 or 3 months.

Other than that I don't like my work and can't get leave to come home I'm in pretty good health. My rear end gives me some trouble every now and then but eventually that should leave.

I'm looking forward for the end of this war but as yet I just can't begin to see an end. It also looks like I'll be going out for the third time and have another crack at them.

Do you still get my allottment check regularly? By the way mother, I lost track of how much money I have in bank. Next letter, why let me know. When I leave for sea again I may increase the size of the allottment.

Haven't heard from any of you for some time, I magine thats because you have been using my old hospital address. Don't forget my new address

W.C. Lineaweaver ARM 1/c USN

Bombing Squadron 84

c/o F.P.O.

San Francisco, Calif.

How is everything at home? going along smoothly I hope. Doesn't look like the draft is going to catch Fat or Dave but it may last long enough to catch Nat.

I know your wondering what the three stars on my wings stand for so I'll explain. They are for three types of combat 1. Plane against plane 2. Plane against ship 3. Plane against enemy installations. You have to engage the enemy in each one.

Was just interrupted to check planes coming in. They'll be going out again soon so I'd better close for now. Please write when you find time.

Your loving son
Wilson

May 19th 1944

Dear Mother:

Enclosed are a few pictures I had taken recently, hope you like them. Some are not so hot and one of them will take you some time to figure out. I was standing on my hands when it was snaped.

Some other pictures were taken since so as soon as their printed I'll send you some if you wish.

Wishing everyone in the best of health & happiness I'll close remaining

Your loving son
Wilson

W.C. Lineaweaver ARM½ U.S.N.
VB-84
% F.P.O.
San Francisco Calif.

5-10-44
Also
5-19-44

SAN DIEGO
MAY 20
8ᴬᴹ AM
1944
CALIF.

Mr & Mrs. Robert Lineaweaver
1240 E. Cumberland St.
Avon, Penna.

May 19th 1944

Dear Mother:

Enclosed are a few pictures I had taken recently, hope you like them. Some are not so hot and one of them will take you some time to figure out. I was standing on my hands when it was snaped.

Some other pictures were taken since so as soon as their printed I'll send you some if you wish.

Wishing everyone in the best of health & happiness I'll close remaining

Your loving son
Wilson

[Postmark is San Diego, Calif., May 20, 1944, 8:30 AM]
Mr & Mrs. Robert Lineaweaver
1240 E. Cumberland St.
Avon, Penna.

[Return Address:]
W.C. Lineaweaver ARM 1/c
VB-84
c/o F.P.O.
San Francisco Calif.

May 22nd -44

Dear Mother:

Your letter arrived this morning and I was very glad to hear from you. I'm glad to know that everything is going along swell at home and all of you are in good health. I'm feeling fine and just about normal again only I'm a little stiff and get around like an old man, with a little exercise this should leave me.

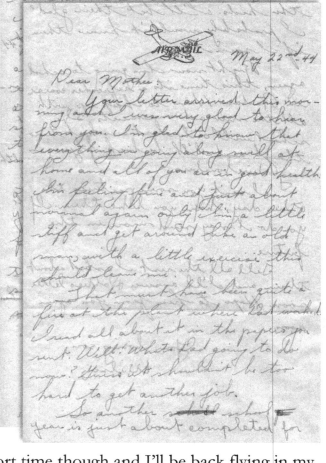

That must have been quite fire at the plant where Dad worked. I read all about it in the papers you sent. Well! Whats Dad going to do now? Guess it shouldn't be too hard to get another job.

So another school year is just about completed for the kids. I'll bet their glad? I probably wouldn't know them if I seen them.

Right now I'm going to school again, this time its a refresher course in Radar. Have to keep up with all the new advancements. The school will only last a short time though and I'll be back flying in my dive bombers.

I sent you some pictures the other day, hope you like them. If you do I may send more in the future.

Tell all the rest I asked about them and I'll answer Dotties letter soon. Hope to hear from you again soon

Your loving son
Wilson

[Postmark is U.S. Navy, May 23, 1944, 11:30 AM]
Mr & Mrs Robert Lineaweaver
1240 E. Cumberland St. / Avon Penna

[Return Address:]
W.C. Lineaweaver ARM 1/c
VB-84 c/o F.P.O.
San Francisco, Calif.

The fire on May 2, 1944, was at the National Radiator Company Plant (the Boiler Works) at Fourteenth and Buttonwood Streets in Lebanon. According to The Lebanon Daily News Centennial Edition, *Lebanon, Pa., Saturday, Sept. 30, 1972, page C-9, it was the largest fire in monetary loss in county history (as of 1972), having caused a million dollars in damage. Wilson's father Robert was working here up until the time of the fire. Following are photos taken of the fire that were sent to Wilson. He returned them with his letter dated September 21, 1944. When he returned them, he also wrote a note on the back side of the top picture, shown below.*

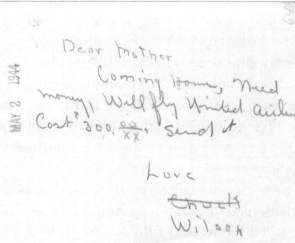

May 23rd -44

Dear Dorothy:

I'm awfully sorry that I avoided writing you recently, so I hope these few lines make up a little for my laziness.

In a few weeks another school year will be completed. Are you glad? I'm glad to know that you have got as far as you are and hope you continue on until your schooling is completed. Talking about school, right now I'm going again and at my age, but the stuff that I learn isn't what I'd like to because after all when I get out of this navy I don't expect to go around killing anybody.

So you still write to Sam McLean, thats nice of you. Keep it up because Sams a swell fellow and I think a lot of him. He's a man worth knowing.

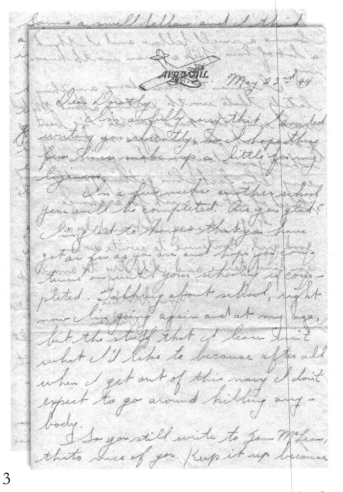

I haven't been doing anything lately thats worth writing about. My work isn't too hard you see I've been doing it for over 3 yrs so knowing what your doing makes your work easy. In fact I'm getting pretty tired of it and wish for a change.

Take it easy Dot and be a good girl. Continue to write when you find time and I'll try to answer.

Your brother
Wilson

[Postmark is U.S. Navy, May 23, 1944, 11:30 AM]
Miss Dorothy Lineaweaver
1240 E. Cumberland St.
Avon, Penna.

[Return Address:]
W.C. Lineaweaver ARM 1/c
VB-84   c/o F.P.O.
San Francisco, Calif.

June 19 - 44

Dear Mother:

Sorry that I have been lax the last few weeks in my writing to you. Your letters have been coming through regularlly but I haven't as yet recieved the newspapers that you sent.

The last two weeks I spent down on the Mexican border learning some more about airial gunnery and doing lots of machine gun firing. Seems to me mother that the navy is always sending me to school but what they teach me won't be much help once I come home after all this is over

Talking about coming home I'm sure disappointed not getting the chance to come home before going to sea again but it looks like thats whats going to happen although I expect to stay here in the states for a few more months.

Glad to hear that everyone's in good health and getting along fine. As for me, I guess I'm doing O.K. Still have slight pain but other than that I'm fully recovered.

In this new squadron we are training pretty hard and I do a lot of flying.

I'm hoping Jim isnt sent across now because I think its plenty hot over there.

Give every one my regards. Take care of yourself and write often.

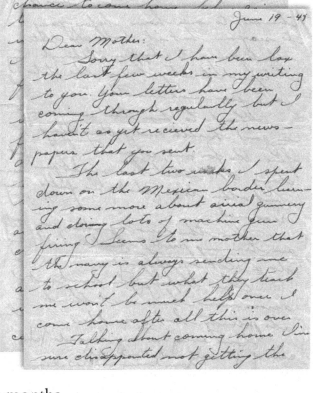

Your loving son
Wilson

[Postmark is San Diego, Calif., June 20, 1944, 12 M]
Mr & Mrs. Robert Lineaweaver
1240 E Cumberland St.
Avon, Penna.

[Return Address:]
W.C. Lineaweaver ARM 1/c
Bombing 84
c/o F.P.O.
San Francisco, Calif

June 29 - 44

Dear Mother:

Haven't heard from you for quite some time and I'm wondering if everythings O.K., hoping it is.

Had a letter from Jim last week and everything seems to be going along fine with him and family only he's expecting to go overseas soon and that isn't too good.

I am sending some pictures that were taken the last time I crossed the equator. It is always a big day aboard ship on that day and a lot of fun. All men who are crossing for the first time get initiated. Put the pictures away and save them for me.

They all were taken on the flight deck of the U.S.S. Sangamon last October on our way to the Southwest Pacific.

We are still doing lots of flying and in a few days we will start night flying which will last for a few week's.

Don't forget to expect a phone call in the next month or two and it will probably be early in the morning.

Give my best wishes & regards to Dad and the rest. Take good care of yourself and write soon.

Your loving son
Wilson

[See October 27, 1943, for the pictures referenced in this letter.]

[Postmark is San Diego, Calif., June 29, 1944, 11:30 AM]
Mr & Mrs Robert Lineaweaver
1240 E Cumberland St.
Avon, Penna.

[Return Address:]
W.C. Lineaweaver ARM 1/c
c/o F.P.O.
VB-84
San Francisco, Calif

6th July, 1944

Dear Mother:

Here it is, two O'clock in the morning and I'm restless and not sleepy a bit. Just think, that makes it five O'clock at home, almost time for you to be getting up and starting work. The difference being three hours or three thousand miles, just a hop, skip & a jump.

The 4th of July was just another day to me, we carry on just like any other day. Hope all of you had a pleasant time over the holiday. I suppose you went up to Hershey Park or maybe to Colemans. How was the weather?

Out here the weather is fair most of the year but right now you have it much warmer than I.

We are working hard and doing lots of flying and it shouldn't take too long before being sent against the enemy. My fellow sailors that are out their right now seem to be doing a grand job. Maybe we can end this war in another year.

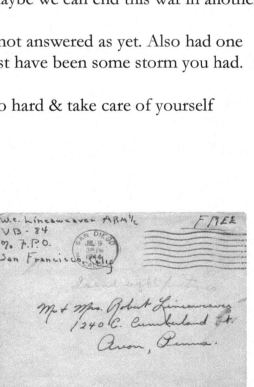

Had a letter from Jimmie last week but have not answered as yet. Also had one from you. The papers arrived as usual, that sure must have been some storm you had. Was there very much damage around Avon.

Hoping all are in good health. Don't work too hard & take care of yourself

Your loving son
Wilson

[Postmark is San Diego, Calif., July 6, 1944, 3:30 PM]
Mr & Mrs. Robert Lineaweaver
1240 E. Cumberland St.
Avon, Penna.

[Return Address:]
W.C. Lineaweaver ARM 1/c
VB-84
c/o F.P.O.
San Francisco, Calif

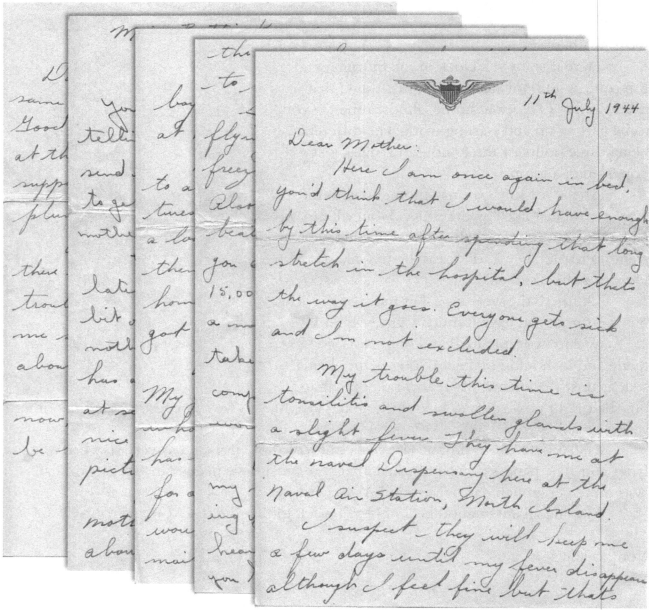

11th July 1944

Dear Mother:

Here I am once again in bed. You'd think that I would have enough by this time after spending that long stretch in the hospital, but that's the way it goes. Everyone gets sick and I'm not excluded.

My trouble this time is tonsilitis and swollen glands with a slight fever. They have me at the naval Dispensary here at the Naval Air Station, North Island.

I suspect they will keep me a few days until my fever disappears although I feel fine but that's

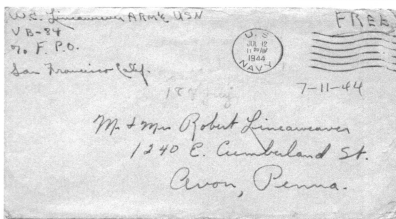

[Postmark is U.S. Navy, July 12, 1944, 11:30 AM]
Mr & Mrs Robert Lineaweaver
1240 E. Cumberland St.
Avon, Penna.

[Return Address:]
W.C. Lineaweaver ARM 1/c USN
VB-84
c/o F.P.O.
San Francisco, Calif.

11th July 1944

Dear Mother:

Here I am once again in bed, you'd think that I would have enough by this time after spending that long stretch in the hospital, but thats the way it goes. Everyone gets sick and Im not excluded.

My trouble this time is tonsilitis and swollen glands with a slight fever. They have me at the naval Dispensary here at the Naval Air Station, North Island.

I suspect they will keep me a few days until my fever disappears although I feel fine but thats the navy for you, they don't want to take any chances.

Guess my trouble comes from flying because one minute your freezing and the next its hot. Also your body takes quite a beating while dive bombing as you can imagine when you dive 15,000 ft with a sudden pull out in a matter of a few seconds. Do not take me wrong mother, I'm not complaining because this is my work.

One of the boys brought down my mail and I just finished reading your letter. It was swell to hear from you. Im glad all of you had an enjoyable holiday and boy how I'd like to spend a day at Hershey Park.

By the way mother, I mean't to ask before how the colored pictures came out? You see I never had a look at them. Some friends took them and promised to send them home for me. Thats how the name got all mixed up.

Would you do me a favor Mother! My girl friend here in San Diego whom I met while in the hospital has been after me for some time for a picture. So I'd like if you would pick out a nice one and mail it to her.

Her address is

Miss Bettie Knepper

3211 ½ Felton St.

San Diego Calif.

You can enclose a short note telling her that I asked you to send it because pictures are hard to get. I know you'll do this mother and I appreciate it, thanks.

Bettie is a very nice girl and lately we've been seeing quite bit of each other although there's nothing serious between us. She has also promised to write me while at sea so I thought it would be nice if you could send her a picture

I hope your in good health mother, you never say very much about yourself in your letters

Does Dad still work at the same place since it burned down? Good jobs shouldn't be hard to get at this time. Dave & Mahlon I suppose are still the blacksmith & plumber respectfully

What are Jake & Harold doing on there vacation? getting into a lot of trouble as usual. Have them write me some letters telling me all about what their doing.

Guess I'll be closing for now, wishing you good health and be happy

Your loving son
Wilson

"...from a small town in Iowa"

Wilson met Bette Knepper (often he spelled it Bettie) while in the U.S. Naval Hospital in San Diego in 1944. Wilson had a friend while stationed overseas by the name of Lane. This friend told his mother about Wilson being in the hospital, and she visited him nearly every day. Also, this friend had a brother, Jack Lane, whose girlfriend worked at a bank in San Diego. One of the girlfriend's co-workers was Bette Knepper, and they introduced her to Wilson. To Bette and their friends, Wilson was known as "Chuck", which came from his middle name of Charles, and was what his buddies in the Navy called him.

Wilson's last visit home to Avon was in October 1944. At that time, his sister Lucille overheard Wilson and their pop in a conversation while sitting on the porch. Wilson was talking about being worried Bette could meet someone else when he goes out to sea again and "a ring wouldn't mean anything." Even so, in Wilson's letter dated November 24, 1944, he told his Mother that he gave Bette an engagement ring and was "getting real close to the hanging" (i.e. getting married!). Bette was a member of the Catholic Church, and in his December 7, 1944, letter, Wilson told his mother that he became a Catholic. He previously was a member of the United Brethren church.

Above and below, Wilson and his fiancé Bette

Bette and Wilson's mother Earlene corresponded frequently until a few years after Wilson's death. Eventually, time found Bette moving on with her life and she married Anthony Helling and they had three children. Anthony died in 1992. As of 2016 and at the age of 94, Bette was in Dubuque, Iowa, still in her own home and living alone, though recovering from the effects of a stroke. Her daughter, Beth Hunemuller, said that Bette still had an ID bracelet that belonged to Wilson, and a paper ring that he had made for her. She also had a bundle of letters returned to her after Wilson's death. They came back tied with a black ribbon and had a black X on them, but she never read some of them as she said it would have been too sad to do so. Bette still has the unread letters and numerous photos of Wilson and mementos from the time they spent together.

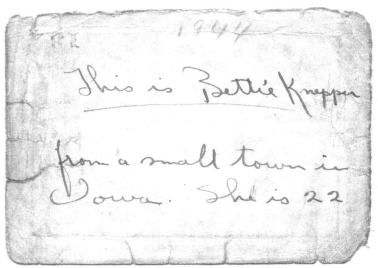

The above picture with ragged edges, front and back, is one Wilson carried in his wallet and mentioned in his letter dated August 10, 1944.

23rd July 1944

Dear Mother:

Well! I finally got around to make the phone call but I was very disappointed in the fact that I couldn't hear you most of the time. All in all though it was worth it to hear you.

Enclosed are the pictures that you wished returned. I liked all of them but especially the one with Nate & Harold in long pants. So if your able please send me one.

Everything is still the same here in San Diego. I'm feeling fine and expect shortly to be going to sea. This will be my third trip to the war zone, others haven't even been out but thats the way my luck runs. If I was able to stay here in the states I think Id probably get married. If I don't soon I'll wind up being an old bachelor.

Got the Hershey pictures and yours and Dots letter the other day. And Mother, some of fellows in my squadron are from Pa. and they enjoyed seeing those Hershey pictures too.

Don't forget to pay for that phone call out of my money.

I will be writing soon, until then I'll close remaing

Your loving son
Wilson

[Postmark is San Diego, Calif., July 24, 1944]
Mr & Mrs. Robert Lineaweaver
1240 E Cumberland St.
Avon, Penna.

[Return Address:]
W.C. Lineaweaver ARM 1/c
VB-84
c/o F.P.O.
San Francisco, Calif.

⚓ ════════════════ ⚓

AIR MAIL

29ᵗʰ July 1944

Dear Mother:

Recieved your letter yesterday and also one from Dottie and Martha. Was very glad to hear the news from home. Martha's letter was quite a surprise

Glad to hear everyones in good health and that your getting along fine (This pen is on the blink so excuse this scratching)

Sorry about that telephone call, it was disgusting not being able to hear all the time and it sorta ruined things but I'm not too disappointed, after all I did hear your voice and managed to say a few things

Don't forget to let me pay for the call. It should run about twenty dollars. Isn't a telephone a wonderful thing mother.

I am in good health mother and doing as well as can be expected. Not working too hard but still fly a lot and had a few close ones recently.

Their has been a long delay in writing this but now having a better pen I'll continue

FREE

Mr & Mrs Robert Lineaweaver
1240 E Cumberland St.
Avon, Penna.

[Return Address:]
W.C. Lineaweaver ARM 1/c
VB-84
c/o F.P.O.
San Francisco, Calif.

W.C. Lineaweaver ARM⅟c
VB-84
% F.P.O.
San Diego, Calif.

Mr & Mrs Robert Lineaweaver
1240 E Cumberland St.
Avon, Penna.

29th July 1944

Dear Mother:

Recieved your letter yesterday and also one from Dottie and Martha. Was very glad to hear the news from home. Martha's letter was quite a surprise.

Glad to hear everyones in good health and that your getting along fine (this pen is on the blink so excuse this scratching)

Sorry about that telephone call, it was disgusting not being able to hear all the time and it sorta ruined things but I'm not too disappointed, after all I did hear your voice and managed to say a few things.

Don't forget to let me pay for the call. It should run about twenty dollars. Isn't a telephone a wonderful thing mother.

I am in good health mother and doing as well as can be expected. Not working too hard but still fly a lot and had a few close ones recently.

Their has been a long delay in writing this letter but now having a better pen I'll continue it

Here it is almost August, how the time is flying. Doesn't seem like I'm going on twenty six. Will soon be an old man.

Too bad about Jim having to go across soon but I'm praying that it may be all over before he gets there which is very probably the way things are going recently.

Mother! Some time ago I ask you to send a picture of me to my girl friend here in San Diego but as yet she hasn't recieved one. Have you forgot?

Not much news out this way, what I mean is, nothing that would interest you.

You know mother, I've been away from home so long that I can't remember lots of things about Lebanon. What has me wondering is, will I come back there to live when this is all over. In my wondering around I found many places that I like better than Lebanon. It is now well over 1 ½ years since I last seen you and thats a long time. All of you have changed and perhaps I've changed some too and I'll be a stranger among you.

Hope you find a better house mother, that place you live at now is a dump and you deserve something better.

Wishing all of you health & happiness I'll close for now

Your loving son
Wilson

Glad you liked the pictures. Have you noticed a great deal of change since I last seen you.

to hear about it. This girl that I've been going with the past four... is very nice and I like her a... would like to get married bu... doubtful due to the war, my... of work and to top it off, I'll... be going to sea soon. Enclosed i... picture that I've been carrying... in my wallet, hope you like...

Bettie is also waiting... for the pictures you are going to... her.

Glad to hear mother t... are fine and everything seem... going along swell. I'm in goo... and doing fine only some days... long hours of work but the... sense in complaining.

Take care of yourself and... often

Your loving so...

Wilson

---

10 August 1944

Dear Mother:

Here it is midnight and we have just finished flying. It was a tough day for me, I flew all day and three hours tonight and not being sleepy at all I'm decided to scratch out this letter.

It was nice that Jim got the chance to come home again and it would have been nicer if I could have been there too. Looks like I should have picked the army instead of the navy so I could come home more often but I don't begrudge Jim all the leave he can get, all the more power to him. But Mother, shouldn't he be going overseas soon?

You asked, Mother, in one of your last letters if I was married or getting married. What a foolish question to be asking because you know that if anything like that did happen, you would be the first

---

FREE

U.S.
AUG 11
11 30 AM
1944
NAVY

Mr & Mrs Robert Lineaweaver
1240 E. Cumberland St.
Avon, Penna.

10 August 1944

Dear Mother:

Here it is midnight and we have just finished flying. It was a tough day for me, I flew all day and three hours tonight and not being sleepy at all I've decided to scratch out this letter.

It was nice that Jim got the chance to come home again and it would have been nicer if I could have been there too. Looks like I should have picked the army instead of the navy so I could come home more often but I don't begrudge Jim all the leave he can get, all the more power to him. But Mother, shouldn't he be going overseas soon?

You asked, Mother, in one of your last letters if I was married or getting married. What a foolish question to be asking because you know that if anything like that did happen, you would be the first to hear about it. This girl that Ive been going with the past four months is very nice and I like her a lot. She would like to get married but I'm doubtful due to the war, my type of work and to top it off, I'll probably be going to sea soon. Enclosed is an old picture that I've been carrying around in my wallet, hope you like her.

Bettie is also waiting impatiently for the pictures you are going to send her.

Glad to hear mother that you are fine and everything seems to be going along swell. I'm in good health and doing fine only some days I have long hours of work but theirs no sense in complaining.

Take care of yourself and write often

Your loving son
Wilson

[Postmark is U.S. Navy, Aug. 11, 1944, 11:30 AM]
Mr & Mrs Robert Lineaweaver
1240 E. Cumberland St.
Avon, Penna.

[No return address remains on the envelope.]

8/11/44

Dear Mother:

Recieved your letter this morning and I was very glad to hear from you and to find out that everything is "O.K." at home.

I spent yesterday with Bettie at Tijuana, Mexico. It's not very nice there but its something different and we sorta enjoyed it.

We went to the horse races but didn't lose any money because we didn't know how to bet, although Bettie picked one winner and I picked one.

Enclosed are a few things we picked up for you hoping you would like something from Mexico and made by Mexicans. There were so many things, a choice was hard but heres hoping you like our choice.

The butterfly is very fine work and done by hand, you can wear it on your dress. I think it will look nice

Still in good health and doing fine. Thanks for the quick response in sending the money.

Your loving son
Wilson

We also sent some post cards.

[No envelope remains with this letter.]

[Note: This is a letter written by Wilson's girlfriend, Bette Knepper.]

August 16, 1944

Dear Mrs. Lineaweaver,

I have received your letters and the pictures of Wilson and I really appreciate them. The pictures were all good although I must admit I'm a bit partial to the colored one. It's so natural and like him.

He's been doing a little night flying for the past couple of weeks but other than that I think the Navy is spoiling him.

He has shown me the pictures of your family and I'm beginning to know you all from everything he tells me. He was also so proud of the folder from Hershey Park.

We've been having some really beautiful weather here. Imagine you are probably really having some hot sweltering days that are far from being pleasant.

Don't worry about Wilson going out as I imagine from all reports he'll be in for several more months as yet, and then of course we're always hoping for those possibilities that he'll be staying here.

Thank you so much for the pictures.

Bette

[Postmark is San Diego, Calif., Aug. 18, 1944, 2:30 PM]
Mrs. E. Lineaweaver
1240 E. Cumberland St.
Avon, Pa.

[Return Address:]
3211 ½ Felton St.
San Diego 4, Calif.

Aug 20ᵗʰ - 44

Dear Mother:

Here it is Sunday night and I'm spending a quite evening at home with Bettie, she decided to write some letters so who am I to be different.

Today being my day off we went to the beach for some sun and both of us got a little red. Tomorrow I'll be back flying again.

Sat. morning Mother, I had to stand Admirals inspection and I past with flying colors. Medals were presented to some of the men by the Admiral prior to the inspection. You should have seen the ceremonies

Your letter containing the pictures arrived last week. Bettie also recieved the ones you sent her and she is quite proud of them and likes them a lot.

Mother! I would write Jim If I only knew his address, will you pleas send it. Do you think he'll be sent to Europe or out my way?

Still in the best of health but best of all, I'm still in the states. How long I can't tell.

In a few more weeks the kids will be trotting off to school again, how time does fly.

Hoping to hear from you again soon I'll close remaining

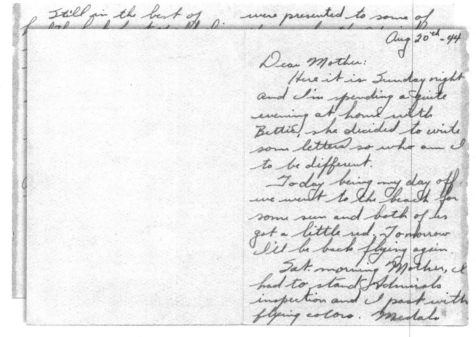

Your loving son
Wilson

[Postmark is San Diego, Calif., Aug. 21, 1944, 11 AM]
Mr & Mrs Robert Lineaweaver
1240 E. Cumberland St.
Avon, Penna.

[Return Address:]
W.C. Lineaweaver
VB-84
c/o Fleet Post Office
San Francisco, Calif.

28th Aug. 44

Dear Mother:

Recieved your last letter a few days ago and I must say your letters are always welcome. But I was sorry to learn that Jake is sick in bed. Hope by now he is up and jumping around per usual.

School days for the kids is just around the corner Are they all set for the opening bell and by the way, what grades are they in. I never can keep tract of them.

Just finished writeing Jim a letter. Should have written him months ago. Thanks for his address. I suppose Jim has left the country or is ready to leave in the very near future.

Haven't you found another place to live as yet. Seems to me by this time you should have. Why doesn't Fat or Dave give you a hand in finding a better place to live.

How are all the married pubes & their families doing. Don't imagine there's chance of them being drafted anymore, the lucky ducks.

By the way mother, what did that phone call cost? You never did tell me.

I'm doing as well as can be expected. Still flying but awfully sick of it and wish I could get out of it and do something else.

Give everyone my regards and I'll be waiting impatiently for your next letter. Take care of yourself and I'll be writing soon

Your loving son
Wilson

[Postmark is San Diego, Calif., Aug. 29, 1944, 3:30 PM]
Mr & Mrs Robert Lineaweaver
1240 E. Cumberland St.
Avon, Penna.

[Return Address:]
W.C. Lineaweaver ARM 1/c USN
VB-84
c/o F.P.O.
San Francisco, Calif

me 300⁰⁰ dollars.

Do you think you could arrange to meet me in Harrisburg. Perhaps you could get Dave to pick me up go to too much trouble though send a telegram giving you my arrival time in Harrisburg

I'll probably be home about first of October but it isn't definite Be seeing all of you soon, give my love to mother and the rest.

your son
Wilson

9/21/44

Dear Pop:

I'm returning the pictures mom sent. They are good pictures and what a fire it must have been. I can't quite place where the plant was that you worked at, but after all I'm away from that part of the country a long time.

What kind of work are you doing now? Hope everything is going along smoothly and that you're in good health.

Are you doing much pinochle playing. Bet I could beat the pants off of you.

Here's a surprise — I'm coming home soon. I expect to get about ten days so I'm going to fly. It will take me about twenty hours from here to Harrisburg and will cost

[Postmark is San Diego, Calif., Sept. 22, 1944, 11 AM]
Mr Robert Lineaweaver
1240 E. Cumberland St.
Avon, Penna.

[Return Address:]
W.C. Lineaweaver ARM 1/c
VB-84
c/o F.P.O.
San Francisco, Calif.

9/21/44

Dear Pop:

I'm returning the pictures mom sent. They are good pictures and what a fire it must have been. I can't quite place where the plant was that you worked at, but after all I'm away from that part of the country a long time. *[See May 22, 1944.]*

What kind of work are you doing now? Hope everything is going along smoothly and that your in good health.

Are you doing much pinochle playing. Bet I could beat the pants off of you.

Here's a surprise - I'm coming home soon. I expect to get about ten days so I'm going to fly. It will take me about twenty hours from here to Harrisburg and will cost me 300.00 dollars.

Do you think you could arrange to meet me in Harrisburg. Perhaps you could get Dave to pick me up. Don't go to too much trouble though. I'll send a telegram giving you my arrival time in Harrisburg.

I'll probably be home about the first of October but it isn't definite. Be seeing all of you soon, give my love to mother and the rest.

Your son
Wilson

A Western Union Telegram dated September 7, 1944 reads:
DEAR MOTHER PLEASE SEND $200.00 NOT IN TROUBLE JUST SPLURGING CARE WESTERN UNION SAN DIEGO CALIF LOVE= WILSON.

Western Union Telegram, below, dated September 22/23, 1944 reads:
DEAR MOTHER COMING HOME FLYING WILL COST $300.00 PLEASE SEND LOVE=
WILSON.

[Note: $300.00 in 1944 is equivalent to over $4,000.00 in 2016.]

Western Union Telegram, opposite page top, dated Sunday, September 24, 1944 reads:
DELAY: WILL BE IN HARRISBURG. FRIDAY OR SATURDAY. RECEIVED MONEY. WILL
SEND TELEGRAM LATER= WILSON.

Western Union Telegram, opposite page bottom, dated Friday, September 29, 1944 reads:
DELAY IN CHICAGO BE HOME SATURDAY= WILSON.

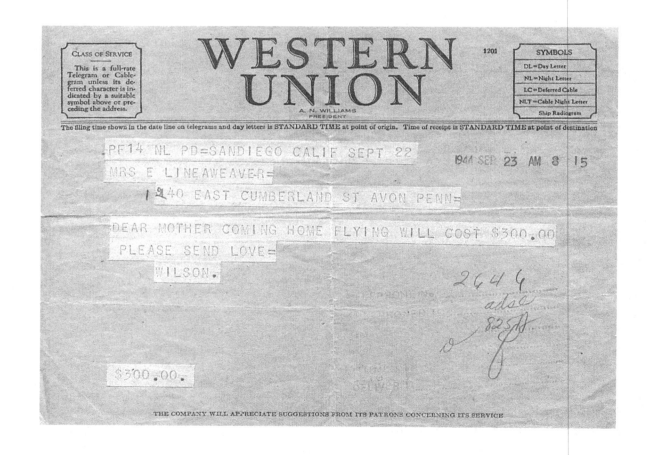

WESTERN UNION

1201

CLASS OF SERVICE

This is a full-rate Telegram or Cablegram unless its deferred character is indicated by a suitable symbol above or preceding the address.

A. N. WILLIAMS
PRESIDENT

(22)..

SYMBOLS

DL = Day Letter
NL = Night Letter
LC = Deferred Cable
NLT = Cable Night Letter
Ship Radiogram

The filing time shown in the date line on telegrams and day letters is STANDARD TIME at point of origin. Time of receipt is STANDARD TIME at point of destination

PE37 NL PD=SANDIEGO CALIF SEPT 24   1944 SEP 24 PM 4 24

MRS ERLINE LINEAWEAVER=

1240 EAST CUMBERLAND ST BA=

DELAY. WILL BE IN HARRISBURG FRIDAY OR SATURDAY.
RECEIVED MONEY. WILL SEND TELEGRAM LATER=
WILSON.

THE COMPANY WILL APPRECIATE SUGGESTIONS FROM ITS PATRONS CONCERNING ITS SERVICE

WESTERN UNION

1201

CLASS OF SERVICE

This is a full-rate Telegram or Cablegram unless its deferred character is indicated by a suitable symbol above or preceding the address.

A. N. WILLIAMS
PRESIDENT

316p.

SYMBOLS

DL = Day Letter
NL = Night Letter
LC = Deferred Cable
NLT = Cable Night Letter
Ship Radiogram

The filing time shown in the date line on telegrams and day letters is STANDARD TIME at point of origin. Time of receipt is STANDARD TIME at point of destination

PBH23 6 TOUR=EDG CHICAGO ILL SEPT 29 156P   1944 SEP 29 PM 3 19

MR AND MRS ROBERT LINEAWEAVER=

1240 EAST CUMBERLAND ST=

DELAY IN CHICAGO BE HOME SATURDAY=
WILSON.

THE COMPANY WILL APPRECIATE SUGGESTIONS FROM ITS PATRONS CONCERNING ITS SERVICE

and did she get a big bang out of them
Perhaps I'll send them
maybe give some to her.
to see me return and

And mother, he
Jimmie and how he
my regards to Dad + the
again soon hoping that
writing yourself.

yo

10/17/44

Dear Mother:
Its about time I let you know
that I got back last Friday just in
time to report in after a long 12 hr. layover in Chicago. The plane ride across
country was uneventful other than the
long stop in Chicago. Did you get my
telegram?

I was glad to get the opportunity
to come home and I enjoyed myself
immensely. Tell Dave, thanks for me.
His about the best taxi service I ever
had. Also Mother, the dinners were tops.
I could really go for some of that
chicken right now.

Recieved your letter this morning,
thanks for the key + token although I
~~not only~~ really didn't need them
because I had another key. Did you
enjoy yourself in Harrisburg? I could
see you + Dave standing there from a
window in the plane as we took off.
I showed Bettie the pictures

W.C Lineaweaver ARM 1/c USN
VB-84
℅ F.P.O.
San Francisco, Calif.

FREE

SAN DIEGO
OCT 17
11 AM
1944
CALIF.

10-17-44

Mr. + Mrs Robert Lineaweaver
1240 E. Cumberland St.
Avon, Penna.

[Postmark is San Diego, Calif., Oct. 17, 1944, 11 AM]
Mr. & Mrs Robert Lineaweaver
1240 E. Cumberland St.
Avon, Penna.

[Return Address:]
W.C. Lineaweaver ARM 1/c
USN
VB-84
c/o F.P.O.
San Francisco, Calif.

10/17/44
[October 17, 1944, was a Tuesday.]

Dear Mother:

Its about time I let you know that I got back last Friday just in time to report in after a long 12 hr layover in Chicago. The plane ride across country was uneventful other than the long stop in Chicago. Did you get my telegram? *[See below.]*

I was glad to get the opportunity to come home and I enjoyed myself immensely. Tell Dave, thanks for me. He's about the best taxi service I ever had. Also Mother, the dinners were tops. I could really go for some of that chicken right now.

Recieved your letter this morning, thanks for the key & token although I really didnt need them because I had another key. Did you enjoy yourself in Harrisburg? I could see you & Dave standing there from a window in the plane as we took off.

I showed Bettie the pictures and did she get a big bang out of them. Perhaps I'll send them home soon, or maybe give some to her. She sure was glad to see me return and I her.

And Mother, keep me posted on Jimmie and how he's making out. Give my regards to Dad & the rest. I will write again soon hoping that you do some writing yourself.

Your loving son
Wilson

LEBANON DAILY N

LEAVE ENDED

Petty Officer First Class Wilson Lineaweaver returned to his base at San Diego, Calif., yesterday by plane after spending a fourteen day leave at home with his parents, Mr. and Mrs. Rober Lineaweaver of 1240 East Cumberland Street. He also visited his friends and relatives.

Enlisting in January, 1941, he trained at Norfolk, Va., and Jacksonville, Fla., and has served in the South Pacific.

This newspaper clipping appeared in the *Lebanon Daily News*, Lebanon, PA, on Friday, October 13, 1944, page 20.

A Western Union Telegram dated [Thursday] October 12, 1944 reads:
STUCK IN CHICAGO GOD ONLY KNOWS WHEN ILL GET BACK TOUGH GOING DONT WORRY IM NOT PAST THAT STAGE BAD WEATHER LOVE.= WILSON..

much but were on 48 hrs notice to go to sea. So mother, the time is just about nigh.

Has Harold received the parts for his Rector Set as yet? Are the two boys still picking potatoes

And Mother, I believe that I forgot to thank Betty for the use of Jimmie's ~~~clothing~~ clothing so will you do that for me. Also give my thanks to Dave for the swell taxi service and the ride to Harrisburg.

Enclosed are a bunch of stamps that I got hold of and thought that I bet could use

The news in the Pacific has been very good recently, maybe this war will be ending sooner than we think. Which we all hope.

Whats the news concerning Jimmie? Safe and well I hope.

With lots of love to you and all I remain.

your loving son
Wilson

10/29/44

Dear Mother:

This is Sunday noon, Bettie and I just returned from church. While waiting for dinner I'll write you these few lines.

Your package arrived last week, the things were very nice and good. Its a good thing that you mailed it to Bettie's or I still would not have it.

Bettie is terribly sorry that she did not answer your letter or after the package came.

W.C. Lineaweaver ARM½ USN
VB-84
⁊. F.P.O.
San Francisco Calif.

FREE

SAN DIEGO
OCT 30
11 AM
1944
CALIF.

10-19-44

Mr & Mrs. Robert Lineaweaver
1240 E. Cumberland St.
Avon, Penna.

[Postmark is San Diego, Calif., Oct. 30, 1944, 11 AM]
Mr & Mrs. Robert Lineaweaver
1240 E. Cumberland St.
Avon, Penna.

[Return Address:]
W.C. Lineaweaver ARM 1/c USN
VB-84
c/o F.P.O.
San Francisco Calif.

10/29/44

Dear Mother:

This is Sunday noon, Bettie and I just returned from church. While waiting for dinner I'll write you these few lines.

Your package arrived last week, the things were very nice and good. Its a good thing that you mailed it to Bettie's or I still would not have it.

Bettie is terribly sorry that she did not answer your letter or after the package came.

Enclosed are a bunch of stamps that I got hold of and thought that maybe fat could use them. I don't know whether he can use them or not but its not doing any harm sending them. Let me know if he wanted them or not, or maybe he had them?

As I told you in my last letter, I got back here to San Diego on time but just on time. Since then we have not been doing much but were on 48 hrs notice to go to sea. So mother, the time is just about nigh.

Has Harold recieved the parts for his Rector Set as yet? Are the two boys still picking potatoes?

And Mother, I believe that I forgot to thank Betty for the use of Jims clothing so will you do that for me. Also give my thanks to Dave for the swell taxi service and the ride to Harrisburg.

The news in the Pacific has been very good recently, Maybe this war will be ending sooner than we think. Which we all hope.

Whats the news concerning Jimmie? Safe and well I hope.

With lots of love to you and all I remain.

Your loving son
Wilson

outfit is in the thick of it and it makes me shudder to think how tough the going is for them. All [I] can do is hope and pray for the [best].

And now mother, this is Sunday evening, Supper is just about ready and [th]en we will be off to a [movie]. Betties sister Eileen is here with [her] son Billie. In a few more weeks [both] of them will be going home to Ia[...] just as soon as [I] go to sea.

I was very thankful for [the] chance to come home for a [short] time before going out again. E[very]thing seems to be going swe[ll] in the Pacific at the present [as] you probably read in the new[s] paper but theirs a lot more [to] come & I'll be in the thick o[f] it. Lets hope this whole thing ends soon.

Give my thanks to Lucille [for] her trouble in getting togethe[r the] Christmas package, it must [have] been lots of trouble. your lovi[ng] W[...]

19th Nov. 1944

Dear Mother:

This is early Sunday morning and its really a beautiful morning, warm and sunny. In a few minutes I'll be going to church, you must at this time be finishing Sunday dinner.

Your Christmas package came last Thursday, it was a pleasant surprise and I'm very grateful. We had night flying all last week so the cookies & candy went swell as a snack late at night.

The time is drawing near when it will be anchors aweigh once more. It makes me feel funny knowing that I have to go out again but thats the way its to be and theres nothing I can do about.

Whats the news about Jimmie, and hows Jimmie Jr. doing? I noticed in the paper recently that Jims

---

Mr & Mrs. Robert Lineaweaver
1240 E. Cumberland St.
Avon, Penna.

[Return Address:]
W.C. Lineaweaver ARM 1/c USN
VB-84
c/o F.P.O.
San Francisco, Calif.

19th Nov. 1944

Dear Mother:

This is early Sunday morning and its really a beautiful morning, warm and sunny. In a few minutes I'll be going to church, you must at this time be finishing Sunday dinner.

Your Christmas package came last Thursday, it was a pleasant surprise and I'm very grateful. We had night flying all last week so the cookies & candy went swell as a snack late at night.

The time is drawing near when it will be anchors aweigh once more. It makes me feel funny knowing that I have to go out again but thats the way its to be and there's nothing I can do about.

Whats the news about Jimmie, and hows Jimmie Jr. doing? I noticed in the paper recently that Jims outfit is in the thick of it and it makes me shudder to think how tough the going is for them. All we can do is hope and pray for the best.

And Now Mother, this is Sunday evening, Supper is just about ready and then we will be off to a movie. Betties sister Eileen is here with her son Billie. In a few more weeks both of them will be going home to Iowa, just as soon as I go to sea.

I was very thankful for the chance to come home for a short time before going out again. Everything seems to be going swell in the Pacific at the present as you probably read in the newspaper but theirs a lot more to come & I'll be in the thick of it. Lets hope this whole thing ends soon.

Give my thanks to Lucille for her trouble getting together my christmas package, it must have been lots of trouble.

Your loving son
Wilson

policy that you will receive will
explain everything. Also the poli[cy]
is only life and does not cover ac[cident]
or anything else. It is the same
Navy insurance called National [Life?]

After this my mail will be cen[sored]
so if I want to say anything it [will]
have to be now. From all that [I]
can gather we will be aboard a
carrier and most likely be opera[ting]
in the Philipinos area.

Give my best regards to D[ad]
& the rest, take care of yoursel[f]
and write often

Your loving son
Wilson

Gave Bettie a ring recently an[d]
she is quite proud of it. Getting
real close to the hanging.

Dear Mother: Nov 24 1944
I recieved your letter the other
day and I was very glad to hear from
you. Also as I said in my last letter,
the Christmas package arrived. Thanks
a million to you & Lucille for your
time & trouble.

Sending Bettie that package
was alright, in fact it was th ideal
thing to do because I got it much
quicker and the package was saved
from all the extra handling

Well Mother! Its happening, when
you recieve this letter I'll be once
again on the high seas heading west
and I cant see anything easy ahead.
As much as I hate going out, thats
the way it is.

A few weeks ago I took out
$10,000. insurance going into affect the
first of Dec. You should be hearing
something pretty soon and the policy

[Postmark is San Diego, Calif., Nov. 25, 1944, 3 PM]
Mr & Mrs. Robert Lineaweaver
1240 E. Cumberland St.
Avon, Penna.

[Return Address:]
W.C. Lineaweaver ARM 1/c USN
VB-84
c/o F.P.O.
San Francisco, Calif.

[The top portion of the letter appears to have been cut off. Nov 24 1944 was written at a later time in pencil at top right.]

Dear Mother:

I recieved your letter the other day and I was very glad to hear from you. Also as I said in my last letter, the Christmas package arrived. Thanks a million to you & Lucille for your time & trouble.

Sending Bettie that package was alright, in fact it was the ideal thing to do because I got it much quicker and the package was saved from all the extra handling.

Well Mother! Its happening, when you recieve this letter I'll be once again on the high seas heading west and I can't see anything easy ahead. As much as I hate going out, thats the way it is.

A few weeks ago I took out $10,000 insurance going into affect the first of Dec. You should be hearing something pretty soon and the policy policy that you will recieve will explain everything. Also the policy is only life and does not cover accident or anything else. It is the same as Jim's insurance called National Life.

After this my mail will be censored so if I wish to say anything it will have to be now. From all that I can gather we will be aboard a carrier and most likely be operating in the Philapino area.

Give my best regards to Dad & the rest, take care of yourself and write often

Your loving son
Wilson

Gave Bettie a ring recently and she is quite proud of it. Getting real close to the hanging.

I professed my faith to Father Sullivan and then received conditional baptism. The catholic religion to my belief is the true religion and I shall be an active member of the catholic church. I only hope mother, that you'll understand and won't feel bad because I'm doing what I think is right according to my own way of thinking.

My trip to sea was short and I never expected to be back so soon. At the present it looks like I'm going to be in the states for Xmas and New Years.

Mother, lately your letters have been few and far between, I'm always looking impatiently for your letter so I hope in the future your letters will arrive more often.

So in closing I'm wishing all of you the best of health and that you are getting along swell.

Your loving son
Wilson

Dec 7th 1944

Dear Mother,

Having just returned from sea where we completed lots of advanced training, your letters with the sad news about Jim was waiting for me. I really don't know what to say or think about Jim being seriously injured, it was quite a shock. The only thing is to hope and pray for the best and let me know mother, as soon as you hear more news.

Today is the third year of this cock eyed war and I'm really getting tired of it as most people are. Also the end is not in sight, I suppose it will probably drag on for a few more years.

A few weeks ago mother I changed my religion and became a member of the catholic church.

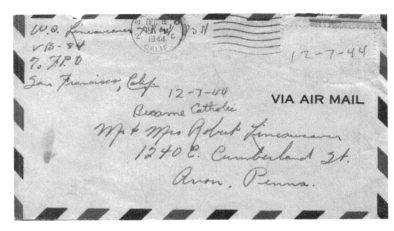

[Postmark is San Diego, Calif., Dec. 8, 1944, 5 PM]
Mr & Mrs Robert Lineaweaver
1240 E. Cumberland St.
Avon, Penna.

[Return Address:]
W.C. Lineaweaver ARM 1/c USN
VB-84
c/o F.P.O.
San Francisco, Calif.

Dec 7th 1944

Dear Mother

    Having just returned from sea where we completed lots of advanced training, your letter with the sad news about Jim was waiting for me. I really don't know what to say or think about Jim being seriously injured, it was quite a shock. The only thing is to hope and pray for the best and let me know mother, as soon as you hear more news.

    Today is the third year of this cock eyed war and I'm really getting tired of it as most people are. Also the end is not in sight, I suppose it will probably drag on for a few more years.

    A few weeks ago mother I changed my religion and became a member of the catholic church. I professed my faith to Father Sullivan and then recieved conditional baptism. The Catholic religion to my belief is the true religion and I shall be an ardent member of the catholic church. I only hope mother, that you'll understand and won't feel bad because I'm doing what I think is right according to my own way of thinking.

    My trip to sea was short and I never expected to be back so soon. At the present it looks like I'm going to be in the states for Xmas and New Years.

    Mother, lately your letters have been few and far between, Im always looking impatiently for your letters so I hope in the future your letters will arrive more often.

    So in closing I'm wishing all of you the best of health and hope you are getting along swell.

Your loving son
Wilson

PFC. JAS. LINEWEAVER SERIOUSLY WOUNDED

Mrs. Elizabeth Hartman Lineweaver of 243 South Tenth Street was informed Monday that her husband, Private First Class James L. Lineweaver (above) was seriously wounded in France on November 8 while serving with the 26th Infantry (Yankee) Division.

He is the son of Mr. and Mrs. Robert Lineweaver of 1240 East Cumberland Street, and has a year-old youngster, James, Jr.

Previous to his induction in February 1943, he was employed at the Textile Printing Company. He was also a popular caddy at the Lebanon Country Club.

He took his basic training at Fort Jackson, South Carolina, and was assigned to Camp Gordon, Georgia, and Camp Campbell, Kentucky, before arriving overseas in October, 1943.

Private Lineweaver is the 151st Lebanon County serviceman now listed as wounded in action during the present conflict.

The above newspaper clipping appeared in the *Lebanon Daily News*, Lebanon, PA, on Nov. 22, 1944. Jim was wounded in his right leg while fighting in France. For hours he lay unconscious in cold water which clotted his blood and kept him from bleeding to death.

A Western Union Telegram dated December 13, 1944 reads:
BACK. PLEASE SEND $100.00 IMMEDIATELY LETTER FOLLOWING. LOVE= WILSON=

a storm with plenty snow. How
many inches was it at home? You
mother, the last snow that I saw
was two years ago on my thirty day
leave.

Glad to hear that every one
in good health and getting along
swell, as for myself, I'm doing
fine and in the best of health.

I had my picture taken the other
day and I hope to be able to
send you one by Xmas. Would you like
that mother?

Hoping all of you have a nice
Xmas I'll close remaining

Your loving son
Wilson.

14th Dec. 1944

Dear Mother:
Yesterday I received your letter
and was very glad to hear from you. The
news concerning Jim sounds good in
a way. Have you gotten word how he
was hurt or how bad. Let me know
as soon as you hear anything new.

The money arrived today, while
waiting to find out if it was there a
few of the service men were turned
down and seemed highly disappointed
but I just said to myself, I can
always count on my mother. Thanks
a million.

Just got back from a little trip
to sea and boy am I glad to be
back. But not for long I imagine, just
so I'm here for Christmas and maybe
New Years, then I'll be satisfied

From what I gather reading the
newspapers you must have had quite

[Postmark is San Diego, Calif., Dec. 15, 1944, 3:30 PM]

Mr & Mrs. Robert Lineaweaver
1240 E. Cumberland St.
Avon, Penna.

[Return Address:]
W.C. Lineaweaver ARM 1/c USN
VB-84
c/o Fleet Postmaster
San Francisco, Calif.

14th Dec. 1944

Dear Mother:

Yesterday I recieved your letter and was very glad to hear from you. The news concerning Jim sounds good in a way. Have you gotten word how he was hurt or how bad. Let me know as soon as you hear anything new.

The money arrived today, while waiting to find out if it was there a few of the service men were turned down and they seemed highly disappointed but I just said to myself, I can always count on my mother. Thanks a million.

Just got back from a little trip to sea and boy am I glad to be back. But not for long I imagine, just so I'm here for Christmas and maybe New Years, then I'll be satisfied

From what I gather reading the newspapers you must have had quite a storm with plenty of snow. How many inches was it at home? You know mother, the last snow that I seen was two years ago on the thirty days leave.

Glad to hear that every ones in good health and getting along swell, as for myself, Im doing fine and in the best of health.

I had my picture taken the other day and I hope to be able to send you one by Xmas. Would you like that mother?

Hoping all of you have a good Xmas I'll close remaining

Your loving son
Wilson.

[Reduced to 40% of original.]

This is the Christmas card Wilson sent home in 1944. Mailed Dec. 18, 1944 from San Diego, California.

I just can't unde[...]
Pop is out of work wit[...]
jobs floating around [...]
many. Here's hoping [...]
soon.

Beth said she'd w[...]
after I leave and she [...]
And Mother if anythin[...]
to [...] be sure and let [...]
she won't have to wor[...]

So mother! I thin[...]
till after I get to sea [...]
little more time for [...]
ridden her from now o[...]
be censored and I wo[...]
say anything.

[...] best of hea[...]
hoping to hear from you[...]

Your [...]
U[...]

20th Jan. 1945

Dear Mother:

Lately I didn't have much time
for writing, our days have been filled up
getting ready to go overseas. Today is
the day prior to our departure so
I thought I'd better get hot and
write you.

We ship out tomorrow on the
"Bunker Hill," one of our largest carriers,
and will join the "Third Fleet" under
Admiral Halsey. This fleet is operating
off the Phillipines and China coast at
the present. I figure by the middle
of next month we'll be in the
thick of it.

A few of your letters came the past
few weeks and also one from Nathan.
Jim also wrote a letter which came the
other day. I was sure glad to hear
that he was doing O.K. and would
soon be rejoining his Company.

W.C. Linaweaver ARM 1/c
VB - 84
% F.P.O.
San Francisco Calif.

U.S. NAVY
JAN 2
12 - M
1945

Mr & Mrs Robert [...]
1240 E. Cumber[...]
Avon, Pen[...]

20th Jan. 1945

Dear Mother:

Lately I didnt have much time for writeing, our days have been filled up getting ready to go overseas. Today is the day prior to our departure so I thought I'd better get hot and write you.

We ship out tomorrow on the "Bunker Hill", one of our largest carriers, and will join the "Third Fleet", under Admiral Halsey. This fleet is operating off the Phillipines and China coast at the present. I figure by the middle of next month we'll be in the thick of it.

A few of your letters came the past few weeks and also one from Nathan. Jim also wrote a letter which came the other day. I was sure glad to hear that he was doing O.K. and would soon be rejoining his Company.

I just can't understand why Pop is out of work with all these war jobs floating around including big money. Here's hoping he gets work soon.

Bettie said she'd write you soon after I leave and she returns to Iowa. And Mother if anything should happen to me be sure and let her know so she won't have to worry.

So mother! I think I'll close till after I get to sea and have a little more time for writing. But remember from now on my mail will be censored and I won't be able to say anything.

The best of health to all and hoping to hear from you soon I remain

Your loving son
Wilson

[Postmark is U.S. Navy, Jan. 21, 1945, 12-M]
Mr & Mrs Robert Lineaweaver
1240 E. Cumberland St.
Avon, Penna.

[Return Address:]
W.C. Lineaweaver ARM 1/c
VB-84
c/o F.P.O.
San Francisco Calif.

I guess I've ever seen because I don't remember that much. I'll bet the kids are enjoying it with plenty of sledding.

Do you still get my allotment checks on time? How much does my bank roll say. As far as I can figure it should be about $400.00

At the present I'm still in good health but the life is ragged. Give my best regard to all the rest of the family. Thinking of you I'll close

Your loving son
Wilson

W.C. Lineaweaver ARM½
VB-84

W.C. Lineaweaver ARM½
VB-84   2 Feb 1945

Dear Mother:

I have been recieving a few of your letters in the week and I'm very grateful. My own writing has been almost none at all; my laxity his an excuse though very feeble. We have been pretty busy lately.

Had a letter from Jim the other day and I was glad to hear that he's getting along swell. He says his knee is stiff and doesn't think it ever will be O.K. Just so they don't send him back to Germany. Perhaps they'll send him home, which would be what he wants.

By the way mother, Did you get any letters from Bette. She said that she would write you soon after I left. You see mother, in case anything would happen to me, you could write and let her know because there's no other way for her to find out.

All the reports that I hear from around good old Penna. is cold weather and snow. You have more snow than

[No envelope remains with this letter.]

W.C. Lineaweaver ARM 1/c
VB-84
2 Feb 1945

Dear Mother:

I have been recieving a few of your letters in the weeks and I'm very grateful. My own writing has been almost none at all, my laxity has an excuse though very feeble. We have been pretty busy lately.

Had a letter from Jim the other day and I was glad to hear that he's getting along swell. He says his knee is stiff and doesn't think it ever will be O.K. Just so they don't send him back to Germany. Perhaps they'll send him home, which would be what he wants

By the way mother, Did you get any letters from Bette. She said that she would write you soon after I left. You see mother, in case anything would happen to me, you could write and let her know because there's no other way for her to find out.

All the reports that I hear from around good old Penna. is cold weather and snow. You have more snow than I guess Ive ever seen because I don't remember that much. I'll bet the kids are enjoying it with plenty of sledding.

Do you still get my allottment checks on time? How much does my bank roll say. As far as I can figure it should be about $400.00

At the present Im still in good health but the life is ragged. Give my best regard to all the rest of the family. Thinking of you I'll close

Your loving son
Wilson

W.C. Lineaweaver ARM 1/c
VB-84

[Note: This letter was written by Wilson's fiance, Bette Knepper, to his mother.]

squadron, or for any reason, will you please write me? I would so appreciate it.

I hope the winter has broken a little by now. From the papers out here, it seems you really have had a long hard winter. We have been having simply beautiful spring weather the past days.

I will enjoy hearing from you at any time.

Sincerely,
Bette

Feb. 8, 1945
Thurs. night

Dear Mrs. Lineaweaver,

Before Wilson left he asked if I would send the Valentine to you when the approximate time rolled around. To prevent any false hope by receiving it at this time, with a U.S.A. post-mark on it, I decided it would help to write a little note to send along with it.

I had a letter on the 27th which I presumed had been mailed from Honolulu. I rather expect another with more definite news since it's been over a week when I received the other one.

My sister and I certainly miss him since he spent most of his free time here. Everything is so empty without having him here.

If ever you get news which means I won't be receiving any mail for a length of time, such as change of base,

D. Knepper
3211½ Felton St.
San Diego 4, Calif.

Mrs. Robert Lineaweaver
1240 E. Cumberland St.
Avon, Pa.

Feb. 8, 1945
Thurs. night

Dear Mrs. Lineaweaver,

Before Wilson left he asked if I would send the Valentine to you when the approximate time called around. To prevent any false hopes by receiving it at this time, with a U.S.A. post-mark on it, I decided it would help to write a little note to send along with it.

I had a letter on the 27th which I presumed had been mailed from Honolulu. I rather expect another with more definite news since it's been over a week when I received the other one.

My sister and I certainly miss him, since he spent most of his free time here. Everything is so empty without having him here.

If ever you get news which means I won't be receiving any mail for a length of time, such as change of base, squadron, or for any reasons, will you please write me? I would so appreciate it.

I hope the winter has broken up a little by now. From the papers, out here, it seems you really have had a Long hard winter. We have been having simply beautiful spring weather the past days.

I will enjoy hearing from you at any time.

Sincerely,
Bette

[Postmark is San Diego, Calif., Feb. 9, 1945, 11 AM]
Mrs. Robert Lineaweaver
1240 E. Cumberland St.
Avon, Pa.

[Return Address:]
B. Knepper
3211 ½ Felton St.
San Diego 4, Calif.

#2

W.C. Lineaweaver ARM1/c
VB-84

26th February 1945

Dear Mother:

It has been quite some time since my last letter but you see mother, we are awfully busy and also I'm unable to get air mail stamps. It takes a long time for you to get mail sent free but I have to resort to this method.

My health is as good as can be expected, its only that my nerves are getting a little ragged and I hope and pray to come home to you soon. All I want to do is fall on that new Chesterfield that Lucille bought and rest without having the heavy engines.

Did you hear from Bettie Knepper since I left. She said that she was going to write you. In the letter I sent Jim recently, I also enclosed a picture of Bette. Wonder if he received it. I sent the letter to his hospital address in England. Perhaps by now he is back in Germany in the front lines and his mail situation is rough but eventually it catches up to you sooner or later.

Boy! that snow your getting back home is something. Never in all my years at home have I experienced that much unless it was back in about 1936. We had some deep snows that year. Guess all the kids liked all that snow if it keeps them out of school.

In the last of your letters you said that Dad started to work for Keystone Fruit Co. How does he like it? Guess it doesn't pay too much.

There very little that I can say about what were doing, in fact I can't say anything, but even so the newspapers and radio can do a better job than I could.

I hope everything is getting along swell at home mother. Give my regards to all the rest. Heres hoping for a quick ending of that hard winter and an early nice Spring.

This will surely get you, mother. I have a moustache and swore that it won't shave off until my return to the states or unless navy makes me. It looks just like pop's did when he was younger.

Gosh mom! Just think, another birthday around the corner. My 26th. Am getting old and going on my fifth year in the Navy. Ought to be getting a promotion soon to Chief Petty officer which is equivalent to a master sergeant in the army. Same rate that cousin ____ has.

Well! It's so long for now mother. Best of everything to you and all the rest. Take good care of yourself. Can still see you standing at the Harrisburg airport when I left.

your loving son
Wilson

W.C. Lineaweaver ARM1/c
VB-84
% Fleet Post office
San Francisco, Calif.

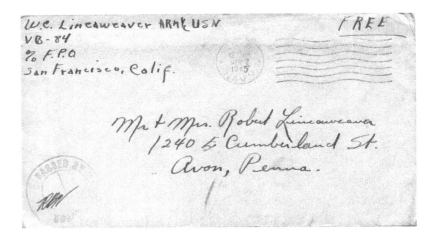

W.C. Lineaweaver ARM1/c USN
VB-84
% F.P.O
San Francisco, Calif.

FREE

Mr & Mrs. Robert Lineaweaver
1240 E. Cumberland St.
Avon, Penna.

[Postmark is U.S. Navy, March 2, 1945, 12:30 PM, with a "Passed by Naval Censor" stamp]

Mr & Mrs. Robert Lineaweaver
1240 E. Cumberland St.
Avon, Penna.

[Return Address:]
W.C. Lineaweaver ARM 1/c USN
VB-84
c/o F.P.O.
San Francisco, Calif.

W.C. Lineaweaver ARM 1/c
VB-84
26th February 1945

Dear Mother:

It has been quite some time since my last letter but you see mother, we are awfully busy and also I'm unable to get air mail stamps. It takes a long time for you to get mail sent free but I have to resort to this method.

My health is as good as can be expected, its only that my nerves are getting a little ragged and I hope and pray to come home to you soon. All I want to do is fall on that new Chesterfield that Lucille bought and rest without having the hear engines.

Did you hear from Bettie Knepper since I left. She said that she was going to write you. In the letter I sent Jim recently, I also enclosed a picture of Bette. Wonder if he recieved it. I sent the letter to his hospital address in England. Perhaps by now he is back in Germany in the front lines and his mail situation is rough but eventually it catches up to you sooner or later.

Boy! that snow your getting back home is something. Never in all my years at home have I experienced that much unless it was back in about 1936. We had some deep snows that year. Guess all the kids like all that snow if it keeps them out of school.

In the last of your letters you said that Dad started to work for Keystone Fruit Co. How does he like it? Guess it doesn't pay too much.

There's very little that I can say about what were doing, in fact I can't say anything, but even so the newspapers and radio can do a better job than I could.

Hope everything is getting along swell at home mother. Give my regards to all the rest. Heres hoping for a quick ending of that hard Winter and an early nice Spring.

This will surely get you, mother. I have raised a moustache and swore that I won't shave it off until my return to the states or unless the navy makes me. It looks just like pop's did when he was younger.

Gosh Mom! Just think, another birthday around the corner. My 26th, Am getting old fast and going on my fifth year in the Navy. Ought to be getting a promotion soon to Chief Petty officer which is equivalent to a master sergeant in the army. Same rate that cousin Chester has.

Well! Its so long for now mother. The best of everything to you and all the rest. Take good care of yourself. Can still see you & Dave standing at the Harrisburg airport when I took off

Your loving son
Wilson

W.C. Lineaweaver ARM 1/c
VB-84
c/o Fleet Post office
San Francisio, Calif.

These pages of Bombing Squadron 84 Narrative are a few of the pages from the History of Bombing Squadron Eighty Four which covers the time period of May 1944 thru June 1945. This is part of the "World War II War Diaries, 12/7/1941 - 12/31/1945" series in Record Group 38: Records of the Office of the Chief of Naval Operations, 1875 - 2006 housed at the National Archives. Wilson (W. C.) Lineaweaver is recorded as the aircrewman for pilot Lt. (jg) W. R. Lamb. According to Pacific Fleet Confidential Letter 2CL-44, dated January 1, 1944, war diaries were identified by the Navy as "the principal means by which the day-to-day experience of the Navy is recorded for current study and future historical use." Narrative copies obtained through fold3.com.

CONFIDENTIAL

USS BUNKER HILL

25 February 1945

MISSION:
    Bomb Nakajima Aircraft assembly plant, Koizumi, Japan.

FLIGHT:
    Take off.....................0830
    Over target.................1040
    Return......................1245
    Average hours in air............... 4h 15m

PLANES:
    On mission....................13
    Recovered.....................13
    Damaged (combat)...........0
            (operational).......1*
            (total)...................... 1
    Lost (combat)..............0
         (operational).........0
         (total)........................ 0

PERSONNEL:
    Out..................26
    Back.................26
    Wounded............. 0
    Lost................. 0

OTHER UNITS:
    13 TBM VT-84
    24 F4U VMF-221

BOMBS DROPPED ON TARGET:
    1,000#GP............. 12 ....12,000 pounds
      250#GP............. 22 .... 5,500 pounds
                         34 bombs   17,500 pounds

AMMUNITION:
    30 caliber............3,600 rounds
    20 mm.................1,800 rounds

*Barrier crash, minor.

Pages from the History of Bombing Squadron 84, National Archives' WWII War Diaries, Record Group 38, "VB-84"

CONFIDENTIAL
AIRCRAFT ACTION REPORT CVG 84 Report No. 8   VB report no. 8

Sheet 4 of 5   VT report no. 7

VF report no. 10

VMF221 report no. 6

BOMBING SQUADRON EIGHTY-FOUR NARRATIVE

1st DIVISION

Plane	1st Section	
201	BARROWS, J. E. Lt. USNR	SELL, L. ARM1c, USNR
213	AVERY, D. C. Lt.(jg), USNR	LYNCH, R. E. ARM3c, USNR
205	STAFFORD, C. B. Lt.(jg), USNR	SCHMELING, W. A. ARM3c, USNR
	2nd Section	
207	JACKS, W. T. Lt. USNR	PETERSEN, H. S. ARM2c, USNR
203	TURPIN, R. C. Lt.(jg), USNR	WILLIAMS, J. J. ARM2c, USNR
214	DOMONKOS, A. H. Lt.(jg), USNR	NEWHOUSER, W. L. ARM3c, USN
204	TIMM, H. O. Lt.(jg), USN	REGAN, P. E. ARM2c, USN

2nd DIVISION

	1st Section	
208	STONE, M. M. Lt, USN	ROSENBERG, M. ARM1c, USN
211	JOHNSTON, I. L. Lt.(jg), USNR	MOISER, J. M. ARM3c, USNR
206	ANDERSON, W. I. Lt.(jg), USNR	VAN BOMMEL, J. M. ARM3c, USN
	2nd Section	
202	LAMB, W.R. Lt.(jg), USNR	LINEAWEAVER, W. C. ARM1c, USN
209	PORTER, G. E. Ensign, USNR	DYKES, W. H. ARM3c, USNR
210	ELLIOTT, R. H. Lt.(jg), USNR	RICE, O. G. ARM3c, USN

Thirteen seemed to be a lucky number for the bombers. On its first combat mission that number had blasted the Nakajima aircraft assembly plant in Ota and this same number was to return to the same area to attack the Nakajima assembly plant in Koizumi, three miles to the southeast.

That was the way it turned out and with equally good results. However, the Koizumi plant was not the objective when the bombers were launched under low hanging rain clouds at 0830. Assignment was to attack the Nakajima Masashino aircraft engine plant in Tokyo. The latter plant was directly across the street from Nakajima Tama, hit so effectively by the bombers on their second mission the previous week.

The bomber element of the group strike from the BUNKER HILL was lead by Lt. BARROWS, with Lt. Comdr., SWANSON, skipper of the Torpedo Squadron, as OTC. All scheduled planes got off the deck, rendezvoused at 1,500 feet and were joined by the other squadrons.

It wasn't long after the formation had headed for Fuji San and the Nakajima Masashino plant that it was evident that the weather over the target was too low for bombing. It was decided to turn northward for the lucrative Koizumi plant lying untouched along the northern shore of winding tone Gawa.

Climbing steadily to 10,000 feet the formation raised the coast of Japan north of Inubo Saki to find that the entire plain was covered with a light blanket of snow. The crazy quilt pattern of rice fields that had appeared green brown on the first flight over the area the previous week now formed tiny lines etching hollow squares in the whiteness. It was as though some giant doodler had scribbled hundreds of tick-tack-tee patterns on a freshly laid table cloth.

-6-

Pages from the History of Bombing Squadron 84, National Archives' WWII War Diaries, Record Group 38, "VB-84"

CONFIDENTIAL

It was a little breathtaking to watch this odd design passing beneath the planes. But then the sobering realization came that the head lines were highways running to airfields and that the solik blocks of black were landing strips and bomber bases. Across the plain 70 miles from the coast lay the most important criss cross of black on white. The Nakajima Koizumi aircraft assembly plant stood out clearly against the snow, a mile south of the black airfield between it and the Ota plant that had been hit on the last strike.

From 13,000 feet pilots could select their point of aim: the center of the 2,500 feet square that produced approximately 20 per cent of the Empires total combat aircraft. From its productions lines came the Imperial Navy's Zeke, Jills, Irvings, Lizes, Franceses and Myrts a total of 450 aircraft a month.

As the bombers began their high speed approach sending the needle past 200 knots the pilots could see the sawtooth roofs of the larger buildings. Pushing over at 10,000 feet the bombers dived at 70° and released at 2,500, completing pullouts at 1,200. Below the thin lines of darkness against the white were turning to rolling clouds of black. Flashes blossomed from the buildings and fire melted the snow covered roof tops.

Twelve 1,000 pound GP's erupted in the build up area and twenty two 250 pounds added to the destruction. After the first few hits, blackness of smoke covered the exact location of later bursts, but each falling bomb seemed to make its contribution to the growing pall of smoke that rose from the plant.

Hitting 310 knots the bombers raced away from the target toward the still whiteness of unmarred landscape to the east. Rally was completed with the accompanying torpedo and fighter planes and the trip back to the coast was over the same undisturbed blanket of snow.

Only four or five enemy fighters were observed during the passage over 150 miles of Tokyo plain. Down on several of the airfields tiny narrow twin black lines indicated that a few fighters had belatedly started taking off. But these Nipponese never came within gun range of the formation.

There was a chance for some of the bombers to turn aside and strafe a pair of Zekes taking off from one of the fields, but the position was such that a diversion would have disrupted the formation. Having accomplished their primary mission, the bombers let lesser targets alone and continued their homeward course.

Landing aboard the carrier was effected with but one mishap. Lt.(jg) STAFFORD floated across the wires and caught the barrier. The prop and engine were creamed, and wheel cowlings were twisted, but the plane could be ready to fly next morning.

The score was 27,500 pounds of generalpurposes bombs hitting the target against no losses.

It was the third disastrous strike against Nakajima aircraft plants.

AIRCRAFT ACTION REPORT   CVG 84 Report No. 8   VB84 Report No. 8
                                                         VF84 Report No. 10
                                                         VT84 Report No. 7
                                                         VMF221 Report No. 6

Video of Wilson and his pilot W.R. Lamb

On this Narrative, Wilson and his pilot are in Helldiver plane #202. Search online for a video titled "Aerial Views Over Okinawa, USS Bunker Hill (CV-17), 2/25/1945". On the video at 6:39 is plane #202 which has just landed on the Bunker Hill. It has W.R. Lamb as the pilot and Wilson as the radioman/gunner (though Wilson is not readily seen in the video, he is behind the pilot). Immediately following on the video, plane #205 piloted by Lt. Stafford caught the barrier on the deck, as described in this Narrative. Wilson's mother Earlene and Lt. Stafford had a brief correspondence after the war. Stafford's letter is included later in this book.

–7–

Courtesy of Debra Goodale

William Raymond Lamb

Wilson's pilot on the USS *Bunker Hill* was William Raymond Lamb. In the National Archives' Bombing Squadron Eighty-Four Narrative, Wilson was listed as Lamb's aircrewman (radioman/gunner) from February to May 1945. Raymond was born in Louisiana, but grew up just east of Livingston, TX. His daughter, Debra Goodale of Cleveland, TX, said that her father went to the Navy recruiter to enlist as a pilot, but was told he had to go to college beforehand. After attending one year of college classes, Raymond again applied to enlist as a pilot, and on this attempt was accepted. His score on the pilot's test, according to his brother Max, was the highest score ever achieved up until that time.

After the war, Raymond suffered from what we now call PTSD, but at the time was called "battle fatigue." World War II took a tremendous psychological toll on its servicemen like Raymond. As a result of battle experiences, these men often suffered deep emotional wounds which never healed. Watching close friends being maimed or killed, experiencing guilt from escaping death while others didn't, and even feeling guilt in killing the enemy, was tremendously painful. On December 21, 1955, eight days before his 34th birthday, Raymond took his own life with a shotgun. The December 29, 1955, the *Polk County Enterprise* newspaper (Livingston, TX) reported that he was a "much decorated Navy pilot during World War II," was an employee of the Shell Oil Refinery, and was survived by his parents, his wife, three daughters, and three siblings.

Courtesy of Debra Goodale

Raymond Lamb (left) & Wilson Lineaweaver (right)

Jim Krombach of the Naval Air Station Wildwood (NJ) Aviation Museum, explains that on the photo at left "the radioman/gunner is standing on the right. He is distinguished by his black shoes (enlisted and ship board officers wore black shoes, aviators wore brown shoes unless wearing flight boots) and is wearing an M-426 flight suit over what is presumed to be his chambray shirt and denim pants. His flight gear includes a mid to late war AN-H-15 Helmet, AN 6530 goggles and mid-late war B4 life vest with dye marker. Dye marker for survival, when opened, is a yellow/green powder and makes about a 30 foot circle around the person to be seen more easily by rescue aircraft. He is also wearing a QAS (Quick Attach Seatpack) parachute harness. Parachutes were heavy and cumbersome. They were left on the seat in the aircraft. The pilot or crewman sat down and his harness was clipped onto rings on the chute. His flightsuit pockets on legs would have contained rayon maps, and radio frequencies to be used for the misson. The pilot is standing on the left and is wearing his khaki work uniform, brown shoes, early-mid war M450 flight helmet, same B4 type life vest and carrying his flight gloves. They are standing in front of an SB2C Helldiver."

Pages from the History of Bombing Squadron 84, National Archives' WWII War Diaries, Record Group 38, "VB-84"

CONFIDENTIAL

USS BUNKER HILL

1 March 1945

MISSION:
    Bomb Installations around Naha Airfield, Okinawa Jima, Nansei Shoto.

FLIGHT:
    Take off....................1315
    Over target................1530
    Return.....................1655
    Average hours in air................. 3h 40 m

PLANES:
    On mission....................13
    Recovered....................13
    Damaged (combat)...........0
            (operational)......0
            (total)....................... 0
    Lost (combat)...............0
         (operational).........0
         (total)....................... 0

PERSONNEL:
    Out.........................26
    Back........................26
    Wounded...................... 0
    Lost........................ 0

OTHER UNITS:
    12 TBM VT-84
    16 F4U VF-84

BOMBS DROPPED ON TARGET:
    500#GP................ 26 .... 13,000 pounds
    250#GP................ 24 .... 6,000 pounds
                          50   19,000 pounds

AMMUNITION:
    30 caliber............. 1,600 rounds
    20 mm.................. 900 rounds

Pages from the History of Bombing Squadron 84, National Archives' WWII War Diaries, Record Group 38, "VB-84"

CONFIDENTIAL

AIRCRAFT ACTION REPORT   CVG 84   Report No. 13   VF84 Report #12
                                                                VB84 Report #10
Sheet 4 of 5   VT84 Report # 9

BOMBING SQUADRON EIGHTY-FOUR NARRATIVE

1st DIVISION

1st Section

Plane	Pilot	
207	BARROWS, J. E., Lt., USNR	SELL, L., ARM1c, USNR
202	AVERY, D. C., Lt.(jg), USNR	LYNCH, R. E., ARM3c, USNR
201	STAFFORD, C. B., Lt.(jg)	SCHMELING, W. A., ARM3c, USNR

2nd Section

214	JACKS, W. T., Lt., USNR	PEDERSEN, H. S., ARM1c, USN
211	TURPIN, R. C., Lt.(jg), USNR	WILLIAMS, J. J., ARM2c, USNR
213	DOMONKOS, A. H., Lt.(jg), USNR	NEWHOUSER, W. L., ARM3c, USN
209	SWEARINGEN, F. A., Lt.(jg), USNR	PICKERING, H. E., ARM2c, USN

2nd DIVISION

1st Section

210	STONE, M. M., Lt., USN	ROSENBERG, M., ARM1c, USN
215	JOHNSTON, L. L., Lt.(jg), USNR	MOSIER, J. M., ARM3c, USNR
206	ANDERSON, W. I., Lt.(jg), USNR	VAN BOMMEL, J. M., ARM3c, USN

2nd Section

212	LAMB, W. R., Lt.(jg), USNR	LINEAWEAVER, W. C., ACRM, USN
204	DITTO, H. B., Lt.(jg), USNR	SMITH, C. W., ARM3c, USN
208	PORTER, G. E., Ens., USNR	DYKES, W. H., ARM3c, USNR

Having done what appeared to be a good morning's work on the small industrial plant south of Machinato the bombers turned southward three miles to Naha airfield for the afternoon target. At least there would be more installations on which to put pippers.

Rendezvous was at 1,500' after the launching and the formation of bombers, fighters and torpedo planes headed for Okinawa Jima seventy miles to the west. Feeling out gun positions again from 13,000' the bombers decided on an east-west line of attack and circled the north end of Naha Airfield in their high speed approach.

The target was nearly obscured by clouds but through occasional holes the 5,000-foot runway with its two 4,000-foot legs could be spotted. Dive angle was a trifle shallow — 60°, releases were made at 2,500' and pull outs effected at 1,000'.

Points of aim varied. Seven of the planes dove on installations around the triangular field. Lt.(jg) JOHNSTON picked out a revetment on the southeastern tip of the field; Lt.(jg) LAMB put his sight on another nearby and Lt.(jg) SWEARINGEN chose one closer to the taxiway at the south end.

Lt. STONE's target was a group of small buildings east of the elbow of the field; Lt.(jg) DITTO aimed for shops in that vicinity. Lt.(jg) ANDERSON dove on a tower at the southern end of the field and Ens. PORTER drew a bead on a building near the field.

All bombs were dropped on the targets except two 250 pounders from wing rack (Lt.(jg) JOHNSTON and Ens. PORTER) and one 500 pounder (Lt.(jg) ANDERSON). These were jettisoned.

-2-

W.C. Lineaweaver ACRM (AA)
VB-84
℅ F.P.O.
San Francisco, Calif.

1st March 1945

Dear Mother:

The other day we had a mail call, the first in a long time and I received some of your letters. It was good hearing from you and all the news from home.

The weather man is sure treating you rough but the kids must like it getting all those weeks off from school. Here's hoping that better weather is in the near future.

Glad to hear that your hand is O.K. again mother, and that Dad started to work at Lebanon Valley. They do mostly all Navy work there, don't they?

As you probably have noticed from the above address, there is a change from ARM⅛ to ACRM. Just got a promotion to "Chief". The letters mean aviation chief Radioman. This is the highest enlisted mans rating in the navy and a change of uniform goes with it which I plan to show you when I'm able to come home.

This trip out is pretty tough, more so than my previous trips. My nerves are really on edge and I don't know how I'll be able to stand up under the strain, but with the help of God I hope to pull through.

The papers will give you a better idea of what were doing than I could tell if able to.

So for now I close. Best of everything to you I remain

Your loving son
Wilson

[No envelope remains with this letter.]
[Notice that the name of the ship underneath the ship picture was removed.]

W.C. Lineaweaver ACRM (AA)
VB-84
c/o F.P.O.
San Francisco, Calif.
1st March 1945

Dear Mother:

The other day we had a mail call, the first in a long time and I recieved some of your letters. It was good hearing from you and all the news from home.

The weather man is sure treating you rough but the kids must like it getting all those weeks off from school. Heres hoping that better weather is in the near future.

Glad to hear that your hand is O.K. again Mother, *[see below]* and that Dad started to work at Lebanon Valley. They do mostly all Navy work there, Don't they?

As you probably have noticed from the above address, there is a change from ARM 1/c to ACRM. Just got a promotion to "Chief". The letters mean Aviation chief Radio Man. This is the highest enlisted mans rating in the navy and a change of uniform goes with it which I plan to show you when I'm able to come home.

This trip out is pretty tough, more so than my previous trips. My nerves are really on edge and I don't know how I'll be able to stand up under the strain, but with the help of God I hope to pull through.

The papers will give you a better idea of what were doing than I could tell if able to.

So for now I close, Best of everything to you I remain

Your loving son
Wilson

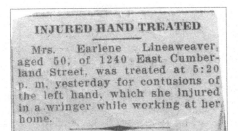

INJURED HAND TREATED

Mrs. Earlene Lineaweaver, aged 50, of 1240 East Cumberland Street, was treated at 5:20 p. m. yesterday for contusions of the left hand, which she injured in a wringer while working at her home.

This newspaper clipping appeared in the *Lebanon Daily News*, Lebanon, PA, on January 18, 1945.

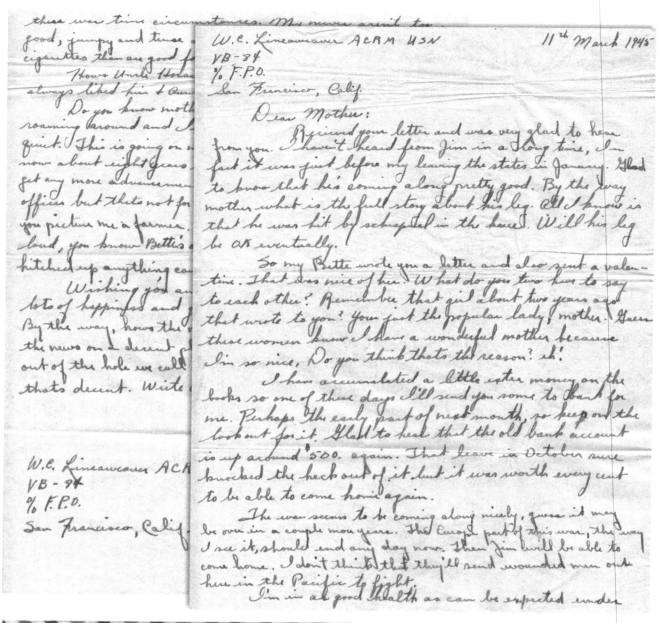

there was these circumstances. My nerves aren't too
good, jumpy and tense and [I'm] smoking more
cigarettes than are good for [me].

How's Uncle Hollis, [I've]
always liked him + Aunt [...]

Do you know moth[er I'm]
roaming around and [...]
quiet. This is going on [...]
now about eight years [...]
get any more advancement
officer but that's not for [...]
you picture me a farmer [...]
loud, you know Bette's [...]
hitched up anything ca[...]

Wishing you an[...]
lots of happiness and [...]
By the way, how's the [...]
the news on a decent [...]
out of the hole we call [...]
that's decent. Write [...]

W.C. Lineaweaver ACR[M]
VB-94
℅ F.P.O.
San Francisco, Calif.

W.C. Lineaweaver ACRM USN
VB-84
℅ F.P.O.
San Francisco, Calif.

11th March 1945

Dear Mother:

Received your letter and was very glad to hear
from you. I haven't heard from Jim in a long time, in
fact it was just before my leaving the states in January. Glad
to know that he's coming along pretty good. By the way
mother what is the full story about his leg. All I know is
that he was hit by schrapnel in the house. Will his leg
be OK eventually.

So my Bette wrote you a letter and also sent a valentine. That was nice of her. What do you two have to say
to each other? Remember that girl about two years ago
that wrote to you? Your just the popular lady, mother. Guess
these women know I have a wonderful mother because
I'm so nice. Do you think that's the reason? eh!

I have accumulated a little extra money on the
books so one of these days I'll send you some to bank for
me. Perhaps the early part of next month, so keep on the
lookout for it. Glad to hear that the old bank account
is up around $500. again. That leave in October sure
knocked the heck out of it but it was worth every cent
to be able to come home again.

The war seems to be coming along nicely, guess it may
be over in a couple more years. The Europe part of this war, the way
I see it, should end any day now. Then Jim will be able to
come home. I don't think that they'll send wounded men out
here in the Pacific to fight.

I'm in as good health as can be expected under

[Postmark is U.S. Navy, March 12, 1945,
12:30 PM, with a "Passed by Naval Censor" stamp]

Mr & Mrs. Robert Lineaweaver
1240 E. Cumberland St.
Avon, Penna.

[Return Address:]

W.C. Lineaweaver ACRM USN
VB-84
c/o F.P.O.
San Francisco, Calif.

W.C. Lineaweaver ACRM USN
VB-84   c/o F.P.O.
San Francisco, Calif.
11th March 1945

Dear Mother:

Recieved your letter and was very glad to hear from you. I haven't heard from Jim in a long time, In fact it was just before my leaving the states in January. Glad to know that he's coming along pretty good. By the way mother what is the full story about his leg. All I know is that he was hit by schrapnel in the knee. Will his leg be O.K. eventually.

So my Bette wrote you a letter and also sent a valentine. That was nice of her. What do you two have to say to each other? Remember that girl about two years ago that wrote to you? Your just the popular lady, mother. Guess these women know I have a wonderful mother because I'm so nice. Do you think thats the reason? eh!

I have accumalated a little extra money on the books so one of these days I'll send you some to bank for me. Perhaps the early part of next month, so keep on the look out for it. Glad to hear that the old bank account is up around $500. again. That leave in October sure knocked the heck out of it but it was worth every cent to be able to come home again.

The war seems to be coming along nicely, guess it may be over in a couple more years. The Europe part of this war, the way I see it, should end any day now. Then Jim will be able to come home. I don't think that they'll send wounded men out here in the Pacific to fight.

I'm in as good health as can be expected under these war time circumstances. My nerves aren't too good, jumpy and tense all the time. Also I smoke more cigarettes than are good for me.

Hows Uncle Horace doing since the heart attack? I always liked him & Aunt Eva.

Do you know mother, I'm getting very tired of this roaming around and I'm really in need of some peace and quiet. This is going on my fifth year in the navy and its now about eight years since I'm away from home. Can't get any more advancements unless its to become a commissioned officer but thats not for me. Maybe I'll start farming, can't you picture me a farmer. Guess I'd better not say that too loud, you know Bette's a farm girl from Iowa and if we get hitched up anything can happen.

Wishing you and all the rest the best of everything, lots of happiness and good health, I'll close for now. By the way, hows the new furniture coming along and what the news on a decent place to live. I wish you could get out of the hole we call home and really find some place thats decent. Write often

Your loving son
Wilson

W.C. Lineaweaver ACRM USN
VB-84   c/o F.P.O.
San Francisco, Calif.

hu cause I just don't know I'll take
the responsibility after being care free all
these years.

Its rugged going out here moth
you can gather reading in paper and
ing to the radio. I say my prayer
Over in Europe things are beginning t
a little rosey and it ought to en
Maybe then they'll let Jim come
I sure hope his leg comes aroun
good as new. The infantry always g
tough fighting, also I should
dive bombing.

Hoping for the best out of t
awful mess and wishing you the
of health & happiness I close re

Your loving so
Wilson

W.C. Lineaweaver ACRM USN
VB-84
% F.P.O.
San Francisco, Calif.

W.C. Lineaweaver ACRM USN   29th March 1945
VB-84 % F.P.O.
San Francisco, Calif.

Dear Mother:
Received your V-letter dated March 4th
and I was awfully glad to hear from you and
home. Glad that everything is all O.K. and
everyone in the best of health.

Its about time the weather is changing for the better after that tough long
winter. Now to complicate things you
have a bus strike. How does Dad go
back and forth from work? Does Joe like
his new work and what does he do?

Give everyone my regards, I think
of all of you often and many times getting
homesick. I'm really tired of this
roaming and want peace & quiet in a
bad way.

In a few more days is my birthday
as you well know, 26 years old. About
time I settle down and start raising
a family of my own, Don't you think?
Well! If everything works out alright,
when I get back to the states this time
I'll get married. Will probably have
to bring her home and have you fix

[Postmark is U.S. Navy, April 2, 1945, 12:30 PM, with a "Passed by Naval Censor" stamp]
Mr & Mrs Robert Lineaweaver
1240 E. Cumberland St.
Avon, Penna.

[Return Address:]
W.C. Lineaweaver ACRM
VB-84   c/o F.P.O.
San Francisco, Calif.

W.C. Lineaweaver ACRM USN
VB-84 c/o F.P.O.
San Francisco, Calif.
29th March 1945

Dear Mother:

Recieved your V-letter dated March 4th and I was awfully glad to hear from you and home. Glad that everything is all O.K. and everyone in the best of health.

Its about time the weather is changing for the better after that tough long winter. Now to complicate thing you have a bus strike. How does Dad go back and forth from work? Does he like his new work and what does he do?

Give everyone my regards, I think of all of you often and many times getting homesick. I'm really tired of this roaming and want peace & quiet in a bad way.

In a few more days is my birthday as you well know, 26 years old. About time I settle down and start raising a family of my own, Don't you think? Well! if everything works out alright, when I get back to the states this time I'll get married. Will probably have to bring her home and have you feed her cause I just don't how I'll take the responsibility after being care free all these years.

Its rugged going out here mother as you can gather reading in papers and listening to the radio. I say my prayers regularly. Over in Europe things are beginning to look a little rosey and it ought to end soon. Maybe then they'll let Jim come home. I sure hope his leg comes around as good as new. The infantry always gets the tough fighting, also I should include dive bombing.

Hoping for the best out of this awful mess and wishing you the best of health & happiness I close remaining

Your loving son
Wilson

W.C. Lineaweaver ACRM USN
VB-84
c/o F.P.O.
San Francisco, Calif.

Every sortie or combat mission had a corresponding report. The next eight pages are an example of a report for an action in which Wilson was involved, and in which he and his pilot W.R. Lamb's bomb hit a Japanese destroyer. Not every report was this detailed.

These reports are held at the National Archives and this copy was obtained through fold3.com.

OPNAV-16-223
Form ACA-1
Sheet 1 of 5

AIRCRAFT ACTION REPORT

RESTRICTED
(Reclassify when filled out)

I. GENERAL

(a) Unit Reporting **VB-84**   (b) Based on or at **USS BUNKER HILL**   (c) Report No. **35**

(d) Take off: Date **7 April, 1945** Time (LZT) **1015 I** (Zone); Lat. **27-10 N.** Long **129-30 E**

(e) Mission **Strike on Jap Fleet Unit**   (f) Time of Return **1515 I** (Zone)

II. OWN AIRCRAFT OFFICIALLY COVERED BY THIS REPORT.

TYPE (a)	SQUADRON (b)	TAKING OFF (c)	ENGAGING ENEMY A/C (d)	ATTACKING TARGET (e)	BOMBS AND TORPEDOES CARRIED (PER PLANE) (f)	FUZE, SETTING (g)
SB2C-4	VB-84	10	0	10	2-500# or 1-1000# 2-250#	No record

III. OTHER U. S. OR ALLIED AIRCRAFT EMPLOYED IN THIS OPERATION.

TYPE	SQUADRON	NUMBER	BASE	TYPE	SQUADRON	NUMBER	BASE
F4U-1D	VB-84	15	USS BUNKER HILL				
TBM-1	VT-85	14	USS BUNKER HILL				
F6F (p)	VF-84	2	USS BUNKER HILL				

IV. ENEMY AIRCRAFT OBSERVED OR ENGAGED (By Own Aircraft Listed in II Only).

(a) TYPE	(b) NO. OBSERVED	(c) NO. ENGAGING OWN A/C	(d) TIME ENCOUNTERED	(e) LOCATION OF ENCOUNTER	(f) BOMBS, TORPEDOES CARRIED; GUNS OBSERVED	(g) CAMOUFLAGE AND MARKING
NONE			(ZONE)			
			(ZONE)			
			(ZONE)			

(h) Apparent Enemy Mission(s) ▬ ▬ ▬ ▬ ▬ ▬ ▬ ▬ ▬ ▬ ▬

(i) Did Any Part of Encounter(s) Occur in Clouds? ▬ ▬ ▬ If so, Describe Clouds ▬ ▬ ▬ ▬ ▬ ▬ ▬
    (YES OR NO)   (BASE IN FEET, TYPE AND TENTHS OF COVER)

(j) Time of Day and Brilliance of Sun or Moon **Mid-morning - overcast** (k) Visibility **0-10**
    (NIGHT, BRIGHT MOON; DAY, OVERCAST, ETC.)   (MILES)

V. ENEMY AIRCRAFT DESTROYED OR DAMAGED IN AIR (By Own Aircraft Listed in II Only).

(a) TYPE ENEMY A/C	(b) DESTROYED OR DAMAGED BY:				(c) WHERE HIT, ANGLE	(d) DAMAGE CLAIMED
	TYPE A/C	SQUADRON	PILOT OR GUNNER	GUNS USED		
	NONE					

ALLECT - MFG. BY THE EGRY REGISTER CO., PATENTED

149

OPNAV-16-223
Form ACA-1
Sheet 2 of 5

AIRCRAFT ACTION REPORT

RESTRICTED
(Reclassify when
filled out)

REPORT No. 35

VI. LOSS OR DAMAGE, COMBAT OR OPERATIONAL, OF OWN AIRCRAFT (of those listed in II only).

	(a) TYPE OWN A/C	(b) SQUADRON	(c) CAUSE: TYPE ENEMY A/C, TYPE GUN, OR OPERATIONAL CAUSE	(d) WHERE HIT, ANGLE (List armor, self-sealing tanks, equipment hit)	(e) EXTENT OF LOSS OR DAMAGE (Give Bureau serial number of planes destroyed)
1	SB2C-4	VB-84	Medium A.A.	wing root	total strike
2					
3					
4					
5					
6					
7					
8					
9					
10					
11					
12					
13					
14					

VII. PERSONNEL CASUALTIES (in aircraft listed in II only; identify with planes listed in VI by Nos. at left).

(a) NO	(b) SQUADRON	(c) NAME, RANK OR RATING	(d) CAUSE	(e) CONDITION OR STATUS
	NONE			

VIII. RANGE, FUEL, AND AMMUNITION DATA FOR PLANES RETURNING

(a) TYPE A/C	(b) MILES OUT	(c) MILES RETURN	(d) AV. HOURS IN AIR	(e) AV. FUEL LOADED	(f) AV. FUEL CONSUMED	(g) TOTAL AMMUNITION EXPENDED .30	50	20MM	MM	(h) NO. OF PLANES RETURNING
SB2C	255	255	5	320	305	NO RECORD				10

IX. ENEMY ANTI-AIRCRAFT ENCOUNTERED (Check one block on each line).

CALIBER	NONE	MEAGER	MODERATE	INTENSE
HEAVY — Time-fused shells, 75mm and over				X
MEDIUM — Impact-fused shells, 20mm-50mm				X
LIGHT — Machine gun bullets, 6.5mm-13.2mm	X			

X. COMPARATIVE PERFORMANCE, OWN AND ENEMY AIRCRAFT (use check list at left).

SPEED, CLIMB,
  at various altitudes

TURNS
DIVES
CEILINGS
RANGE
PROTECTION
ARMAMENT

150

ALLSET — MFD. BY THE EGRY REGISTER CO., PATENTED

OPNAV-16-223
Form ACA-1
Sheet 3 of 5

AIRCRAFT ACTION REPORT

RESTRICTED
(Reclassify when filled out)

(OMIT THIS SHEET IF NO ATTACK WAS MADE)

REPORT No. 35

XI. ATTACK ON ENEMY SHIPS OR GROUND OBJECTIVES (By Own Aircraft Listed in II Only).

(a) Target(s) and Location(s) **Takanami Cl DD** (FOR SHIPS INCLUDE ALL IN AREA UNDER ATTACK) (b) Time Over Target(s) **1258 I** (Zone)

(c) Clouds Over Target **3,500 ft.** **9/10 cover** - (BASE IN FEET, TYPE AND TENTHS OF COVER)

(d) Visibility of Target **Hazy-partially obscured by clouds** (CLEAR, HAZY, PARTIALLY OBSCURED BY CLOUDS, ETC.) (e) Visibility **0-10** (MILES)

(f) Bombing Tactics: Type **glide** (LEVEL, GLIDE OR DIVE) Bomb Sight Used **MK-8** (TYPE)

Bombs Dropped per Run **4** (NUMBER) • Spacing **Salvo** (FEET) Altitude of Bomb Release - - - (FEET)

(g) Number of Enemy Aircraft Hit on Ground: Destroyed - - - Probably Destroyed - - - - Damaged - - -

(h) AIMING POINT	(i) DIMENSIONS OR TONNAGE	(j) NO. A/C ATTACKING (k) SQUADRON	(l) BOMBS AND AMMUNITION EXPENDED EACH AIMING POINT	(m) NO HITS On Aiming Point	(n) DAMAGE (None, slight, serious, destroyed or sunk)
1 Destroyer		10	(all bombs)	3	probably sunk
2		VB-84	1500 lb. per plane		
3					
4					
5					
6					
7					
8					

(o) RESULTS: (For all hits claimed on ship targets and for land targets of special interest, draw diagram, top or side view or both, as appropriate, showing type and location of hits. For all targets give location and effect of hits, and identify by numbers above. Use additional sheets if necessary)

1. Three definite hits were seen on the D.D., left it burning, dead in the water (see photos attached)

(p) Were Photographs Taken? **YES** Photographs of Damage, When Taken, Should Be Attached By Staple.

151

ALLSET — MFD. BY THE EDDY REGISTER CO., PATENTED

OPNAV-16-223
Form ACA-1
Sheet 4 of 5

AIRCRAFT ACTION REPORT

RESTRICTED
(Reclassify when
filled out)

REPORT No. 35

XII. TACTICAL AND OPERATIONAL DATA. (Narrative and comment. Describe action fully and comment freely, following applicable items in check list at left. Use additional sheets if necessary.)

ENGAGEMENT WITH ENEMY
OWN AIRCRAFT
Disposition
Altitudes
Speeds
Approach Tactics
Use of Cover, Deception
Angles of Attack and
Their Effectiveness
Distance of Opening Fire
Defense Tactics and
Their Effectiveness
ENEMY AIRCRAFT
Method of Locating, Distance
Disposition
Altitudes
Speeds
Approach Tactics
Use of Cover, Deception
Angles of Attack
Distance of Opening Fire
Defensive Tactics
COMMENTS AND
RECOMMENDATIONS
Own Weaknesses
Enemy Weaknesses
Offensive Tactics, Own
"   "   , Enemy
Defensive Tactics, Own
"   "   , Enemy
Flexible Gunnery, Own
Escort Tactics
Fighter Direction
Use of Radar
Night Fighting
Recognition, Aircraft

ATTACK
OWN TACTICS
Method of Locating Target
Approach to Target
Altitudes, Speeds
Approach
Dive
Pull-Out
Dive Angle
Strafing
Retirement
Defensive Tactics
Use of Jamming
DEFENSE, ENEMY
Evasive Tactics, Ships
Concealment
Searchlights
Night Fighter Tactics
Use of Jamming
COMMENTS AND
RECOMMENDATIONS
Bombing Tactics
Torpedo Tactics
Effectiveness of
Bombs, Torpedoes
Selection of Targets
Fuzing
Strafing Tactics
Defensive Tactics
Use of Radar
Reconnaissance
Photography
Briefing

OPERATIONAL
Navigation
Homing
Rendezvous
Recognition, Ships
Communications
Flight Operations
Search and Tracking
Base Operations
Maintenance

1st DIVISION

Plane   1st Section

201   CONN, J.P., Lt.Comdr.   DOUGHERTY, L.F., ACRM
209   HOLLADAY, R.W., Lt(jg)   SAYLOR, G.E., ARM2c
215   GORDINIER, H.R., Lt(jg)   MAUDE, R.H., ARM3c

2nd Section

212   TILLEY, H.W., Lt.   OLSEN, V.C., ARM1c
205   HICKS, L.T., Lt(jg)   SANCHEZ, A.E., ARM2c

2nd DIVISION

1st Section

202   KORNEGAY, W.B., Lt(jg)   RAWLINGS, V.C., ARM1c
208   SWEARINGEN, F.A., Lt(jg)   PICKERING, H.E., ARM2c
210   ELLIOTT, R.H., Lt(jg)   RICE, O.C., ARM3c

2nd Section

211   LAMB, W.R., Lt(jg)   LINEWEAVER, W.C., ACRM
204   PORTER, G.E., Ensign   DYKES, W.H., ARM3c

Reports that the target would be warships of the Japanese Fleet made this mission one that all pilots wanted to fly. There had been some juicy targets in Kure harbor about three weeks previously, but the current operation was the first for the squadron against enemy warships underway.

Composition of the force was fairly well known. Rounding the southern end of Kyushu during the night, the enemy had been sighted by a scout and the word was given to go in for the kill. Principal warship and pride of the fading Nipponese Navy was the battleship Yamato. Around her was a screen of about eight destroyers and a light cruiser of the Agano class.

With this information, the squadron rendezvoused with other planes in the group, which in turn joined up on other groups in the force and headed for a contact southwest of southern Kyushu. Course was set to the northwest across the Ryukus. Overcast at about 7,000 feet kept the formation low as it passed over rocky Amami O Shima and sped over East China Sea.

Blips on the radar screen in the squadron commander's plane appeared at thirty-two miles, altitude 6,500 feet. By the time the formation was twenty miles away the enemy disposition was well defined. Reports of these contacts were made to the strike leader.

152

OPNAV-16-223
Form ACA-1
Sheet 5 of 5

AIRCRAFT ACTION REPORT

REPORT No. _____

XIII. MATERIAL DATA. (Comment freely on performance or suitability, following check list at left Use additional sheets if necessary).

ARMAMENT
Guns, Gunsights
Turrets
Ammunition
Bombs, Torpedoes
Bomb Sights
Bomb Releases

COMMUNICATIONS
Radio, Radar
Homing Devices
Visual Signals
Codes, Ciphers

RECOGNITION
IFF
Signals
Battle Lights
Procedures

PROTECTION
Armor; Points and Angles
of Fire Needing Further
Protection
Leak Proofing

EMERGENCY EQUIPMENT
Parachutes
Life Belts, Life Rafts
Safety Belts
Emergency Kits
Rations, First Aid

NAVIGATIONAL EQUIPMENT
Compasses
Driftsights
Octants
Automatic Pilots
Charts
Field Lighting

INSTRUMENTS
Flight
Power Plant

OXYGEN SYSTEM

**CAMOUFLAGE AND
DECEPTION DEVICES**

STRUCTURE
Airframe
Control Surfaces
Control System
Dive Flaps
Landing Gear
Heating System
Flight Characteristics
At Various Loadings

POWER PLANT
Engines
Engine Accessories
Propellers
Lubricating System
Starters
Exhaust Dampers

HYDRAULIC SYSTEM

ELECTRICAL SYSTEM
Auxiliary Plant
Lights

FUEL SYSTEM

FLIGHT CLOTHING

MAINTENANCE

BASE FACILITIES
Plane Servicing Equipment
Personnel Facilities

Despite the knowledge of the whereabouts and composition of the Japanese force, it still was surprising to look over the sides of cockpits and actually see it below. Reports had been accurate, there was the Yamato with her screen of one cruiser and eight destroyers. But even more surprising was absence of opposition. The entire formation of more than 300 planes flew directly over the Jap force at 6,500 feet and did not draw a shot.

Following the load of other groups, the bombers circled north of the force awaiting orders. After some minutes no direct word had come from the strike leader and the bomber commander, mindful of his planes' diminishing gas load, decided to attack. When the decision was made a destroyer was seen speeding below the squadron and it was designated as the target.

Apparently the destroyer was one of the force's pickets, as it was several miles from the battleship and her screen. However, the exact position of the destroyer to the battleship was not known at that time because of cloud cover over the area. From photographs and other evidence the position of the enemy at the time of attack has been drawn and a plot is on the following page.

When the bombers came in for their attack, flying under the clouds at about 3,500 feet, they approached from the starboard side of the destroyer's wake. The diagram, second page follows, shows the tactics used in the attack.

It was further noted that the destroyer ceased its anti-aircraft fire when second runs were made on the ship. Fighter escort planes also observed the lack of AA fire when they made passes to drop their bombs. Furthermore the destroyer stopped dead in the water, although it had been making what appeared to be full speed before the attack began.

The white smoke continued to pour from the forward stack for several minutes. Pictures in the Photo folder show the destroyer at this stage and also earlier when it was under attack. Before the bombers completed their rally, the destroyer stopped smoking. A short while afterward, three pilots and five gunners observed a terrific explosion aft of No. 3 turret. First there was a red-orange blast, then the fantail seemed to heave and shudder. Immediately afterward black smoke billowed upward. Observers believed they saw the vessel settling at the stern.

REPORT PREPARED BY: APPROVED BY

SIGNATURE | RANK AND DUTY | SIGNATURE | RANK AND DUTY | DATE

153

AIRCRAFT ACTION REPORT

OPNAV-16-223
Form ACA-1
Sheet 5 of 5

RESTRICTED
(Reclassify when filled out)

REPORT No 35

XIII. MATERIAL DATA. (Comment freely on performance or suitability, following check list at left
Use additional sheets if necessary).

ARMAMENT
 Guns, Gunsights
 Turrets
 Ammunition
 Bombs, Torpedoes
 Bomb Sights
 Bomb Releases

COMMUNICATIONS
 Radio, Radar
 Homing Devices
 Visual Signals
 Codes, Ciphers

RECOGNITION
 IFF
 Signals
 Battle Lights
 Procedures

PROTECTION
 Armor; Points and Angles
 of Fire Needing Further
 Protection
 Leak Proofing

EMERGENCY EQUIPMENT
 Parachutes
 Life Belts, Life Rafts
 Safety Belts
 Emergency Kits
 Rations, First Aid

NAVIGATIONAL EQUIPMENT
 Compasses
 Driftsights
 Octants
 Automatic Pilots
 Charts
 Field Lighting

INSTRUMENTS
 Flight
 Power Plant

OXYGEN SYSTEM

**CAMOUFLAGE AND
DECEPTION DEVICES**

STRUCTURE
 Airframe
 Control Surfaces
 Control System
 Dive Flaps
 Landing Gear
 Heating System
 Flight Characteristics
 At Various Loadings

POWER PLANT
 Engines
 Engine Accessories
 Propellers
 Lubricating System
 Starters
 Exhaust Dampers

HYDRAULIC SYSTEM

ELECTRICAL SYSTEM
 Auxiliary Plant
 Lights

FUEL SYSTEM

FLIGHT CLOTHING

MAINTENANCE

BASE FACILITIES
 Plane Servicing Equipment
 Personnel Facilities

Further observation was denied because of cloud cover and the squadron turned for base.

Witnesses of the various hits and explosions are known to be reliable. They include Lt.Comdr. CONN, Lt(jg) KORNEGAY, Lt(jg) GORDINIER, MAUDE, RAWLINGS, PICKERING, SANCHEZ AND DYKES, each of whom verify that hits were made. Those who observed the explosion in the stern include Lt(jg) KORNEGAY, Lt(jg) SWEARINGEN, Ensign PORTER, SAYLOR, MAUDE, OLSEN, SANCHEZ AND DYKES.

A direct hit made by a fighter plane, identified as that of Lt(jg) DIXON, was observed by RAWLINGS.

On the basis of the observation made on the scene and the interpretation of pictures taken, the squadron has listed the destroyer as probably sunk. Observation of another destroyer breaking in two and sinking was discounted because its position was not that of the destroyer attacked by VB-84. From staff photo interpreters a shipping plot was obtained and this has been included to show the relative position of the destroyer to the other ships in the force.

REPORT PREPARED BY:

APPROVED BY

J.E. NAYMAN, 1st Lieut. ACIO   J.P. CONN, Jr. Lt.Comdr. C.O.   5-26-45

SIGNATURE   RANK AND DUTY   SIGNATURE   RANK AND DUTY

154

The Japanese Takanami class destroyer, lower left as "J" on the diagram, is the one hit by Wilson and his pilot in their dive bombing.

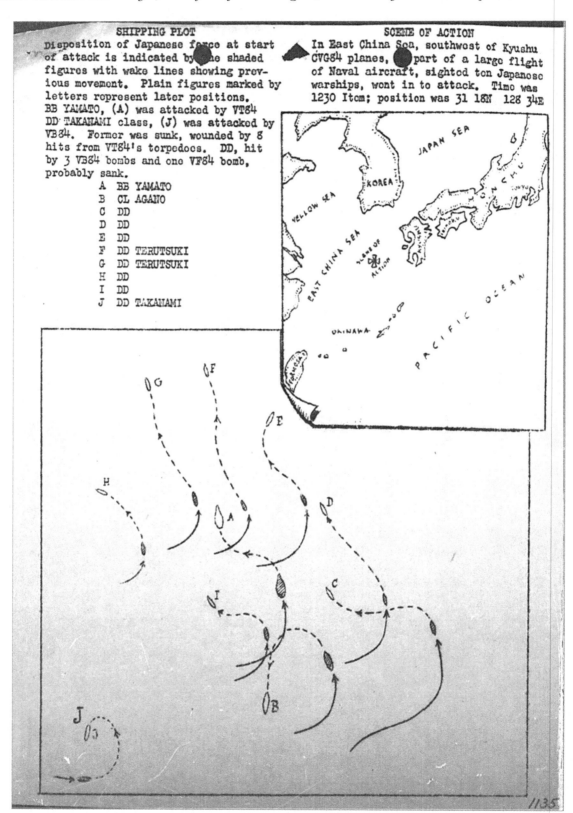

SHIPPING PLOT

Disposition of Japanese force at start of attack is indicated by the shaded figures with wake lines showing previous movement. Plain figures marked by letters represent later positions. BB YAMATO, (A) was attacked by VT84 DD TAKANAMI class, (J) was attacked by VB84. Former was sunk, wounded by 8 hits from VT84's torpedoes. DD, hit by 3 VB84 bombs and one VF84 bomb, probably sank.

A BB YAMATO
B CL AGANO
C DD
D DD
E DD
F DD TERUTSUKI
G DD TERUTSUKI
H DD
I DD
J DD TAKANAMI

SCENE OF ACTION

In East China Sea, southwest of Kyushu CVG84 planes, part of a large flight of Naval aircraft, sighted ten Japanese warships, went in to attack. Time was 1230 Item; position was 31 18N 128 34E

1135

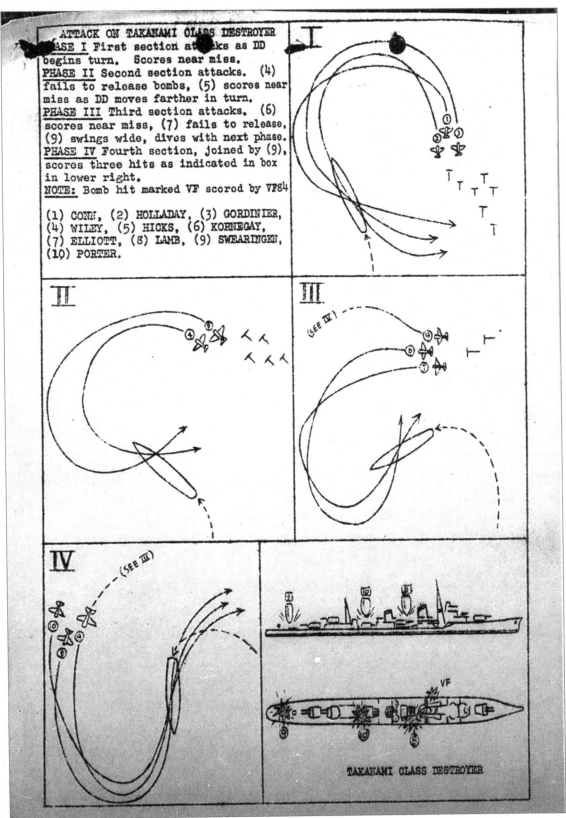

ATTACK ON TAKANAMI CLASS DESTROYER
PHASE I First section attacks as DD begins turn. Scores near miss.
PHASE II Second section attacks. (4) fails to release bombs, (5) scores near miss as DD moves farther in turn.
PHASE III Third section attacks. (6) scores near miss, (7) fails to release, (9) swings wide, dives with next phase.
PHASE IV Fourth section, joined by (9), scores three hits as indicated in box in lower right.
NOTE: Bomb hit marked VF scored by VF84

(1) CONN, (2) HOLLADAY, (3) GORDINIER,
(4) WILEY, (5) HICKS, (6) KORNEGAY,
(7) ELLIOTT, (8) LAMB, (9) SWEARINGEN,
(10) PORTER.

TAKANAMI CLASS DESTROYER

Wilson and his pilot W.R. Lamb are designated as plane (8) on these diagrams.

Diagram I: Planes left to right are 2, 1, 3.

Diagram II: Planes left to right are 4, 5.

Diagram III: Planes top to bottom are 9, 6, 7.

Diagran IV: Planes left to right are 10, 8, 9.

Diagram of bomb hits are left to right 9, 10, 8, VF.

you read in the pape...
than what I could...

Some of the big...
were the Tokyo raid...
again a week later...
Jima campaign, aid...
the Island again + ag...
our actions. What r...
flying as far as 60 m...
fully know how much...
these things probabl...
way, so I'll wait...
anything you want...
know that your littl...
right in the middle...
Keep up your prayer...
cause I know you...
Wishing you...
and Well! just the...
I received...
also your cards and...
a pleasant feeling...
and knowing som...
Please, don't...
thing cause I can g...

W.C. Lineaweaver ACRM
VB-84 % F.P.O.
San Francisco, Cali...

W.C. Lineaweaver ACRM
VB-84 % F.P.O.
San Francisco, Calif.

14th April, 1945

Dear Mother:

I had been some time since I heard from you but the other day I had another "V" letter. Glad to hear the news from home. Thanks Mom.

I'm getting along as well as can be expected, feel O.K. and in pretty good health. We are having a rough time of it out here and its beginning to get me down especially my nerves which are always on edge. About the only thing that I think about is getting back to the states and what I'll do. O happy day when I see that "Frisco" bridge again.

You should be having nice weather by this time, mother. Spring to my way of thinking is about the best season of the year. Maybe thats because its been five years since my last spring. Thats hard to believe but its true. I seen my first snow in years and that I didn't particularly care to see under the circumstances cause it was over Tokyo.

The navy has lifted the censorship regulation on past actions somewhat so I'm able to tell you some of the things I've been doing out here. Although the navy communique's do a good job in giving out the dope and what

---

Envelope:

W.C. Lineaweaver ACRM USN
VB-84
% FPO
San Francisco, Calif.

Actions he was in!

Mr & Mrs Robert Lineaweaver
1240 E. Cumberland St.
Avon, Penna.

[Postmark is U.S. Navy, 1945, 12:30 PM, with a "Passed by Naval Censor" stamp]
Mr & Mrs Robert Lineaweaver
1240 E. Cumberland St.
Avon, Penna.

[Return Address:]
W.C. Lineaweaver ACRM USN
VB-84
c/o FPO
San Francisco, Calif.

W.C. Lineaweaver ACRM
VB-84 c/o F.P.O.
San Francisco, Calif.
14th April, 1945

Dear Mother:

It had been some time since I heard from you but the other day I had another "V" letter. Glad to hear the news from home. Thanks Mom.

I'm getting along as well as can be expected, feel O.K. and in pretty good health. We are having a rough time of it out here and its beginning to get me down especially my nerves which are always on edge. About the only thing that I think about is getting back to the states and what I'll do. O' happy day when I see that "Frisco" bridge again.

You should be having nice weather by this time, mother. Spring to my way of thinking is about the best season of the year. Maybe thats because its been five years since my last spring. Thats hard to believe but its true. I seen my first snow in years and that I didn't particularly care to see under the circumstances cause it was over Tokyo.

The navy has lifted the censorship regulation on past actions somewhat so I'm able to tell you some of the things I've been doing out here. Although the Navy communique's do a good job in giving out the dope and what you read in the papers will give you a better account than what I could.

Some of the big actions that I participated in were the Tokyo raids of Feb 16th & 17th and then again a week later. Also participated in the Iwo Jima campaign, aiding our marines by dive bombing the Island again & again. Okinawa was another of our actions. What really scared me mostly was flying as far as 60 miles inland over Japan. I don't fully know how much or what I can talk about and these things probably don't interest you too much anyway, so I'll wait until I get home and tell you anything you want to know. Just want you to know that your little sailor for the third time is right in the middle of it and the going is tough. Keep up your prayers mother. Need I say this cause I know you do.

Wishing you the best of health & happiness and Well! just the best of everything.

I recieved your letter as of March 14th also your cards and one from Nat & Harold. It's a pleasant feeling being about 7000 miles away and knowing someone thinks of you.

Please don't go to any trouble sending anything cause I can get just about everything.

Your loving son
Wilson

W.C. Lineaweaver ACRM USN
VB-84 c/o F.P.O.
San Francisco, Calif.

The following are copies of pages from the Bunker Hill's deck log housed at the National Archives. A Navy ship's deck log consists of chronological entries documenting its daily activities, including a ship's location and daily movements.

DECK LOG—TITLE PAGE
NAVPERS 137 (REV. 1-44)

JUN 5 1945

CONFIDENTIAL

LOG BOOK

OF THE

U. S. S. _____ BUNKER HILL _____

_____ CV-17 _____
IDENTIFICATION NUMBER

COMMANDED BY

_____ G. A. SEITZ, Captain _____ , U. S. N.

Attached to {
_____ 58.3 _____ Division,

_____ Squadron,

_____ Flotilla,

_____ Fifth _____ Fleet,
}

Commencing _____ 1 April _____ , 19⁴⁵ ,

at _____ Sea _____ ,

and ending _____ 30 April _____ , 19⁴⁵ ,

at _____ Sea _____

_____

TO BE FORWARDED DIRECT TO THE BUREAU OF NAVAL PERSONNEL AT THE END OF EACH MONTH

PAGE ____

NAVPERS, 13 (FORMERLY CHRMOG)   DECK LOG—ADDITIONAL REMARKS SHEET

UNITED STATES SHIP _____ BUNKER HILL   CV17   Sunday   1   April 19 45

(Day) (Date) (Month)

ADDITIONAL REMARKS

0000-0400 Steaming as a station unit of Task Group 58.3 on base course 330° T, speed 18 knots, 132 r.p.m., zigzagging in accordance with plan #6. The formation is in cruising disposition 5-ROGER, axis 080° T, with the guide in the U.S.S. ESSEX bearing 170° T, distance 4,760 yards from this ship. All boilers are on the line. The watch is in condition III, and material condition of readiness modified "ABLE" is set. 0001 Ceased zigzagging. Changed course to 180° T. 0020 Commenced zigzagging in accordance with plan #6. 0040 Ceased zigzagging. Changed course to 090° T. 0042 Changed course to 100° T. 0047 Changed speed to 24 knots. Commenced landing aircraft. 0052 Changed course to 105° T. Completed landing 2 VF(N) from target combat air patrol. 0054 Changed speed to 18 knots. Changed course to 000° T. 0112 Changed course to 105° T. 0121 Changed course to 270° T. 0135 Commenced zigzagging in accordance with plan #6. 0249 Ceased zigzagging. Changed course to 090° T. 0252 Changed speed to 24 knots. 0253 Changed course to 085° T. 0259 Changed speed to 22 knots. 0302 Changed course to 090° T. 0306 Changed speed to 18 knots. 0310 Commenced catapulting aircraft. 0311 Completed catapulting 2 VF(N) for target patrol. 0312 Changed course to 235° T. 0331 Commenced zigzagging in accordance with plan #6.

R. C. Santee
R. C. SANTEE,
Lt. (D), USNR.

Plane crashes →

0400-0800 Steaming as before. 0515 Manned all General Quarters Stations and set condition "ABLE". 0516 Ceased zigzagging and resumed base course 235° T. 0516 Rotated formation axis left to 090° T. 0531 Changed speed to 25 knots. 0540 Changed course to 085° T. 0543 Commenced catapulting aircraft. 0545 Changed course to 080° T. 0547 Changed course to 075° T. 0550 Completed catapulting 7 VF for "H-55" hour strike. 0553 Commenced launching aircraft. 0555 Changed speed to 26 knots. 0558 Changed course to 080° T. 0600 Changed speed to 25 knots. 0603 Changed speed to 23 knots. 0606 Changed speed to 25 knots. 0608 An F4U, piloted by First Lt. R. K. MARBLE, USMCR, crashed in the water on the take-off due to inability to gain altitude. Pilot was not recovered. 0609 An F4U, piloted by First Lieut. J. E. MERCER, USMCR, crashed in the water on the take-off due to either a spin or temporary loss of control. Pilot was not recovered. 0615 Secured from General Quarters, set condition III and material condition of readiness modified "ABLE". Gunnery Department set condition "ONE-EASY". 0633 Completed launching 9 VT and 9 VB for "H-55" hour strike, 26 VF for "H-45" hour strike, and 2 VF, Air Coordinator, and 3 VF(P) and 1 VF for photo mission. 0634 Changed course to 270° T. 0635 Changed speed to 23 knots. 0642 Changed course to 080° T. 0647 Changed course to 270° T. 0714 Changed course to 065° T. 0718 Changed course to 060° T. 0720 Commenced recovering aircraft. 0730 Completed recovering 1 VF(N) and 1 VF, emergency landing from "H-55" hour strike. 0732 Changed speed to 18 knots. 0740 Changed course to 230° T. 0740 Secured from condition "ONE-EASY" and set condition III in the Gunnery Department. Mustered crew on stations. No absentees. 0752 Changed course to 060° T. 0756 Recovered one VF(N) from patrol. 0758 Changed course to 220° T.

J. J. HASBURGH, JR.,
Lt. (D), USNR.

0800-1200 Steaming as before. 0807 Rotated formation axis left to 060° T. 0822 Received accident report on MICHAELSEN, L. G., Slc, 733,45,00, USNR. Diagnosis: Burns left leg, upper left cheek, left lower eyelid and nose. While fuzing a napalm bomb on the flight deck, fuze pin dropped out. The man recovered the fuze and attempted to throw it over the side. Fuze exploded causing injury. Treatment: Burns cleaned and treated. Patient returned to duty. 0841 Changed course to 055° T. 0845 Changed speed to 21 knots. 0846 Commenced recovering aircraft. 0910 Changed speed to 19 knots. 0911 Completed landing 1 VF and 1 VF(P) from photo mission, 11 VF, 9 VB and 9 VT from "H-55" hour strike and 3 VF from "H-45" hour strike. 0918 Commenced landing aircraft. 0951 Completed landing 21 VF from "H-45" hour strike; 2 VF, Air Coordinator; 2 VF(P) from special photo mission and 1 VF from U.S.S. YORKTOWN. 0953 Changed course to 210° T. 1000 Made daily inspection of magazines and smokeless powder samples. Conditions normal. 1005 Changed speed to 21 knots. 1024 U.S.S. ENGLISH came alongside for transfer of mail and personnel. 1029 U.S.S. ENGLISH cast off, having transferred aboard the following men: Lt. B. E. BARRY, (A1), USNR, JOHNSON, C. P., ARM1c, USNR, and MEPLAR, C. E., AOM1c, USNR, of VT-84. 1042 Changed course to 230° T. 1052 Changed course to 050° T. 1110 Changed speed to 18 knots. 1121 Changed course to 210° T. Changed speed to 21 knots. 1143 Changed course to 045° T. 1145 Commenced launching aircraft. 1147 Changed course to 050° T. 1150 Changed course to 055° T. 1151 Completed launching 12 VF for combat air patrol and 1 VF to U.S.S. YORKTOWN. 1153 Changed speed to 18 knots. 1156 Changed course to 210° T.

J. T. HAYES,
Lt. (jg), (D), USNR.

APPROVED: EXAMINED:

G. A. SEITZ, Captain, U.S.N. COMMANDING.   C. E. ODEND'HAL, JR., Comdr., U.S.N. NAVIGATOR

TO BE FORWARDED DIRECT TO THE BUREAU OF NAVAL PERSONNEL AT THE END OF EACH MONTH

CONFIDENTIAL

NAVPERS 135 (REV.1-44)

DECK LOG—ADDITIONAL REMARKS SHEET

PAGE

UNITED STATES SHIP ___BUNKER HILL   CV-17___   Wednesday   11   April , 19 45
                                                      (Day)   (Date)   (Month)

ADDITIONAL REMARKS

1200-1600 Continued:
1406 Commenced firing all guns. 1408 Changed course to 085° T. 1409 Ceased firing. 1410 Changed course to 355° T. 1411 Changed speed to 25 knots. 1411 Commenced firing to port. 1412 Ceased firing. The following men were injured during the enemy air attack and were treated at their battle stations: LENEHAN, D. J., TMV2c, 708-82-36, USNR, was struck by shrapnel in the right hand. Prognosis: Good. He was returned to duty. PARADIS, F. J., Slc, 202-81-54, USNR, was struck by shrapnel in the right ear. Prognosis: Good. Returned to duty. GRIX, R. J., Slc, 894-93-41, USNR, received contusion of the right leg. Prognosis: Good. GRIX returned to duty. VINDIGNI, S. J., Slc, 710-35-10, USNR, crushed his left hand. Prognosis: Good. He returned to duty. SCHEMMEL, H. S., Slc, 868-17-25, USNR, received contusion of the left toe. Prognosis: Good. SCHEMMEL returned to duty. VALLEY, L. C., Slc, 761-72-58, USNR, received contusion of the back. Prognosis: Good. He returned to duty. BOYD, J. T., Slc, 783-81-06, USNR, received shrapnel in the right hand. Prognosis: Good. BOYD returned to duty. BLACK, J. E., S2c, 557-47-16, USNR, received laceration of the left third finger. Prognosis: Good. BLACK returned to duty. NEWCOMB, R. W., 802-10-40, Y3c, USNR, received laceration of the right index finger and little finger left hand. Prognosis: Good. NEWCOMB returned to duty. SIEGFRIED, W. V., Slc, 909-79-87, USNR, received laceration of the face. Prognosis: Good. He was admitted to the sick list. KOIS, J. S., Slc, 822-58-31, USNR, received shrapnel in the forehead. Prognosis: Critical. KOIS was admitted to the sick list. 1412 Changed course to 265° T. 1413 Changed course to 175° T. 1418 Changed course to 085° T. 1420 Changed course to 030° T. 1422 Changed course to 330° T. 1428 Changed course to 060° T. 1432 Changed course to 350° T. 1450 Commenced launching aircraft. 1455 Completed launching 12 VF for target combat air patrol and 1 VF for U.S.S. YORKTOWN. 1456 Changed course to 090° T. 1457 Changed speed to 25 knots. 1458 Changed course to 180° T. 1500 Commenced firing. A small fire was observed on the U.S.S. ENTERPRISE and was later identified as a plane on starboard catapult on fire due to strafing. It was catapulted, putting the fire out. 1501 Ceased firing. Changed course to 000° T. 1503 Changed course to 090° T. 1504 Commenced firing. 1505 Changed course to 180° T. 1506 Plane shot down on the port bow. 1508 Changed course to 270° T. 1509 Ceased firing. 1511 Changed course to 000° T. 1512 Changed course to 090° T. 1512 Commenced firing. 1512½ Ceased firing. 1515 Changed course to 180° T. 1521 Changed course to 270° T. 1525 Changed course to 180° T. 1526 Changed course to 270° T. 1529 Changed course to 180° T. 1535 U.S.S. KIDD rejoined the formation. She had been hit by an enemy aircraft early in the afternoon. Changed speed to 20 knots. 1551 Changed course to 355° T. 1558 Changed course to 345° T.

R. K. HALL,
Lt. (jg), (D), USNR.

1600-2000 Steaming as before. 1606 Commenced landing aircraft. 1610 Changed course to 355° T. 1616 Changed course to 025° T. 1616 C.I.C. reported bogie bearing 140° T, distance 12 miles. 1617 Changed course to 000° T. Ceased landing aircraft due to emergency maneuvering. 1618 Changed course to 330° T. 1619 Changed course to 300° T. 1620 Changed course to 030° T. 1621 Changed speed to 25 knots. 1622 Changed course to 120° T. 1622 C.I.C. reported bogie bearing 160° T, distance 10 miles. 1625 Changed course to 000° T. 1628 Changed speed to 20 knots. 1630 Commenced landing aircraft. 1634 Ceased landing aircraft due to emergency maneuvering. 1634 Changed course to 060° T. 1636 Changed course to 000° T. 1645 Commenced landing aircraft. 1646 Changed course to 060° T. Ceased landing aircraft due to emergency maneuvering. 1649 Changed course to 000° T. 1655 Resumed landing aircraft. 1705 Completed landing 14 VF from combat air patrol, 12 VF from target combat air patrol and 3 VF(P) from special photo mission. One VF, piloted by Ensign R. E. McCARTHY, (A1), 368968, USNR, from the target combat air patrol, was hit by anti-aircraft fire and made an emergency landing on the U.S.S. BATAAN. Later the VF was jettisoned. 1707 Changed course to 300° T. 1708 Changed course to 240° T. Commenced firing at an enemy plane. 1709 Changed course to 000° T. 1711 Changed course to 355° T. Ceased firing. Splashed one "JUDY". 1735 Changed course to 180° T. Changed speed to 27 knots. 1755 Secured from General Quarters, set condition III and material condition of readiness modified "ABLE". 1821 Changed course to 355° T. Changed speed to 18 knots. 1824 Commenced landing aircraft. 1825 Changed speed to 20 knots. 1838 Completed landing 19 VF from target combat air patrol and 2 VF from combat air patrol. 1845 Manned all General Quarters Stations and set condition "ABLE". 1846 Destroyer Division 96 rejoined the formation. 1903 Changed course to 270° T. 1907 Changed course to 355° T. Changed speed to 18 knots. 1912 Changed course to 325° T. 1913 Changed course to 265° T. Changed speed to 25 knots. 1914 Changed course to 175° T. 1921 Changed course to 215° T. 1925 Changed course to 245° T. 1929 Changed course to 195° T. 1938 Two flares were dropped off the port beam beyond the screen. 1946 Changed speed to 25 knots. 1949 Changed course to 155° T. 1949 Commenced firing on an enemy plane. 1950 Ceased firing. 1959 Changed course to 215° T.

J. J. HASBURGH, JR.,
Lt. (D), USNR.

APPROVED:

G. A. SEITZ, Captain,   U.S.N   COMMANDING.

EXAMINED:

C. J. ODEND'HAL, JR., Comdr., U.S.N.   NAVIGATOR

TO BE FORWARDED DIRECT TO THE BUREAU OF NAVAL PERSONNEL AT THE END OF EACH MONTH

Injuries from enemy air attack →

DECK LOG — ADDITIONAL REMARKS SHEET

PAGE _____

UNITED STATES SHIP BUNKER HILL CV17 — Monday 16 April 19 45
(Day) (Date) (Month)

ADDITIONAL REMARKS

1200-1600 Steaming as before. 1200 Commenced launching aircraft. 1202 Manned all Torpedo Defense Stations. Bogie reported bearing 095° T, distance 12 miles. 1204 Completed launching 8 VF for combat air patrol. 1209 Commenced landing aircraft. 1214 Completed landing 7 VF from combat air patrol. Major H. H. LONG, USMC, of VMF-451, pilot of an F4U on combat air patrol, bailed out, landed in the water and later was picked up by a destroyer. 1221 Commenced landing aircraft. 1235 Manned all General Quarters Stations. 1238 Secured from General Quarters, set condition III and material condition of readiness modified "ABLE". The Gunnery Department remained at Torpedo Defense. Completed landing 8 VF from combat air patrol and 20 VF from sweep #1. A VF, piloted by Lt. (jg) J. C. DIXON, (A1), 282937, USNR, on sweep #1 of VF-84 was seen to bail out over Kushira and landed in enemy territory. A VF, piloted by Lt. E. J. LITTLEJOHN, (A1), 129981, USNR, on sweep #1 of VF-84 was not seen after the attack on Kushira. No details available at this time. 1248 Changed course to 210° T. 1300 Changed course to 020° T. 1305 Changed course to 015° T. 1306 Commenced landing aircraft. 1310 Completed landing 8 VF from combat air patrol. 1314 Changed course to 190° T. 1329 Manned all General Quarters Stations and set condition "ABLE". 1329 Maneuvered on various emergency courses while repelling enemy air attack. 1357 Commenced catapulting aircraft. 1359 Completed catapulting 2 VF for Amami combat air patrol. 1400 Published the findings and sentences in the cases of the following men tried by a summary court martial: DAVIS, D. W., SF3c, 642-37-82, USNR, offense: Sleeping on watch. Tried: 19 January 1945. Findings: Specification proved by plea. Sentence: Reduction to the next inferior rating and to perform extra police duties for a period of sixty days. Approved by the Convening Authority on 13 March 1945, but the reduction to the next inferior rating is remitted on condition that he maintains a satisfactory record for six months. Approved by the Immediate Senior in Command on 1 April 1945. BERES, W. N., S1c, 708-46-92, USNR, offense: Absent over leave. Tried: 4 February 1945. Findings: Specification proved by plea. Sentence: To perform extra police duties for a period of two months, and to lose thirty-three dollars per month of his pay for a period of four months, total loss of pay amounting to one hundred thirty-two dollars. Approved by the Convening Authority on 11 March 1945 and by the Immediate Senior in Command on 31 March 1945. WOOLERY, R. A., Pfc., 870506, USMCR, offense: Violation of the censorship regulations. Tried: 27 January 1945. Findings: Specification proved by plea. Sentence: To lose twenty dollars per month of his pay for a period of two months, total loss of pay amounting to forty dollars. Approved by the Convening Authority on 11 March 1945 and by the Immediate Senior in Command on 31 March 1945. MEANEY, T. P., S1c, 762-04-61, USNR, offense: Absent without leave, breaking his arrest and having in his possession an identification card not issued by proper authority. Tried: 1 February 1945. Findings: Specification proved by plea. Sentence: To be confined for a period of twenty days, and to lose twelve dollars per month of his pay for a period of six months, total loss of pay amounting to seventy-two dollars. Approved by the Convening Authority on 11 March 1945 and by the Immediate Senior in Command on 31 March 1945. 1402 Commenced launching aircraft. 1406 Completed launching 10 VF for Amami combat air patrol. 1455 Commenced launching aircraft. 1500 Completed launching 12 VF for combat air patrol. 1502 Secured from General Quarters, set condition III and material condition of readiness modified "ABLE". The Gunnery Department remained at Torpedo Defense. 1510 Commenced landing aircraft, on course 005° T, speed 25 knots. 1520 Completed landing 4 VF from combat air patrol. 1525 Changed course to 180° T. 1544 Changed course to 005° T. 1551 Changed course to 010° T. 1551 Commenced recovering aircraft. 1553 Completed recovering 4 VF from combat air patrol. 1554 Changed course to 040° T.

J. T. HAYES,
Lt. (jg) (D), USNR.

1600-1800 Steaming as before. 1601 Changed course to 045° T. 1603 Manned all General Quarters Stations and set condition "ABLE". 1611 Secured from General Quarters, set condition III and material condition of readiness modified "ABLE". Gunnery Department remained at Torpedo Defense. 1623 Changed speed to 18 knots. 1632 Secured from Torpedo Defense and set condition "ONE-EASY" in the Gunnery Department. 1637 Changed course to 090° T. 1647 Commenced zigzagging in accordance with plan #6. 1703 Ceased zigzagging. Changed course to 270° T. 1727 Changed course to 045° T. 1738 Changed course to 180° T.

K. K. HALL,
Lt. (jg), (D), USNR.

APPROVED: G. A. SEITZ, Captain, U.S.N. COMMANDING.
EXAMINED: C. J. ODEND'HAL, JR., Comdr., U.S.N. NAVIGATOR

TO BE FORWARDED DIRECT TO THE BUREAU OF NAVAL PERSONNEL AT THE END OF EACH MONTH

CONFIDENTIAL

NAVPERS (X) (REV C-44) 3142

DECK LOG—ADDITIONAL REMARKS SHEET

PAGE

UNITED STATES SHIP _____ BUNKER HILL — CV-17 ————— Thursday 26 April, 19 45

(Day) (Date) (Month)

ADDITIONAL REMARKS

1200-1600 Steaming as before. 1203 Changed course to 005° T. 1208 Changed course to 165° T. 1233 Changed course to 000° T. Changed speed to 23 knots. 1239 Maneuvered independently while rotating formation axis right to 165° T. 1256 On station with guide in the U.S.S. ESSEX bearing 255° T, distance 4,000 yards from this ship. 1258 Changed course to 165° T. C Changed speed to 25 knots. 1303 Changed course to 185° T. 1314 Changed course to 000° T. 1322 Changed course to 185° T. 1328 Commenced launching aircraft. 1330 Changed course to 180° T. 1336 Completed launching 16 VF for target combat air patrol. 1337 Changed course to 190° T. 1341 Commenced landing aircraft. 1345 U.S.S. WILKES-BARRE, LIND and WEEKS left the formation on rescue mission for downed plane. 1353 Changed course to 200° T. 1354 Changed course to 210° T. 1355 Changed course to 220° T. 1356 Changed course to 230° T. 1358 Changed course to 250° T. 1359 Changed course to 270° T. 1401 Changed course to 280° T. 1403 Changed course to 290° T. 1404 Completed landing 4 VF, 10 VT and 11 VB from support mission. 1407 Changed course to 320° T. Changed speed to 23 knots. 1409 Maneuvered independently while rotating formation axis right to 225° T. 1419 Maneuvered independently while rotating formation axis right to 285° T. 1426 Changed course to 290° T. Changed speed to 20 knots. 1434 Commenced launching aircraft. 1436 Changed speed to 23 knots. 1438 Completed launching 12 VF for combat air patrol. 1445 Commenced landing aircraft. 1449 Changed course to 295° T. 1450 Changed course to 300° T. 1453 On station with guide in the U.S.S. ESSEX bearing 015° T, distance 4,000 yards from this ship. 1454 Changed speed to 20 knots. 1455 Completed landing 11 VF from combat air patrol. 1510 Published the findings and sentences in the following cases tried by deck courts: DeRUSHA, W. E., S1c, 726-52-59, USNR, offense: Absent from flight quarters. Tried on 18 April 1945. Findings: Specification proved by plea. Sentence: To solitary confinement on bread and water for a period of five days with full ration every third day, and to lose twenty dollars per month of his pay for a period of one month, total loss of pay amounting to twenty dollars. Approved by the Convening Authority on 19 April 1945. GREENFIELD, H., S1c, 653-49-94, USNR, offense: Disobedience of orders. Tried on 18 April 1945. Findings: Specification proved by plea. Sentence: To solitary confinement on bread and water for a period of five days with full ration every third day, and to lose eleven dollars per month of his pay for a period of two months, total loss of pay amounting to twenty-two dollars. Approved by the Convening Authority on 22 April 1945. VALLEY, L. C., S2c, 761-72-58, USNR, offense: Disobedience of orders. Tried on 23 April 1945. Findings: Specification proved by plea. Sentence: To solitary confinement on bread and water for a period of ten days with full ration every third day. Approved by the Convening Authority on 24 April 1945. 1517 Changed course to 060° T. Changed speed to 20 knots. 1518 U.S.S. WILKES-BARRE, LIND and WEEKS rejoined the formation. 1520 Maneuvered independently while rotating formation axis right to 300° T. 1538 Changed course to 080° T. 1540 On station with guide in the U.S.S. ESSEX bearing 030° T, distance 4,000 yards from this ship.

W. A. Pitcher
W. A. PITCHER,
Lt. (jg), (D), USNR.

1600-1800 Steaming as before. 1600 By order of the Commanding Officer, MOLAND, A., STM1c, 839-09-87, USNR, was placed in confinement on bread and water for a period of three days in execution of a sentence at Captain's Mast. 1620 Changed course to 290° T. 1621 Commenced landing aircraft. By order of the Commanding Officer, BROWN, W., STM1c, 846-69-27, USNR, was placed in solitary confinement on bread and water for a period of five days with full ration on third day in execution of sentence given at Captain's Mast. HAYNES, J. W., STM1c, 575-29-78, USNR, was placed in solitary confinement for a period of five days on bread and water with full ration on fifth day, in execution of sentence given at Captain's Mast. 1623 Changed course to 305° T. Changed speed to 23 knots. 1628 Changed speed to 21 knots. 1632 Changed course to 315° T. 1635 Completed landing 16 VF from target combat air patrol and 1 VT from support mission. 1639 Changed course to 325° T. 1646 Rotated formation axis right to 335° T. 1655 Changed course to 090° T. 1657 Changed speed to 18 knots. 1701 Commenced zigzagging in accordance with plan #6. 1752 Ceased zigzagging and remained on course 110° T.

A. L. Julian
A. L. JULIAN,
Lt. U. S. Navy.

1800-2000 Steaming as before. 1803 Changed course to 040° T. 1807 Maneuvered independently while rotating formation axis right to 035° T. 1812 Changed speed to 22 knots. 1817 U.S.S. BLACK, BULLARD, MARSHALL and LEWIS HANCOCK rejoined the formation screen. 1812 Changed course to 035° T. 1829 Commenced landing aircraft. 1833 On station with guide in the U.S.S. ESSEX bearing 125° T, distance 4,000 yards from this ship. 1835 Completed landing 12 VF from combat air patrol. 1838 Changed course to 150° T. Changed speed to 21 knots. 1851 Commenced zigzagging in accordance with plan #6. 1905 By order of the Commanding Officer, MOLAND, A., STM1c, 839-09-87, USNR, was released from confinement having served three hours and five minutes of his three days solitary confinement.

APPROVED:

G. A. SEITZ, Captain, U.S.N COMMANDING.

EXAMINED:

C. C. ODEND'HAL, JR., Comdr., U.S.N. NAVIGATOR

TO BE FORWARDED DIRECT TO THE BUREAU OF NAVAL PERSONNEL AT THE END OF EACH MONTH

Deck court sentences → (margin note)

Captain's Mast sentences → (margin note)

(see 1905 below) (margin note)

W.C. Lineaweaver ACRM
VB-84 c/o F.P.O.
San Francisco, Calif.
18th April, 1945
At sea

Dear Mother:

Enclosed is a Government check for $200.00 dollars which I'd like you to deposit on to my savings account. Please let me know immediately upon recieving this.

Still getting along O.K. mother but sure wish I was home. Haven't had any recent letters from you so I'm looking forward to one any day now.

Glad to hear that there going to keep Jim out of combat. Sure hope his leg comes around alright and they send him home. From the reports I hear out here, the Germans seem to be on their last leg.

Wishing all of you the best of everything I'll close remaining

Your loving son
Wilson

[Postmark is U.S. Navy, April 18, 1945, 12:30 PM, with a "Passed by Naval Censor" stamp]
Mr & Mrs. Robert Lineaweaver
1240 E. Cumberland St.
Avon, Penna.

[Return Address:]
W.C. Lineaweaver ACRM
VB-84
c/o FPO
San Francisco, Calif.

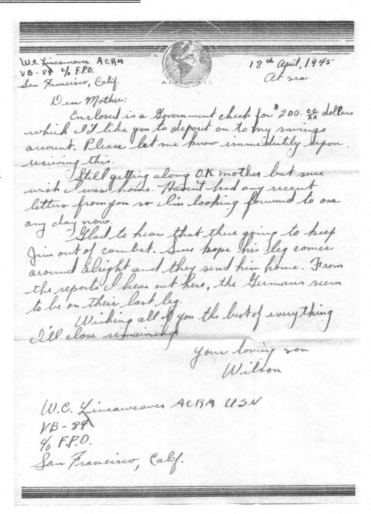

W.C. Lineaweaver ACRM USN
VB-84
c/o F.P.O.
San Francisco, Calif.

[This letter is reproduced here at its original size.]

This past week, and plenty of rain, a month
ago...

April 22, 1945
Avon, Pa

Dear Son Wilson

Sunday after noon just now
finished a letter to your girl, I had a letter
from her on the 9th and this Thursday a
Souvenir folder from her, In her letter she
says she arrived home in Bernard, Iowa.
We were all very glad to hear from you
Happy to hear that you are doing fine, I sure
wish for you all to be at home again soon.

I received a letter from Jim day
before your's and it only took nine days to
come here, Will sent you his new address
along. He said they had beautiful weather and
was assigned and is in the 27th Station compliment Squadron attached to the 96th Bomber
group and in the 8th air Force. also said he
was waiting to be put to work and said he
has good sleeping quarters and good eats
and the Base is spread over a wide area
and must ride the bus to go to eat, Betty
would like to have him at home and little
Jimmie sure is getting pretty Jim said
I was to sent you his love and Best regards.
and I will sent him your address again.

We were thinking of you on your
Birthday Did you receive many greetings
on time. We are having very cold weather

[Note: This is a letter written to Wilson from his mother. It was likely among his things which were returned to the family after his death, and is the only letter we have to Wilson from his mother. There is no envelope with the letter.]

April 22, 1945
Avon Pa

Dear Son Wilson

Sunday after noon just now finished a letter to your girl. I had a letter from her on the 9th and this Thursday a Souvenir folder from her. In her letter she says she arrived home in Bernard, Iowa. We were all very glad to hear from you Happy to hear that you are doing fine. I sure wish for you all to be at home again soon.

I received a letter from Jim day before your's and it only took nine days to come here, Will sent you his new address along. He said they had beautiful weather and was assigned and is in the 27th Station Compliment Squadron attached to the 96th Bomber group and in the 8th Air Force. also said he was waiting to be put to work and said he has good sleeping quarters and good eats and the Base is spread over a wide area and must ride the bus to go to eat, Betty would like to have him at home and little Jimmie sure is getting pretty. Jim said I was to sent you his love and Best regards. and I will sent him your address again.

We were thinking of you on your Birthday Did you receive many greetings on time. We are having very cold weather This past week, and plenty of rain. a month ago we had real summer weather like July days. That bus strike was the end of January and lasted three weeks. People either walked to work are stayed at home are had others take them to work Your dad went with some one in a car. Your dad is home since last Wednesday he strained his left side. He goes back to work Tuesday. His side is o.k. again.

Please Wilson I would like to sent you a box what would you like me to sent you I think the mail is slow for the past weeks. What was your feeling toward the Death of our President. Here for three days we all felt his passing. We hear Plenty on the radio and in newspaper I sure wish it was over and have an everlasting Peace for all time

Just now Harold is doing his school work and Lucille is looking at a fashion book. Dorothy and Nathan are up town to a show and your dad is lying on the Chesterfield taking it easy and howling at every move we make, I want to write to Jim yet this afternoon Tonight we go to church. You should see our three rooms how nice they look with the new furniture but I wish to get away from here. We are all well and doing fine hoping this letter finds you in the best of health and happiness. God Bless you and keep you safe always. I think of you boys often and hope to see you again in not to many months. I close for now Write soon again With all my love We remain

Mother & family

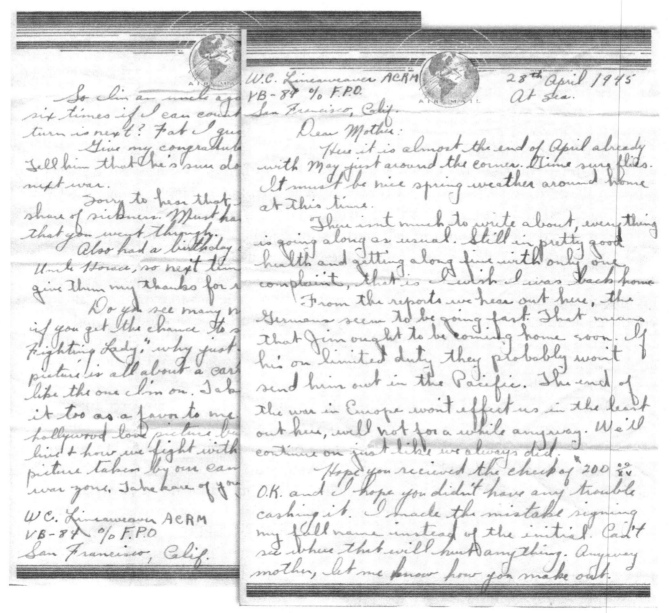

So I'm an uncle ag——
six times if I can count——
turn is next? Fat I gue——

Give my congratula——
Tell him that he's sure do——
next war.

Sorry to hear that,——
share of sickness. Must ha——
that you went through.

Also had a birthday a——
Uncle Horace, so next tim——
give them my thanks for w——

Do you see many m——
if you get the chance to s——
Fighting Lady," why just——
picture is all about a carr——
like the one I'm on. I ta——
it too as a favor to me——
hollywood love picture b——
line & how we fight with——
picture taken by our cam——
war zone. Take care of yo——

W.C. Lineaweaver ACRM
VB-84 % F.P.O.
San Francisco, Calif.

W.C. Lineaweaver ACRM   28th April 1945
VB-84 % F.P.O.   At Sea.
San Francisco, Calif.

Dear Mother:

Here it is almost the end of April already
with May just around the corner. Time sure flies.
It must be nice spring weather around home
at this time.

There isn't much to write about, everything
is going along as usual. Still in pretty good
health and getting along fine with only one
complaint, that is I wish I was back home.

From the reports we hear out here, the
Germans seem to be going fast. That means
that Jim ought to be coming home soon. If
his on limited duty they probably won't
send him out in the Pacific. The end of
the war in Europe won't effect us in the least
out here, well not for a while anyway. We'll
continue on just like we always did.

Hope you received the check of $200 00/xx
O.K. and I hope you didn't have any trouble
cashing it. I made the mistake signing
my full name instead of the initial. Can't
see where that will hurt anything. Anyway
mother, let me know how you make out.

W.C. Lineaweaver ACRM
VB-84
% FPO
San Francisco, Calif

Via Air Mail

Mr & Mrs Robert Lineaweaver
1240 C. Cumberland St.
Avon, Penna.

[Postmark is U.S. Navy, April 28, 1945, 12:30
PM, with a "Passed by Naval Censor" stamp]
Mr & Mrs Robert Lineaweaver
1240 E. Cumberland St.
Avon, Penna.

[Return Address:]
W.C. Lineaweaver ACRM
VB-84
c/o FPO
San Francisco, Calif

W.C. Lineaweaver ACRM
VB-84 c/o F.P.O.
San Francisco, Calif.
28th April 1945
At sea.

Dear Mother:

Here it is almost the end of April already with May just around the corner. Time sure flies. It must be nice spring weather around home at this time.

There isnt much to write about, everything is going along as usual. Still in pretty good health and getting along fine with only one complaint, that is I wish I was back home.

From the reports we hear out here, the Germans seem to be going fast. That means that Jim ought to be coming home soon. If he's on limited duty they probably won't send him out in the Pacific. The end of the war in Europe won't effect us in the least out here, well not for a while anyway. We'll continue on just like we always did.

Hope you recieved the check of $200.00 O.K. and I hope you didn't have any trouble cashing it. I made the mistake signing my full name instead of the initial. Can't see where that will hurt anything. Anyway mother, let me know how you make out.

So I'm an uncle again, that makes about six times if I can count correctly. Whose turn is next? Fat I guess.

Give my congradulations to Dave & Liz. Tell him that he's sure doing his part for the next war. *[Faye Elizabeth Lineaweaver, born March 24, 1945.]*

Sorry to hear that the kids had there share of sickness. Must have been the tough winter that you went through.

Also had a birthday card from Aunt Eva & Uncle Horace, so next time you pay them a visit give them my thanks for remembering.

Do you see many movies Mother? Well! if you get the chance to see the picture, "The Fighting Lady," why just for me, see it. The picture is all about a carrier in the Pacific like the one I'm on. Take pop along to see it too as a favor to me. Its not the usual hollywood love picture but all about how we live & how we fight with every picture a real picture taken by our cameras out here in the war zone. Take care of yourself.

Your loving son
Wilson

W.C. Lineaweaver ACRM
VB-84 c/o F.P.O.
San Francisco, Calif.

> ***The Fighting Lady*** *- This military documentary presents life aboard an American aircraft carrier (later revealed to be the USS Yorktown) operating in the Pacific theater during World War II. It depicts the daily routines on the massive ship and the intensity of aerial and naval conflict in battles with Japanese forces. It can be viewed at numerous places on the internet.*

there but you know wh[...]
yins.

Please don't attemp[...]
package mother cause [...]
get it. You know what [...]
other one. I realize th[...]
but honestly I can m[...]
the things that are ar[...]

You ought to see m[...]
Have been working on it [...]
months and it really loo[...]
shave it before coming h[...]

Take care of your[...]
too hard. Give my regard[...]
and write often.

Y[...]

W.C. Lineaweaver AC[...]
VB-84
% F.P.O.
San Francisco, Calif

W.C. Lineaweaver ACRM   1st May 1945
VB-84 % F.P.O.   At sea.
San Francisco, Calif.

Dear Mother:

Recieved your letter as of April 12th and
was very glad to hear from you. Sorry that
I haven't written more often. We are plenty
busy but thats no excuse, its just that I'm
not in a writing mood very often due to the type
of life we have to lead out here. Also the things
we do I don't care to write about and I'm sure
they wouldn't interest you anyway.

Sure was glad to hear that Jim is O.K.
and back to duty. Are they going to make
him a ground crew man in the Air Corps? I'd
write him but I don't know his address so
when he gets a permanent one, send it to me.
Jim should complain about my writing, the
total of his letters this year so far have
been just one letter and I've done better
than that.

How many letters has my girl friend
written you and what does she find to write
about? Let me know.

Hope you got the check O.K. What does
my bank roll come to at this time? Sure wish
I can keep it going higher and have it sta[...]

W.C. Lineaweaver ACRM
VB-84
% FPO
San Francisco, Calif.

29 March letter you in

Mr. & Mrs. Robert Lineaweaver
1240 E. Cumberland St.
Avon, Penna.

Via Air Mail

[Postmark is U.S. Navy, May 3, 1945, 12:30 PM, with a "Passed by Naval Censor" stamp]
Mr. & Mrs. Robert Lineaweaver
1240 E. Cumberland St.
Avon, Penna.

[Return Address:]
W.C. Lineaweaver ACRM
VB-84
c/o FPO
San Francisco, Calif.

W.C. Lineaweaver ACRM
VB-84 c/o F.P.O.
San Francisco, Calif.
1ˢᵗ May 1945
At sea.

Dear Mother:

Recieved your letter as of April 12ᵗʰ and was very glad to hear from you. Sorry that I havent written more often. We are plenty busy but thats no excuse, its just that I'm not in a writing mood very often due to the type of life we have to lead out here. Also the things we do I don't care to write about and I'm sure they wouldn't interest you anyway.

Sure was glad to hear that Jim is O.K. and back to duty. Are they going to make him a ground crew man in the Air Corps? I'd write him but I don't know his address so when he gets a permanent one, send it to me. Jim should complain about my writing, the total of his letters this year so far have been just one letter and I've done better than that.

How many letters has my girl friend written you and what does she find to write about? Let me know.

Hope you got the check O.K. What does my bank roll come to at this time? Sure wish I can keep it going higher and have it stay there but you know what happened in past years.

Please don't attempt to send me a package mother cause I'll probably never get it. You know what happened to the other one's. I realize the sweet intentions but honestly I can manage easily on the things that are available out here.

You ought to see my mustache, mother. Have been working on it the past couple months and it really looks slick. Guess I'll shave it before coming home though.

Take care of yourself and don't work too hard. Give my regards to all the rest and write often.

Your loving son
Wilson

W.C. Lineaweaver ACRM USN
VB-84
c/o F.P.O.
San Francisco, Calif.

To: Mrs Erline Lineaweaver
        1240 E. Cumberland St.
        Avon, Penna.

From: W.C. Lineaweaver ACRM
        VB-84
        c/o FPO
        San Francisco, Calif
        5th May, 1945

Pre-printed note reads:

MOTHER

TO MOTHER

This brings a wish on Mother's Day,
That's in my heart while I'm away,
That God is kind and keeps you well,
Until we hear the Victory Bell.

I love you, miss you, pray each day,
I'll soon be home with you to stay,
Until I do, I'll go my way,
Making each morn my Mother's Day.

Your Loving Son,
[signed] Wilson

[Postmark is U.S. Postal Service No. 1,
May 23, 1945, 8 PM; Note: This postmark
is 12 days after Wilson was killed.]

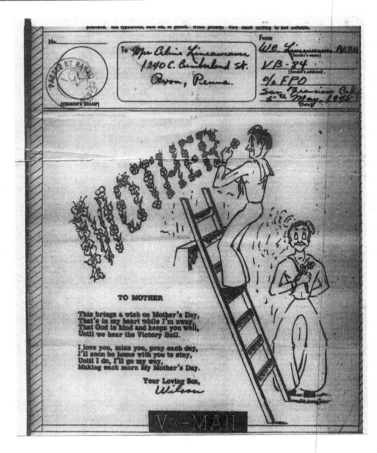

Hundreds of millions of letters were processed annually during World War II. Competing for limited overseas cargo space needed for food, fuel, ammunition, and other supplies, was this tremendous amount of mail. The importance of mail for the armed forces during World War II was second only to food. The 1942 Annual Report to the Postmaster General stated: "The Post Office, War, and Navy Departments realize fully that frequent and rapid communication with parents, associates, and other loved ones strengthens fortitude, enlivens patriotism, makes loneliness endurable, and inspires to even greater devotion the men and women who are carrying on our fight far from home and friends. We know that the good effect of expeditious mail service on those of us at home is immeasurable". In 1944, Navy personnel received over 272 million pieces of regular first class mail and 38 million pieces of

National Archives 111-SC-142-170365-B

V-mail. In 1945, over 838 million total pieces of mail items were received by the Navy.

To help alleviate the burden of transporting literally tons of mail, and inspired by the British Airgraph Service, Victory Mail, or V-Mail, was launched on June 15, 1942. A person who wanted to send a letter by V-Mail obtained a standard pre-printed form from the local post office or five and dime store. The form included space for the address of the military recipient, address of sender, circular area for censor's stamp of approval, and a message area, or could have a pre-printed message like the one Wilson used for Mother's Day 1945. When the form was completed it was folded, sealed, and made its way to a processing center. There it was opened, censored, and photographed on 16mm film. At its destination's processing center, the V-Mail was then printed from the film

National Archives 111-SC-818-384767

onto 4" x 5" black and white photographic paper and delivered to its recipient. V-Mail service was discontinued on November 1, 1945.

One roll of film 100 feet long could hold up to 1700 messages. Thirty-seven mail bags required to carry 150,000 one-page letters could be replaced by a single mail sack. The weight of that same amount of mail was reduced dramatically from 2,575 pounds to a mere 45. V-Mail ensured that thousands of tons of shipping space could be reserved for crucial war materials.

(V-Mail information was obtained from the Smithsonian's National Postal Museum website.)

[Note: There is no envelope with this letter as it was never mailed. After Wilson's mother received it with Wilson's personal effects, she shared the letter with Bette.]

11th May 1945
at sea

My Dear Bette:

Gosh honey! I have left quite a few days slip by with out writing in which I'm sincerely sorry. For punishment you have my permission to smack each cheek as often as you wish after I get back with the condition that you don't use your hands. How's that?

The mail situation out here is pretty lousy lately although I did get one of your letters this morning dated april 14th having the usual one month interval. It was the one containing pictures.

Thanks a million for these pictures which I'm very grateful for honey. Will try to get one for you including the mustache before I shave it off. One thing for certain sweetheart, I'm not coming home with it.

Like your pictures immensely but honest honey, you look so different from the gal I use to know. Hardly know you sweetheart. It's the hair what ever you done to it. Like it though and this is the first time I've seen

---

(partially visible overlapping page, left:)

you wearing a hat other then that little purple o... you used to wear when we went to church.
...brown...
Speak... there... to go to... days a... books... out thou... Catholi... carry... glad... help... heart... as far... helpful... so be... and now...

Weig... at 152... like my... is it st... stand a... myself... We get... world...

(partially visible overlapping page, far left:)

through out our ship announcing
the su...
day. N...
a little...
the N...
were r...
is sent...
was s...
sweethe...
as far...
also w...
is doin...
have I...

Aunt I...
amuse...
I'm co...
dishies...

ner...

11th May *[1945]*
at Sea

My Dear Bette:

Gosh honey! I have left quite a few days slip by with out writing in which I'm sincerely sorry. For punishment you have my permission to smack each cheek as often as you wish after I get back with the condition that you don't use your hands. Hows that?

The mail situation out here is pretty lousy lately although I did get one of your letters this morning dated April 14th having the usual one month interval. It was the one containing pictures.

Thanks a million for these pictures which I'm very grateful for honey. Will try to get one for you including the mustache before I shave it off. One thing for certain Sweetheart, I'm not coming home with it.

Like your pictures immensely but honest honey, you look so different from the gal I use to know, Hardly know you sweetheart. Its the hair what ever you done to it. Like it though and this is the first time I've seen you wearing a hat other then that little purple one you used to wear when we went to church. Seems like I also remember a little brown tan affair that you wore a few times

Speaking of church, I almost forgot that there are other day's besides Sunday I have to go to mass. Yesterday was one of those day's and I even had to look up in my books what holy day it was. Didn't miss out though. but honey I guess Im a poor Catholic when I continuously have to carry my book around. will sure be glad when you can look after me and help me along. But not to boast sweet heart I feel proud of my advancement as far as it goes and every body is so helpful. only hope that you too will also be proud of me. Love you honey, lots and more if thats possible.

Weighed myself today and I'm still at 152. That seems to be my average. I like my 105 lb gal with the 18 waist or is it still. Gosh I hope so Just couldn't stand anybody changing that other than myself.

We get very little news of the out side world but the other day word was passed through out our ship accounceing the surrender of Germany. Happy day. Now maybe things will become a little easier for us and the rest of the navy out this way. Only hope we're not forgotten and as much effort is sent our way as before plus what was sent over Europe way.

Still in pretty good health. sweetheart and I'm getting along swell as far as my duties are concerned. also were told that our war effort is doing some good too. Many medals have been won so far

Remember the dishwashing Aunt Het cartoon that you sent along. amuseing but not quite true as far as I'm concerned, no kisses, no washie dishies

By for now my love Please write

Yours always
Chuck   new suit.

[This three page letter was written and mailed by Wilson on the day he was killed. Reduced to 83% of original.]

W.C. Lineaweaver ACRM
VB-84 ℅ F.P.O.
San Francisco, Calif.

11th May 1945
Somewhere at sea.

Dear Mother:

It has been a considerable long time since I recieved your last letter but the old saying goes, "No news is good news." Only hope that you and all the rest are in good health and everything going along swell.

This is May now and I'll bet its nice around home, the leaves and everything out and the farmers having all their fields plowed. It sure gets tiresome looking at just plain water month in and month out and flying continuously. How I'd like to get back to good solid ground again!

Guess the kids are winding up another year of schooling and are beginning to look forward to summer vacation. Hows the little boy scouts making out? I was going to send them money for scout uniforms and could have easily spared it but after considering how easy it is for kids to pick up money here and there, it would do them good to

W.C. Lineaweaver ACRM   #2
VB-84

AIR MAIL

earn it. Also they'd be pestering me all the
time for other favors that they could very easily
do themselves.

We have lost contact pretty much with
the outside world but word was passed on
our ship about the unconditional surrender
of Germany. It sure sounded good and now
the chances of Jim getting back into combat
are just about nil the way I look at it. All
we have to do now is finish off these little
yellow monkeys and the boys will be coming
home to stay. All but me, as you know I'm
regular navy.

Was there any celebrating on what they
called V-E day? Will the people at home get all
the gas they want, tires etc. and how about
the ration system, will that stay as before until
Japan is defeated?

Did you get the "200⁰⁰/₀₀ check O.K. and what
does my bank roll consist of?

So you finally got a lot of new furniture,
guess I won't know the place next time I come
home. Sure was nice of Lucille to put a large

share of her spending money into it. Now if you could only get a decent place to live.

Still in good health and getting along swell and sincerely hope it is that way at home. Take care of yourself mother and don't work so hard, it isn't at all necessary. With only a few at home your work should be lightened a lot and you have Nate & Harold to do heavy work if the occasion arises.

Give my best regards to all the rest and please write. Hoping to hear from you soon I remain

Your loving son
Wilson

W.C. Lineaweaver ACRM USN
VB-84
% F.P.O.
San Francisco Calif.

[This is the envelope for the preceding three page letter. The letter's transcription follows on the next two pages.]

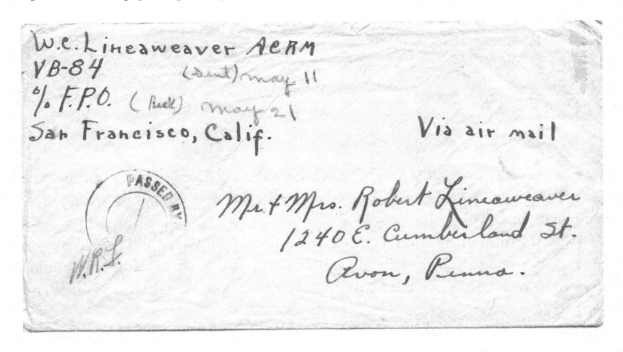

[Postmark is missing and perhaps was on a postage stamp that was removed; with a "Passed by Naval Censor" stamp]
[Handwritten later on envelope is: "(Sent) May 11 (Rec'd) May 21"]
Mr. & Mrs. Robert Lineaweaver
1240 E. Cumberland St.
Avon, Penna.

[Return Address:]
W.C. Lineaweaver ACRM
VB-84
c/o FPO
San Francisco, Calif.

[This is the transcription for the preceding three page letter.]

W.C. Lineaweaver ACRM
VB-84 c/o F.P.O.
San Francisco, Calif.
11ᵗʰ May 1945
Somewhere at sea.

Dear Mother:

It has been a considerable long time since I recieved your last letter but the old saying goes, "No news is good news". Only hope that you and all the rest are in good health and everything going along swell.

This is May now and I'll bet its nice around home, the leaves and everything out and the farmers having all their fields plowed. It sure gets tiresome looking at just plain water month in and month out and flying continuously. How I'd like to get back to good solid ground again!

Guess the kids are winding up another year of schooling and are beginning to look forward to summer vacation. Hows the little boy scouts making out? I was going to send them money for scout uniforms and could have easily spared it but after considering how easy it is for kids to pick up money here and there, it would do them good to earn it. Also they'd be pestering me all the time for other favors that they could very easily do themselves.

We have lost contact pretty much with the outside world but word was passed on our ship about the unconditional surrender of Germany. It sure sounded good and now the chances of Jim getting back into combat are just about nil the way I look at it. All we have to do now is finish off these little yellow monkeys and the boys will be coming home to stay. All but me, as you know I'm regular navy.

Was there any celebrating on what they called V-E day? Will the people at home get all the gas they want, tires etc. and how about the ration system, will that stay as before until Japan is defeated?

Did you get the $200.00 check O.K. and what does my bank roll consist of?

So you finally got a lot of new furniture, guess I won't know the place next time I come home. Sure was nice of Lucille to put a large share of her spending money into it. Now if you could only get a decent place to live.

Still in good health and getting along swell and sincerely hope it is that way at home. Take care of yourself mother and don't work so hard, it isn't at all necessary. With only a few at home your work should be lightened a lot and you have Nate & Harold to do heavy work if the occasion arises.

Give my best regards to all the rest and please write. Hoping to hear from you soon I remain

Your loving son
Wilson

W.C. Lineaweaver ACRM USN
VB-84
c/o F.P.O.
San Francisco, Calif.

USS *Bunker Hill* Deck Log record of Friday, May 11, 1945, from the hours of 0800 to 1200

0800-1012 Steaming as before. 0805 Set condition "ONE-EASY" in the Gunnery Department. 0838 Changed speed to 26 knots. 0841 Changed course to 190° T. 0846 Commenced launching aircraft. 0850 Changed course to 185° T. 0854 Changed course to 180° T. Completed launching 16 VF for Kikai support mission and 2 VF for Yontan mail trip. 0856 Commenced landing aircraft. 0857 Manned all Torpedo Defense Stations. 0859 Changed course to 200° T. 0900 Manned all General Quarters Stations and set condition "ABLE". Formed cruising disposition 5-VICTOR. Changed course to 210° T. 0901 Changed course to 220° T. 0903 Ceased landing aircraft. 0904 Changed course to 230° T. 0910 Changed course to 235° T. Commenced landing aircraft. 0920 Secured from General Quarters, set condition III and material condition of readiness modified "ABLE". Gunnery Department remained at Torpedo Defense. 0938 Completed landing 8 VF from Kikai support mission and 12 VF, 11 VT and 11 VB from special strike. 0939 Changed course to 050° T. Changed speed to 21 knots. 0942 Set condition "ONE-EASY" in the Gunnery Department. 0943 Rotated formation axis right to 235° T. 1005 The ship was hit by an enemy suicide bomber on flight deck just aft of #3 elevator. 1006 The ship was hit again by second suicide plane inboard of #2 elevator; general alarm sounded but operation doubtful; bridge ship service telephones out.

J. N. HORROCKS,
Lt. (jg), (D), USNR.

1012-1200 Steaming as before. 1012 Changed speed to 25 knots. Emergency 9 turn, changed course to 140° T. 1017 Emergency 9 turn, changed course to 230° T. 1020 Flight deck burning fiercely, issuing dense black smoke. 1025 Own ship's anti-aircraft fire splashed a "ZEKE" on the starboard beam. 1026 Changed course to 140° T. 1028 Damage control in full progress. 1035 Changed course to 090° T. 1050 Ship has a 4° starboard list. 1050 Changed speed to 20 knots. 1057 Emergency 5 turn, changed course to 040° T. 1058 Changed speed to 15 knots. 1059 U.S.S. SPERRY is standing by port side. 1100 Emergency 9 turn, changed course to 310° T. 1101 Fire on flight deck aft and on fantail is out. Fire on hangar deck is inaccessible. Planes moved up to #1 elevator and over the side to clear hangar deck. 1103 U.S.S. ENGLISH came alongside to aid in fire fighting. U.S.S. STEMBEL alongside also. 1105 Changed course to 300° T. 1108 Fire on flight deck has broken out again. 1108 U.S.S. ENGLISH is receiving survivors from Quad #15. 1109 All ships alongside aiding in fire fighting are directed to pour water into hangar deck. 1115 U.S.S. WILKES-BARRE is alongside starboard side aft evacuating wounded personnel and putting hoses into hangar deck. 1115 Fire on hangar deck under control. 1125 Ship is receiving bogie reports via T.B.S. as C.I.C. is out of commission. 1125 Ship is proceeding independently of Task Group 58.3 with two destroyers, SPERRY and ENGLISH and one cruiser, WILKES-BARRE, as escorts. 1140 Ship's course is 330° T, speed 10 knots. 1152 Commander Task Group 58.3 set condition "ONE-EASY" in anti-aircraft batteries. U.S.S. BUNKER HILL remained at General Quarters.

C. J. ODEND'HAL, JR.,
Comdr., USN., Navigator.

The Essex class USS *Bunker Hill* (CV-17) was one the U.S. Navy's premier ships of World War II, being one of the most sophisticated, expensive, and well-protected ships ever built. The United States was the only country in the world during World War II having the capability to build an Essex-class type ship. Twenty-four of them were built. The *Bunker Hill* saw more action than most other vessels in the Pacific Theater of operations during World War II. Built for a crew of 2600, by May of 1945 she had some 3,400 men aboard while supporting the invasion of Okinawa. The purpose of the *Bunker Hill* was centered on its pilots and aircrew. The men who fired the boilers, manned the guns, and kept her aircraft flying, were all directed to the final task of having men fly into combat nearly every day.

National Archives 80-G-274266

Black smoke billows from the *Bunker Hill* on May 11, 1945.

On the morning of Friday, May 11, 1945, a combat mission, including 11 bombers from VB-84, took off from the flight deck of the *Bunker Hill* at 0530. Wilson was not on the flight schedule for this mission, so he remained onboard and used some of his time to write two letters. The next combat mission for May 11th was scheduled for noon. It is likely that Wilson was on this flight schedule and at 1004 was probably in the aircrewmen's ready room on the gallery deck waiting to be briefed on his upcoming mission. At 1005 the lives of 3400 men aboard the *Bunker Hill* were forever changed. Those that survived, bore physical and emotional scars for the rest of their lives.

On Friday, May 11, 1945, at 1005 the first of two surprise kamikaze planes to strike the *Bunker Hill* was able to plow through a brief barrage of anti-aircraft fire. The first Zero (a Japanese fighter plane) dropped its bomb just before hitting a U.S. fighter plane parked on the flight deck setting it afire, then it skidded across the flight deck and dropped into the water carrying a catwalk and its men with it.

Wikipedia Commons

USS *Bunker Hill* burns; USS *Pasadena* to the right.

Its bomb pierced the flight deck and the ship's port side exploding just above the water about thirty feet from the ship. Thirty or more planes which sat parked on the flight deck, many with their engines running and propellers spinning, became a burning inferno with persistent explosions. The planes on the flight deck were being prepared for the next mission and were loaded with armaments, napalm, and each had approximately 23,000 gallons of fuel. As each plane caught fire and melted, the inferno burned more intensely, blackening the sky above and the ship below. Rockets ignited and ammunition exploded.

About thirty seconds after the first kamikaze hit, a second Zero kamikaze was also able to make its way to the *Bunker Hill.* Several following kamikazes were shot down before reaching the ship. In some accounts, the second plane was said to have been a Judy (a Japanese dive bomber). Maxwell Taylor Kennedy, while researching his book *Danger's Hour,* was able to prove that it was indeed a Zero. This Zero struck at the base of the island, with its bomb penetrating the flight deck and exploding in a pilot's ready room. It blasted a hole approximately forty feet wide in the flight and gallery decks. Additional intense fires broke

National Archives 80-G-259904

Destroyed planes on the flight deck.

out on the gallery deck and in planes parked on the flight and hangar decks. Gasoline pouring from wrecked planes burst into flames and carried the fire further into the heart of the ship. Less than a minute after the second kamikaze hit, fire hoses were laid out and water was on the fires. A less-than-five-minute delay in getting water turned on for hoses in Bay 4 resulted in 75% of those sprinkler heads being melted. Engine hulks melded and molten aluminum from the planes puddled on the flight deck from the intense heat.

Navsource.org

Island and flight deck after the kamikaze hit.

The ship's main ventilation trunk carried dense smoke from the hangar and flight decks throughout the rest of the ship. Many casualties occurred in the lower decks because smoke was forced in fatal amounts into spaces that otherwise would have been safe. A report from the Navy's World War II Diaries held at the National Archives states: "The casualties were mostly burns and smoke plus a few shrapnel wounds. ... One is struck by the fact that there were relatively few very seriously wounded casualties, they were either spared of a serious wound or killed outright. Smoke was the greatest single factor in the cause of death. Many died of smoke before they were burned enough to die. A great many persons had no choice but to go over the side and some were injured in the process due to the height from which they left the ship. Many were picked up by other ships but several of the missing undoubtedly drowned."[15] The fires burned furiously, but by 1600 only a few isolated fires remained. It wasn't until the next day, May 12th, at 0500 that all fires were determined to be out.

---

[15] World War II Diaries-USS *Bunker Hill: Rep of air ops Against Kyushu & Honshu, Japan, Ryukyu Is & Jap Task force.* National Archives' Record Group 38 via fold3.com. 267.

In Wilson's Bombing Squadron 84 (VB-84), the youngest aircrewman was age 19 and the oldest was 26. Wilson had just turned 26 a month and 5 days before the attack. For this squadron, Navy reports list 2 officers and 19 enlisted men killed on May 11th. Most of the 19 enlisted men were radiomen/gunners like Wilson, and two of the 19 were listed as missing in action. Various sources give differing numbers of total men killed that day. Navy reports held at the National Archives give the numbers as follows: 352 bodies were buried at sea (including Wilson), with 1 more found later and buried at Ulithi (total 353). Of those 353 men, only 329 were able to be identified, making 24 unidentified bodies buried at sea. An additional 43 men were listed as missing.[16] This gives a total of 396 men killed from the kamikaze attack on the *Bunker Hill*. Maxwell Kennedy in his book *"Danger's Hour"* writes that days later on the ship's way to Pearl Harbor, a previously unopened storage room door was opened and two men's bloated bodies were found. These were likely two of the 43 men listed as missing.

National Archives 80-G-259966

San Diego Air and Space Museum

Regarding identification of the dead, the Navy report states: "Since much of the superstructure of the ship was isolated by reason of heat and smoke until dark on the day of the attack, many spaces were not investigated until morning and it was thought that the casualties were about '250' dead. However we were in for a shock when the Gallery Deck spaces were opened and our list grew by leaps and bounds. Many were trapped in the midships section between the two 'hits' and were unable to go in any direction because of: (a) lack of exits. (b) smoke (resulting in darkness). (c) fire. (d) Loss of lighting power. Since 'Bay One', Hangar Deck, was a large space relatively cool and clean, early after the active phase of the attack it was used as a morgue. Bodies were layed out for identification and preparation for burial. The best means of identification were:

San Diego Air and Space Museum

Casualties on the flight deck and burial at sea.

---

[16] World War II Diaries-USS *Bunker Hill: Rep of air ops Against Kyushu & Honshu, Japan, Ryukyu Is & Jap Task force*. National Archives' Record Group 38 via fold3.com. 270. **NOTE:** The ship's Deck Log states 351 men buried at sea, plus the one later buried at Ulithi, so total dead could be 395 or 396.

(1) Identification Tags or Bracelets. (2) Names stencilled on belts (a measure recently adopted). (3) Dental Charts. (4) Last and <u>least</u>, clothing. Many persons were found who were wearing some one's else clothing (in one case - clothing from two other people)."[17]

In preparing the bodies for burial, "the burial crews stretched eighteen-foot strips of dark navy blue canvas across the dining tables like super-long tablecloths, six feet across the table and six feet hanging down from either end. They laid the bodies of their comrades on top and then placed two fifty-five-pound, 5 inch projectiles on top of each body, one cradled along the dead men's chests, the second between their legs. They then folded the extra six feet of canvas over their feet up to their heads. The remaining six feet or so from their heads folded down to their feet. Forty-foot lengths of rough cordage were then wrapped around the body, a half hitch tied every eighteen inches or so, securing each body within their weighted shroud. ... The Navy had never buried so many men at once, and no one knew how long it would take. Ship's carpenters had constructed only three burial chutes originally. But it would have taken all that day and night to bury the dead three at a time. So crewmen hastily added three olive drab stretchers to spill the dead faster into the sea."[18] About 380 miles south-southwest of Okinawa in the Philippine Sea, burial of 352 men (the ship's Deck Log states 351) started at 1203 on Saturday, May 12th, and lasted until 1850 that evening, it being the largest burial at sea of American personnel in the history of the U.S. Navy. "By mid-afternoon, the chaplains were all crying. By the end of the day, exhausted mentally, spiritually, and physically, they could barely mumble the requisite prayers before the assembly line was tipped, and the dead men slid into the sea. ... The burial became too much at times and sailors would drift away. Some wandered to the ship's stern and looked back, horrified at the wake. Despite their efforts, many of the tightly sewn canvas shrouds had filled with air. The bodies rose, bobbing to the surface, then swayed sickly back and forth in the whitewash behind the *Bunker Hill*, marking her path away from Kyushu. ... Sharks followed the *Bunker Hill* for days."[19]

Family stories of how Wilson died include that he was burned alive in a ready room, minutes from being in his plane and in the air. No actual reference to his exact location or manner of death has been found, though his death certificate lists his cause of death as smoke inhalation. An article written by fellow airman Bill Schmeling, quoted in the next paragraph, suggests Wilson's location at the time of the attack was in a ready room. Being likely that Wilson was scheduled for a flight at noon, he was indeed probably waiting in an aircrewman's ready room (pilots and flight crews had separate ready rooms). Most of the enlisted men in Wilson's squadron killed that day were radiomen/gunners, which may also indicate they were waiting together in a ready room. An action report regarding Air Group 84 states that most of their personnel losses occurred in the ready rooms by blast and by being trapped by fire. The ready rooms were located just below the flight deck and above the hangar deck in the gallery deck, which was a suspended mezzanine overlooking the hangar deck. The gallery deck was destroyed in the attack. Some of the men in the ready rooms died quickly from the concussion from the blast and were found still sitting in their chairs. Others, and throughout the ship, died a much more horrible death. The smoke in the air contained a great deal of heat and particulate matter. As the men breathed this into their lungs, their tracheal bronchial tree filled with soot and they died slowly from asphyxiation. Others died from carbon monoxide poisoning while some men burned to death. When the surviving crewmen were gathering bodies, some of the blackened corpses came apart. Bodies stiffened when rigor

---

[17] World War II Diaries-USS *Bunker Hill: Rep of air ops Against Kyushu & Honshu, Japan, Ryukyu Is & Jap Task force*. National Archives' Record Group 38 via fold3.com. 270.
[18] Kennedy, Maxwell Taylor. *Danger's Hour: The story of the USS Bunker Hill and the kamikaze pilot who crippled her*. New York: Simon & Schuster, 2008. 424,425.
[19] Ibid. 424-426.

mortis had set in. In the confusion of the attack and the blackness of the smoke, some of the men lay dead atop each other, entangled together in a terrible knot.

William (Bill) Schmeling, at the age of 85, wrote an article that appeared in *The Denver Post* on May 27, 2010. Bill was a fellow VB-84 radioman/gunner with Wilson on the *Bunker Hill* when it was attacked. Within this article he writes: "One day in May, we were all sitting around the ready room, some playing cards, some half dozing, others writing letters. Uncharacteristically, I went to lay down in my

Bodies of men who tried to escape ready rooms.

Wikimedia Commons

bunk at the front end (focile) of the ship. Suddenly, there was a loud boom. I ran up to the flight deck. "My God," I thought, "we've been bombed!" Black smoke was billowing out from the base of the island; sailors were scurrying around in all directions. I was in utter shock. A chief finally yelled at me to get down to the hanger deck and try to help. I gave a black sailor CPR for at least a half an hour but could not save him. A Japanese suicide bomber (kamikaze) had crashed into the base of the superstructure with 1,100 pounds of bombs. Thirty seconds later, a second plane exploded into the side of the carrier, leaving a huge hole. They came in low, under the radar, and no warning was sounded. There was no time to close hatches to prevent the circulation of deadly smoke; everyone was taken by surprise. Our ready room (where I would normally have been) was located very close to where the plane hit. The force of the explosion jammed all of the escape hatches. All the men in our squadron were trapped in a furnace full of acrid, black smoke. But the worst was yet to come. We had to pry the hatch open and retrieve the bodies. They were all bunched up right below the hatch cover; black, charred corpses with barely perceptible terrified expressions frozen on their faces. I helped

in this operation without emotion. I had buried everything deep inside me . . . and it remained there for most of my life. We learned later that six men managed to escape through a port hole and my pilot [Carlos B. Stafford] and others located in a different ready room managed to escape."[20]

Of the two letters Wilson wrote on the morning of May 11th, one was finished and sent on its way to his family in Avon, Pa. They received it on May 21st. The family received the Western Union Telegram informing them of Wilson's death on May 28th. The other letter was addressed to his fiancé in Iowa. It was finished and signed but was not

National Archives 80-G-259942

Memorial service on the *Bunker Hill* flight deck, May 20, 1945.

mailed. Instead, it ended up making its way to Pennsylvania with Wilson's personal effects that were shipped to his mother several months later. These letters are reproduced and transcribed just previous to this kamikaze account. It wasn't until July 27, 1945, that news of the kamikaze attack on the *Bunker Hill* was released by the American government and appeared in newspapers across the country.

---

[20] Schmeling, Bill. "A gunner recalls duty on the USS Bunker Hill." *The Denver Post* (Denver, CO), May 27, 2010. Accessed December 22, 2016. http://www.denverpost.com/2010/05/27/a-gunner-recalls-duty-on-the-uss-bunker-hill/.

Western Union Telegram, May 28, 1945, informing Wilson's parents of his death.
No date, place, or other information about his death was provided at that time.

WESTERN UNION

A. N. WILLIAMS
PRESIDENT

1220

647P

CLASS OF SERVICE

This is a full-rate Telegram or Cablegram unless its deferred character is indicated by a suitable symbol above or preceding the address.

SYMBOLS

DL=Day Letter
NL=Night Letter
LC=Deferred Cable
NLT=Cable Night Letter
Ship Radiogram

The filing-time shown in the date line on telegrams and day letters is STANDARD TIME at point of origin. Time of receipt is STANDARD TIME at point of destination

PY108 78 GOVT=WASHINGTON DC MAY 28 558P

MR & MRS ROBERT JOSEPH LINEAWEAVER=

:1240 EAST CUMBERLAND ST BA=

28 PM 7 17

THE NAVY DEPARTMENT DEEPLY REGRETS TO INFORM YOU THAT YOUR
SON WILSON CHARLES LINEAWEAVER AVIATION CHIEF RADIOMAN USN
WAS KILLED IN ACTION WHILE IN THE SERVICE OF HIS COUNTRY.
THE DEPARTMENT EXTENDS TO YOU ITS SINCEREST SYMPATHY IN YOUR
GREAT LOSS. HIS REMAINS WERE BURIED AT SEA WITH FULL
MILITARY HONORS. IF FURTHER DETAILS ARE RECEIVED YOU WILL
BE INFORMED. TO PREVENT POSSIBLE AID TO OUR ENEMIES PLEASE
DO NOT DIVULGE THE NAME OF HIS SHIP OR STATION=

VICE ADMIRAL RANDALL JACOBS CHIEF OF NAVAL
Regional Office #10   PERSONNEL.

INDEXED

NO RECORD
MILITARY FILE

THE COMPANY WILL APPRECIATE SUGGESTIONS FROM ITS PATRONS CONCERNING ITS SERVICE

GOOD EVENING

Ret. Jimmy Doolittle won't recognize the old town of Tokyo on his next visit there.

V Lebanon Daily News. V

and The Lebanon Daily Times.

THE WEATHER

Eastern Penna.—Fair with moderate temperature today. Increasing cloudiness and cooler tonight, Wednesday, showering and cooler.

73rd YEAR—No. 223.   Single Copy Three Cents; Published Every Evening Except Sunday   LEBANON, PA., TUESDAY EVENING, MAY 29, 1945.   Entered as second class matter at the postoffice at Lebanon, Pa., under the Act of March 2, 1879   8 PAGES—THREE CENTS

Yokohama Set Ablaze By 500 Superforts

County Lashed By Heavy Storm; Barn Is Destroyed

Severe Electrical Disturbance Causes Damage Monday

HAIL AND RAIN

Moyer Barn Near Bellegrove Hit By Lightning, Razed

Terrorizing flashes of lightning and terrific claps of thunder, accompanied by a deluge of rain and a downpour of hail, swept the high-lights of a severe spring storm early Monday evening which caused considerable damage in some parts.

A number of barns in Central Pennsylvania were set on fire by the lightning, one of them near Bellegrove, resulting in a loss of nearly $7,000. Some damage was caused by the hail and also from high water. Roofing cellars and downing chickens on the outskirts of the city and in the county districts. Electrical, telephone and telegraph wires were reported down in a number of places.

Annville and vicinity were hard hit among other places. A bolt of lightning struck the transformer on the outskirts of the community, and knocked out power wires. While no homes were in darkness, some of the machines at the Fink and Fenwaid bakeries were rendered powerless. Herman Gebhard, in charge of the service for that district, worked feverishly for some hours to get things in shape, and street lighting was restored after only a brief outage.

A stroke of lightning fired the barn of Charles B. Moyer, Annville, RD 1, on the Black Bridge Road north of Bellegrove. The barn and contents were valued at approximately $7,819.88 as estimated by Assistant Fire Chief John Hopper, of the Union Hose Fire Company of Annville, who responded to the alarm sent in at o'clock. A full force of firemen was on hand to combat the fire which lit the cloud-darkened sky for miles around. The barn, 40 by 60 feet in dimensions, was totally destroyed. The loss is covered by insurance.

Besides the structure, some destroyed farm implements were destroyed including a milk separator which Mr. Moyer recently installed at a cost of $215.89. It was estimated that late firemen in a bucket stand saved approximately $15,000 including eighteen head of cattle, two horses, two tractors, the implement shed, milk house and the residence. Fortunately an ample stream of water flowed from the house was available to the firemen and with their hose and pumper were able to prevent total loss of the buildings. They also fought the southern fire in a drenching rain. The ambulance of the fire company accompanied the firemen to the scene, but fortunately was not needed.

At the Metropolitan headquarters

(Continued on Page Eight)

BARN HIT BY LIGHTNING IS RAZED BY FIRE

A barn and hogpen on the farm of Ira Heirich, Grantville R. D. 1, near Shellsville, were destroyed by a fire started when a bolt of lightning struck the larger building during the height of last evening's storm. Damage was estimated by the owner to be in excess of $3,000.

A large number of farm implements and hand products, including about 250 pounds of chicken feed, 50 pounds of potatoes and other odd work shoes. With the exception of several chickens and a litter of four kittens, who were

(Continued on Page Eight)

V.F.W.

Members and Auxiliary REPORT AT HOME 4:45 P. M., May 30th For Memorial Day Parade Uniforms of cape.

SAVE THIS NEWSPAPER

After you have read this paper, please save it. Every bit of paper is vitally needed for war production.

MEMORIAL OBSERVANCE TO HAVE DEEPER SIGNIFICANCE THIS YEAR

With 192 names added during the Second World War to Lebanon County's long list of heroes who made the supreme sacrifice in serving their country, Memorial Day tomorrow will have a deeper significance than ever before. In addition to the 154 killed in action, 14 who met death in other performance of duty, 12 who died natural deaths, and 4 who died as the result of accidents, there were scores of widows, orphans, sons, nephews and other relatives of local people who pass their time in the name of world freedom and were registered from other sections. Boys and girls of young

(Continued on Page Four)

LIST OF SIXTEEN NEW INDUCTEES IS RELEASED

Local Draft Board three, Annville, today released the names of sixteen registrants who were inducted into the armed services at Harrisburg last May 23. Fourteen were assigned to the Army, and one each to the Navy and Marine Corps. This is the first group of registrants to leave Lebanon County after the order to suspend induction of men thirty years and over, was issued by Selective Service. The list follows:

Army

Ray Irvin Eberhole, 462 Maple street, Annville.   John Clair Edris, Jonestown.

AUTO CLUB ADDS 69 TO ITS MEMBERSHIP

Sixty-nine new members were enrolled at the May meeting of the Palmyra-Lebanon County Automobile Club, held in the club rooms at Palmyra on Monday evening, under the direction of the president, George D. Ferry.

H. K. Brandt, of Sheridan Road 1, was named as chairman of a special committee to recommend to the State Secretary of Highways needed improvements to the important highways in Lebanon Valley.

Among the projects advocated by the committee are the rebuilding of U. S. 422 between Womelsdorf and Palmyra and between Womelsdorf and Sinking Springs, modernization of Pa. 501 between Myerstown and Lititz, Pa. 72, Lebanon to Manheim, and also improvements to certain portions of U. S. 322 and to Pa. 897 between Schaefferstown and Lebanon.

Secretary D. J. Grace reported that the membership was 3,213 at the beginning of May. A 10,000 membership contest was approved by the Club. New members and membership cards are to participate in a prize drawing to be made when the club reaches its membership goal.

PFC. ISRAEL G. WERTZ HAS BEEN LIBERATED

Once feared dead because he had failed for many weeks to receive word from him, Pfc. Israel G. Wertz, who was liberated as a German war prisoner camp, PFC. Israel G. Wertz, reduced to now liberated in this hospital on his way home. His widowed mother Mrs. Kate Wertz, of 416 Guilford

(Continued on Page Eight)

THE LEBANADROME ROLLER RINK

Memorial Day Party WEDNESDAY, MAY 30th Skating from 8:30 to 12:00

HARRY STARK, Well Known Organist

HATS — BLOW OUTS GAMES and PRIZES

Parents or relatives who accompany children will be admitted free of charge.

MEMORIAL DAY PROGRAM PLANS ARE COMPLETED

Parade Formation Is Announced By Committee Head

LIST PROGRAM

Affair Will Be Conducted Late Tomorrow Afternoon

Frederick S. Frantz, chairman of the general committee arranging for the celebration of Memorial Day today issued the "general order" which is to govern the parade formation for the march through town to Mt. Lebanon cemetery late in the afternoon tomorrow.

At the same time he announced the program that will mark the annual Memorial Day ceremony at the soldiers Block on Mt. Lebanon cemetery, to be featured with an address by Rev. Calvin Reber, of Palmyra, a retired missionary from China who was interned by the Japanese. The Perseverance Band and the High School Band will have a part in the cemetery program and there will be the usual memorial touches such as Logan's general order and Lincoln's Gettysburg address to be presented by High School Seniors Duellie J. Erdley and Nell Roger respectively. Eugene M. Gaines is master of ceremonies.

The parade will form in the vicinity of Eighth and Chestnut Streets and will move north on Eighth to Maple Street and east to the cemetery. In event of rain however the same order and program will be in effect on Thursday at the same time.

The general order follows:

The parade will form, promptly at 3:30, K. 7:45" A.V. all to be ready to march at 4:15 when drill. Marshal will report to Chief Marshal.

Head of formation Eighth and Chestnut Streets.

Units will take their place by routes that do not interfere with formation of parade.

1 Division — Military and Re-Auxiliaries and Gold Star Mothers.

1 Division—Red Cross and relatives of persons in the Armed forces.

(Continued on Page Four)

MONKEY BUSINESS

Decatur, Ill., May — (P)— B. O. Wood, a railway express clerk, doesn't think a crate of monkeys is so much fun.

A family of three monkeys he shipped from St. Louis to Detroit escaped from the crate. Before the train arrived in Decatur, Wood said, the monkeys had taken refuge in a box, studies an orange from the conductor's hat, and awaked their tails in his face.

They were hiding in a corner when the train arrived here. Railway express agents decided to let their colleagues in Detroit capture them.

KILLED IN PACIFIC

WILSON C. LINEAWEAVER

REPORT WILSON C. LINEAWEAVER KILLED AT SEA

Aviation Chief Radioman Wilson Charles Lineaweaver was killed in action while serving on an aircraft carrier in the Pacific according to a telegram received by his parents, Mr. and Mrs. Robert Lineaweaver, of 1240 East Cumberland Street. The message did not give the date or place but it is presumed he have occurred near Japan, as the Navy three home in his letters that his carrier was often cruising close to Japan waters. The message stated further that a few three weeks before he died, his mother received further instructions as to his treatment on board the U. S. S. Monnet. On his second trip overseas he was wounded and sent back to the states for treatment arriving at San Diego, Calif. Upon his recovery he went home to here and then sent out again to the Pacific at which time he met with his death.

The local navy man holds the Air Medal and the presidential

(Continued on Page Eight)

PFC. HAROLD HARTMAN AGAIN FREE MAN

Pfc. Harold W. Hartman, laborer, one-time shoe repairman, and later an employe of the Old cleaning establishment, is again a free man, having been liberated from a German prisoner-of-war camp in Germany. A cablegram to the effect from the soldier himself was received to his

(Continued on Page Three)

Air Raid Made After Nip Suicide Planes Hit Ships

One Light American Vessel Was Sunk And Twelve Other Fleet Units Damaged In All-Night Raid Made On U. S. Shipping Around Okinawa — Yokohama Is Blasted By Huge Force Of Superforts

(By the Associated Press)

Approximately 500 fighter-escorted Superforts scorched Yokohama today with 3,200 tons of fire bombs in their greatest daylight raid, made 24 hours after Japanese suicide planes wound up their most damaging attack on U. S. shipping around Okinawa Island.

One light American ship was sunk and 12 other fleet units were damaged in the night-long Nipponese attack, ending Monday morning. At least 77 Japanese planes were shot down.

The enemy air strike didn't stop American divisions from cloaking sweeping advances on both flanks of the sodden Okinawa front, giving them control of two thirds of Naha and half-encircling Shuri, keystone fortress.

Unconfirmed reports emanating from Chungking said recent Japanese reverses in West Central China have "laid a solid foundation for launching a general counteroffensive," to be spearheaded by Generalissimo Chiang Kai-shek's American-trained Sixth Army.

Development of Okinawa, 325 miles south of Japan as a base for assaulting Japan is progressing ahead of schedule, said Commodore A. G. Bissell, who described it as "the biggest construction job ever attempted in the Pacific."

Today's hour, and a half B29 raid on Yokohama was the first Japan-bound blow of the day and followed almost two days of continuous action. To the south, in Manila's waterfront the 38th Division appeared on the verge of sealing Wawa Dam.

Australian gains were reported on Tarakan off the Borneo coast and on Bougainville in the Solomons. Indian troops in Burma fought off a concerted counterattack in one sector and began wiping out an enemy concentration in mainland.

Rumors of actual or impending Japanese withdrawals in China to a line north of the Yangtze were attributed by some Chungking sources to Nipponese moves at possible Russian entrance into the war. Some stories said the invaders were preparing to abandon Ichang, their watersheded bastion 225 miles up the Yangtze from Shanghai.

The emperor's forces in northeast Asia, placed by an escaped French officer at 100,000 in Indo-China alone, were imperiled by both the repeated evacuations and expanding Chinese offensives in south China. Chinese newsmen

(Continued on Page Eight)

WM. BRESSLER, MISSING OVER REICH, LOCATED

Technical Sergeant William R. Bressler, missing with another local service man, Lt. Richard L. Althouse, since April 19, when they were forced to bail out of their B-17, "Mean Widdle Kid," over German-held territory, has been located according to an official message sent his parents, Mr. and Mrs. Ellas Bressler, of Annville on Kay 4, four days earlier by the Fifth Armored Division. The message did not offer any details, and Mr. and Mrs. Bressler have not learned whether their son was a prisoner of the Germans or whether he was able to hide in the woods, as did Althouse, until the American advance made his location safe.

According to an official dispatch, the son along with other members of their crew, bailing out after their entire squadron was attacked by German anti-aircraft guns. A plane flying over Berlin had its wing sheared off by flak that turned a safe crashing down upon the plane which his mechanic, the captain, had the falling wing had taken off his rudder.

Bressler, 23, is a wireless operator with the 457th Bomb Group and wears the Air Medal and two

(Continued on Page Three)

V.F.W. ORDERS PLANS MADE FOR NEW HOME

Veterans of Foreign Wars, of Fredrick Fuhrman Post, at their meeting last evening held in the post home, 719 Chestnut Street, authorized the building committee to proceed with preliminary plans looking toward the eventual erection of the post's new home on the site now occupied by frame dwellings at 116 to 118 South Eighth Street. The site was recently purchased from John K. Bashore, Alien M. Vlogel is chairman of the building committee.

Commander Charles D. Horner conducted the business session which was attended by more than forty members, despite the bad weather conditions. Commander Horner was elected as the post representative at the State Encampment to be held in Harrisburg on June 21. He will officially represent the post's quota of ninety delegates at the state convention which is limited this year to one day of streamlined business matters, with no social touches.

Twenty new members, representing service men from all over the country, were invited, and hope that he had been wounded in action. Two members were nominated for their enlisted

(Continued on Page Eight)

SIXTY L.H.S. SENIORS ARE NOW IN SERVICE

Sixty members of the class of 1945, Lebanon Senior High School have entered the service at their country, according to a statement made today by Principal Charles E. Gunkins. The young men will receive their diplomas in absentia at commencement exercises which will take place on Thursday evening June 7 in the high school stadium.

There are 373 members in the class of 1945, 113 of whom are boys. The sixty who have left for the service represent almost fifty per cent of the total class enrollment of the young men of the

(Continued on Page Eight)

NEARLY 6,000 WORKERS STILL OUT ON STRIKE

(By The Associated Press)

Nearly 15,000 workers in Detroit, Buffalo and Berwick, Pa. returned to their jobs today but approximately 6,000 others in the nation were idle and further work stoppages appeared imminent.

The Berwick Industrial Division on the east Okinawa flank wheeled nearly half-way across the Island in order two villages south of Shuri, Hashkawa Nipponese in Shuri fought off attacks by the First Marines, 77th and 96th Infantry Divisions.

ESCAPES WITH WRIST INJURY IN 7 FOOT FALL

Nelson Jones, 22 year old negro laborer at the Veterans Hospital, making his home at 1144 Federal Street, fell seven feet from the top of a building at his work on Monday and suffered a fracture of the left wrist. He was sent to the Good Samaritan Hospital for treatment, where four sutures were taken in the wound and a tetanus injection given him, after which he was discharged.

LEARN K. L. M'NEIL WAS WOUNDED

In a V-mail letter which was received by his mother, Mrs. A. D. Lukens, 115 North Fifth Street, T/5 Kenneth L. (Frank) MacNeil officially revealed for the first time that he had been wounded in action on the three hundred and

(Continued on Page Eight)

GRADUATION AT HEIDELBERG TOWNSHIP H. S.

Sixteen seniors of Heidelberg Township High School were graduated on Monday evening at the premiere commencement exercises in the Schaefferstown School auditorium. Rev. Lawrence Baly, professor of practical theology at Franklin and Marshall Seminary, was commencement speaker.

The program was opened with a stirring march, played by the school orchestra. Rev. A. H. Bachman, pastor of St. Paul's Reformed Church of Schaefferstown, pronounced the invocation, after which the girls' chorus sang.

Mary Louise Horst, an outstanding pianist of the graduating class, played Liszt's Hungarian Rhapsody Number Two. "Citizenship and School Spirit," was the topic on which John Layser, valedictorian of the class, spoke. In excellent oratorical style, he pointed out the close tie between loyalty of a good citizen and being a good student.

Layser's speech was followed by two songs by the mixed chorus. The last, "America the Beautiful," was accompanied with a trumpet obligato played by Harry Heiney.

Rev. Baly's address was featured by the presentation of diplomas to the graduates by Harry C. Moyer, superintendent of county

(Continued on Page Three)

JUST A LITTLE LATE

Boise, Idaho, Today — (P)— Georgie Oird, city editor of the Idaho Statesman, was stumped when a subscriber asked for a "free gramophone." But the "idea" of produced a copy of Sunday's edition which said:

"The Statesman's free gramophone offer for Bodies will close at 6 o'clock this evening."

Diei then explained the item was in the "40 years ago" column.

SPEAKING OF BONDS

Washington, Today — (P) — A war bond statement by Lt. Gen. Ben Lear, deputy commander, European Theater of Operations:

"Purchase of war bonds is the daily which every man, woman and child owes to his country."

Attention Legionnaires

Report to Legion Home WEDNESDAY AFTERNOON at 5 o'clock for Memorial Day Parade

Servicemen and Ex-servicemen invited to participate.

Harry Miller, Commander

MISS C. GABLE ENDS 45 YEARS OF TEACHING

School directors and faculty members of South Lebanon Township held a surprise party in the school rooms of the Iona School on Monday afternoon in honor Miss Charlotte Gable, who completed her last day of teaching on Monday. After 45 years of service in schools of Heidelberg and South Lebanon Township.

Ray A. Kurtz, supervising principal of the schools, on behalf of the faculty and school board, presented Miss Gable with a number of attractive gifts, including a billfold and a fine piece of table cloth accompanying remarks. He compressed the wishes of all and expressed the regret of all at her retirement.

Miss Gable says that she has been in school state after attending first grade. After her graduation from Millersville State Teachers College, she began immediately to

(Continued on Page Four)

ARMY TO TAKE MEN WITH MINOR DEFECTS

Local draft boards have been notified by defective Service headquarters that a limited number of men under twenty-six, who do not meet the physical standards for general military service because of minor defects, will be accepted by the Army. While the number of such men was not announced, Selective Service said the number would be limited.

In order to determine which registrants undergo through physical examination without any approval from the State Director. Registrants previously rejected for general military service or found qualified for limited service.

"It is assumed," the order said, "that local boards will use reasonable judgment and discretion, so that no registrant in this age group will again be forwarded for preinduction physical examination who has an obvious defect."

KILLED IN PACIFIC

WILSON C. LINEAWEAVER

REPORT WILSON C. LINEAWEAVER KILLED AT SEA

Aviation Chief Radioman Wilson Charles Lineaweaver was killed in action while serving on an aircraft carrier in the Pacific according to a telegram received by his parents, Mr. and Mrs. Robert Lineaweaver, of 1240 East Cumberland Street. The message did not give the date or place but it is presumed to have occurred near Japan as the boy wrote home in his letters that his carrier was often cruising around in Jap waters. The message stated however that a more explanatory letter would follow.

He is the 159th Lebanon Countian to be reported killed.

Enlisting in January, 1941, he underwent his recruit training at Norfolk, Va., and upon its completion was assigned to further instructions at Jacksonville, Fla. In January, 1942 he left the states for foreign duty on board the U. S. S. Hornet. On his second trip overseas he was wounded and sent back to the states for treatment arriving at San Diego, Calif. Upon his recovery he was home on leave and then sent out again to the Pacific at which time he met with his death.

The local navy man holds the Air Medal and the presidential

(Continued on Page Eight)

REPORT WILSON C. LINEAWEAVER KILLED AT SEA

(Continued from Page One)

citation for bravery in action during aerial naval operations against the Japs.

He passed his twenty-sixth birthday on the sixth of April. Lineaweaver graduated from Lebanon High School in 1937, and was a member of the United Brethren in Christ faith.

Surviving him are his parents, Robert Joseph, and Nettie Earline nee Haag Lineaweaver. The following brothers and sisters: David and Mahlon, of this city, Private First Class James Lineaweaver with the U. S. Army in England, and Lucille, Dorothy, Nathan and Harold at home.

File No.

Serial:

U. S. S. BUNKER HILL (CV17)
℅ FLEET POST OFFICE
SAN FRANCISCO, CALIF.
25 May 1945.

My dear Mrs. Lineaweaver,

  Before this letter reaches you, you will already have received the sad news from the Navy Department that your son, Wilson C. Lineaweaver, ACRM, USN, was killed in action against the enemy. Although I realize fully that there is little I can say which will help to alleviate your natural grief, I do want to assure you of the very deep sympathy of every officer and man aboard this ship.

  Your son's death on 11 May 1945 was caused by enemy bombing attacks against this vessel while operating in the forward combat area near Japan. Insofar as I can ascertain his death was without suffering and in all probability instantaneous. Due to battle conditions, it was of course necessary to bury his body at sea. This was done with all dignity and reverence on 12 May 1945 with burial services conducted by our Roman Catholic Chaplain. In addition, memorial services with full military honors were held on 20 May 1945 with the ship's company in attendance.

  Wilson was an excellent aircrewman and was of great value to his pilot. His friendly and cheerful nature had won him the affection of his shipmates as his ability had won him their respect.

  Whatever were recovered of your son's valuables and other personal effects, not destroyed by battle damage, have been carefully inventoried and are being shipped to: "Personal Effects Distribution Center, Naval Supply Depot, Clearfield, Utah," for forwarding as soon as possible to you. Any further communication concerning them should be addressed to that activity direct. Information concerning pension, insurance, etc. will be sent to you shortly by "The Bureau of Naval Personnel, Casualty and Allotments Section, Navy Department, Washington 25, D.C." Since we have forwarded all your son's records, any further questions concerning his affairs should be addressed to that office.

  Again may I extend my heartfelt sympathy. Please try to take at least some measure of comfort in your sorrow in the thought that your son died as only a brave man can, fighting for those ideals and values and verities which we believe to be more important than even life itself. I can assure you that we who have been granted the opportunity to carry on the fight for him are determined that his death shall not have been in vain.

Very sincerely yours,

G. A. SEITZ,
Captain, U. S. Navy,
Commanding.

Mrs. Eslene Lineaweaver,
1240 E. Cumberland Street,
Lebanon, Pennsylvania.

ADDRESS REPLY TO
COMMANDANT
FOURTH NAVAL DISTRICT
AND REFER TO NO.

FOURTH NAVAL DISTRICT
DISTRICT STAFF HEADQUARTERS
BUILDING NO. 4
NAVY YARD, PHILADELPHIA 12. PA.

P6-2

4 June 1945

Mr. and Mrs. Robert J. Lineaweaver
1240 E. Cumberland St.
Lebanon, Pa.

Dear Mr. and Mrs. Lineaweaver,

Information from the Bureau of Naval Personnel
has been received by the Commandant, Fourth Naval District
that your son, Wilson Charles Lineaweaver, Aviation Chief
Radioman, has been reported dead in the performance of his
duty and in the service of his country. The Commandant regrets that it is not possible for a Navy Chaplain to call
and extend his personal condolences. The NavyDepartment
will supply you with further accurate information as it is
received and can be released.

This letter is sent that you may know the Navy
Department is fully cognizant of the great loss which you
have sustained.

It is the hope and prayer of the undersigned
Chaplain that you may be Divinely sustained in the days that
lie ahead.

Yours sincerely,

E. W. Davis

E. W. DAVIS
Captain (ChC), U. S. Navy
District Chaplain

File No.

Serial:

U. S. S. BUNKER HILL (CV17)
℅ FLEET POST OFFICE
SAN FRANCISCO, CALIF.

14 June 1945.

Mrs. Eslene Lineaweaver
1240 E. Cumberland St.
Lebanon, Pa.

Dear Mrs. Lineaweaver:

You have received the sad news of the death of your son from the Navy Department. I am not writing with the expectation that any words of mine will relieve you of your sorrow for I realize how severe this blow has been to you. In times like this words of consolation and sympathy seem so empty and inadequate. I shall feel that I have accomplished much if I can but help a little in lightening the burden.

In life more important than anything else, is that we be prepared for eternity. You have lost one most dear to you and your grief is intense, yet consolation can be found in the fact that by teaching and example he knew the way to God and I believe that he has followed it. While the Sacraments could not all be given, absolution was, and facing eternity, who of us, trained in the faith, would not grasp the mercy of God. The day before he died, the Feast of the Ascension, he was at Holy Mass. He did his duty. When danger threatened he did not falter. We pray that the supreme sacrifice of his life will be accepted by God for any transgressions of his youth.

Each day that the Holy Sacrifice of the Mass is offered aboard this ship, your son will be remembered. We shall offer the Mass, too, that you may receive the strength to carry the burden of your loss. May God love you.

Sincerely yours in Christ,

Robert E. Delaney
Chaplain

RED:hsj

THE SECRETARY OF THE NAVY
WASHINGTON

2 July 1945

Mr. and Mrs. Robert Joseph Lineaweaver
1240 East Cumberland Street
Lebanon, Pennsylvania

My dear Mr. and Mrs. Lineaweaver:

I offer to you my personal condolence in the death of your son,
Wilson Charles Lineaweaver, Aviation Chief Radioman, United
States Navy, which occurred in action 11 May 1945.

Sincere sympathy is extended to you in your loss. It is hoped
that you may find comfort in the thought that his sacrifice
was made in order that the freedom of his country might be
preserved.

Sincerely yours,

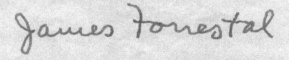

James Forrestal

REPORT OF CASUALTY
NAVPERS-2059 (REV. 1-45)   CF. 6526

NAME (Last)	(First)	(Middle)	RANK OR RATING	BRANCH	STATUS	FILE OR SERV. NO.
LINEAWEAVER	Wilson	Charles	ACRM(AA)(T)	USN	Active	258 32 24

CASUALTY CONTROL NO.	DUTY ATTACHMENT		CASUALTY STATUS
29625-A-458-284	VD-84		Dead

CASUALTY CODE	ENEMY ACTION	CAUSE OF CASUALTY
0121	Yes	Enemy Action

DATE OF CASUALTY	PLACE OF CASUALTY	AREA
11 May 1945		Asiatic

DATE OF APPT. OR ENLIST.	PLACE OF ENLISTMENT	PREVIOUS DUTY
6 Jan 1941	Baltimore, Maryland	USNH San Diego, Calif.

STATE CREDIT	(Street)	(City)	(County)	(State)	NAVAL DISTRICT
1240 E. Cumberland St.	Lebanon	Lebanon	Pennsylvania	

DATE OF BIRTH	PLACE OF BIRTH (City)	(State)	MARITAL STATUS	DEPEND.	RACE
6 Apr 1919	Elizabeth	New Jersey	Single	Yes	White

NOTIFICATION OF NEXT OF KIN

☐ By Local Activity	☐ By Letter	☒ By BuPers 2-0 ☐ By Telegram	☐ No Notification

NAME(S) OF NEXT OF KIN	RELATIONSHIP(S)	ADDRESS(ES)
*Arlene Betty Lineaweaver	Mother	1240 E. Cumberland St., Lebanon, Penna.
Robert Joseph Lineaweaver	Father	Same

Report of death rec'd 25 May 1945	DATE 30 May 1945

FINISHED FILE - Pers 5324

DEATH PAYMENTS

FINISHED FILE - Pers 5324

BY DIRECTION OF THE CHIEF OF NAVAL PERSONNEL

A. C. JACOBS
CAPTAIN, U. S. N. R.
DIRECTOR OF THE DEPENDENTS
WELFARE DIVISION

16—43230-1   U. S. GOVERNMENT PRINTING OFFICE

NMS-Form N
(1940)

CERTIFICATE OF DEATH

From: U.S.S. BUNKER HILL CV17   29625-A-458-281

To: *Bureau of Medicine and Surgery, Navy Department, Washington, D. C.*
(See Circular Letter R-6, Appendix D, Manual of the Medical Department, for instructions)

1. Name LINEAWEAVER, Wilson Charles,   258-32-24   Rank or rate ARM 1c, USN.

2. Born: Place New Jersey   Date 4-6-19

3. Nationality W-US   Religion Catholic
(White—U. S., Colored, Samoan, etc.)   (Denomination)

4. Eyes Blue   Hair Sandy   Complexion Fair   Height 67   Weight 146

5. Marks, scars, etc. (noted in health record) ANT:2 PS forehead; S ½" lower lip;
S ½" right knee; S ½" left knee; S ½" right foreleg; 2 BMK
2½" x 1"right foreleg. POST: Vs 1"d left arm; S ½"d left elbow; S ½" right elbow.

FINGERPRINT   NOT AVAILABLE

State which finger _____
(Right index preferred)

6. Relation, name and address of next of kin or friend Mother: Mrs. Zalene LINEAWEAVER,
1240 1. Cumberland St., Lebanon, Pa.

7. Original admission: Place USS BUNKER HILL CV17   Date 11 May 1945
(Ship or station to which attached when first admitted to sick list)

8. Died: Place USS BUNKER HILL CV17   Date 11 May 1945   Hour 1045

9. Cause of death { Principal SMOKE INHALATION, (ship's fire), #2549. Key Letter K
Contributory _____

10. Death is not the result of own misconduct and is in the line of duty.
(Is or is not)   (Is or is not)

11. Disposition of remains Buried at sea.

RECEIVED
JUL 24 1945
INTAKE & FILES UNIT

12. Summary of facts relative to the death: 1. Within Command.
2. Work.
3. Negligence not apparent.
4. Fatally injured during a dive bombing attack by
determined Japanese planes against this ship at 1005 this date.

Finished File, Casualties
and Allotments Section

Finished File, Casualties
and Allotments Section

16—15556   (Continue on back of this form)

Naval Unit
PERSONAL EFFECTS DISTRIBUTION CENTER
U. S. Naval Training and Distribution Center
Farragut, Idaho

PEDC/L19/
Serial 7-3039/gf

_____
(Date)

To: Mrs. Erlene N. Lineaweaver
     1240 E. Cumberland Street
     Lebanon, Pennsylvania

                                      (Deceased).
Subject: LINEAWEAVER, Wilson Charles, ACRM, 258 32 24, USN,
          Inventory of Personal Effects; Certified copy of.

       1. An inventory of the subject's personal effects
was held this date and consists of the following listed items.
These effects have been turned over to the Supply Officer for
shipment to you at the above address. Upon receipt of these
effects, please sign and return the attached receipt, using
the enclosed envelope (no postage required):

                CLOTHING   MISCELLANEOUS

 3 Grey overseas caps   1 Ditty bag
 5 Nainsook drawers   1 Whisk broom
11 Handkerchiefs   3 Pillow covers
 5 White hats   1 Sewing kit
 1 Dress blue jumper   1 Shoe shining kit
 1 Undress blue jumper   1 Hunting knife; 1 sheath
 1 Neckerchief   1 Fountain pen
 3 Chambray shirts   1 Pipe
 1 Grey shirt   3 Towels
 1 pr., High black shoes   1 Magnifying glass
 1 pr., Low black shoes   1 U.S.N. pin
 1 pr., Shower shoes
 6 pr., Black socks
 1 pr., White socks   NOTE:
 3 pr., Heavy wool socks   The sum of $22.10 made
 1 Blue trouser   out to you will be forwarded
 3 Dungaree trousers   when released by the Navy
 1 Grey trouser   Department.
 6 Cotton undershirts

                                   J. E. HUNT
                                   Captain, SC, U. S. Navy
                                   Supply Officer in Command

                                   By Direction

                              (1)

Case No. 3300
Inspector 1j1
Recorder

VALUABLES RECEIVED

BUREAU OF SUPPLIES & ACCOUNTS
PERSONAL EFFECTS DISTRIBUTION CENTER
Farragut, Idaho

258 32 24, LINEAWEAVER, Wilson, Charles, ACRM, USN
(Ser. No.)   (Name)   (Rate)   (Branch)

Regular Mail
Registered
No.

From:

INVENTORY

QUANTITY	DESCRIPTION
1	Sunday Missal
1	Mass Book
2	Photos
15	Snapshots

NOTE:

NOTE: $22.10 has been deposited in the United States
Treasury awaiting permission from the Navy Department to forward check to you.

NOTE: In the event any bulk effects are received
you will be notified accordingly.

Received .... the above mentioned articles from: C2A. EDMONSON, CPC, USN
                                                                           OinC "Valuables"
                                                                                                    3300
Name   Rate

USNT&DC FARR., IDA. 9-26-45-30M-4-up-544   **ORIGINAL**

spence it.
Will try to
later date.
From someone
your son and
and will miss

impression that he
"happy go-lucky
wanted to be.
I am sending
of Wilson which
at Xmas time.
you knew him
was when he left
he made "Chief," as
think he had an
having a picture ta
new uniform.
I received Lacet
letter Saturday.
Would you send me
the article in your
This has been a
attempt at saying
I have in my min
cannot put into wor

Dear Mrs. Lineaweaver & family,
Some how I haven't been able
to bring myself to write you under
the circumstances but realize it
must be done.
Please accept my most
sincere sympathy
Although I had steeled myself
against receiving news such as
that, it was still almost unbelievable it could mean the
end of someone on earth who
was as vitally alive as
Wilson.
When he went out this
time he knew his chance of
a safe return was slim but
he still gave everyone the

B. Knepper
Bernard, Iowa

DUBUQUE
JUN 11
3 PM
1945
IOWA

Via Air Mail

Mr & Mrs Robert Lineaweaver &
Family
1240 E. Cumberland St.
Avon, Pa.

[This is a letter from Wilson's fiancé Bette Knepper to Wilson's mother, one of several correspondences after Wilson's death.]

Dear Mrs. Lineaweaver and family,

Somehow I haven't been able to bring myself to write you under the circumstances but realize it must be done.

Please accept my most sincere sympathy

Although I had steeled myself against receiving news such as that, it was still almost unbelievable it could mean the end of someone on earth who was as vitally alive as Wilson.

When he went out this time he knew his chance of a safe return was slim but he still gave everyone the impression that he was that "happy go-lucky sailor" he wanted to be.

I am sending you a photo of Wilson which was taken at Xmas time. I imagine you know him still as he was when he left the states, before he made "Chief", as I do. Don't think he had an opportunity of having a picture taken in his new uniform.

I received Lucille's very nice letter Saturday. Thank you. Would you send me a copy of the article in your paper?

This has been a very feeble attempt at saying so many things I have in my mind & heart but cannot put into words. Please excuse it.

Will try to do better at a later date.

From someone who loved your son and brother very much and will miss him more

Bette

[Postmark is Dubuque, Iowa, June 11, 1945, 3 PM]
Mr and Mrs Robert Lineaweaver and Family
1240 E. Cumberland St.
Avon, Pa.

[Return Address:]
B. Knepper
Bernard, Iowa

Dad & the boys & girls,
Good night mother and
God Bless _____
ways. _____
much soo_____
to write th_____
mother _____
you. My _____
hope to se_____

I'm still well mother
and I'm _____
hope to _____
all soon, _____
very long_____
is over.
We are _____
to move _____
the two _____
and we're _____
hines to _____
the move _____
leave Se_____
We go _____
Instead o_____
we're gett_____
guess we _____
almost m_____
I hope _____
stay well_____

was asking myself why it
couldn't have happened 4 months
ago. We all _____
much mot_____
tears in my_____
of him.
I went _____
"chuck." We_____
and I've s_____
only had on_____
I sent both_____
give you o_____
it mother_____
spoiled it_____
my hat on_____
We saw _____
and Sund_____
saw the _____
Princess_____
a lot of ot_____
they were_____
the Than_____

Tue. Aug. 21st
1945

My Darling Mother:
I love you with all my
heart mother and I miss you
all an awful lot.
I received 2 letters from
you to-day mother, and
3 from Betty, it was the first
mail in over a week. I was
very happy to hear from
you.
We changed A.P.O.'s last
week, it 557 now, that
stopped the mail a couple
days and then V.J.-Day came
and that stopped everything.
We had off Wed. + Thur. and
we really celebrated, but all
the time, but all the time I

[Postmark is U.S. Army Postal Service A.P.O., 592, Aug. 23, 1945]

Mrs. Robert Lineaweaver
Avon, (Lebanon County)
Pennsylvania

[Return Address:]
Pfc. Jim L. Lineaweaver
661st Air Material Sqd.
411th Air Service Group
A.P.O. 557 (33500943)
c/o P.M., New York City

[This is one of numerous letters written by Wilson's brother Jim to his mother at home. At the time of this letter, Jim was with the U.S. Army stationed in England and here refers to his brother, whom he called "Wils" in other letters.]

Tue. Aug. 21st 1945

My Darling Mother:

I love you with all my heart mother and I miss you all an awful lot.

I received 2 letters from you to-day mother, and 3 from Betty, it was the first mail in over a week. I was very happy to hear from you.

We changed A.P.O.'s last week, its 557 now, that stopped the mail a couple days and than VJ-Day came and that stopped everything.

We had off Wed. & Thur. and we really celebrated, but all the time, but all the time I was asking myself why it couldn't have happened 4 months ago. We all loved him so awful much mother, I always get tears in my eyes when I think of him.

I went to London Friday with "Chuck". We had our picture taken and I've sent them to Betty. I only had one big envelope so I sent both to Betty and she'll give you one. I hope you like it mother but I think I spoiled it by not having my hat on the right way.

We saw 3 shows in London, and Sunday after noon we saw the King & Queen, the two Princesses, Churchill, Attle, and a lot of other English Big Shots. They were at St. Pauls for the Thanksgiving Services.

I'm still well mother and I'm taking good care. I hope to be home with you all soon, it shouldn't take very long now since the war is over.

We are finally getting ready to move to Germany. We closed the two coke bars yesterday and we're packing up the machines to move. They closed the movie too. I think we'll leave Sept. some time.

We go for rations to-morrow. Instead of getting 2 weeks rations we're getting 6 weeks, so I guess we'll be working until almost mid-night.

I hope your all well and stay well. Give my love to Dad & the boys & girls.

Good night mother and God Bless you all always. I'll write again soon, much sooner than it took me to write this one. I love you mother and I never forget you. My love to all, and I hope to see you all soon.

Your Loving Son
Your Jimmie Sr.

again.

I know you have been more
than busy
and now
boys atten
I would
again soo

My h
your fam

the bombing. You are very
fortunate t
letter wa
rather spe
my birth
have it.

You
in so
could neve
helped
him.
you so

I wa
erronou
religion
his newly

Has
home? I
and kno
will he

3.

diary he was keeping among
them?
It was r
him. If
thing sai
a person
wouldn't
would ime
me to e
them and
anything

I am
you asker
visit to m
they are.
the le
on the 11
been only

2.

Tues. night
Sept. 4, 1945

Dear Mrs. Lineaweaver,

It has been quite some time
since my last letter from you
and I'm sorry I was so long
in returning the letter you inclosed,
but I wanted a copy of it and
until a week ago I didn't have
the opportunity to type it.

Have you heard from any-
one who was with Wilson on
the ship? I would appreciate
the address of anyone who knew
anything concerning his last few
months. Did you receive his
personal belongings? Was the

[Postmark is Bernard, Iowa, Sept. 5, 1945, PM]
Mrs. Earlene Lineaweaver
1240 E. Cumberland St.
Avon, Pa.

[Return Address:]
B. Knepper
Bernard, Iowa

[This is a letter from Wilson's fiancé Bette Knepper to Wilson's mother, one of several correspondences after Wilson's death.]

Tues. night
Sept. 4, 1945

Dear Mrs. Lineaweaver,

It has been quite some time since my last letter from you and I'm sorry I was so long in returning the letter you enclosed, but I wanted a copy of it and until a week ago I didn't have the opportunity to type it.

Have you heard from anyone who was with Wilson on the ship? I would appreciate the address of anyone who knew anything concerning his last few months. Did you receive his personal belongings? Was the diary he was keeping among them? Also his white scarf? It was rather a keep-sake for him. If there is any little thing such as papers, pictures or personal things which you wouldn't miss too much, it would mean everything nice to me to even just see or read them and I promise to return anything you want.

I am sending the pictures you asked for at the first visit to my sister's house where they are.

The letter Wilson wrote you on the 11th of May must have been only a short time before the bombing. You are very fortunate to have that. My last letter was dated May 6th a rather special one since that was my birthday. I am so happy to have it.

You have been very thoughtful in so many things and you could never know how it has helped just to hear things about him. I appreciate it & thank you so very much.

I was sorry to see the erronous statement as to his religion. He was so proud of his newly adopted Catholic faith.

Has your son Jimmie returned home? I so often think of him and know what a consolation it will be to have him with you again.

I know you have been more than busy this time of the year and now especially with the two boys attending school again but I would like to hear from you again soon.

My best regards to all your family.

Sincerely,
Bette

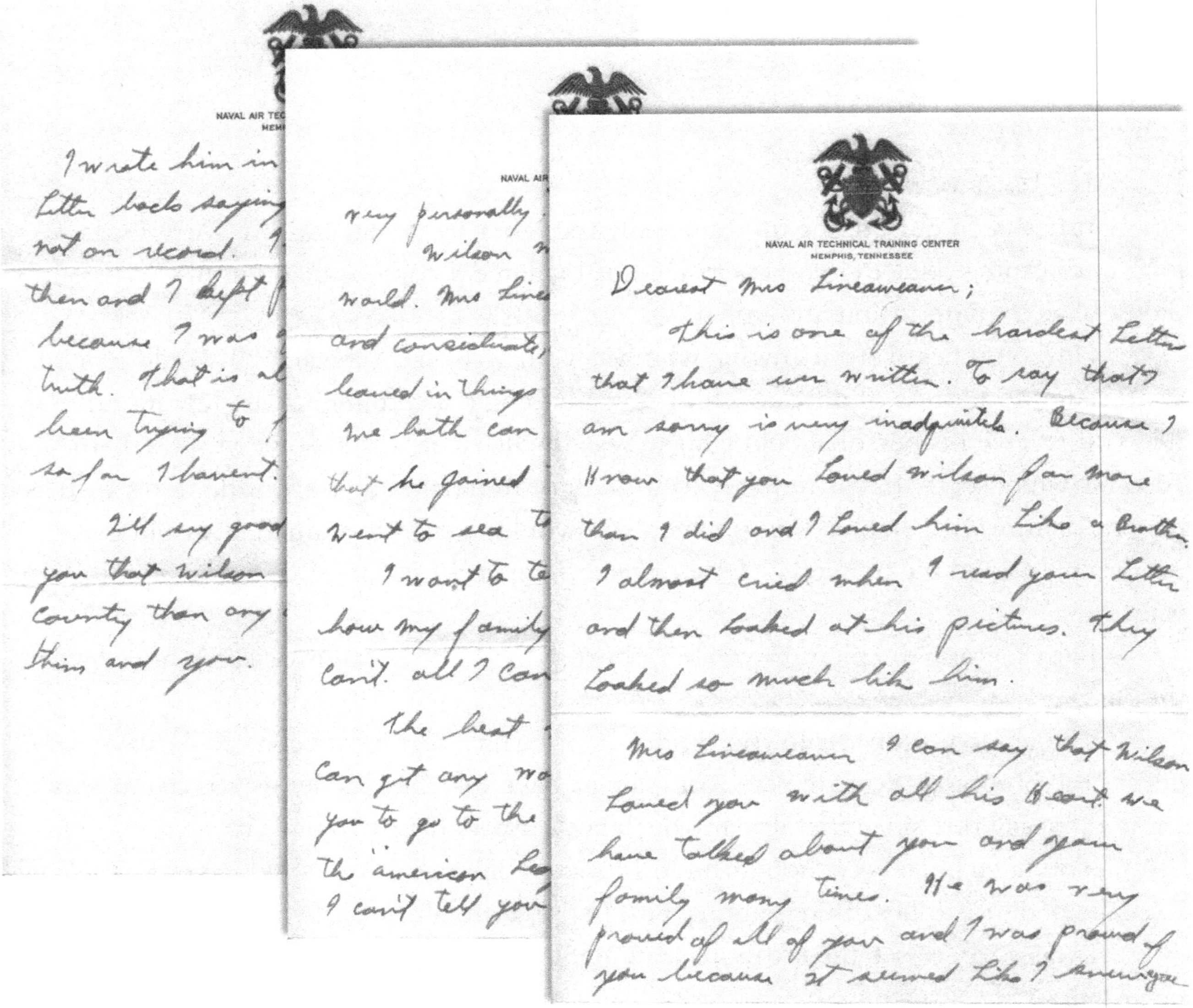

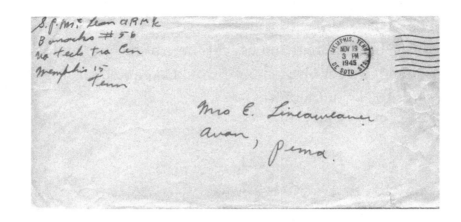

Page 1 (leftmost, partial):

I wrote him in
letter back saying
not on record. 1
then and I kept f
because I was
truth. that is al
been trying to f
so far I haven't.

I'll say good
you that Wilson
country than any
thing and you.

Page 2 (middle, partial):

NAVAL AIR
MEM

very personally
Wilson
world. Mrs Linea
and considerate,
leaned in things
we both can
that he gained
went to sea

I want to te
how my family
can't. all I can

the heat
can get any wo
you to go to the
the American Le
I can't tell you

Page 3 (rightmost):

NAVAL AIR TECHNICAL TRAINING CENTER
MEMPHIS, TENNESSEE

Dearest Mrs Lineaweaver;

this is one of the hardest letters
that I have ever written. To say that I
am sorry is very inadequate. Because I
know that you loved Wilson far more
than I did and I loved him like a brother.
I almost cried when I read your letter
and then looked at his pictures. they
looked so much like him.

Mrs Lineaweaver I can say that Wilson
loved you with all his heart we
have talked about you and your
family many times. He was very
proud of all of you and I was proud of
you because it seemed like I knew you

Envelope:

S. f. Mc Lean aRMk
Barracks #56
na tech tra Cen
Memphis 15
Tenn

MEMPHIS, TENN
NOV 19
3 PM
1945
DE SOTO ST

Mrs E. Lineaweaver
Avan,
Penna.

[Note: This letter was written by Wilson's good friend, Sam McLean, to Wilson's mother.]

Dearest Mrs Lineaweaver;

This is one of the hardest Letters that I have ever written. To say that I am sorry is very inadqwitch. Because I know that you Loved Wilson far more than I did and I Loved him Like a Brother. I almost cried when I read your Letter and then Looked at his pictures. They Looked so much like him.

Mrs Lineaweaver I can say that Wilson Loved you with all his Heart. We have talked about you and your family many times. He was very proud of all of you and I was proud of you because it seemed Like I knew you very personally.

Wilson was the greatest man in the world. Mrs Lineaweaver. He was good and considerate, had Lots of fun and beleaved in things that he should. We both can be very glad and happy that he Joined the church before he went to sea this last time.

I want to tell you how I feal and how my family and wife feal but I can't. all I can say is that "I am sorry."

The best way I know that you can get any word of his death is for you to go to the Red Cross and then to the "American Ledgon". I am sorry but I can't tell you any thing about it.

I wrote him in May and then I got the letter back saying that his address was not on record. I was afraid for him then and I kept putting it off writting you because I was afraid to find out the truth. That is all that I know. I have been trying to find out all I can but so far I havent.

I'll say good by for now and tell you that Wilson did more for his country than any one I know. God Bless him and you.

Your Friend
Sam

[Postmark is Memphis, Tenn., De Soto Sta., November 19, 1945, 3 PM]
Mrs E. Lineaweaver
Avon, Penna.

[Return Address:]
S.P. McLean ARM 1/c
Barracks #56
Na Tech Tra Cen
Memphis 15 Tenn

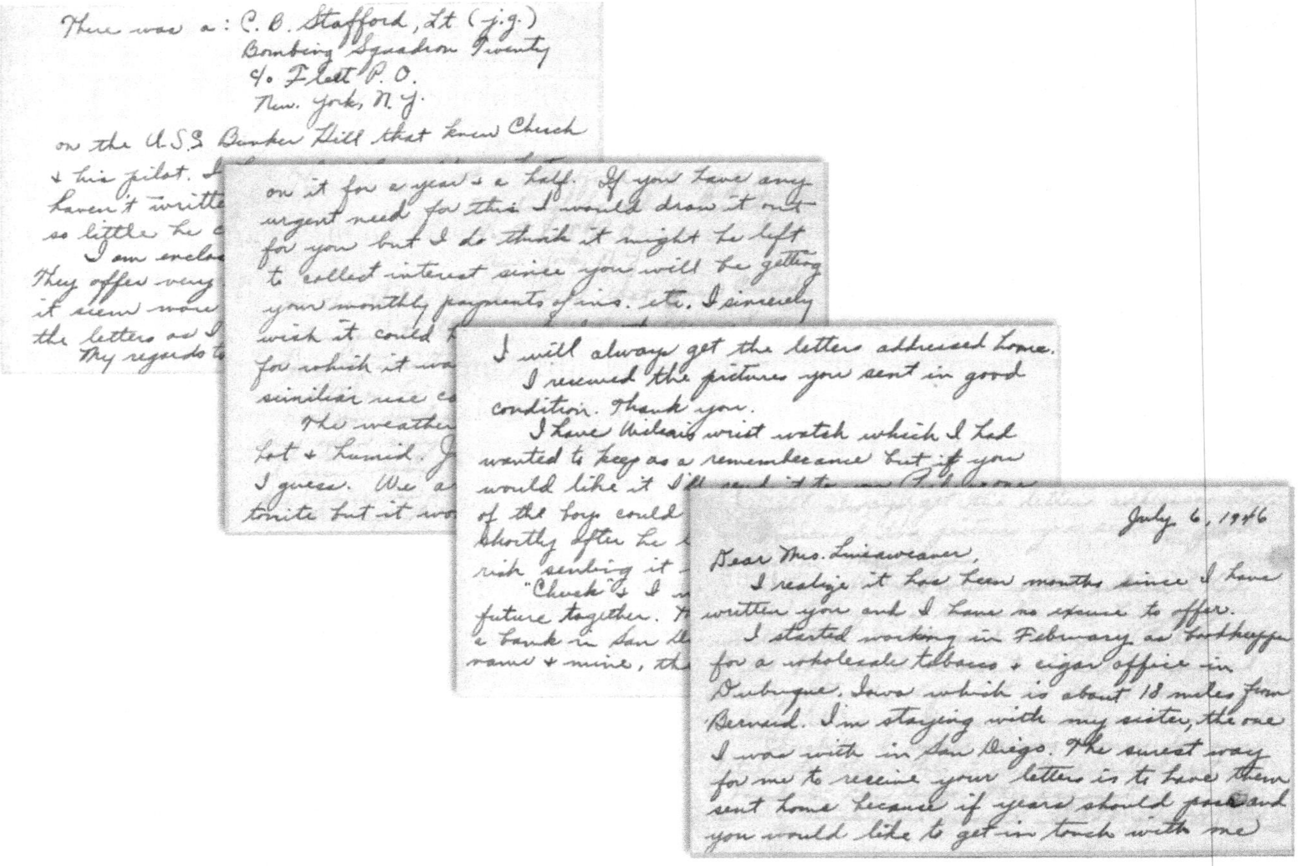

There was a: C. B. Stafford, Lt (j.g.)
Bombing Squadron Twenty
c/o Fleet P.O.
New York, N.Y.
on the U.S.S. Bunker Hill that knew Chuck
+ his pilot.
haven't writte
so little he c
I am enclos
They offer very
it seem more
the letters as I
My regards to

on it for a year & a half. If you have any
urgent need for this I would draw it out
for you but I do think it might be left
to collect interest since you will be getting
your monthly payments of ins. etc. I sincerely
wish it could
for which it wa
similar use c
The weather
hot + humid.
I guess. We a
tonite but it wo

I will always get the letters addressed home.
I received the pictures you sent in good
condition. Thank you.
I have Wilson's wrist watch which I had
wanted to keep as a remembrance but if you
would like it I'll send it to
of the boys could
Shortly after he
risk sending it
"Chuck" & I
future together.
a bank in San D
name + mine, the

July 6, 1946
Dear Mrs. Lineaweaver,
I realize it has been months since I have
written you and I have no excuse to offer.
I started working in February as bookkeeper
for a wholesale tobacco + cigar office in
Dubuque, Iowa which is about 18 miles from
Bernard. I'm staying with my sister, the one
I was with in San Diego. The surest way
for me to receive your letters is to have them
sent home because if years should pass and
you would like to get in touch with me

[Postmark is Dubuque, Iowa, July 11, 1946, 2 PM]
Mrs. Earlene Lineaweaver
1240 E. Cumberland St.
Lebanon, Pa.

[Return Address:]
B. Knepper
Bernard, Iowa

[Note: This letter was written by Wilson's fiance, Bette Knepper, to his mother.]

July 6, 1946

Dear Mrs. Lineaweaver,

I realize it has been months since I have written you and I have no excuse to offer.

I started working in February as bookkeeper for a wholesale tobacco & cigar office in Dubuque, Iowa which is about 18 miles from Bernard. I'm staying with my sister, the one I was with in San Diego. The surest way for me to receive your letters is to have them sent home because if years should pass and you would like to get in touch with me I will always get the letters addressed home.

I received the pictures you sent in good condition. Thank you.

I have Wilson's wrist watch which I had wanted to keep as a rememberance but if you would like it I'll send it to you. Perhaps one of the boys could wear it. I had it repaired shortly after he left but he didn't want me to risk sending it because mail was so uncertain.

"Chuck" & I were saving money for our future together. This is in a savings acct. in a bank in San Diego. The account is in his name & mine, the amount is $325. plus the interest on it for a year & a half. If you have any urgent need for this I would draw it out for you but I do think it might be left to collect interest since you will be getting your monthly payments of ins. etc. I sincerely wish it could be used for the purpose for which it was saved but perhaps some similiar use can be found for it.

The weather here has been unbearably hot & humid. Just a typical summer seige I guess. We are having a light shower tonite but it won't amount to much.

There was a:	C.B. Stafford, Lt (j.g.)
	Bombing Squadron Twenty
	c/o Fleet P.O.
	New York, N.Y.

on the U.S.S. Bunker Hill that knew Chuck & his pilot. I have had his address but haven't written to him. Seems like there's so little he could write us about.

I am enclosing two other letters I received. They offer very little information but they make it seem more real. Will you please return the letters as I would like to keep them.

My regards to your family. Please write.

Bette.

[This is a letter written by Lt. C.B. Stafford who served with Wilson aboard the USS Bunker Hill.]

BOMBING SQUADRON TWENTY
c/o FLEET POST OFFICE
NEW YORK, N. Y.

9 September 1946

Dear Mrs. Lineaweaver,

I am writing to you in regard to "Chuck" Lineaweaver, with whom I had the pleasure of serving aboard ship with, on the "Bunker Hill".

"Chuck" flew in my division for quite some time and was very efficient as an AirCrewman. I can remember quite well that many times I have looked over in his direction and found a reassuring look. Our aircrewmen swore by their pilots and aided a great deal to ease the strain of combat. Lineaweaver's performance aboard ship was excelent, and I am sure that to the last he did his share in helping to save the ship and crew.

His Pilot was Lieut. Lamb, from Lubbock, Texas, and as far as I have heard he is out of the service now. I was in NewPort, R.I., a few week-ends ago and saw our old Commanding Officer, Comdr. J.P.Conn, he is attending the General Line School there. His address is 12B. Constelation St. The Anchorage, NewPort, R.I.

Someone sent a book to me a few days ago in which there was several stories about Air Group 84, the name was the new edition of "Helldiver Squadron".

I am now Personnel and Administrative Officer for Air Group (Bombing Squadron-20) 20, stationed in Charlestown, Rhode Island. Still flying the Helldiver.

Mrs Lineaweaver, if there is anything you would like to know, or that I can do for you, please do not hesitate to call on me.

Give my regards to Mrs. Behney.

Sincerely,

Lt. C. B. Stafford, USN

[Note: This letter was written by Wilson's fiancé, Bette Knepper, to his mother.]

November 3, 1946

Dear Mrs. Lineaweaver,

As usual I make apoligies for my delay in writing to you but time seems to be slipping by so quickly one can't keep up to it. It doesn't seem possible we're in the first week of Nov. already. Summer just seemed to have come and now it's winter again. We've been having simply beautiful weather for this time of the year, there hasn't even been a killing frost as yet. Our flowers are still in bloom which isn't at all natural for now.

I have been attending quite a number of football game this fall but declined a chance to go today because it's dark and quite cold this afternoon. I imagine you have much football talk with the two boys. Saw the Notre Dame-Iowa game last week which was quite a thrill.

I remember Wilson mentioning about leaving the books on the plane. He had said perhaps they would be of some help to the person picking them up. We didn't really think they would bother to return them. He left them on the plane at Chicago, I believe, when he was put off because of proirity.

Have you received any correspondence from Mrs. Lane, the people Wilson spent so much time with in San Diego?

Please write again.

Bette

[Postmark is Dubuque, Iowa, Nov. 5, 1946, 4 PM]
Mrs E. Lineaweaver
1240 E. Cumberland St
Avon, Pa.

[Return Address:]
B. Knepper
Bernard, Iowa

Monday afternoon
January 20, 1947

Dear Mrs. Lineaweaver,

My sister, Eileen, was out home Sunday and brought in your letter of Jan, 9th.

The Mrs. Lane I wrote about was the lady of the couple where Wilson stayed so much of the time when he first got out of the hospital. It was through her son, Jack, who was going with my girl friend at the bank, that I first met Wilson. I think Wilson mentioned that she had written to you when he was still in the hospital. She used to visit him almost every day. They own a real estate agency in San Diego. I haven't heard from her but thought perhaps you had. It seems Wilson met these people through knowing their other son who was stationed overseas.

Mrs. Lineaweaver it isn't right for you to feel you could have helped Wilson's status any by doing one thing or the other. He knew the danger he was in and mentioned it many times. When he first went back to duty after being hurt that time he could have "pulled strings" to get something but didn't want to do it because of the ill feelings he had against certain fellows who had done the same. After we started being together more he tried to get stationed in the States but it was too late then. One reads so often of fellows who had gone throught so much in the war then came home only to be killed in some simple accident. Also Wilson had mentioned so many times that he would much sooner not come back than to be crippled or blind as so many were. You have to try to believe that it was, somehow, for the best. You make it so hard for yourself by having people write about him to keep the memory of him fresh in your mind. I know it is none of my business and I haven't the right to write this way but it would be so much more to Wilson's liking to center your attentions around the rest of your family who still have a life to map out for themselves and help them get a right start so they can become the wonderful, sweet tempered, lovable personality Wilson was.

The money in the savings account at San Diego is still there for any necessity which might arise.

We have been having simply wonderful weather for the middle of winter, I know we haven't had more than a week of really cold wintery weather so far. We had a little snow today and it is to get down to 5°below zero by morning, so perhaps we'll get our share yet. Still when a person thinks that there can't be more than two months of winter anymore it doesn't seem so bad at all.

I changed jobs about two weeks ago, and I don't have to work as hard and steady as I did before. I feel so much better now --Perhaps I can gain a little weight. I've been trying for so long to gain but I just can't seem to. When Wilson left the States I weighed more than I ever had but lost it when he left and have never been able to gain it back. I only weigh 102½ and would happy to weigh 112. That is rather unusual for someone to want to gain, because most girls would give anything if they could lose. I guess there is a happy medium though.

I really should close and get back to my work again, so until I hear from you again, I will close with best regards to all----- Write !!

as ever
Bette

Wilson's Girl (?)

1-20-47

Mrs. Earlene Lineaweaver
1240 E. Cumberland St.
Avon, Pa.

[Postmark is Dubuque, Iowa, Jan. 20, 1947, 8 PM]
Mrs. Earlene
      Lineaweaver
1240 E. Cumberland St.
Avon, Pa.

[No Return Address]

[Note: This letter was written by Wilson's fiance, Bette Knepper, to his mother.]

Monday afternoon
January 20, 1947

Dear Mrs. Lineaweaver,

My sister, Eileen, was out home Sunday and brought in your letter of Jan, 9th.

The Mrs. Lane I wrote about was the lady of the couple where Wilson stayed so much of the time when he first got out of the hospital. It was through her son, Jack, who was going with my girl friend at the bank, that I first met Wilson. I think Wilson mentioned that she had written to you when he was still in the hospital. She used to visit him almost every day. They own a real estate agency in San Diego. I haven't heard from her but thought perhaps you had. It seems Wilson met these people through knowing their other son who was stationed overseas.

Mrs. Lineaweaver it isn't right for you to feel you could have helped Wilson's status any by doing one thing or the other. He knew the danger he was in and mentioned it many times. When he first went back to duty after being hurt that time he could have "pulled strings" to get something but didn't want to do it because of the ill feelings he had against certain fellows who had done the same. After we started being together more he tried to get stationed in the States but it was too late then. One reads so often of fellows who had gone through so much in the war then came home only to be killed in some simple accident. Also Wilson had mentioned so many times that he would much sooner not come back than to be crippled or blind as so many were. You have to try to believe that it was, somehow, for the best. You make it so hard for yourself by having people write about him to keep the memory of him fresh in your mind. I know it is none of my business and I haven't the right to write this way but it would be so much more to Wilson's likeing to center your attentions around the rest of your family who still have a life to map out for themselves and help them get a right start so they can become the wonderful, sweet tempered, lovable personality Wilson was.

The money in the savings account at San Diego is still there for any necessity which might arise.

We have been having simply wonderful weather for the middle of winter, I know we haven't had more than a week of really cold wintery weather so far. We had a little snow today and it is to get down to 5° below zero by morning, so perhaps we'll get our share yet. Still when a person thinks that there can't be more than two months of winter anymore it doesn't seem so bad at all.

I changed jobs about two weeks ago, and I don't have to work as hard and steady as I did before. I feel so much better now -- Perhaps I can gain a little weight. I've been trying for so long to gain but I just can't seem to. When Wilson left the States I weighed more than I ever had but lost it when he left and have never been able to gain it back. I only weigh 102 ½ and would happy to weigh 112. That is rather unusual for someone to want to gain, because most girls would give anything if they could lose. I guess there is a happy medium though.

I really should close and get back to my work again, so until I hear from you again, I will close with best regards to all ----- Write!!

As ever,
Bette

II

He told me a lot ~~that~~ of how good
friend they ...
on liberty ...
Tommorow ...
I'll tell you ...
told me.
    I'll say ...
write again ...

all the ships he was on. His accident
which I will tell you about later in
another letter ...
ever since ...
went thru ...
    He called ...
& said every ...
a excellent ...
squadron ...
I don't me ...
enlisted m ...
Many thing ...
Sam (He) was a ...
was transfe ...
pictures al ...
see them ...
to ask hi ...
    Jame is ...
about 5'7" ...
like that ...
looking. ...
rest of the ...
    I was al ...
started tal ...
crying whe ...
the things.

July 9, 1952
Wensday

Dear Mother,
    This letter will be the most welcomed
~~few~~ letter to you I have ever written.
Every other letter I write I tell you
only of my self. This time I'll tell you
of some ~~one~~ dear to you.
    Tonigh Wensday was a big clean
up at school. We worked in a little office
We had finished & I went in a little
room to get my book. Lewis a colored
fellow from Carliel Pa, who I work with
said "I mean we can get more." A cheif said
just "I mean we can," By this time I was
setting on a bench again. He said what
state are you from I said Pa. He said
Avon. I said "Yea" "Do you know
"Chuck." that all I heard. It was
Sam Mc Dean. He came over & was
shaking my hand. I was taken by
surprise & was stunned. My knees were
shakey. We talked for about ½ hr.
& Beleve me. By what He said Wils
was every thing I ever thought he
was & even more. We disgused.

[No envelope remains with this letter.]

[Note: This letter was written by Wilson's youngest brother, Harold, to their mother, when Harold was in the U.S. Navy.]

July 9, 1952
Wensday

Dear Mother,

This letter will be the most welcomed letter to you I have ever written. Every other letter I write I tell you only of myself. This time I'll tell you of some one dear to you.

Tonigh Wensday was a big clean up at school. We worked in a little office We had finished & I went in a little room to get my book. Lewis a colored fellow from Carlial. Pa., who I work with said, "Lineaweaver get mine." A cheif said just "Lineaweaver" By this time I was sitting on a bench again. He said what state are you from I said Pa. He said Avon. I said "Yea" "Do you know "chuck." thats all I heard. It was Sam McLean. He came over & was shaking my hand. I was taken by suprise & was stunned. My knees were shakey. We talked for about ½ hr. & Believe me. By what He said Wils was every thing I ever thought he was. & even more. We disgused all the ships he was on. His accident. which I will tell you about later in another letter. They had been buddies ever since boot camp in Norfolk. They went thru Jacksonville together.

He called him "Chuck" all the time & said every one liked him & that he was a excellent radio man the best in the squadron. He was Cheif radio man I [??] me rate. All the other enlisted men were under him. Many things he told me about him. Sam (He) was at Rhode Iseland but he was transferred back. He is bringing pictures along tomorrow. So I can see them. I am thinking of Question to ask him.

Sam is about the same size as Wils about 5'7" 5'6" 5'8" something like that. He is about 30-35. Good looking. He ask about you & the rest of the family & about Dot.

I was all nervous when we first started talking. I felt a little like crying when he told me some of the things.

He told me a lot of how good freinds they were & what fun they had on liberty together. He is a cheif. Tommorow when I can think clearer I'll tell you some of the stories he told me.

I'll say Good night now & I'll write again tommorow

Sincerely
Harold.

[Note: The location is unknown of any letter Harold may have written regarding the things Sam McLean told him about Wilson.]

Got to stop now.
I'll write tommorow

(2)

So it ... lol held me in my hir t a
a park ... a Country Youth Fellowship & H ask the
to do. ... girl & Jackie & I went along. From T hen
I th ... on. H went with her
letter ... Well ...
take a ... oldest
times ... mornin
Bet ... again
long ti ... next F
don't ... & I ma
lady. ... I got ho
W ... of whi
It is a ... I
paid. ... questi
pane ... on it.
W ... grade
wear ... on la
would ... school
on the ... study
That ... gradua
chute ... dom t
don t ... give in
We ... of Ja
... 5 big
... up. Bo
... what
... nights
... I want

August 7, 1952
Thursday.

Dear Mother,

Received 3 letters today One from
Dick one from Jackie & one from you.
Well just 12 more day time sure goes
slow now.
We only flew once this week. Then
Wensday it rained like o mad Tommoron
we are supposed to go up, but I think they
may change the schedul. I hope not: the
one time I was up I liked it very much
well at least I was up any way.
I met another fellow that new Wilson.
I couldn't talk to him long. We had to
go. He was with him up tell 4-2 I don't
know his name maybe I'll see him again.
He works in the hangers where we get our
parachute & harnesses. I'll try to find
him again.
Jackie Hains send me a clipping
of the accident down at the ⟵ Sounds
rough.
She also send a clipping of the Wedding
y Wilson Miller Jr. So Cap married the
girl Not bad. I was with the first
night he took the girl home. We were t

[No envelope remains with this letter.]

[Note: This letter was written by Wilson's youngest brother, Harold, to their mother, when Harold was in the U.S. Navy.]

August 7, 1952
Thursday.

Dear Mother,

Received 3 letters today One from Dick one from Jackie & one from you.

Well Just 12 more day time sure goes slow now.

We only flew once this week. Then Wensday it rained like mad Tommorow we are susposed to go up, but I think they may change the schedule. I hope not: the one time I was up I liked it very much well at least I was up any way.

I met another fellow that new Wilson. I couldn't talk to him long. We had to go. He was with him up till 1942. I don't know his name maybe I'll see him again. He works in the hangers where we get our parachute & harnesses. I'll try to find him again.

Jackie Hains send me a clipping of the accident down at the *[Harold drew a picture of a Y intersection here]* Sounds rough.

She also send a clipping of the Wedding of Wilson Miller Jr. So Cap married the girl Not bad. I was with the first night he took the girl home. We were at a County Youth Fellowship & He ask the girl & Jackie & I went along. From Then on. He went with her

Well Today is the last evening for the oldest company on the base tommorow morning they leave for South side again Just like we will next Friday Then we will leave a Tuesday & I may be home on a Wensday. When I get home I wear a real starched pr of whites to Church.

I passed the final test 120 questions. I think I did very good on it. I'm not sure. We find our grades out soon. Tommorow we have our last test we will have in this school. Right now I'm sorry I didn't study harder. Right like when I graduated from High school. Here they don't have graduation. They just give us a certificate like we got at Jacksonville & thats it. We get 2 big locker inspections coming up. Boy I gott the blue of it. Thats what I've been going the last few nights stensling clothing Last Night I went to volentary night school So it would help me in my big test.

I'm very glad to hear we are going to a park. I can't think of any thing nicer to do.

I think you had better send the last letter the 14. on a Thursday. Because it take a good 2 days to get here some times 3.

Betty's Aunt's staying at Jims a long time. Usually things like that don't last long. She must be a good lady.

We don't have to take out insurance It is automatic. I have $10,000 Government paid. It goes automaticly to both parents (if alive) in case if not to the family.

We had to fill out sheets Because we are flying. In case something would go wrong. No one was killed on the flights we go on in 7 years. Thats a good record. We have chutes anyway

All the accidents happen at once don't they.

Well time to sign off now

Got to stop now.

I'll write tommorow

Sincerely Yours
Harold.

life.

desire

numb

My se

electr

day an

skin t

finger

I beca

built

My ma

sample

own i

only a

master

never

a diff

had to

bargai

---

fewe

leave

much

know

of my

The d

my de

sorou

the tree

numb

to the p

was c

office

Christn

on the

home

metal

momen

Much better.

My Favorite Toy

H Lineaweaver
Eng 11-C
9-20-57
C-

for Christmas in 1942 I received an erector set. This erector set became my most treasured toy because of my desire for it, and because it now has a special meaning. I was eight years old, and from the clothing people gave to us, and from the house we lived in I knew that our family was not well-to-do. However, we were not hungry. Erector sets were expensive, especially the larger sets, and because of the war there were not many sets for sale.

It is very difficult to imagine one-self a young boy, especially a boy with a desire for such a toy. I remember staring, for a long time, at these toys in the basement of the Bon Ton. My desire was intense; how-ever, I never felt the impulse to steal one, and I did not desire a large number 10 set, but only a number 1 set. I often went to look at these toys, and the closer Christmas came the

[Note: This is a paper Wilson's youngest brother Harold wrote for his college English class in 1957.
He received a grade of C-. The erector set he later gave to a nephew.]

H Lineaweaver
Eng 11-C
9-20-57

My Favorite Toy

For Christmas in 1942 I received an erector set. This erector set became my most treasured toy; because of my desire for it, and because it now has a special meaning. I was eight years old, and from the clothing people gave to us, and from the house we lived in I knew that our family was not well-to-do. However, we were not hungry. Erector sets were expensive, especially the larger sets, and because of the war there were not many sets for sale.

It is very difficult to imagine oneself a young boy, especially a boy with a desire for such a toy. I remember staring, for a long time, at these toys in the basement of the Bon Ton. My desire was intense; however, I never felt the impulse to steal one, and I did not desire a large number 10 set, but only a number 1 set. I often went to look at these toys, and the closer Christmas came the fewer were the sets that remained.

My brother Wilson came home on leave from the Navy. I did not know much about the war at that time, but I did know Wils was a hero by the conversation of my family, which later I understood. The day he came home I hinted to him my desire for the prized set.

Christmas morning came, and to my sorrow there was no erector set under the tree for me. I had hoped for at least a number 1 set. Then my mother sent me to the post office. In our small town it was customary for the one room post office to be open for a couple hours on Christmas to disperse the mail that came on the morning train. When I returned home with the mail I saw a bright red metal box under the tree. The next few moments were the most exciting in my life. I knew my other brothers had no desire for an erector set, and I knew a number 1 set came in a cardboard box. My set was a number 6; it had an electric motor with many gears. That day and many days afterwards I wore the skin thin on my thumbs and index fingers building examples from the book. I became very familiar with the set, and built hundred's of examples. My masterpiece was a mixture of three samples from the book, and some of my own ideas. When I was finished there were only a few pieces not used. I kept my masterpiece a long time to show Wils, but he never saw it. Later I learned Wils had a difficult time getting my set for me. He had to go to the Bon Ton's warehouse and bargain for it.

Note: The first Air Medal given to Wilson in January 1943 for action on October 26, 1942, is the only medal and award listed here that was not given posthumously. In addition, see his letter dated May 10, 1944, where he states he was given three stars on his wings [aircrew badge] for engaging the enemy in combat of: plane against plane, plane against ship, and plane against enemy installation.

PURPLE HEART

The Purple Heart is awarded to members of the Armed Forces of the United States who after April 5, 1917, have been wounded or killed in action against an enemy of the United States or an opposing armed force, while serving with friendly foreign forces engaged in an armed conflict, as the result of acts of enemy or hostile opposing forces, as a result of terrorist attacks or attacks on peacekeeping forces since March 28, 1973, or by friendly fire in circumstance as described above.

DISTINGUISHED FLYING CROSS

The Distinguished Flying Cross is awarded to a member of the United States Armed Forces who distinguished himself or herself by heroism or extraordinary achievement while participating in aerial flight. An act of heroism must be evidenced by voluntary action above and beyond the call of duty. Extraordinary achievement must have resulted in an accomplishment so exceptional and outstanding as to clearly set the individual apart from others in similar circumstances. Awards will only be made to recognize single acts of heroism or extraordinary achievement, and not in recognition of sustained operations.

AIR MEDAL - FIRST

The Air Medal is awarded to a person who, while serving with the United States Armed Forces, has distinguished himself or herself by meritorious achievement while participating in aerial flight. Awards may recognize single acts of heroism or merit, or may recognize sustained meritorious service over a period of six months or more. The Air Medal primarily recognizes personnel on flight status requiring frequent participation in aerial flight. It may be awarded to personnel not on flight status whose duties require frequent flight other than in a passenger status. The Air Medal ranks behind the Distinguished Flying Cross in order of precedence.

GOLD STAR In Lieu Of AIR MEDALS - SECOND, THIRD, FOURTH

The Gold Star is awarded and worn for the second and subsequent awards of the same medal, to a maximum of four. It is attached to the medal's ribbon.

PRESIDENTIAL UNIT CITATION And RIBBON BAR With STAR

The Presidential Unit Citation (PUC) is awarded to units of the United States Armed Forces, and those of allied countries, for extraordinary heroism in action against an armed enemy on or after December 7, 1941. The unit must display such gallantry, determination, and esprit de corps in accomplishing its mission under extremely difficult and hazardous conditions so as to set it apart from and above other units participating in the same campaign. The collective degree of valor (combat heroism) against an armed enemy by the unit nominated for the PUC is the same as that which would warrant award of the individual award of the Distinguished Service Cross, Air Force Cross, or NAVY CROSS.

AMERICAN DEFENSE SERVICE MEDAL
The American Defense Service Medal is awarded to personnel in the Armed Forces who served on active duty between September 8, 1939, and December 7, 1941. Wording on the reverse of the medal reads: "For Service During the Limited Emergency Proclaimed by the President on September 8, 1939 or During the Unlimited Emergency Period Proclaimed by the President on May 27, 1941".

WORLD WAR II VICTORY MEDAL
The World War II Victory Medal is awarded to all members of the Armed Forces of the United States who served on active duty in World War II at any time between December 7, 1941 and December 31, 1946.

AMERICAN CAMPAIGN MEDAL
The American Campaign Medal is awarded for service within the American Theater between December 7, 1941, and March 2, 1946, under any of the following conditions: (1) On permanent assignment outside the continental limits of the United States. (2) Permanently assigned as a member of a crew of a vessel sailing ocean waters for a period of 30 days or 60 non-consecutive days. (3) Permanently assigned as a member of an operating crew of an airplane actually making regular and frequent flights over ocean waters for a period of 30 days. (4) Outside the continental limits of the United States in a passenger status or on temporary duty for 30 consecutive days or 60 days not consecutive. (5) In active combat against the enemy and was awarded a combat decoration or furnished a certificate by the commanding general of a corps, higher unit, or independent force that he actually participated in combat. (6) Within the continental limits of the United States for an aggregate period of one year.

ASIATIC-PACIFIC CAMPAIGN MEDAL
The Asiatic-Pacific Campaign Medal is awarded to members of the U.S. Armed Forces for at least 30 consecutive (60 non-consecutive) days service (less if in combat) within the Asiatic-Pacific Theater between December 7, 1941 and March 2, 1946.

GOOD CONDUCT MEDAL
The Navy Good Conduct Medal is awarded to enlisted personnel of the United States Navy and Naval Reserve (active duty) for creditable, above average professional performance, military behavior, leadership, military appearance and adaptability based on good conduct and faithful service for three-year periods of continuous active service.

PRESIDENT HARRY TRUMAN'S CONDOLENCE CERTIFICATE
An official certificate from the U.S. President to honor those killed in action in military service.

PURPLE HEART Letter

In reply address not the signer of this
letter, but Bureau of Naval Personnel,
Navy Department, Washington, D. C.
Refer to No.

Pers-68- AA
MM/258 32 24

17 SEP 1945

NAVY DEPARTMENT

BUREAU OF NAVAL PERSONNEL

WASHINGTON 25, D. C.

FOR VICTORY
BUY
UNITED
STATES
WAR
BONDS
AND
STAMPS

Mr. Robert Joseph Lineaweaver
1240 East Cumberland Street
Lebanon, Pennsylvania

Dear Mr. Lineaweaver:

The Bureau has the honor to inform you of the Award of the Purple
Heart and certificate to your late son, Wilson Charles Lineaweaver,

Aviation Chief Radioman, United States Navy,

in accordance with General Order 186 of January 21, 1943 which reads
in part as follows:

> "The Secretary of the Navy is further author-
> ized and directed to award the Purple Heart
> posthumously, in the name of the President of the
> United States, to any persons who, while serving
> in any capacity with the Navy, Marine Corps or
> Coast Guard of the United States, since December 6,
> 1941, are killed in action or who die as a direct
> result of wounds received in action with an enemy
> of the United States, or as a result of an act of
> such enemy."

The medal is being forwarded under separate cover. Please acknowledge
receipt on the enclosed form.

By direction of Chief of Naval Personnel.

Sincerely yours,

R. J. HARDY
Commander, U.S.N.
Enlisted Performance Division

PURPLE HEART Certificate

THE UNITED STATES OF AMERICA

TO ALL WHO SHALL SEE THESE PRESENTS, GREETING:

THIS IS TO CERTIFY THAT

THE PRESIDENT OF THE UNITED STATES OF AMERICA
PURSUANT TO AUTHORITY VESTED IN HIM BY CONGRESS
HAS AWARDED THE

PURPLE HEART

ESTABLISHED BY GENERAL GEORGE WASHINGTON
AT NEWBURGH, NEW YORK, AUGUST 7, 1782

TO

Wilson Charles Tineaweaver, Aviation Chief Radioman, United States Navy

FOR MILITARY MERIT AND FOR WOUNDS RECEIVED
IN ACTION

resulting in his death May 11, 1945

GIVEN UNDER MY HAND IN THE CITY OF WASHINGTON
THIS 30th DAY OF August 1945

James Forrestal
THE SECRETARY OF THE NAVY

VICE ADMIRAL, UNITED STATES NAVY
CHIEF OF NAVAL PERSONNEL

Letter For:
DISTINGUISHED FLYING CROSS
SECOND AIR MEDAL
FOURTH AIR MEDAL

2 July 1948

Mrs. Erlene N. Lineaweaver
1240 E. Cumberland Street
Lebanon, Pa.

      It is with a deep sense of the
great loss which you have sustained that I herewith forward to you, as the next of kin of the
late Wilson Charles Lineaweaver, ACRM, USN, the
Distinguished Flying Cross, and Gold Stars in lieu
of the Second and Fourth Air Medals presented to
him by the President of the United States with
citations signed by the Secretary of the Navy.

                                J. L. KAUFFMAN
                             Rear Admiral, U.S.NAVY
                 Commandant, FOURTH Naval District

Encls.
1. HW- Three Citations
2. HW- Two Gold Stars

DISTINGUISHED FLYING CROSS Citation And Medal

THE SECRETARY OF THE NAVY
WASHINGTON

The President of the United States takes pride in presenting the DISTINGUISHED FLYING CROSS posthumously to

WILSON CHARLES LINEAWEAVER
AVIATION CHIEF RADIOMAN
UNITED STATES NAVY

for service as set forth in the following

CITATION:

"For heroism and extraordinary achievement in aerial flight as Radioman-Gunner of a Dive Bomber in Bombing Squadron EIGHTY FOUR, attached to the U.S.S. BUNKER HILL, during operations against enemy Japanese forces in the vicinity of Iwo Jima, Okinawa and the Japanese Homeland from February 19 to April 29, 1945. Completing his twentieth mission during this period, LINEAWEAVER rendered valuable assistance to his pilot in inflicting extensive damage on hostile airfields, gun positions and installations. His courage and devotion to duty were in keeping with the highest traditions of the United States Naval Service."

For the President,

Secretary of the Navy

Gold Star In Lieu Of SECOND AIR MEDAL Citation

THE SECRETARY OF THE NAVY
WASHINGTON

The President of the United States takes pride in presenting the GOLD STAR in lieu of the Second Air Medal posthumously to

WILSON CHARLES LINEAWEAVER
AVIATION CHIEF RADIOMAN
UNITED STATES NAVY

for service as set forth in the following

CITATION:

"For meritorious achievement in aerial flight as a Radioman-Gunner of a Bomber Plane in Bombing Squadron EIGHTY FOUR, attached to the U.S.S. BUNKER HILL, in action against enemy Japanese forces during the invasion of Iwo Jima and in the vicinity of Okinawa, Tokyo and Kyushu from February 19 to March 18, 1945. Completing his fifth mission during this period, LINEAWEAVER contributed materially to the success of his squadron. His courageous devotion to duty in the face of grave hazards was in keeping with the highest traditions of the United States Naval Service."

For the President,

John L. Sullivan

Secretary of the Navy

Gold Star In Lieu Of FOURTH AIR MEDAL Citation

THE SECRETARY OF THE NAVY
WASHINGTON

      The President of the United States takes pride in presenting the GOLD STAR in lieu of the Fourth Air Medal post-humously to

WILSON CHARLES LINEAWEAVER
AVIATION CHIEF RADIOMAN
UNITED STATES NAVY

for service as set forth in the following

CITATION:

      "For meritorious achievement in aerial flight as Radioman-Gunner of a Dive Bomber in Bombing Squadron EIGHTY FOUR, attached to the U.S.S. BUNKER HILL, during operations against enemy Japanese forces in the vicinity of Okinawa and the Japanese Homeland from March 30 to April 19, 1945. Completing his fifth mission during this period, LINEAWEAVER rendered valuable assistance to his pilot in inflicting extensive damage on hostile, airfields, gun positions and installations and contributed materially to the success of his squadron. His courage and devotion to duty were in keeping with the highest traditions of the United States Naval Service."

For the President,

John L. Sullivan

Secretary of the Navy

Gold Star In Lieu Of THIRD AIR MEDAL Letter

In reply address not the signer of this
letter, but Bureau of Naval Personnel,
Navy Department, Washington 25, D. C.

Refer to No.

.Pers-101T-rph
258 32 24

NAVY DEPARTMENT
BUREAU OF NAVAL PERSONNEL
WASHINGTON 25, D. C.

for PEACE
OF
MIND—
BUY
SAVINGS
BONDS

2 4 MAY 1948

.Mrs. Erlene N. Lineaweaver,
1240 E. Cumberland Street,
Lebanon, Pennsylvania.

Dear Mrs. Lineaweaver,

The Chief of Naval Personnel takes pride in forwarding the
permanent citation for the Gold Star in lieu of the Third Air Medal
awarded to your son, the late Wilson Charles Lineaweaver, Aviation
Chief Radioman, United States Navy.

Navy Department records indicate that the medal for the enclosed award has been presented.

By direction of the Chief of Naval Personnel.

J. M. BUNCH,
LT., U. S. Navy,
Assistant to Director,
Medals and Awards Activity.

Gold Star In Lieu Of THIRD AIR MEDAL Citation

THE SECRETARY OF THE NAVY
WASHINGTON

The President of the United States takes pride
in presenting the GOLD STAR in lieu of the Third Air
Medal posthumously to

WILSON CHARLES LINEAWEAVER
AVIATION CHIEF RADIOMAN
UNITED STATES NAVY

for service as set forth in the following

CITATION:

"For meritorious achievement in aerial
flight as Radioman-Gunner of a Dive Bomber
Plane in Bombing Squadron EIGHTY FOUR, attached to the U.S.S. BUNKER HILL, in action
against enemy Japanese forces in the vicinity
of Okinawa, from March 23 to 27, 1945. Completing his fifth mission during this period,
LINEAWEAVER contributed materially to the success of his squadron. His courage and devotion
to duty was in keeping with the highest traditions of the United States Naval Service."

For the President,

Secretary of the Navy

PRESIDENTIAL UNIT CITATION And RIBBON BAR With STAR - 1st Letter

In reply address not the signer of this
letter, but Bureau of Naval Personnel,
Navy Department, Washington 25, D. C.

Refer to No.

NAVY DEPARTMENT
BUREAU OF NAVAL PERSONNEL
WASHINGTON 25, D. C.

Pers-102C jld
MM/ 258 32 24

-3 FEB 1947

Erlene Lineaweaver
1240 E. Cumberland St.
Lebanon, Pa.

Dear Mr. Lineaweaver;

The Chief of Naval Personnel takes pride in forwarding
the following award made to your son, the late Wilson
Charles Lineaweaver, Aviation Radioman First
Class, United States Navy

for meritorious conduct as a member of the Naval service:

Facsimile and ribbon bar with star of the Presidential Unit
Citation awarded the USS BUNKER HILL for extraordinary
heroism displayed by her crew in action against
enemy Japanese forces in the air, ashore and afloat
in the Pacific War Area from 29 January 1944 to 8
April 1945.

By direction of Chief of Naval Personnel:

Sincerely yours,

JOE H. FLOYD
Lt. Comdr. USN, Director
Enlisted Processing and Transmittal
Medals and Awards

Enclosure: (2)

C-90150

PRESIDENTIAL UNIT CITATION And RIBBON BAR With STAR - 2nd Letter

In reply address not the signer of this
letter, but Bureau of Naval Personnel,
Navy Department, Washington 25, D. C.

Refer to No.

Pers-1013-bed
MM/258 32 24

1 October 1948

NAVY DEPARTMENT
BUREAU OF NAVAL PERSONNEL
WASHINGTON 25, D. C.

Mrs. Erlene B. Lineaweaver,
1240 East Cumberland Street,
Lebanon, Pennsylvania.

Dear Mrs. Lineaweaver:

The Chief of Naval Personnel takes pride in forwarding the
facsimile of the Presidential Unit Citation and Ribbon Bar
with star to which your son, the late Wilson C. Lineaweaver,
Aviation Chief Radioman, United States Navy, was entitled
by virtue of his service in the U.S.S. BUNKER HILL or her
attached Air Groups.

By direction of the Chief of Naval Personnel:

Sincerely yours,

K. STEEN
Lieutenant Commander, USN
Director, Medals and Awards

Encl: (2)

PRESIDENTIAL UNIT CITATION

[Note: An identical citation as below was sent for each of the two previous letters.]

THE SECRETARY OF THE NAVY
WASHINGTON

The President of the United States takes pleasure in presenting the PRESIDENITAL UNIT CITATION to the

U.S.S. BUNKER HILL

and her attached Air Groups participating in the following operations:

November 11, 1943, to February 23, 1944, Rabaul, Gilberts, Nauru, Kavieng, Marshalls, Truk, Marianas: AG-17 (VF-18, VB-17, VT-17, Part of VFN-76).

March 29 to April 30, 1944, Palau, Hollandia, Truk; June 11 to August 5, 1944, Marianas, Bonins, Palau; September 6 to October 21, 1944, Philippines, Palau, Yap, Ryukyus, Formosa: AG-8 (VF-8, VB-8, VT-8, Part of VFN-76).

November 11 to 25, 1944, Luzon: AG-4 (VF-4, VB-4, VT-4).

February 16 to May 11, 1945, Japan, Bonins, Ryukyus: AG-84 (VF-84, VB-84, VT-84, VMF-221, VMF-451).

for service as set forth in the following

CITATION:

"For extraordinary heroism in action against enemy Japanese forces in the air, ashore and afloat in the South, Central, Southwest and Western Pacific, from November 11, 1943, to May 11, 1945. Spearheading our concentrated carrier-warfare in the most forward areas, the U.S.S. BUNKER HILL and her air groups struck crushing blows toward annihilating Japanese fighting power; they provided air cover for our amphibious forces; they fiercely countered the enemy's aerial attacks and destroyed his planes; and they inflicted terrific losses on the Japanese in Fleet and merchant marine units sunk or damaged. Daring and dependable in combat, the BUNKER HILL with her gallant officers and men rendered loyal service in achieving the ultimate defeat of the Japanese Empire."

For the President,

James Forrestal

Secretary of the Navy

C-73273

Letter For:
AMERICAN DEFENSE SERVICE MEDAL
WORLD WAR II VICTORY MEDAL

In reply address not the signer of this
letter, but Bureau of Naval Personnel,
Navy Department, Washington 25, D.C.

Refer to No.

Pers-10

MM/ 258 32 24

2 JAN 1947

NAVY DEPARTMENT
BUREAU OF NAVAL PERSONNEL
WASHINGTON 25, D.C.

Mr. Robert J. Lineaweaver
1240 E. Cumberland St.
Lebanon, Pa.

Dear Mr. Lineaweaver:

The Chief of Naval Personnel has the honor to forward herewith the
awards of the American Defense Service Medal and World War II Victory
Medal made posthumously to your son, the late Wilson C. Lineaweaver,
Aviation Chief Radioman, United States Navy.

In order that you may understand the significance of the above awards
there is enclosed a bulletin which sets forth the regulations governing
their issuance. For your further information the area campaign medals
to which he may be entitled will not be ready for distribution until a
much later date.

Please acknowledge receipt on the enclosed form.

By direction of Chief of Naval Personnel:

Sincerely yours,

Mark Lanham

Assistant to Director,
Medals and Awards

Encls. - 4

Letter For:
AMERICAN CAMPAIGN MEDAL
ASIATIC-PACIFIC CAMPAIGN MEDAL
GOOD CONDUCT MEDAL

In reply address not the signer of this
letter, but Bureau of Naval Personnel,
Navy Department, Washington 25, D. C.

Refer to No.

Pers-10/rab
MM/258 32 24

7 July 1948

NAVY DEPARTMENT
BUREAU OF NAVAL PERSONNEL
WASHINGTON 25, D. C.

Mr. Robert J. Lineaweaver
1240 E. Cumberland St.
Lebanon, Pa.

Dear Mr. Lineaweaver:

The Chief of Naval Personnel has the honor to forward herewith the
awards of the American Campaign Medal, the Asiatic-Pacific Campaign
Medal and the Good Conduct Medal made posthumously to your son,
the late Wilson C. Lineaweaver, United States Navy.

In order that you may understand the significance of the above awards
there is enclosed a bulletin which sets forth the regulations governing their issuance.

By direction of Chief of Naval Personnel:

Sincerely yours,

J. L. YOUNG
LTJG., USN,
Medals and Awards

Encls-4

PRESIDENT HARRY TRUMAN'S CONDOLENCE CERTIFICATE

IN GRATEFUL MEMORY OF

Wilson Charles Lineaweaver

WHO DIED IN THE SERVICE OF HIS COUNTRY

At Sea, Asiatic Area, attached Bombing Squadron-84, 11 May 1945

HE STANDS IN THE UNBROKEN LINE OF PATRIOTS WHO HAVE DARED TO DIE

THAT FREEDOM MIGHT LIVE, AND GROW, AND INCREASE ITS BLESSINGS.

FREEDOM LIVES, AND THROUGH IT, HE LIVES—

IN A WAY THAT HUMBLES THE UNDERTAKINGS OF MOST MEN

Harry Truman

PRESIDENT OF THE UNITED STATES OF AMERICA

Thursday, August 26, 1948 -- U.S. Naval Reserve Training Center, Municipal Airport, Reading, Pa.

U. S. Naval - Marine Corps Reserve
Training Center
Sixteenth Battalion
Municipal Airport, Reading, Pa.

26 Augu t 1948

MEMORIAL SERVICE

Naval Reserve Training Center, Thursday
evening, 26 August 1948 at 7:30 P.M. in
memory of:

'ilson Charles Lineaweaver, ACRM, USN

1900   Marches by U. .Naval band recordings

1930   Formation at Flag Staff by Officers and Men
        from Division 4-52

1935   a. Commander 5. L. Francis, USN, Inspector-
        Instructor, U. 5.Naval Reserve Training Cen-
        ter, Reading, Pa. introductory remarks.

        b. Introduction of Lt. G. Jay Umberger, Chaplain,
        USNR

        c. Ritual, Prayer and Benedictory by Chaplain
        Umberger.

        d. Citation and medal presentation by Lt. Comdr.
        E. V. Burchill, Commanding Officer, Battalion
        4-16 of the Organized Naval Reserves.

        e. Taps and lowering of colors.

Posthumous Awards Made at Municipal Airport

Mrs. Erlene N. Lineweaver, of 1240 East Cumberland St., Lebanon, is shown here receiving posthumous naval awards for her son, Wilson C. Lineweaver. The presentation took place at the Reading Municipal Airport last night. Left to right are: Lieut. Commander Nevin Hollinger, acting assistant inspector-instructor; Commander Dennis L. Francis, inspector-instructor; Mrs. Lineweaver, and Lieut. Commander E. V. Burchill, commander of Battalion 4-16, Organized Naval Reserve.　　(Eagle Staff Photo.)

Mother Gets Son's Awards From Navy

The Distinguished Flying Cross and gold stars in lieu of additional Air Medals were presented posthumously last night to Wilson Charles Lineaweaver, aviation chief radioman at a ceremony at the Naval Reserve Training Center, Reading Municipal Airport

The awards were accepted by the hero's mother, Mrs Erlene N Lineaweaver, of Lebanon, and were made for heroic and extraordinary achievement as a radio gunner on a dive bomer based on the aircraft carrier USS Bunker Hill

Officers participating in the presentation ceremony were: Commander Dennis L. Francis, inspector-instructor in the Reading area; Lieut G. Jay Umberger, Naval Reserve chaplain for the Pennsylvania state staff; Lieut. Comdr. E. V. Burchill, commanding officer of the U. S. Naval Reserve Organized Surface Battalion 4-16, and Lieut. Comdr. Nevin H. Hollinger, commanding officer of Division 6, Organized Naval Reserves.

Newspaper clipping from the *Reading Eagle*, Reading, PA, Friday, August 27, 1948

In Loving Memory
of Our Son
A. C. R. M. Wilson Charles Lineaweaver

who was killed in action on the U.S.S. Bunker Hill one year ago today.

We loved him, yes, we loved him,
But the angels loved him more;
And they have sweetly called him,
To yonder shining shore.
The golden gates were opened,
A gentle voice said, "Come!"
And with farewells unspoken,
He calmly entered home.

Sadly missed by
Parents, Brothers and Sisters

Parents Receive Award Of Gold Star To Son

Wilson C. Lineaweaver

Mr. and Mrs. Robert Lineaweaver, 1240 East Cumberland Street, recently received from the War Department the Gold Star in lieu of the Third Air Medal awarded by the President of the United States posthumously to their son, Chief Radioman Wilson Charles Lineaweaver, who was killed in action in the Pacific on May 11, 1945.

The citation accompanying the medal reads as follows:

For meritorious achievement in aerial flight as a Radio-Gunner of a Dive Bomber plane in Bombing Squadron Eighty-four attached to the USS Bunker Hill in action against the enemy Japanese forces in the vicinity of Okinawa from March 23 to 27, 1945. Completing his fifth mission during this period, Lineaweaver contributed materially to the success of his squadron. His courage, devotion to duty was in keeping with the highest traditions of the United States Naval Service.

The above was signed by John L. Sullivan, secretary of the Navy. Lineaweaver enlisted in the naval service in January, 1941.

Flying Cross Award Is Made Posthumously

Wilson C. Lineaweaver, aviation chief electronicsman, USN, son of Mr. and Mrs. Robert J. Lineaweaver, of 1240 East Cumberland Street, has been posthumously awarded the Distinguished Flying Cross by Secretary of the Navy John L. Sullivan for the President.

Lineaweaver served as a radioman-gunner of a dive bomber in Bombing Squadron 84 during operations against enemy Japanese forces in the vicinity of Iwo Jima, Okinawa and the Japanese homeland from February 19 to April 29, 1945. He rendered valuable assistance to his pilot in inflicting extensive damage on hostile airfields, gun positions and installations. He was killed when shot down while in aerial flight on a dive bomber attached to the USS Bunker Hill.

During the war citations were temporary, or incomplete, for security reasons.

Text of the complete citation is as follows:

"For heroism and extraordinary achievement in aerial flight as radioman-gunner of a dive bomber in Bombing Squadron 84, attached to the USS Bunker Hill, during operations against enemy Japanese forces in the vicinity of Iwo Jima, Okinawa and the Japanese homeland from February 19 to April 29, 1945. Completing his 20th mission during this period, Lineaweaver rendered valuable assistance to his pilot in inflicting extensive damage on hostile airfields, gun positions and installations. His courage and devotion to duty were in keeping with the highest traditions of the U. S. Naval service."

Newspaper clippings from the *Lebanon Daily News*, Lebanon, PA. Middle clipping appeared June 26, 1948. Far right clipping appeared July 22, 1948.

LINDSLEY EDGAR J
CHIEF PHARMACIST'S MATE · USN · ILLINOIS
LINDSLEY JOHN H
FIREMAN 3C · USN · ILLINOIS
LINEAWEAVER WILSON C
AVN CHIEF RADIOMAN · USN · PENNSYLVANIA
LINEBARGER HENRY F
COXSWAIN · · TEXAS
LINK LEONARD A
SEAMAN 1C · USNR · OKLAHOMA
LINK NORBERT
LIEUTENANT(JG) · USNR · KANSAS
LINK RAYMOND F
SEAMAN 2C · USNR · KANSAS
LINN JOHN A
RADIOMAN 2C · USNR · OREGON
LINNARTZ HAROLD M
FIREMAN 1C · USN · TEXAS
LINSLEY THOMAS H
ELECTRICIAN'S MATE 3C · USNR · PA
LINSON JOHN A
AVN RADIOMAN 1C · USNR · CALIFORNIA
LINTON GEORGE EDWARD
FIREMAN 2C · USN · WYOMING
LINTON THOMAS H
SEAMAN 1C · USNR · SOUTH DAKOTA
LIPARITI FRANK A
SEAMAN 1C · USNR · NEW YORK

FindAGrave.com

Flickr.com (Public Domain)

HONOLULU MEMORIAL HAWAII

The Honolulu Memorial, located within the National Memorial of the Pacific near the center of Honolulu, Hawaii, honors the sacrifices and achievements of American Armed Forces in the Pacific (not including the southwest Pacific) during World War II and in the Korean War. The memorial was later expanded to include the Vietnam War. The names of 28,788 military personnel, 18,094 names from World War II, who are missing in action or were lost or buried at sea in the Pacific during these conflicts, are listed on marble slabs in ten Courts of the Missing which flank the Memorial's grand stone staircase.

CORNWALL CEMETERY
CORNWALL, PA

INDIANTOWN GAP NATIONAL CEMETERY,
ANNVILLE, PA

Made in the USA
Columbia, SC
09 April 2018